MW00416711

CURRENCY AND INTEREST RATE HEDGING

A USER'S GUIDE TO OPTIONS, FUTURES, SWAPS, & FORWARD CONTRACTS

Second Edition

Torben Juul Andersen

NEW YORK INSTITUTE OF FINANCE
New York London Toronto Sydney Tokyo Singapore

Library of Congress Cataloging-in-Publication Data

Andersen, Torben Juul.

Currency and interest rate hedging : a user's guide to options, futures, swaps, and forward contracts / Torben Juul Andersen. —2nd ed.

p. cm.

Includes bibliographical references and index.

ISBN 0-13-226101-4

1. Foreign exchange futures. 2. Hedging (Finance) 3. Financial futures. 4. Interest rate futures. 5. Options (Finance) I. Title.

HG3853.A53 1993

332.64'5—dc20 93-23811 CIP

This book is dedicated to

Mette & Christine

Printed in the United States of America

10 9 8 7 6 5 4 3 2 1

New York Institute of Finance
(NYIF Corp.)
2 Broadway
New York, New York

Contents

Preface

Events in the financial markets have taken interesting turns since the release of the first edition of *Currency and Interest Rate Hedging* in 1987. The dramatic interim changes in the foreign exchange rates between the major international currencies, not to mention the extreme pressures imposed on the European Monetary System during 1992–93, have more than ever reemphasized the importance of hedging underlying currency and interest rate exposures.

This new edition of the book updates economic events and financial statistics. Given the apparent volatility of financial variables, some of the original examples and case studies reappearing in this edition employ the foreign exchange and interest rate levels prevalent in the mid-1980s, whereas the new examples added to the book reflect the financial situation of the early 1990s. This approach should remind the reader that there is nothing predetermined when it comes to absolute foreign exchange and interest rate values.

It is a prerequisite for the proper handling of financial exposures that these are appropriately recorded and monitored. Therefore, the new edition of the book includes a discussion of how to measure currency and interest rate exposures, pointing to possible ways of managing these financial risks. This new edition discusses relevant concepts such as duration and efficient sets of assets and liabilities. The book also points to the potential applicability of the different hedging instruments in portfolio management.

The discussion attempts to account for major market developments that have taken place over recent years, such as the expansion of futures exchanges in the European markets and the introduction of new financial futures products. The aim is to complement the existing range of products, some of which also seek to compete directly with the expanding market for bank-traded OTC products.

The expanding product range in the bank-driven OTC market is included in this new edition. The markets for forward rate and swap products have become highly active markets in the major currencies, and today in many respects they resemble the liquidity of the traditional foreign exchange and money markets. Other newer hedging products are adapted to serve more specific hedging requirements. The market participants offering these newer instruments show great ingenuity, not the least of which is in terms of linguistics. It is entirely possible that a few product terms slipped my recognition, but such products are likely varieties of instrument combinations already described. Once the basic instruments are understood, any new product can be analyzed by decomposing it into the generic product elements. This is true whether the product is structured on floors, caps, swaps, or other types of instruments. A range of these more complex structures is included in the new edition.

In the choice of the appropriate instruments, the resulting hedge position should be analyzed and measured against likely market trends in foreign exchange and interest rates. In reality, any hedging decision will eventually involve taking some sort of view on the most likely market developments. Hence, the book also includes a comparative section that aims to perform such analysis.

It is my sincere wish and hope that this enhanced second edition of *Currency and Interest Rate Hedging* will be considered a positively improved book, and will serve as a useful tool for any person, professional, student, or layman who seeks more insights into the markets for hedging instruments, as well as provide a deeper understanding of their potential use.

Finally I wish to express my appreciation to Fred Dahl at Inkwell Publishing Services and to Drew Dreeland at Paramount Publishing for their invaluable support in the completion of this book.

Torben Juul Andersen
Frederiksberg, Denmark

I

THE ARGUMENT FOR HEDGING

1

International Trade and Payments

Over longer periods of time the cross-border net-payment flows emanate from, and are eventually a consequence of, international trade transactions. The payments relate directly to compensation for export and import of goods and services, or they relate to international capital transactions caused by surpluses or deficits on the current balance of payments. To the extent that there is imbalance between the incoming and outgoing payments on trade transactions in a country, private institutions or the central government will either deposit (invest) or borrow funds on the international financial markets. Hence a significant part of international cash flows relates to debt service and interest compensation from international borrowers and investors. The interest payments are registered on the country's current balance of payment, whereas repayment of principal is included in the capital balance section of the balance of payment account.

Both international borrowers and investors have become more actively engaged in the current management of their portfolios. A borrower might want to refinance and restructure the loan portfolio in view of new market developments. This is done not only through transactions directly in the capital markets, but also through transactions in the foreign exchange market, which can serve to change the characteristics of the loan portfolio. Similarly, investors can quickly switch large parts of their liquid security investments in the securities markets to a more preferred currency composition as the result of new market developments, or change the characteristics of their invested portfolios through engagements in foreign exchange contracts.

In the short run, substantial payment flows can relate to current transactions in the foreign exchange market. Many of these transactions are carried out by market participants in the form of intermediaries, speculators, and hedgers in the currency market all of whom are interested in the current management of currency exposures. During certain periods in recent years, the short-term behavior in the foreign exchange market has become quite detached from the economic fundamentals underpinning the trade balances among different currency jurisdictions. The size of the foreign exchange market has risen to a very significant size. In 1992 the Bank for International Settlement (BIS) has estimated that the foreign exchange transaction volume in the United Kingdom, the United States, and Japan amounted to around US$ 15½ billion during the month of April, corresponding to an annualized trading volume of US$ 185 billion in these major currency markets. Compared to a similar estimate made in 1989, the foreign exchange market has grown by approximately 50% during the three-year period.

THE INTERNATIONAL FINANCIAL SYSTEM

Since World War II, many attempts have been made to further unrestricted international trade, to the economic benefit of the countries involved. Negotiations in the late 1940s among the major Western countries led to the General Agreement on Tariffs and Trade (GATT), in which the countries agreed to eliminate tariff barriers on imported goods. The agreement has since been revised a few times, and today continues to play an important role in international political discussions. Under the auspices of the United Nations, attempts have been made to standardize international trade practice and international trade law in order to reduce the inherent risks of intercountry trade transactions. The liberalization of international trade has had a visible effect on economic growth in the Western world during the 1950s and 1960s.

The *Bretton-Woods Agreement* of 1944 also reflected the vision of rebuilding the world economic system by promoting international trade. For this to succeed, an unrestricted international payment system was required. This was accomplished by creating a "clearing center" where countries with a current balance of payment deficit could get temporary credit until stabilizing economic policy measures had reversed unfavorable balance of payments trends. The credit would be provided by the countries with registered balance of payment surpluses. This clearing center was instituted through the establishment of the *International Monetary Fund (IMF)*. At the same time the World Bank was established for the purpose of extending longer-term credits in support of socioeconomic projects in countries in need of funds for their economic development.

Each participating country deposited a certain quota in gold (25%) and the domestic currency (75%) with the IMF, the quota being determined by the relative sizes of the countries' GNPs and international trade volume. The clearing system was arranged so that a country at any time could draw an amount equivalent to the current gold holding of the country's quota. The gold holding was equal in size to the initial gold deposit, plus the amount of gold that other countries had paid in, in exchange for the country's domestic currency. To obtain further drawings on the IMF quota, the countries had to negotiate directly with the IMF, which then set its conditions for further credits, with due regard for the economic situation of the countries in question.

In the IMF system each country determined a fixed foreign exchange rate (value) against gold. The U.S. dollar was fully convertible into gold at a fixed price of US$ 35 per ounce. Hence the U.S. dollar became the international reserve currency which the central banks on request could convert into gold. Each member country was obliged to maintain a foreign exchange rate with a maximum deviation of plus or minus 1% from the fixed foreign exchange rate. Due to the limited supply of gold, *special drawing rights* (*SDRs*) were created in 1970, with the view of creating sufficient international liquidity to further the increase in trade flows. The value of the SDR was determined by a weighted average of sixteen international currencies.

Already in 1968 the gold convertibility of the U.S. dollar was abolished, and in 1971 the *Smithsonian Agreement* widened the maximum allowable variation from the fixed foreign exchange rate to plus or minus 2¼%. Until the final collapse of the instituted international financial system in 1973, the system went through a whole array of crises. The final consequence was a return to freely floating foreign exchange rates.

The increased volatility among the European currencies was found unacceptable by the member countries of the European Economic Community (EEC). So, in 1972 the member countries, plus a few other European countries, agreed to keep swings of their respective currencies within half the allowable band as determined by the *Smithsonian Agreement*. This made up the so-called *snake*, which moved inside the Smithsonian foreign exchange rate boundaries, the *tunnel*.

Following several years of political discussions, a group of EEC member countries initiated the establishment of the *European Monetary System (EMS)* in 1979. In this system each currency *can* move within a band of plus or minus 2¼% from a fixed foreign exchange rate set against each of the participating currencies with certain exceptions (see Figure 1.1).

FIGURE 1.1

The European Monetary System. (Reprinted by permission of Financial Times.)

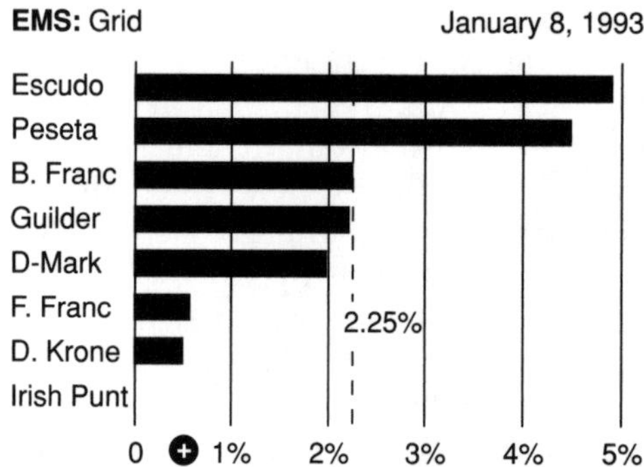

The chart shows the member currencies of the exchange rate mechanism measured against the weakest currency in the EMS's narrow 2.25 percent fluctuation band. In practice, currencies in the narrow band cannot rise more than 2.25 percent from the weakest currency in that part of the system. The Spanish peseta and Portuguese escudo operate with 6 percent fluctuation bands.

The implementation of this fixed rate monetary system was supported by swap arrangements among the countries' central banks, whereby each country could obtain short-term credits in the other European currencies to support the stability of the foreign exchange rate development. The EMS was formalized further by the creation of a *European Currency Unit (ECU)*, the value of which is determined by a weighted average of the EEC currencies. For European visionaries the ECU constitutes the common currency of a future European monetary union. Since the inauguration of the EMS in 1979, ten adjustments of the fixed rate parities had taken place as of 1992. From 1987 and until the summer of 1992, the EMS functioned under fairly stable conditions. As a consequence of the fixed rate parity among the participating currencies, the period showed a relatively strong convergence of long-term interest rates in different EMS currencies (see Figure 1.2).

FIGURE 1.2
Long-Term Interest Rates (10-year government bonds).

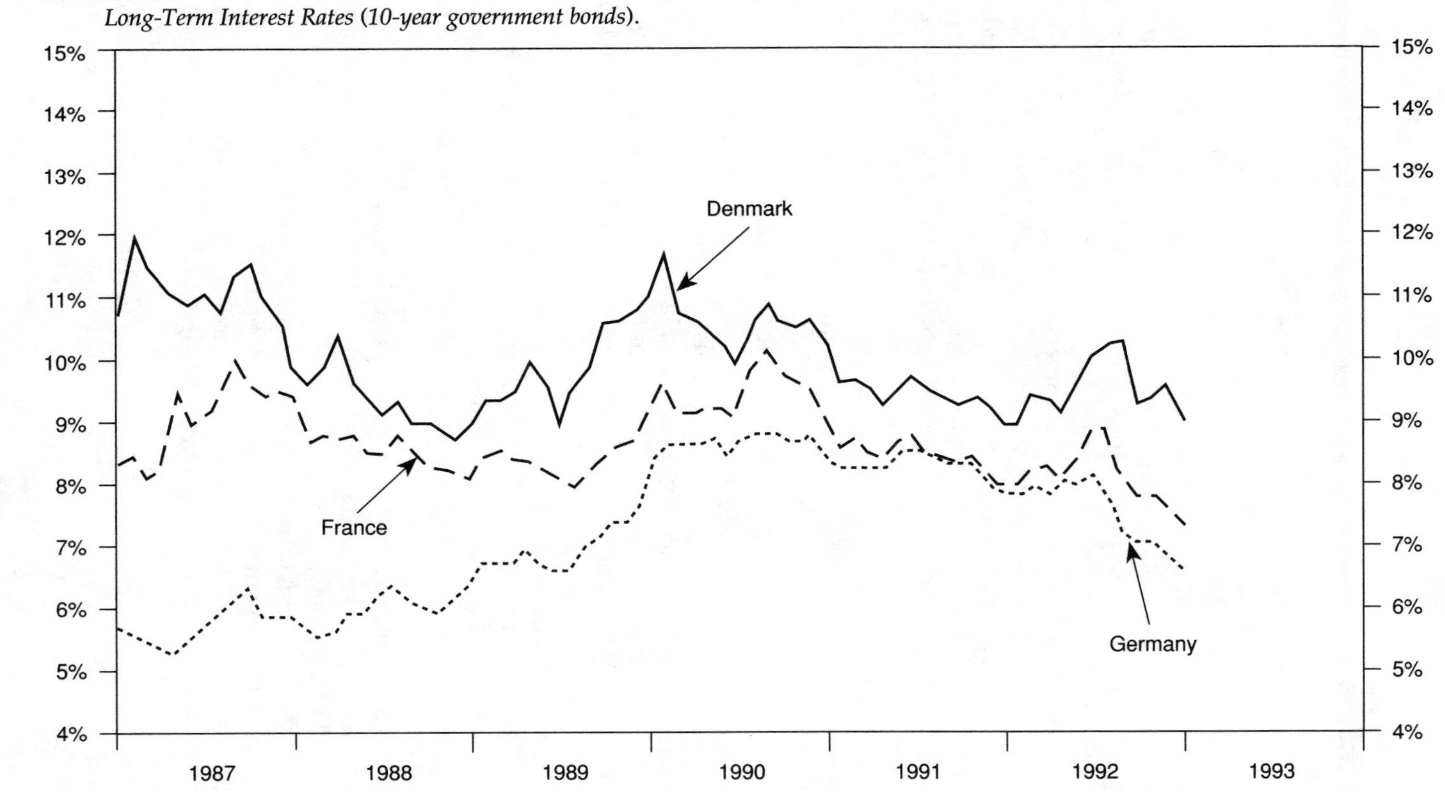

The EEC worked toward a completion of the so-called internal market by the end of 1992. The main idea was to establish common standards and open borders for all types of trade and services, commercial and financial.

The continued development within the EEC was outlined in the *Maastricht Agreement,* which was signed in Maastricht by the European heads of state in late 1991 and planned for the final ratification in each of the European member countries during 1992. The Maastricht Agreement stipulated, among other things, a further monetary integration of the European countries, eventually to be formalized by the establishment of a single common currency by 1999.

A national referendum in Denmark on June 2, 1992 by a marginal majority rejected the Maastricht Agreement, and hence obstructed the ratification of the agreement, which in principle was to be unanimous in all member countries. This outcome inspired further political discussions across Europe, creating uncertainty around the EMS and the currency convergence among the EMS currencies. The effect was a currency crisis within the EMS. On September 14 the Italian lira was devalued 7% against the German mark, and on September 16—just a few days before the French Maastricht referendum—the pound sterling and the Italian lira were forced to leave the EMS. Later the Swedish krona, the Norwegian krone, and the Irish punt were opted out of the EMS peg by market forces. For long periods the French franc and the Danish krone were under similar market pressure. Eventually, by August 2, 1993 the intensity of the market forces led to a widening of the foreign exchange rate bands among the remaining EMS-currencies from the previously agreed 2¼% to 15%, with the exception of Dutch guilder which maintained a 2¼% band around the German mark.

The final outcome of the EMS drama is hard to forecast. If the political will and ability to integrate the economic policies of the European countries are rehabilitated, one must expect a return to some sort of coordinated foreign exchange rate policy. However, the events of 1992–93 have taught market participants a lesson: When market confidence is hampered, the forces of the market will quickly adjust rates to reflect the overall market view.

The European countries have not been the only ones with the coordination of economic policy on the agenda. The same principles, although in a much more informal way, have regularly been pursued with mixed success among the leading industrialized countries in the form of semiannual G7 meetings among the leading industrialized economies (the United States, Japan, Germany, the United Kingdom, France, Canada, and Italy). During 1987 and the following years, the forum tried to "talk" the foreign exchange rate (specifically the U.S. dollar) into place, by indicating how they perceived the appropriate level of the U.S. dollar foreign exchange, and by backing this with coordinated intervention. With hindsight the effect of the talking appears to have merely served as a potential, although a rather uncertain, indicator for future monetary intervention. However, intervention has generally proved to be of limited avail. The market forces have often become the winner in setting appropriate market prices.

The aim of coordinating global economic and monetary policies has on the whole shown appalling results over the five years from 1987 to 1992. In fact, it appears to have never been more uncoordinated. One outcome has been a lowering of short-term U.S. money market rates during 1992 to their lowest level in over 30 years, while at the same time increasing short-term rates in Germany to their highest level in 20 years. The lesson must be that markets do not listen to political intentions, but rather react to the perceived reality of economic conditions.

BALANCE OF PAYMENT DEVELOPMENTS AND INTERNATIONAL CREDIT INTERMEDIATION

In the wake of the increase in the international oil prices in the early 1970s, the energy-importing economies—in developed as well as in developing countries—increasingly registered balance of payments deficits. The balance of payments surpluses of the oil-producing countries were transferred to the countries with balance of payments deficits primarily through the intermediation of the international banks. The balance of payments deficits registered on the European continent and in Japan in the early 1980s triggered a general tightening of fiscal and monetary policies, whereas the United States during the same period appeared to go through an unwarranted fiscal expansion. This reversed the balance of payments pattern over the prior years bringing the United States into a position of a major deficit country. The balance of payments development shows a cyclical pattern reflecting the effects of a generally uncoordinated economic policy among the major industrialized countries. (See Table 1.1.)

The United States continues to be a deficit country, although at a decreasing rate. Japan, on the other hand, has, within a depressed domestic market, registered the highest ever balance of payments surplus during 1992—a staggering ECU 90 billion (US$ 117 billion). The United Kingdom has, since the late 1980s, incurred relatively large balance of payment deficits. Germany has registered a negative trade balance development in recent years in the wake of the unification of East and West. France, Belgium, and Denmark are examples of countries with an improved balance of payment development.

TABLE 1.1
Current Balance of Payment Development (1985–1992).

(ECU Billions)	*United States*	*Japan*	*Germany*	*United Kingdom*
1985	–159.7	64.5	21.7	4.7
1986	–150.0	86.9	40.3	0.1
1987	–141.6	75.5	39.8	–6.4
1988	–107.0	66.6	42.9	–24.3
1989	–91.8	52.4	52.2	–32.3
1990	–70.9	28.3	37.0	–23.8
1991	–3.0	63.0	–16.1	–9.0
1992	–45.3*	90.3	–19.4	–16.1

Source: Various international financial statistics.
*Estimate.

The unevenness in external balance developments will continue to put high demands on the credit intermediation of the international capital markets. The volume of funds raised on the international capital markets continues to be significant (see Table 1.2).

Development in Interest Rates and Foreign Exchange Rates

The interest rates on foreign currencies quoted on the Eurocurrency markets are determined by the domestic interest rate movements, and they relate to the interest rates of other foreign currencies through the interest rate parity factor.

Arbitrage between the domestic money market and the equivalent Eurocurrency market will cause the interest rate level of the two markets to follow each other, given that no regulatory restrictions prevent arbitrage transactions to take place. The domestic interest rate is determined by the economy's current demand for credit and the monetary authorities' regulation of credit availability. The latter is managed in response to the development of the balance of payment, the unemployment rate, the inflation rate, and other economic policy measures. Specifically, in very open economies, cross-border capital movements can periodically exert a significant influence on the credit availability.

In the shorter time span, interest rate movements are also influenced by a variety of factors that can help form the market participants' expectations, such as the implementation of new fiscal policy measures, publication of updated inflation rates or of similar economic indicators, rumors of government resignations, and the like. Specifically, in fixed foreign exchange rate environments (such as the EMS), more extreme

TABLE 1.2

Funds Raised by Main Borrowers on the International Capital Markets.

(%)	*1985*	*1986*	*1987*	*1988*	*1989*	*1990*	*1991*	*1992*
OECD area	83.3	90.0	89.1	91.2	91.4	88.4	87.3	87.9
Developing countries	9.2	5.0	6.7	5.0	4.7	6.6	8.8	7.8
Eastern Europe	1.9	1.0	0.9	1.0	1.0	1.1	0.3	0.2
Others	5.6	3.1	3.3	2.8	2.9	3.9	3.6	4.1
Total	100.0	100.0	100.0	100.0	100.0	100.0	100.0	100.0
(US$ Billions)								
Total	279.6	388.1	392.9	453.5	466.5	434.9	524.9	609.7
of which:								
United States	66.8	72.1	66.2	61.3	66.7	47.1	75.0	95.0
Japan	22.4	47.1	55.2	61.0	107.0	64.5	82.4	75.5
United Kingdom	26.8	30.0	50.4	77.9	46.5	51.4	60.3	70.9
France	15.6	25.8	18.8	28.6	24.5	28.9	37.5	42.5
Canada	11.6	25.8	13.9	24.3	21.4	23.1	30.7	30.2
Germany	3.3	15.1	11.9	13.6	15.6	16.0	19.3	28.4
Italy	10.3	15.9	16.1	14.8	21.2	28.9	20.4	15.1
Australia	18.2	24.5	18.9	21.0	28.5	17.7	12.3	14.7

Source: Financial Market Trends, February 1990/1993, OECD Paris.

market pressure on the currency—that is, where due to selling pressure it becomes difficult to maintain the rate-parity despite currency intervention—the central bank of that currency will have to support the currency by increasing the short-term interest rate, hence making it attractive to place funds and more expensive to borrow in that currency. Consequently there has been a tendency among the EMS currencies to have relatively volatile interest rates. During the fall of 1992 and early 1993, this was in several cases carried to the extreme, with short-term interest rates reaching three-digit figures, such as in the Swedish krona and the Irish punt.

The interest rate of a given currency will be influenced by the interest rate developments of other currencies and the financial markets' expectations on the future foreign exchange rates of the currencies. Due to the prevalence of a forward foreign exchange market, international interest rate arbitrage transactions can easily be closed. Hence a currency's interest rate will be determined vis-à-vis the interest rate of other foreign currencies in accordance with the expected future foreign exchange rates as determined by the quotes on the forward foreign exchange market. The return to floating foreign exchange rates during the 1970s and the uncoordinated economic policies of the Western economies thus have

FIGURE 1.3
Interest Rate Development (Three-Month Eurocurrency Deposits).

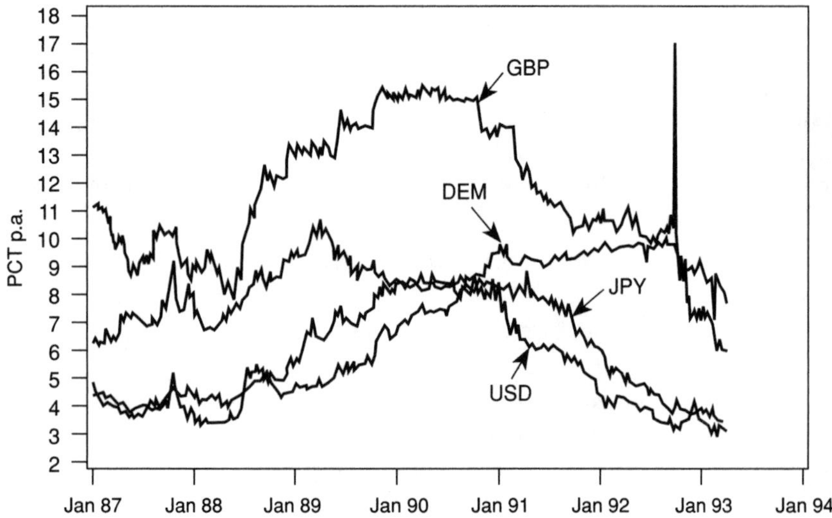

had a destabilizing effect on the interest rate development of the major international currencies (see Figure 1.3).

Keep in mind that the term *interest rate* refers to a wide spectrum of maturities. In general the short-term interest rates (maturities of up to 12 months) are most relevant for the foreign exchange rate market. Usually the central banks intervene in the short-term maturities where a currency is under pressure, and seek to maintain the long-term interest unchanged. The *term structure of interest rates* refers to the interest rate (effective yield) on securities of comparable risk at different maturities. Hence, the effective yields are arranged by the times to the securities' repayment dates. The resulting yield curve illustrates the interest rate prevailing at different maturities.

Changes in short-term and long-term interest rates can differ widely depending on circumstances. A "normal" yield curve is said to be *upward sloping*. For fixed rate securities the price risk is larger for longer maturities, and hence investors are said to require a *risk premium* in terms of a higher interest rate for longer-term commitments.

A *downward sloping* yield curve is said to represent a market expectation of falling interest rates. Investors will then tend to favor longer-term securities, because the potential capital gain is higher. Borrowers will fund themselves in the shorter term, because they expect to be able to refinance themselves more cheaply at maturity. Supply and demand will then make short-term interest rates rise (higher demand for short-

FIGURE 1.4
U.S. Dollar Yield Curves.

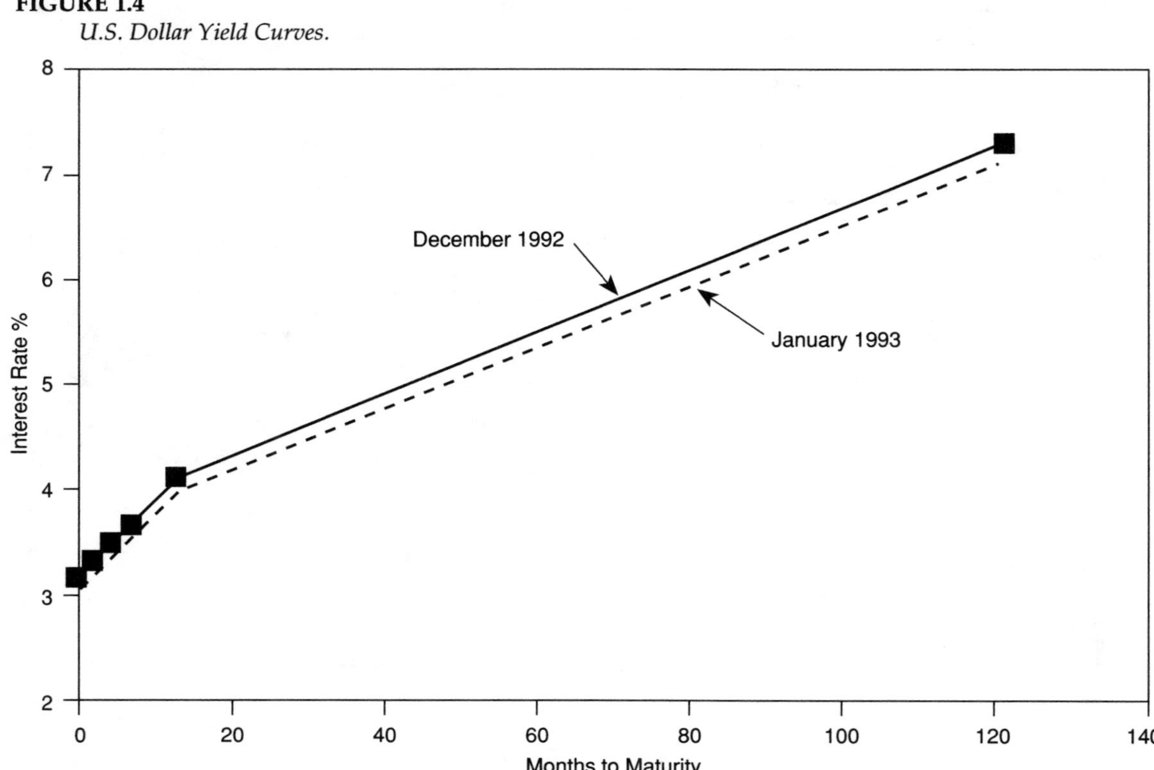

FIGURE 1.5
German Mark Yield Curves.

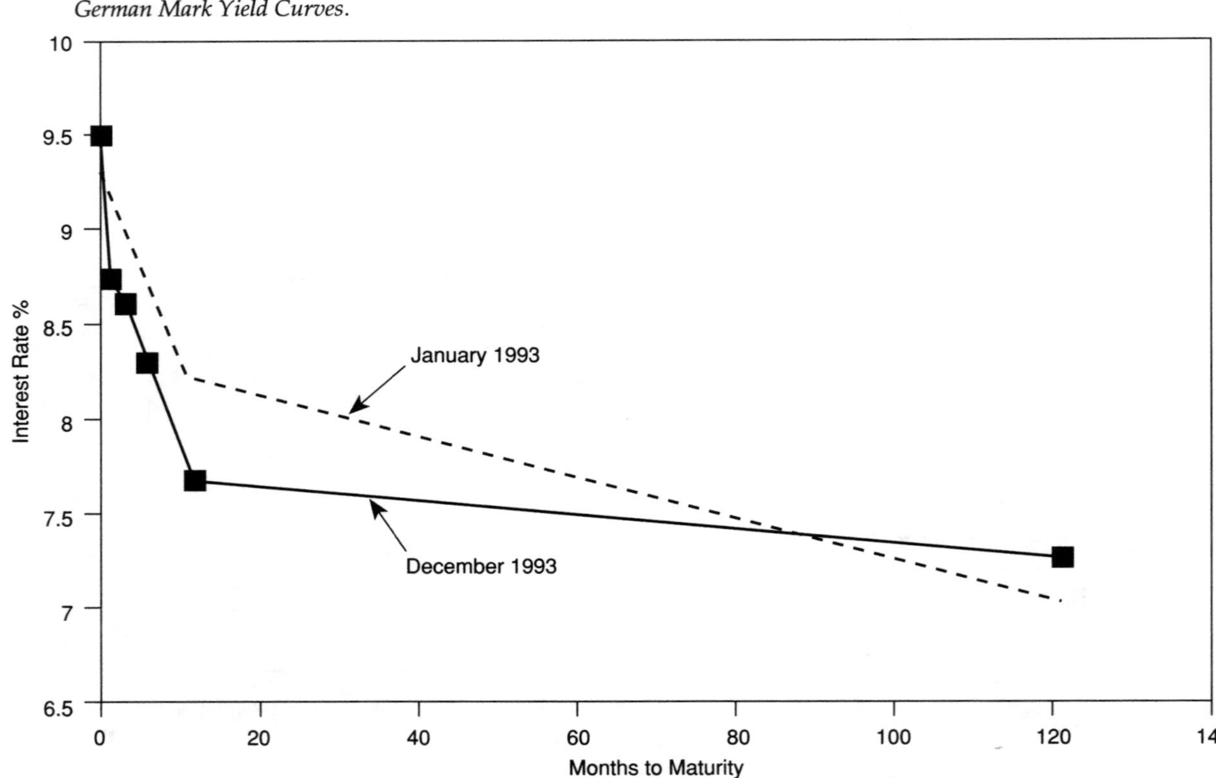

term funds), and will lower the long-term interest rates (higher supply of credit).

An upward sloping yield curve that is steeper than the normal curve is said to represent market expectations of increasing interest rates. In Figure 1.4 the short-term interest rates are low because the Federal Reserve Bank (FED) has tried for long periods to stimulate economic growth by expanding short-term credit availability. In Figure 1.5 the short-term interest rates are high because the German Bundesbank (Buba) has tried to dampen the inflationary development by limiting short-term credit availability. The interesting thing to note is that the long-term interest rates are less volatile, and that the long-term interest rate differential between the two currencies is relatively small (see Figure 1.6).

FIGURE 1.6
U.S. Dollar–German Mark Yield Curve Difference.

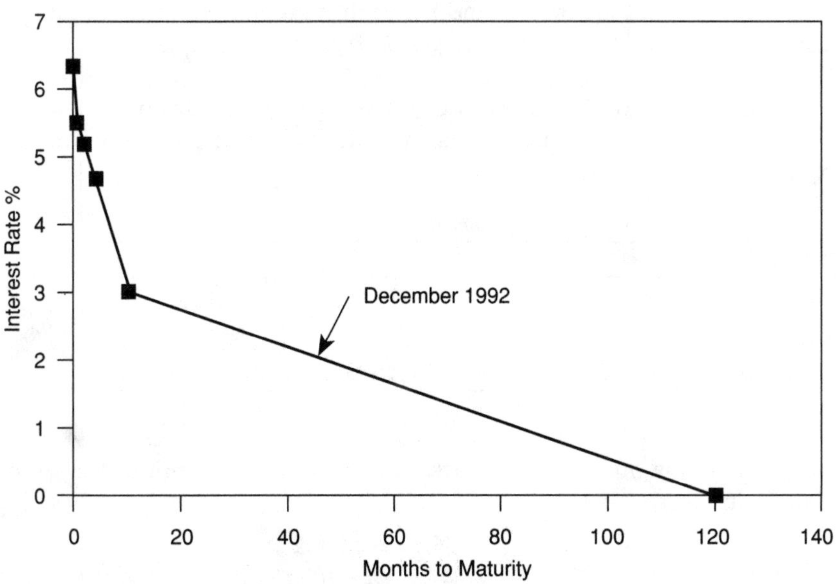

The financial markets often operate with the concept of *zero-coupon interest rates*. The yield of a given security implies that each of its cash flow components (that is, the coupon payments and the repayments of principal) all refer to the same internal rate of return. Alternatively, one could argue that each individual cash flow component represents different interest rates each relating to the specific time span of the payment. These rates are the zero-coupon interest rates.

A *zero-coupon bond* is a security with only two payments, namely the initial investment and the payment at maturity of principal and interest compensation. Hence, any security with a given cash flow pattern can be considered a combination of a series of zero-coupon bonds. Consequently, the price of a security can be looked upon as being the sum of the underlying zero-coupon bond prices.

$$P = \sum_{t=1}^{n} p_t \times d_t$$

where

$d_t = 1/(1+i_t)^t$
p_t = Payment at maturity (time t).
d_t = Discount factor for time period t.
i_t = Zero-coupon interest rate pertaining to period t.

The discount factors (d_t) and hence the zero-coupon interest rate (i_t) can be determined by solving a series of security price equations.

Example: A market consists of three liquid securities of 1, 2, and 3 years' maturity, each structured as a bullet loan and paying an annual coupon of 5%.

Payment Structures

Year:	*0*	*1*	*2*	*3*	*Yield (%)*	*Zero-Coupon (i%)*
Security 1	–99.90	105			5.10	5.1000
Security 2	–99.54	5	105		5.25	5.2515
Security 3	–99.06	5	5	105	5.35	5.3525

The following equations are established to determine the zero-coupon interest rates (i_t):

$$99.90 = 105d_1$$
$$99.54 = 5d_1 + 105d_2$$
$$99.06 = 5d_1 + 5d_2 + 105d_3$$

Hence

$$d_1 = 0.9515 \Rightarrow i_1 = 5.1000\%$$
$$d_2 = 0.9027 \Rightarrow i_2 = 5.2515\%$$
$$d_3 = 0.8551 \Rightarrow i_3 = 5.3525\%$$

where $d_t = 1/(1+i_t)^t$

As it appears from this simple example, the difference between the effective yield and the zero-coupon interest rate is usually fairly small (see Figure 1.7).

An analysis of the cash flow structure of the market's liquid securities shows that the zero-coupon interest rates in principle can be found by solving a set of linear equations. In practice, however, it can be quite difficult to assemble a sufficient set of securities to determine the relevant zero-coupon interest rates. This is typically the case in markets with a limited market of straight zero-coupon bonds and with a more complex bond structure. To overcome this problem, a series of techniques has been developed to make it possible to approximate an appropriate zero-coupon interest rate structure.

The *foreign exchange spot rate* denotes the price at which one currency is traded against another currency today, although the currency amounts normally are cleared two business days later. The price is typically quoted as local currency units per U.S. dollar (international convention) with the exception of pound sterling. It can also be quoted against other currencies (cross-currency rates).

Foreign exchange transactions can also be closed at longer maturities in the forward market, typically up to 12 months ahead, but in certain cases even longer. The foreign exchange rates in the forward market must, under circumstances with no restrictions, be determined in accordance with the equivalent money market rates of the two currencies. Hence the currency of the higher interest rate will be quoted in the forward market at a discount (that is, more currency per unit of the other currency), reflecting the interest rate differential between the two curren-

FIGURE 1.7
Zero-Coupon Yield Curve.

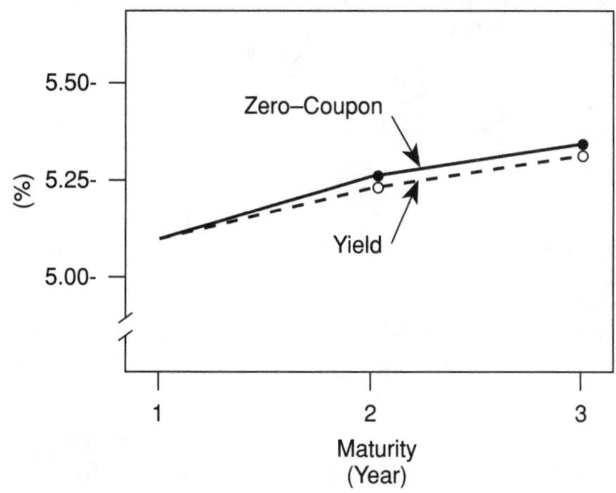

FIGURE 1.8

Foreign Exchange Rate Developments (Monthly Averages).

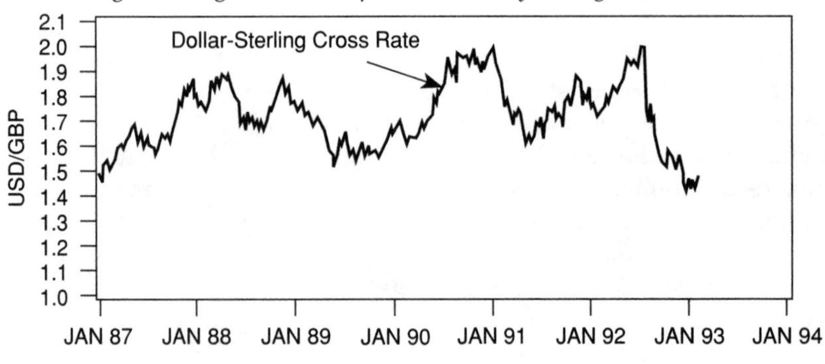

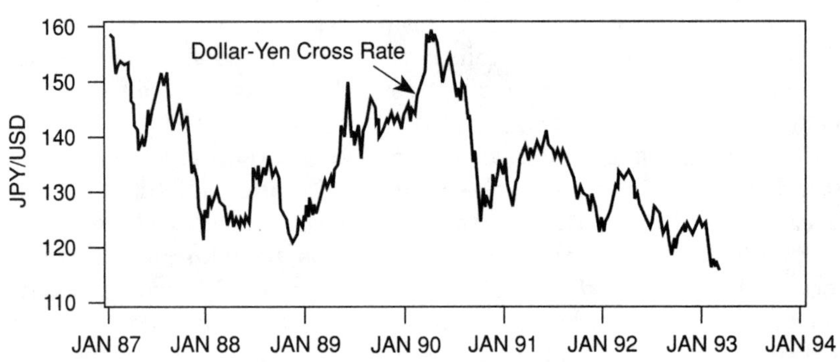

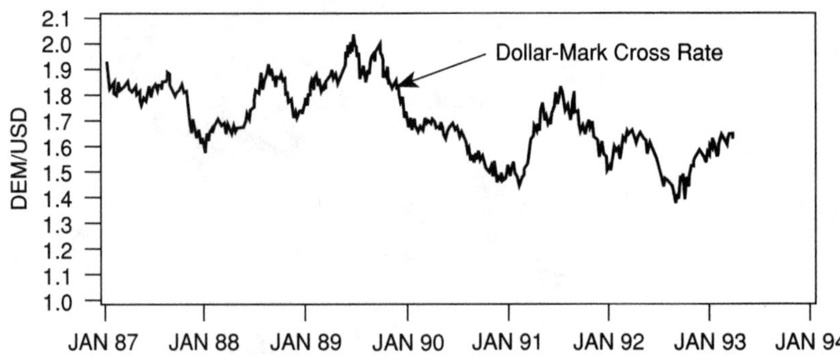

cies (the interest rate parity factor). Consequently, market developments in the foreign exchange market and the interest rate development in the short-term money markets are closely intertwined.

This means that, for example, U.S.-dollar-denominated assets can be sold forward against the German mark at a higher rate than the prevailing foreign exchange spot rate, when the short-term interest rate in the German mark exceeds that of the U.S. dollar.

Under a floating rate regime and even in a managed floating rate environment, the determination of the foreign exchange rates is highly influenced by the expectations of the market participants leading to erratic movements in the foreign exchange rates. The behavior of foreign exchange intermediaries, speculators, and hedgers further contributes to the short-term foreign exchange rate development periodically leading to substantial rate volatility (see Figure 1.8).

CONCLUSION

Substantial currency flows take place between the countries of the world economic system emanating from underlying trade and capital transactions. After World War II, the foreign exchange rates determining the currency exchange relating to these cross-border payments were managed within a fixed rate system under the auspices of the IMF. This system collapsed in the early 1970s leading to freely floating exchange rates. Certain European countries led by the EEC tried to establish a more stable foreign exchange rate zone on the European continent.

These attempts have been challenged during 1992–93, putting severe pressure on the parity system and forcing some participants to leave the EMS. The attempts towards increased economic cooperation between the major industrialized countries, the G7, have so far had limited success. As a consequence of this development, interest rates and foreign exchange rates have become increasingly volatile.

2

Financial Exposure

With the expansion of international financial relationships and the continued liberalization of cross-border cash flows, more and more institutions become exposed to international transactions. These typically take the form of future foreign currency cash receivables and payables caused by trade transactions and foreign currency denominated financial commitments. The increasing exposure requires enforced attention by the financial management of the institutions involved, and the management boards need to establish clear institutional policies stating the acceptable risk levels of the institution's currency and interest rate exposures.

In times of volatility in international interest rates and foreign exchange rates, an excessive financial exposure can have a very significant impact on an institution's financial performance and consequently requires management's constant attention.

An institution's financial exposure can be separated into two broad categories. *Interest rate exposure* arises when financial assets and liabilities have a mismatch in maturity or interest rate basis, or when floating rate financial commitments create uncertainty with regard to future cash flows. *Currency exposure* arises when foreign currency receivables and payables do not match each other in amount and timing because the future conversion value of the net flows into the domestic currency of accounting is unknown.

INTEREST RATE EXPOSURE

The concept of interest rate exposure is best described by means of a few examples.

Example: A company, after updating its liquidity budget in December, realizes that a liquidity gap of US$ 10,000,000 will appear throughout the 12 months commencing in June of the following accounting year, caused by planned engagement of a new project. Assume that the short-term dollar interest rate has moved between 8–12% p.a. over the past year. With a similar volatility in interest rates over the coming year, cash flow calculations on the project will show a variation of US$ 400,000 on interest expenses, which severely jeopardize the profitability of the project. Locking in the future rate would give the company a clearer picture of the project's profitability.

Example: A commercial bank extends floating rate U.S. dollar loans to its corporate client base. The bank itself issues a fixed coupon, dollar-denominated Eurobond to fund its dollar assets. However, the bank's assets carry floating rate interest whereas a part of the bank's liabilities carry a fixed interest rate. A drop in the dollar interest rate, in this combination of interest rate basis on the assets and liabilities, will bring the bank's future profitability in jeopardy.

Example: A leasing company provides long-term financial commitments to its client base with a locked-in return to the institution. The leasing company funds these activities through floating rate loans. In an increasing interest rate environment, the net profit will shrink and possibly even turn into a loss position. Interest rate mis-match situations are illustrated in Figure 2.1.

One solution to such interest-gapping positions is to match the interest rate basis of the assets and the liabilities. The following chapters deal with a wide variety of techniques whereby the interest rate basis of assets and liabilities can be changed without conflicting with the underlying business practice of the institution.

However, the situation might not be as simple as that. Consider a corporation that has placed part of its assets in short-term money market deposits at the overnight rate, at the same time funding the assets by discounting 3- and 6-month notes. This corporation will lose money if the

FIGURE 2.1
Illustration of Types of Interest Rate Exposure.

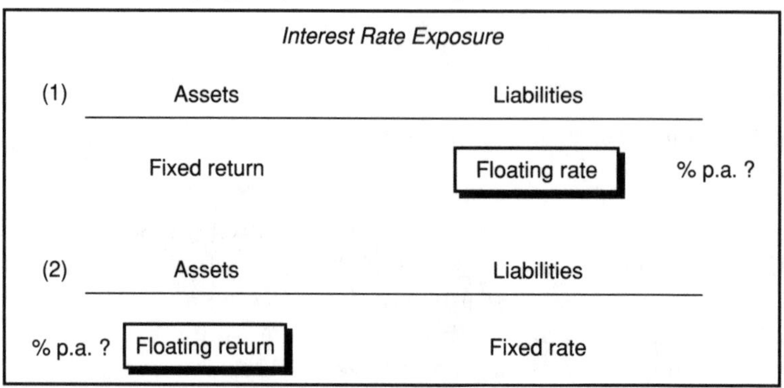

general interest rate level increases or if the yield curve becomes normal and steeper. The corporation will gain if the interest rate level drops or if the yield curve is inverse and tilts further downward.

Conversely consider an institution that is funding a portfolio of 6- and 12-month T-bills by drawing on a money market-based overdraft facility. The institution would lose if the interest rate level rose or if the yield curve became more downward sloping. But the institution would gain if the interest rate fell or if the yield curve turned normal or became steeper.

Therefore, the answer is not so straightforward. Risk is a function of volatility and is reflected in both potential loss and potential gain. Through full hedging, a position is covered against unexpected future losses, but at the same time it excludes potential extraordinary gains and thus carries an opportunity cost. Hence, the art of managing interest rate risk is to monitor, manage, and optimize the total exposure of the institution in accordance with the prevailing corporate policy.

CURRENCY EXPOSURE

Currency exposure arises when future cash inflows and cash outflows have different currency denominations. This in principle is equivalent to a currency mismatch between assets and liabilities since assets and liabilities should reflect the volume of expected cash receivables and cash payables, respectively. Currency exposure can be best explained by an example.

Example: A German trading company makes a major part of its sales in U.S. dollars. The current need of working capital is funded through low-interest Swiss franc loans. If the U.S. dollar depreciates against the Swiss franc, the company's overall profit will be squeezed. On the other hand, if the U.S. dollar strengthens against the Swiss franc, the company would gain from the currency exposure. For an illustration of currency exposure see Figure 2.2.

FIGURE 2.2
Illustration of Currency Exposure.

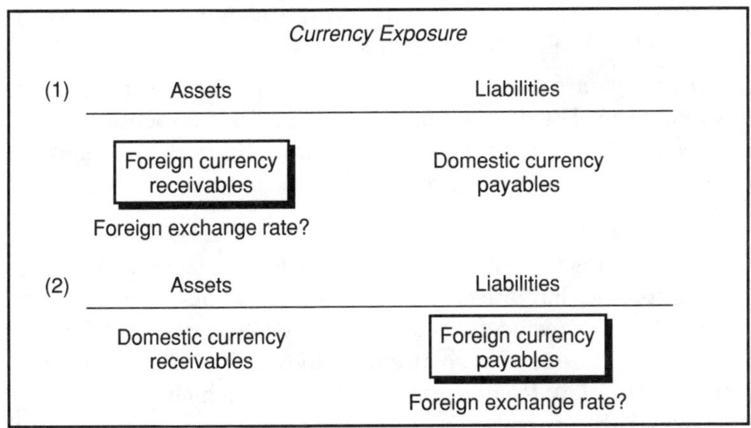

To the extent that the company can match cash inflows and outflows to the same foreign currency, the potential earnings squeeze will be eased. To the extent that the company has a net outflow of Swiss francs or a net inflow of U.S. dollars, the company runs a risk because the future foreign exchange rate, which translates the foreign currency flows into the domestic currency of accounting (German marks), is unknown. If the company has a net outflow of Swiss francs at repayment of the foreign-currency-denominated loans, a strengthening of the Swiss franc against the German mark would cause an increase in the company's interest expense measured in German mark. Conversely, if the company has a net inflow of U.S. dollars from exports, a weakening of the U.S. dollar against the DM will cause a decrease in the company's DM earnings.

One way of eliminating the uncertainty of the currency gapping is to match the currencies of the assets and the liabilities. However, this will also result in the elimination of potential extraordinary gains from the currency position.

Textbooks discussing currency exposure often use a framework that distinguishes among three types of foreign exchange risks:[1]

1. *Translation exposure* relates to the problem of converting long-term foreign-currency-denominated assets and liabilities into the domestic currency of accounting with its implications for the profit and loss statement. The discussion often centers around the accounting issues regarding foreign subsidiaries in a multinational corporation vis-à-vis the United States or other national accounting rules.
2. *Transaction exposure* relates to the expected revenue and expenses over the coming accounting year and performs an analysis on the net income effect as registered on the profit and loss statement, from potential changes in the foreign exchange rates.
3. The *economic exposure* view on the effects of foreign exchange rate trends is long term. The discussion centers on price competition in foreign markets, with its impact on export earnings, import costs, and the implications for coming years' profit and loss statements.

However, it can be argued that cash flows in the end are what really matters to any institution managed according to general business principles. Assets and liabilities, properly stated, should measure the present value of the expected future cash inflows and cash outflows of the institution. Therefore too much attention to translation exposure represents a short-term view to the exposure problem, which might have a negative impact on the institution's long-term cash flows.

The income statement of an institution based on the current accounting year usually doesn't match the actual cash flows of the institution over the accounting period, due to lags in the payment structure of the institution's commitments. Over a longer time span (say ten years), however, the net income registered on the institution's accounts will get very close to reflecting the net cash inflows of the institution. Hence the view that the main focus in a going concern should be on *long-term* cash flows remains valid, as the cash flows eventually will be *fully* reflected in the profitability measures of the institution.

In consequence any analysis of financial exposure must as a starting point involve a longer-term analysis of the institution's domestic as well as foreign-currency denominated cash flows. The analysis will indicate the maturities of both cash outflows and inflows, with a view to the interest rate basis of financial commitments. The simple cash flow statement in Table 2.1 could be utilized with benefit.

With the cash flow statement that provides an overview of the institution's term exposure on interest rates and foreign exchange rates, a view is taken on the short-term volatility and long-term trends of the interest and foreign exchange rates in order to assess the mismatch risk of the foreign currency cash flows. If management's view is that all major

TABLE 2.1
Simplified Cash Flow Statement.[2]

	Cash Inflows		*Cash Outflows*		*Liquidity Forecast Net Cash Inflows*	
Quarters	*Currency*	*Amount*	*Currency*	*Amount*	*Currency*	*Amount*
1.	DM	130,000	DM	210,000	DM	–80,000
	US$	295,000	US$	105,000	US$	190,000
	Sw. frc.	25,000	Sw. frc.	75,000*	Sw. frc.	–50,000
	£ stg.	90,000*	£ stg.	10,000	£ stg.	80,000
	—	—	—	—	—	—
	—	—	—	—	—	—
2.	—	—	—	—	—	—
	—	—	—	—	—	—
	—	—	—	—	—	—
	—	—	—	—	—	—
3.	—	—	—	—	—	—
	—	—	—	—	—	—
4.	—	—	—	—	—	—
5.	—	—	—	—	—	—
6.	—	—	—	—	—	—
7.	—	—	—	—	—	—
.	—	—	—	—	—	—
.	—	—	—	—	—	—
.	—	—	—	—	—	—
.	—	—	—	—	—	—
.	—	—	—	—	—	—
.	—	—	—	—	—	—
.	—	—	—	—	—	—

*Financial commitments on floating rate basis, cash flow estimate based on present interest rates.

currency and interest rate gaps should be closed because they otherwise bring the institution's profitability into jeopardy, a natural response would be to match the foreign exchange and interest rate basis of the cash inflows and cash outflows, or to lock in the future conversion of the net foreign currency cash inflows. The following chapters deal with a wide variety of techniques that convert the currency and/or the interest rate basis of cash flows and that lock in or guarantee the future foreign exchange rate as well as the future interest rate.

MEASURING INTEREST RATE EXPOSURE

The interest rate risk exposure is typically registered by listing the assets and liabilities according to their repricing dates.[3] This is often referred to as the *interest maturity ladder* (see Table 2.2). The establishment of the maturity repricing profile enables management to assess the interest rate repricing risk inherent in the asset and liability position. To limit the size of the interest rate risk exposure, management might impose *interest rate risk limits*, that indicate the maximum allowable interest rate gapping in predefined maturity intervals.

TABLE 2.2
Illustrative Interest Maturity Ladder.

Maturity	*Assets*	*Liabilities*	*Interest Rate Gap*	*Cumulative Gap*
Overnight	10	50	–40	–40
<3 months	17	20	–3	–43
3–12 months	13	23	–10	–53
1–3 years	26	17	+9	–44
3–5 years	38	8	+30	–14
>5 years	16	2	+14	0
Total	120	120		

All assets and liabilities with expected return implications and all financial contracts should be registered. All instruments used to hedge or manage the interest rate exposure (financial futures, swaps, floors, caps, and the like) should be included in assessing the maturity repricing profile. Assets and liabilities with ambiguous repricing maturity dates should be assessed very carefully for stability and expected repricing possibilities. The imposition of interest rate risk limits should involve all the currencies included in the balance sheet (see Table 2.3).

TABLE 2.3
Illustrative Interest Rate Limits.

Currency	*O/N*	*12 Months*	*1–3 Years*	*3–5 Years*	*Cumulative Gap*
US dollar	40	60	30	30	60
German mark	—	—	—	—	—
Pound sterling	—	—	—	—	—
Japanese yen	—	—	—	—	—
French franc	—	—	—	—	—
⋮					

MEASURING CURRENCY EXPOSURE

All institutions should manage their liquidity risk exposure. This risk exposure is registered simply by listing all the assets and liabilities by payment dates and final maturities. This listing is often referred to as the *cash maturity ladder* (see Table 2.4). To perform a full assessment of the liquidity gapping, the maturity profile must be established for every currency included in the balance sheet. To limit the size of the currency exposure, management might impose *cumulative outflow limits* to indicate the maximum allowable currency gapping. All assets and liabilities with expected cash flow implications should be included together with forward foreign exchange contracts, currency swaps, and other related positions.

TABLE 2.4
Illustrative Cash Maturity Ladder.

Maturity (Months)	*Liabilities*	*Assets*	*Net Outflow*	*Cumulative Outflow*
3	54	21	+33	33
6	48	34	+14	47
9	51	52	−1	46
12	46	52	−6	40
24	35	44	−9	31
36	18	30	−12	19
>36	9	28	−19	0
Total	261	261		

The imposition of cumulative outflow limits should involve every currency in which the institution carries significant transactions (see Table 2.5).

TABLE 2.5
Illustrative Cumulative Outflow Limits.

Currency	*<3 Months*	*<12 Months*	*<3 Years*	*Cumulative Outflow*
U.S. dollar	40	30	20	50
German mark	—	—	—	—
Pound sterling	—	—	—	—
Japanese yen	—	—	—	—
French franc	—	—	—	—
⋮				

DURATION

The *market value* of any asset or liability is determined by the discounted value of all the future cash flows relating to the asset or liability in question. In the case of a bond, the market value is determined by the discounted value of the future coupon payments and the final repayment at maturity. In the determination of this value, the discount rate (or the internal rate of return) is held constant throughout the life of the asset.

If the reinvestment rate of the coupon payments is equal to the discount rate throughout the period, then the actual return on the investment will correspond to the discount rate. However, if the reinvestment rate turns out to be lower than the discount rate, then the actual return on the investment will fall correspondingly. If the reinvestment rate rises above the discount rate over the life of the bond, then the actual return on the investment will exceed the discount rate.

The value of an asset, such as the bond, will change over time in accordance with the rate of return required by the market, that is, the prevailing interest rate. If the interest rate increases, the discounted value of the future cash flows is diminished, but the reinvestment rate of the coupons increases. If the interest rate drops, the rediscounted value of the future cash flows increases, but the reinvestment rate of the coupons falls. From this we can conclude that, for a given interest rate level, there must be a specific holding period, during which the potential loss from a marginal change in the interest rate will be offset by the potential gain.

This holding period is the *duration*. The duration of a given asset is defined as the time-weighted value of the asset's future cash flows:

$$D = \frac{\sum_{t=1}^{n} t \times C_t / (1+r)^t}{P}$$

where

$$P = \sum_{t=1}^{n} C_t / (1+r)^t$$

and

t = Time period.
n = Number of periods to final maturity.
C_t = Cash flow in period t.
r = Discount rate (internal rate of return).
P = Market price of the asset.

The duration measure enables a net investor to match a given liability in a particular currency with an asset or security of the same currency, so that the duration of the security approximately corresponds to the expected maturity of the liability. Thereby the investor in a given interest rate environment has provided for a stable return on the invested portfolio until the liability comes due.

The duration can also be used by a net borrower to match a given asset in a particular currency with a loan of the same currency, so that the duration of the loan corresponds to the expected life of the assets. Thereby the borrower has arranged a loan facility, which under the given circumstances establishes a stable interest rate on the funding until the asset is scrapped.

A shortcoming of the duration measure is that it is a function of the interest rate level. A higher interest rate gives a lower duration, and a lower interest rate gives a higher duration. Consequently the asset and liability match by duration must be monitored over time, and adjusted to the changing interest rate environment. Only the duration of zero-coupon securities (where the duration is equal to their final maturity) is insensitive to changes in the interest rate, and hence can play a particularly interesting role in interest rate risk management.

EFFICIENT SETS OF ASSETS AND LIABILITIES

The portfolio theory combines all possible investment alternatives with different cash flow structures and different currency characteristics, arranging them by expected return in the currency of accounting (mean) and risk (standard deviation of the expected return) to form the investment feasibility area. The *efficient set of assets* is the investment portfolio that, for a given risk, provides the highest expected return on the investment. Similarly, an *efficient set of liabilities* can be found as the loan portfolio that, for a given risk, provides the lowest expected cost of borrowing (see Figure 2.3).

The construction of the efficient sets takes into account both interest rate and currency fluctuations. A shortcoming of this structure is that it typically has to be based on historical statistics on interest rate and currency movements. This can be overcome by applying expected future variations in the calculations, but then, of course, there is no guarantee that this is going to be the actual outcome of events. Another shortcoming can be that there is often no obvious most efficient portfolio (the in-

FIGURE 2.3
Efficient Sets of Assets and Liabilities.

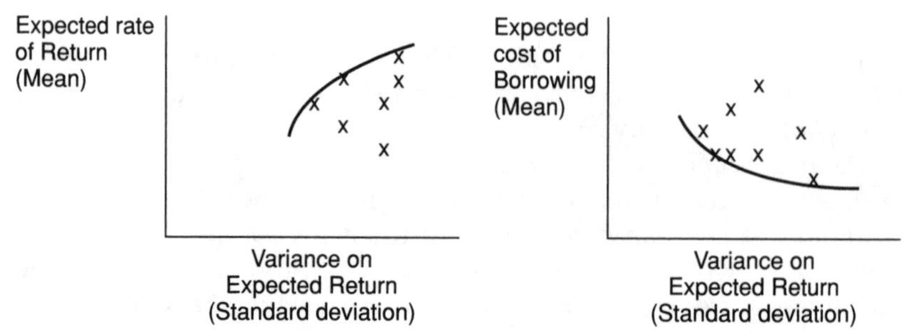

vestment portfolio with the highest return and the cheapest loan portfolio are also the most risky). In that case, the analysis does not provide an obvious optimal solution. Nevertheless, the analysis can with its limitations serve as an additional analytical tool in managing the interest rate and currency structure of investment and loan portfolios.

RISK MANAGEMENT

To enforce interest rate risk and currency risk limits, management must implement the appropriate registration, accounting, and reporting systems to record the exposures on a current basis. Concurrently, an appropriate control system must be put in place. Finally and very importantly, the exposure reports should be in a form for active use in the risk management process.

To serve the management in a satisfactory manner the information system must fulfill certain basic requirements:[4]

- It must provide up-to-date price information (preferably on-line) on *all* instruments making up the institution's exposures.
- It must record *all* instrument exposures accurately.
- It must summarize the exposures in appropriate management reports.
- It must provide sensitivity analysis that substantiates the potential effects of the exposures.

The sensitivity analysis should primarily be based on the effect on the institution's future cash flows, although immediate effects on the profit and loss statement and the balance sheet can be of interest as well. The analysis must spell out the effects of changes in the interest rate level (a parallel change), changes in the interest rate structure (a change in the slope of the yield curve), and changes in the foreign exchange rates. The analysis can, for example, be summarized into most likely, pessimistic, and optimistic scenarios.

FORECASTING INTEREST RATES

The interest rate indicates the market-determined price on the availability of money which brings about an equilibrium between entities demanding funds and entities supplying funds in a given currency. As such the interest rate is determined by supply and demand forces often illustrated by the *Marshallian cross* indicating volumes of funds in demand and supply as a function of the price (see Figure 2.4). The term "interest rate level" is meant to be a general indicator of the interest rates on all the financial instruments available in the financial market which, through substitution effects, will have the same general movement in the interest rate.

The monetary authorities tend to affect the interest rate level by monitoring and managing the reserve position of the commercial banks. This can, for example, take place through open market operations, through restrictions on credit expansion, by imposing reserve requirements on deposit growth, by quantitative regulations of the discount window, and so on. Hereby the supply of loanable funds in the banking system is regulated. If the credit availability is increased, the interest rate level will fall; if the credit availability is tightened, the interest rate level will increase.

In the "Keynesian" models the interest rate is linked to the real

FIGURE 2.4
Interest Rate Level as Determined by Supply and Demand.

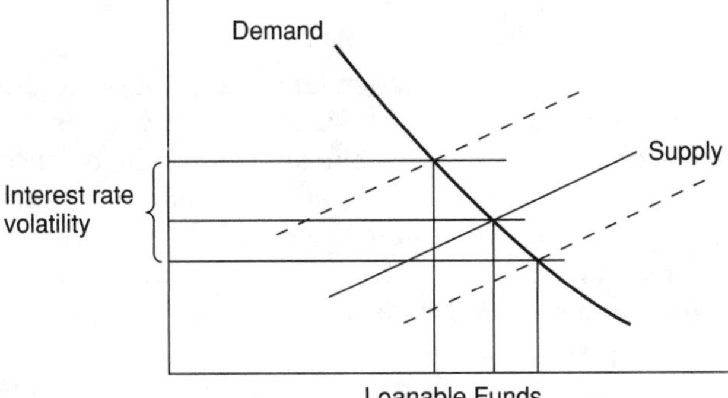

economy through the interest rate sensitivity of investments and savings. For an open economy this has implications for the balance of payments development inasmuch as the discrepancy between the level of investments and the level of savings is equivalent to the balance of payments deficit. Hence if the balance of payment is in deficit, the monetary authorities will tighten the credit expansion, the interest rate level will increase, investment activities will fade, and the volume of savings will increase. Therefore the disposable income available for consumption will drop and the demand for imported goods will ease to the benefit of the balance of payments development. In the event of insufficient savings, the high demand for goods and services will induce an inflationary process.

The "monetarist" models take the view that an expansion in the availability of credit with a given production capacity in an economy will induce an inflationary process with time lags of one to two years. If inflation increases, savers and investors who give up consumption today to obtain consumption at a later point in time will require an extra interest rate compensation in order to secure the same "real" consumption at the future date. This will drive the interest rate level *upward*. The inflationary process will make domestically produced goods more expensive abroad with negative implications for the balance of payments development.

Hence the two economic schools appear to reach contradictory conclusions with regard to the monetary policy's impact on interest rate movements. In the one case a tightening of credit availability induces an increased interest rate level, and in the other case the same phenomenon is spurred by an expansion of the availability of credit. Without going into a detailed discussion of the evolution of the two major schools of thought, it can be said that when the economic profession is in disagreement about how the economic dynamics work, then what really matters is the market makers' perception of the economic realities. If the participants in a financial market believe in one set of economic dynamics vis-à-vis the interest rate, their collective expectations will tend to make their belief come true.

Nevertheless, it becomes crucial to understand the position of the monetary authorities in order to understand their reaction to various developments in the real economy. To some public authorities the balance of payments development constitutes a major concern, to others it is the level of economic activity, and to others again the inflationary process is in focus. Very often forecasting the interest rate level is tantamount to foreseeing the reaction of monetary and fiscal authorities to a worsening of the balance of payments position, the level of unemployment, or to an increase in the inflation rate. If the reaction pattern of the monetary authorities is well understood, the forecasting exercise boils down to the forecast of real economic events and the ability to foresee the political response and market reaction to such developments. However, this is an exercise that is *not* mastered by economic science, but rather that relies solely on the subjective judgment and experience of individuals.

Economic models can forecast the real economic consequences of different events under a given set of preconditions and therefore constitute a good tool for economic policy makers, as it answers their question, "What happens if we introduce this or that policy measure?" To date, however, no forecasting model has been developed that can forecast the future interest rate satisfactorily. The exercise of forecasting interest rates at best is an uncertain task, and relying on interest rate forecasts in consequence is the same as making a bet on the future. So in many cases it is wise to hedge major interest rate gaps.

FORECASTING FOREIGN EXCHANGE RATES

The foreign exchange spot rate is determined by the current supply and demand situation of the two currencies in question (see Figure 2.5). The supply and demand for a country's currency arise partly from trade-related cash flows into and out from the country.

To pay for imports, foreign currency must be bought against the supply of the domestic currency: the higher the supply of the domestic currency, the lower the price on this currency. When an exporter receives payment from an importer in a foreign country the importer demands the exporter's currency against the supply of foreign currency. The higher the demand of the exporter's currency the higher will be the price

FIGURE 2.5
Forecasting Foreign Exchange Rates.

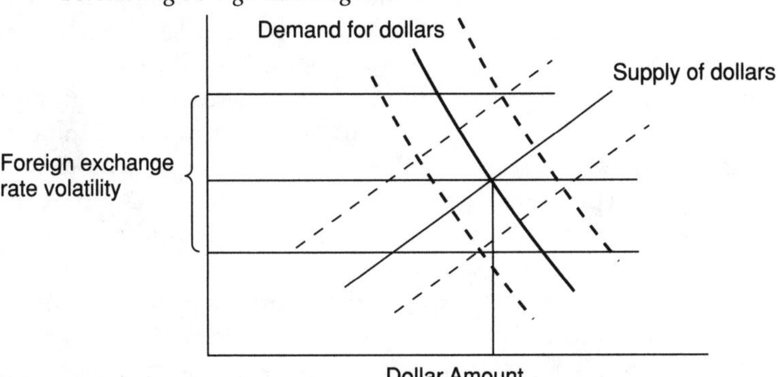

for the exporter's domestic currency. Hence the higher the current balance of payment surplus of a country, the higher the likelihood is that the price of that country's currency will increase.

Yet, as proven by the foreign exchange rate development of the U.S. dollar in the mid-1980s, this rule of thumb is *not* satisfactory in explaining foreign exchange rate movements. This is because it ignores the balance of payments' capital account, which registers cash flows originating from international money and capital market transactions. If foreign entities invest in a country, they will demand the currency of this country against the supply of foreign currency when effecting the investment. The increased demand from these investment transactions will force up the price of the country's currency.

The residual on the overall balance of payments account, including the current account and the capital account, is the country's international reserves. If there is a net cash inflow of foreign currency to the country its international reserve position will improve. Conversely, if a country has a net cash outflow of foreign currency, the country's international reserve position will weaken. Therefore some forecasters have used the international reserves of a country as an indicator of the general supply and demand position of that country's currency. However, even if the reserve position is volatile it might on average remain at a level that secures a stable foreign exchange rate development, and so it does not constitute a satisfactory indicator of foreign exchange rate movements.

A standard rule often used in foreign exchange rate analysis is the *purchasing power parity theory*. This theory basically says that, of two countries, the country with a higher inflation rate will have its currency depreciate against the other country's currency of a magnitude that is inversely related to the inflation rates of the two countries. This is because over time the country with the higher inflation rate will export more expensive goods and the country will receive cheaper imports from the lower inflation country. This will have a negative impact on the balance of payments development in the high inflation country which eventually will enforce a readjustment of the foreign exchange rate. This adjustment process, however, is slow. First of all, the adjustment process might take a long time to materialize; second, the international reserve position of any country makes up a buffer that can extend the duration of the foreign exchange rate adjustment. Hence this is not a satisfactory model for forecasting short-term foreign exchange rate movements. (As it turns out, the model holds fairly true in the long run, but who can forecast the inflation rates ten years ahead of time?)

Which indicators, then, *can* explain the short-term movements in foreign exchange rates? One is the comparison of relative interest rates between different foreign currencies. In countries with liberal foreign exchange rate regulations, the international investors will be attracted to the highest-yielding currency investments. What matters here is not the real interest rate, as indicated by the nominal interest rate minus the inflation rate, but rather the nominal interest rate itself. To foreign investors, the inflation rate of other countries does not matter because they will use the proceeds of the investment in their own country. So what matters is the relative size of different currency areas' nominal interest rates. All other things being equal, foreign investments will be attracted to the currency area of the highest nominal interest rate, which will strengthen the foreign exchange rate of that currency. This being the case, we come back to the problem of forecasting interest rates in order to determine future foreign exchange rates.

The expectation of a continued strengthening of a foreign currency will attract more foreign investors because they see a chance to increase the yield from the investment above the nominal interest rate of that currency area. This attraction vanishes quickly when the foreign exchange rate starts to weaken. This "rational" investor behavior causes the foreign exchange rates to follow cyclical trends, which are very hard to forecast. Another important element in the foreign currency investor behavior is the perceived security of the different alternative currency areas. The security element relates to political stability in the currency area in question and to potential political destabilization in the alternative currency areas.

The underlying factors that induce the behavioristic moves of foreign investors are very hard, if not impossible, to forecast, which appears to be proven by following up on professional foreign exchange rate forecasts. The economic technician would analyze the foreign exchange rate movements, for example, by performing a regression analysis involving a set of explanatory variables:

$$S_t = a + bR + cM + dC + eI + fG + gS_{t-1}$$

where

S_t = Spot foreign exchange rate at time t.
R = Relative change in international reserves.
M = Relative change in money supply (M2).
C = Relative change in the consumer price index (CPI).
I = Relative 3 - month interest rates.
G = Relative yield on 1-year government bonds.
S_{t-1} = Spot foreign exchange rate at time $t-1$.
$a \ldots g$ = Regression coefficients.

Even if all the regression coefficients pass the significance test, we come back to the problem of forecasting the explanatory variables in order to end up with a forecast for the future foreign exchange rate. As already illustrated, this represents the true weakness of consequential models when used for forecasting purposes. In response, a variety of time series techniques has been developed. These models are pure statistical models that base their forecasting ability solely on a statistical analysis of the historical foreign exchange rates as represented in a sufficiently large time series.

A special technique, the so-called *technical analysis*, constitutes a group of the most simple time series analyses developed in the search for objective statistical forecasting methods. These models are usually based on the moving average concept applied on a time series of the historical daily foreign exchange rates. In essence, such a model compares the short-term movement in the foreign exchange rate with the longer-term movement in the foreign exchange rate. If the short-term movement differs significantly from the longer-term movement, the foreign exchange rate movement *might* have come to a turning point.

TABLE 2.1
Technical Analysis.

Day	*(DM/US$)*	*10-day Moving Average*	*5-day Moving Average*	*2-day Moving Average*	
1	2.7500	—	—	—	
2	2.7750	—	—	2.7625	
3	2.8000	—	—	2.7825	
4	2.8100	—	—	2.8050	
5	2.8050	—	2.7880	2.8075	
6	2.8220	—	2.8024	2.8135	
7	2.8500	—	2.8174	2.8360	
8	2.8600	—	2.8294	2.8550	
9	2.8700	—	2.8414	2.8650	
10	2.9000	2.8242	2.8604	2.8850	
11	3.0000	2.8492	2.8960	2.9500	
12	3.2500	2.8967	2.9760	3.1250	
13	3.3000	2.9467	3.0640	3.2750	
14	3.2500	2.9907	3.1400	3.2750	
15	3.2000	3.0302	3.2000	3.2250	
16	3.1500	3.0630	3.2300	3.1750	Sell
17	3.0500	3.0830	3.1900	3.1000	signal 1
18	2.9500	3.0920	3.1200	3.0000	
19	2.9000	3.0950	3.0500	2.9250	Sell
20	2.8500	3.0900	2.9800	2.8750	signal 2

Example: The 10-day, 5-day, and 2-day moving averages have been calculated on a time series of foreign exchange rates. We see that on the 16th day, the 2-day moving average falls below the 5-day moving average. This indicates the beginning of a downward trend in the foreign exchange rate. On the 19th day, the 5-day moving average falls below the 10-day moving average, indicating with higher significance the downward trend in the foreign exchange rate. For a foreign currency investor, this would indicate that the currency in question should be sold. Conversely when the short-term moving averages exceed the long-term moving averages from below, it indicates that the currency in question should be bought. (See Table 2.1 and Figure 2.6.)

The analysis is based on the observation that foreign exchange rates move in cycles where objective statistical measures can indicate the turning points of these cycles. The cyclical movements of the foreign exchange rates are very much a function of the market participants' behavior, which will be discarded when there is intervention in the foreign exchange markets. Hence this type of analysis has its limits, although the models have proven to be useful in managing short-term foreign currency positions, as well as leads and lags in foreign currency flows. The model, however, is reactive in nature and can serve only as an indicator for subjective evaluations on the future foreign exchange rate.

Over recent years a new type of technical analysis, often referred to

FIGURE 2.6

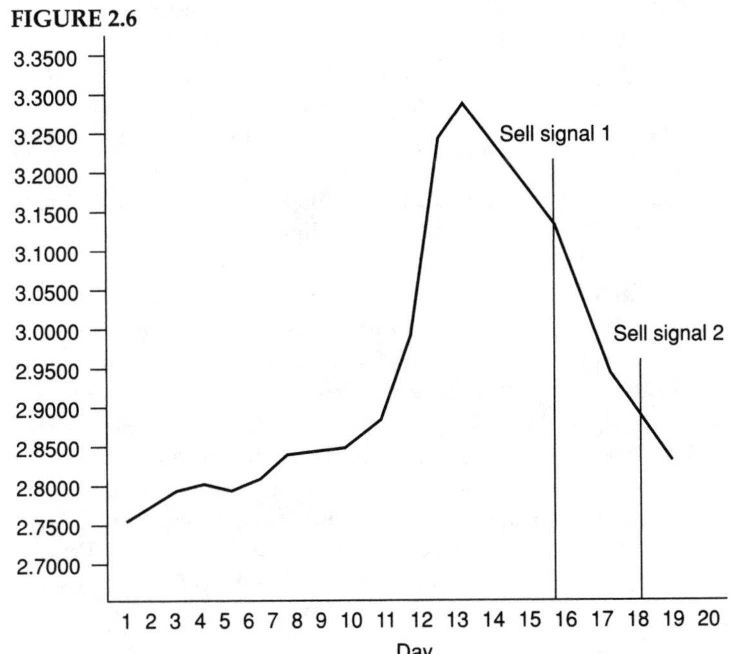

as *chaos theory,* has been applied to describe price movements in the financial markets. The idea is to establish a nonlinear relationship in a given time series. It turns out that quite simple formulas can create seemingly unstructured time series, often referred to as *random walk* or *white noise,* which can then in the best of cases bring order into chaos. Despite the interesting analytical findings, the theoretical concept has not yet been developed into reliable forecasting models. (Refer to the appendix on forecasting techniques for a further presentation of the models.)

Assuming that one day models will be developed to forecast future financial variables with full certainty, then the mere knowledge of the future will be used by market participants to engage in riskless positions. This in itself will eliminate the future price structure as it is forecast, because the future prices immediately will become today's prices. In other words, it is not likely that the ideal and true models will ever be found. What models can do is to explain price movements ex post and to make ex ante analysis.

CONCLUSION

The expansion in the volume of international commercial transactions and the liberalization of the foreign exchange regulations in many industrialized countries have made institutions engaging in international business more vulnerable to interest rate and foreign exchange exposures, a development that will require close attention by management.

There are differing attitudes to the question on whether or not to hedge financial exposure. Some feel that all foreign exchange and interest rate gaps should be closed to minimize the uncertainty of cash flows, while others feel that in the long run losses and gains will even out. The proper answer probably reflects the more balanced view that financial exposure should be managed. Given the volatility of the interest and foreign exchange rates, the apparent difficulties in forecasting their movements, and the increased impact from interest rate and currency gaps, it is often wise to hedge major exposures.

High volatility in interest rates and foreign exchange rates can have a severe impact on an institution's cash flows if rate trends continue to run in an unfavorable direction. Hence it is crucial that management performs a thorough analysis of the institution's financial exposures in order to assess the potential risk of these positions. As forecasting interest rates and foreign exchange rates has proven virtually impossible, maintaining large open positions is to gamble on future rate movements. In response to this, management should define its attitude to these types of risks and institute clear guidelines regarding the level of acceptable financial exposure.

II

FINANCIAL FUTURES

3

The Futures Contract

Futures contracts have their roots in the markets for raw materials, such as agricultural products (corn, soybeans, wheat, sugar, cocoa) and metals (copper, tin, silver, gold, platinum), specifically in the case of silver and gold which also serve as investment vehicles.

As opposed to making forward dealings in commodities, where the goods are physically exchanged at a future date at an agreed price, the idea of the futures contract is to create a standard instrument to be traded on an exchange floor.

An exchange-traded futures contract for a given commodity is interchangeable with other contracts on the same commodity, having common specifications for such terms as size of contract, commodity grade, delivery months, and so on (see Table 3.1). Standardized by the exchange on which it trades, the futures contract therefore is easily traded. A *futures contract* is a legal commitment for the seller to make delivery and for the buyer to take delivery of a standardized quantity and quality of the underlying commodity at a specified point in time (the *expiration date*).

The value of a futures contract depends on the market price of the underlying commodity in the *spot,* or *cash,* market. To determine the

TABLE 3.1
Specifications of a Standard Contract: Gold.

Commodity name	Gold
Exchange name	Commodity Exchange, New York (COMEX)
Size of contract	100 troy ounces
Delivery months	Current calendar month, the next two months, and Feb/Apr/June, Aug/Oct/Dec
First delivery date	First Friday of the delivery month; this is the first day on which delivery may be made.
First notice date	Two business days before the first delivery date; this is the first day on which a seller may issue notice of intention to deliver.
Expiration date	Second Friday before delivery of the futures contract; this is the last day on which an option may be exercised.
Minimum price fluctuation	$0.10 per ounce; this is the smallest change allowable in the price movement of a contract.

value of a contract, one should multiply the spot market price by the size of the contract.

Example: If gold is quoted at $305 per ounce on COMEX, one contract of gold is worth $30,500 ($305 per ounce times 100). A minimum price movement of $0.10 in the price of gold is therefore equal to a $10 change in the price of the contract ($0.10 per ounce times 100 ounces in a contract).

Over the years, the underlying interests of futures contracts have changed and increased in number. For many years, contracts traded exclusively on agricultural commodities, such as corn, wheat, pork bellies, and soybeans, as well as on precious metals. In the early 1980s, futures contracts became available on oil and gasoline, debt instruments, and different stock indexes. Table 3.2 presents a small sampling of the types of contracts available today.

OPENING AND CLOSING TRANSACTIONS

A transaction in futures contracts must be identified as either "opening" or "closing" a position. The initial buying or selling of a futures contract results in an *open position* for the buyer or seller, respectively. The seller's position is open because it is considered *short*—the seller has sold a commodity that he or she does not own. The buyer's position is considered

TABLE 3.2
Representative Futures Contracts.

Commodity Name	*Delivery Months*	*Size of Contract*	*Minimum Price Fluctuation*	*Name of Futures Exchange*
Wheat (hard red winter)	Mar./May/ July/Sept./ Dec.	5,000 bushels ($12.50)	$0.0025 per bu.	Kansas City Board of Trade
Cattle, live	Feb./Apr./ June/Aug./ Oct./Dec.	20,000 pounds	$0.025 per lb. ($5)	Mid-American Commodities
U.S. Treasury Bonds	Mar./June Sept./Dec.	$100,000 face value	1/32 point) ($31.25 8% coupon	Chicago Board of Trade
Standard & Poor's 500 Stock Index	Mar./June Sept./Dec.	500 × S&P stock index value	5 points ($25)	Chicago Mercantile Exchange
U.S. dollar	Mar./June Sept./Dec.	$100,000 U.S. dollars	$0.0001 ($10)	Toronto Futures Exchange
No. 2 heating oil	All months	42,000 gallons	$0.0001 per gal ($4.20)	New York Mercantile Exchange
Japanese yen	Jan./Mar./Apr. June/July/ Sept./Oct./ Dec., and spot month	12,500,000 Japanese yen	$0.000001	Singapore International Monetary Exchange

long because the contract is for a future purchase of the commodity. As a result, the buyer's position is also open.

A *closing* transaction is one that offsets a position. A commitment may be closed in two ways:

1. By an *offsetting* (liquidating) *transaction:* To close, or offset a short position, a *seller* buys a comparable contract (a *closing purchase transaction*). A buyer closes a long position by selling a comparable contract (a *closing sale transaction*). All but a small percentage of positions are closed this way.
2. By *delivering* or *receiving* the commodity: A seller may also close a position by delivering the commodity, a buyer by receiving it.

ROLE OF THE EXCHANGES

A futures exchange provides the trading arena for standardized futures contracts. As in the case of stock exchanges, only members may trade on futures exchanges. Eligibility for membership depends on creditworthiness, past business history, character and integrity.

ROLE OF THE CLEARING HOUSES

The clearing house is an exchange-affiliated agency that clears trades, guarantees performance, and handles fulfillment through delivery.

Clearing

For every trade, the buyer's and seller's firms submit the data on the trade to the clearing house. At the clearing house, data from the buying and selling firms are compared. If the data match, the trade is *cleared.* If not, the data are sent back to the firms for correction. Should the trade data still not match up, the trade is handled on an *out trade*—that is, as a special case.

Guaranteeing Performance

The clearing house thus acts as a third party to all trades. During the course of a trading day, Smith may sell a contract to Jones, Jones to Doe, and Doe to someone else. Once the trade is made, however, the contract no longer exists between the last buyer and seller. Rather, the clearing house becomes the counterpart to each transaction—a buyer to every seller and a seller to every buyer. Purchasers and sellers of the contracts create financial obligations not to one another but to the clearing corporation or to the exchange through its member firms.

Delivery

Although only a few percent of all futures contracts result in physical delivery, clearing corporations usually have to provide the mechanism for delivery of the underlying commodity when necessary.

QUOTATIONS

Figure 3.1 presents futures contract quotations, which are typically listed alphabetically by commodity on the respective futures exchanges with the expiration dates grouped below each commodity. Corn, for example, is listed before soybeans, soybeans before wheat, and so on. Notice also that these commodities all fall under the heading of "Grains and

Oilseeds." Other categories are "Livestock and Meat," "Metals and Petroleums," "Wood," and "Financial," among others. When a commodity is traded on more than one exchange, it is typically repeated with the abbreviation for the exchange in parentheses after the commodity name. Wheat, for instance, is listed three times because it trades on the Chicago Board of Trade (CBT), the Kansas City Board of Trade (KC), and the Minneapolis Grains Exchange (MPLS). These abbreviations are explained in a key at the bottom of the quotation section. Next to the commodity names are the standard contract size, such as 5,000 bushels for corn, and the unit of quotation, such as cents per bushel.

At the top of the columns of quotations are the following headings:

- *Open:* The price at which each contract opened.
- *High/Low:* The high and low prices of the day.
- *Settle:* The price at which the contract closed.
- *Change:* The difference between the closing prices of this day and the previous day.
- *Lifetime High/Low:* The highest and lowest prices at which the contract has traded in its lifetime to date.
- *Open Interest:* The total number of futures contracts (purchases or sales) that have not been offset by an opposite transaction or fulfilled by delivery.

Example: In Figure 3.1, the size of a corn contract on the CBT is 5,000 bushels and the price quotes represent cents per bushel. Five yearly corn contracts settle on the same months: May, July, September, December, and March. As soon as a March contract for one year expires, a new contract begins trading for July of the next year on the CBT.

The May contract opened at 228½ ($2.285) per bushel. During the trading day, the highest price was 229½ ($2.295), and the lowest was 227 ($2.27). It closed at 228 ($2.28), which represents a ¼-point change from the previous day's close. Since the contract began trading, the highest price has been 291¼ ($2.9125) and the lowest, 222½ ($2.225). There are 33,049 positions (buys and sells) in the May contract that have not been offset by an opposite transaction or by delivery.

Expiration months tend to be standardized even from one exchange to another.

Example: Silver, which is traded on the CBT and COMEX, has identical expiration months on either exchange.

FIGURE 3.1

Quotes on Futures Prices. (*Reprinted by permission of Wall Street Journal* [*Europe*], *© Dow Jones & Company, Inc., April 10, 1986. All rights reserved.*)

FUTURES PRICES

Thursday, April 10, 1986.

Open Interest Reflects Previous Trading Day.

–GRAINS AND OILSEEDS–

	Open	High	Low	Settle	Change	Lifetime High	Lifetime Low	Open Interest
CORN (CBT) 5,000 bu.; cents per bu.								
May	228½	229½	227	228	– ¼	291¼	222½	33,049
July	220¼	221¾	218½	219¼	– 1½	286	218½	30,339
Sept	204¼	205¼	202¾	203	– 1¾	270	202¾	8,086
Dec	200½	201¼	199	199¼	– 2	235½	199	37,218
Mar87	209½	210¼	207¾	207¾	– 2	242½	207¾	5,283
May	213½	213¾	212	212¼	– 1½	242	212	1,423
July	215	215	212¾	212¾	– 1¾	222	212¾	175
Est vol 49,000; vol Wed 46,044; open int 115,573, +4115.								
SOYBEANS (CBT) 5,000 bu.; cents per bu.								
May	525	529¼	521½	524¾	+ 1¾	657	489	23,833
July	521½	527¼	518½	522¾	+ 2¾	658	497	27,993
Aug	519½	526	517½	521¼	+ 2	609	498½	3,898
Sept	510½	514	508½	510	....	555½	496	3,265
Nov	509	511¾	504½	507¾	– 1	556½	498	19,093
Jan87	516¼	521	514	516¾	– ½	565	509	1,512
Mar	524½	529	522½	526	– ½	576	519½	1,367
May	531	533¼	527½	530½	– 1½	556	527½	142
Est vol 29,500; vol Wed 28,643; open int 81,115, +1,330.								
SOYBEAN MEAL (CBT) 100 tons; $ per ton.								
May	154.40	156.00	153.50	154.90	+ 1.00	163.90	134.00	15,674
July	153.90	155.40	152.80	154.40	+ 1.00	167.00	134.00	13,588
Aug	153.20	154.80	152.30	154.10	+ 1.20	163.50	135.50	4,603
Sept	151.00	152.60	149.50	151.10	+ .60	159.30	137.50	3,306
Oct	148.10	149.00	146.50	148.50	+ .50	156.00	136.00	4,017
Dec	149.20	150.50	147.50	149.60	+ .40	157.00	136.00	6,910
Jan87	....	....	....	150.70	+ .50	157.50	136.00	820
Mar	....	....	....	151.00	....	159.00	149.00	275
Est vol 12,000; vol Wed 11,530; open int 49,193, –30.								
SOYBEAN OIL (CBT) 60,000 lbs.; cents per lb.								
May	17.50	17.64	17.41	17.43	+ .02	27.45	16.76	16,734
July	17.77	17.97	17.72	17.75	+ .04	25.25	17.03	16,469
Aug	17.85	18.05	17.80	17.88	+ .06	25.15	17.16	5,659
Sept	17.95	18.07	17.95	17.95	....	24.05	17.10	2,959
Oct	18.05	18.15	17.95	17.97	....	22.80	17.25	3,666
Dec	18.45	18.55	18.35	18.40	....	22.50	17.51	7,714
Jan87	18.60	18.65	18.50	18.50	– .05	22.35	17.70	1,127
Mar	19.00	19.05	18.85	18.90	....	20.25	18.20	398
Est vol 12,000; vol Wed 20,055; open int 54,762, +170.								
WHEAT (CBT) 5,000 bu.; cents per bu.								
May	295½	298	285	286¾	– 9¼	350	274	5,224
July	250½	251	246	246¼	– 4½	310	246	16,154
Sept	252	253	248½	249	– 3½	299	248½	6,627
Dec	260¾	260¾	256	256	– 4½	308¼	256	5,442
Mar87	261½	261¾	257	257	– 4¾	287	257	614
Est vol 11,000; vol Wed 8,921; open int 34,105, –269.								
WHEAT (KC) 5,000 bu.; cents per bu.								
May	280	281	272	273¼	– 8½	301	263½	3,898
July	242	242¾	239½	239½	–2½	298½	239½	8,425
Sept	245½	245¾	243½	243½	– 2	281½	243½	1,633
Dec	253½	253½	253	252½	– 2	283	253	799
Mar87	....	....	....	256	– ½	259¾	256½	52
Est vol 2,962; vol Wed 3,115; open int 14,807, +143.								
WHEAT (MPLS) 5,000 bu.; cents per bu.								
May	338½	340	336¾	336¾	– 3¼	363	318¾	3,368
July	300½	301¾	299½	300	– 2½	247½	294	1,454
Sept	276	276	273¾	274	– 2¼	350	273¾	1,221
Dec	282½	282½	281	281	– 2¼	302	281	335
Est vol 1,448; vol Wed 1,036; open int 6,378, –3.								
BARLEY (WPG) 20 metric tons; Can. $ per ton								
May	90.00	90.90	89.60	89.60	– 2.30	130.00	89.60	2,585
July	89.50	90.30	89.50	89.50	– 2.70	119.17	89.50	2,513
Oct	86.50	87.10	86.40	86.40	– 2.30	106.00	86.40	2,759
Dec	87.00	87.80	86.90	86.90	– 2.50	99.50	86.90	1,749
Est vol 2,420; vol Wed 566; open int 9,606, –68.								
FLAXSEED (WPG) 20 metric tons; Can. $ per ton								
May	281.80	281.80	279.70	279.70	– 2.10	352.50	279.60	2,739
July	289.20	289.20	287.30	287.50	– 1.70	326.20	287.30	1,426
[illegible]	[illegible]	[illegible]	[illegible]	[illegible]	[illegible]	[illegible]	[illegible]	1,144

	Open	High	Low	Settle	Change	Lifetime High	Lifetime Low	Open Interest
Dec	38.95	39.15	38.80	38.81	– .35	59.25	38.45	9,459
Mar87	40.00	40.10	39.85	39.85	– .35	49.50	39.50	692
Est vol 3,000; vol Wed 4,119; open int 20,426, –297.								
ORANGE JUICE (CTN)–15,000 lbs.; cents per lb.								
May	94.55	95.00	94.20	94.50	– .95	162.50	82.60	1,706
July	94.40	94.80	93.70	93.70	– 1.00	157.50	83.50	1,823
Sept	93.70	93.90	92.60	92.60	– 1.40	127.25	82.00	1,020
Nov	93.60	93.60	92.50	92.50	– 1.35	125.00	82.50	467
Jan87	93.00	93.00	92.10	92.10	– 1.00	113.00	83.75	270
Mar	93.25	93.25	92.90	92.85	– .80	122.00	83.90	948
May	94.00	94.00	94.00	93.20	– 1.20	94.75	84.50	665
July	....	....	....	93.70	– 1.10	95.00	84.75	306
Est vol 650; vol Wed 743; open int 7,205, –122.								
SUGAR–WORLD (CSCE)–112,000 lbs.; cents per lb.								
May	9.45	9.45	8.85	8.91	– .46	9.58	3.58	31,072
July	9.45	9.45	8.65	8.74	– .61	9.50	3.79	27,053
Sept	9.39	9.42	8.83	8.83	– .50	9.42	4.05	357
Oct	9.38	9.40	8.80	8.80	– .50	9.40	4.02	42,446
Jan87	9.50	9.50	9.50	8.80	– .50	9.50	5.65	169
Mar	9.61	9.64	9.06	9.10	– .45	9.64	6.03	14,198
May	9.80	9.82	9.25	9.27	– .41	9.82	6.75	3,520
July	9.85	9.90	9.32	9.34	– .44	9.92	7.77	1,500
Est vol 28,688; vol Wed 23,784; open int 120,315, +314.								
SUGAR–DOMESTIC (CSCE)–112,000 lbs.; cents per lb.								
July	20.65	20.70	20.62	20.68	....	21.60	19.35	1,295
Sept	20.65	20.70	20.65	20.70	– .03	21.45	19.35	588
Nov	....	....	....	20.62	– .03	21.29	19.65	282
Est vol 100; vol Wed 183; open int 2,165, –113.								
–METALS & PETROLEUM–								
COPPER (CMX)–25,000 lbs.; cents per lb.								
Apr	....	....	....	64.30	+ .40	65.25	63.00	0
May	64.00	64.75	64.00	64.55	+ .40	74.00	60.00	34,680
July	64.75	65.40	64.70	65.25	+ .40	72.55	60.35	26,994
Sept	65.35	65.85	65.35	65.80	+ .40	70.90	60.90	8,197
Dec	65.90	66.60	65.90	66.45	+ .40	70.30	61.60	6,976
Mar87	67.15	67.15	67.15	67.10	+ .40	70.00	62.55	1,558
May	....	....	....	67.45	+ .40	70.00	62.90	437
July	....	....	....	67.85	+ .40	69.95	63.25	197
Est vol 7,700; vol Wed 13,440; open int 79,141, +929.								
GOLD (CMX)–100 troy oz.; $ per troy oz.								
Apr	337.50	339.50	337.50	338.90	– .40	496.80	314.70	1,721
June	339.80	342.80	339.00	341.70	– .50	433.50	320.50	60,368
Aug	343.00	346.00	343.00	345.10	– .50	427.50	328.00	17,586
Oct	347.00	348.60	346.30	348.30	– .50	395.70	331.50	7,271
Dec	349.00	353.00	349.00	351.70	– .50	392.00	336.50	13,538
Feb87	354.50	355.00	354.40	355.20	– .50	397.50	337.30	11,716
Apr	357.00	357.00	357.00	358.30	– .50	405.00	346.30	8,147
June	360.00	360.70	360.00	361.60	– .50	409.00	350.50	7,368
Aug	....	....	....	365.10	– .50	408.50	356.00	6,472
Oct	368.70	366.70	366.70	368.70	– .50	420.00	361.00	4,973
Dec	372.00	372.00	372.00	372.60	– .50	399.40	367.00	1,666
Feb88	....	....	....	376.70	– .50	....	....	230
Est vol 27,000; vol 33,678; open int 141,056, +3,142.								
PLATINUM (NYM)–50 troy oz.; $ per troy oz.								
Apr	428.70	430.50	425.00	427.90	– .80	444.50	264.50	544
July	428.00	435.50	425.50	431.10	+ .10	448.00	273.00	14,448
Oct	430.50	438.30	430.00	434.30	+ .50	450.00	303.50	2,374
Jan87	435.00	440.50	434.00	437.50	+ 1.00	450.00	347.00	835
Apr	437.50	442.50	436.00	440.70	+ 1.60	448.50	361.00	494
Est vol 4,985; vol Wed 5,703; open int 18,695, +743.								
PALLADIUM (NYM) 100 troy oz.; $ per troy oz.								
Apr	....	....	....	105.75	– .30	114.00	106.00	2
June	106.25	107.80	106.25	106.75	– .30	119.30	91.50	4,238
Sept	108.25	109.00	108.25	108.15	– .30	119.00	91.70	1,139
Dec	110.00	110.00	109.75	109.55	– .30	120.00	94.25	576
Mar87	111.75	111.75	111.75	110.95	– .30	127.50	90.00	145
Est vol [illegible]; vol Wed [illegible]; open int [illegible], –85								

Open Interest and Volume

After the quotation of each commodity in Figure 3.1, the listing provides figures for total volume and open interests in each contract.

Volume is the number of contracts that were traded during the day, whether the transactions opened or closed positions. The previous day's volume is included as a point for comparison of the current day's trading.

Open interest is the total number of open contracts, whether buys or sells or different expiry dates, *as of* the close of trading.

Volume and open interest do not necessarily increase or decrease in relationship to each other. Heavy volume during a trading day, for example, could leave open interest almost unchanged from the previous day if the opening and closing transactions are roughly equal in number. Or volume could increase from one day to the next—but decrease open interest if most of the trades were made to close positions.

MARGIN

To ensure that member firms have enough funds to cover their positions in the market, clearing corporations require members to deposit and maintain margin against their positions. Margin in futures trading is roughly analogous to margin in stock and bond trading.

But only roughly. The margin differs in several ways. Whereas margin for a securities transaction is at least 50%, it is typically less than 10% for a futures trade (it varies from one exchange to the other). In securities, buying on margin is optional, but all futures trades require margin payments. Perhaps the most crucial difference is in the purpose of margin payments. In the purchase of a stock or bond, margin is partial payment; the remainder of the purchase is financed by the brokerage firm. In futures transactions the margin is a *performance bond,* or *earnest money;* it ensures that purchasers and sellers will live up to their contractual obligations. Because the margin is not a partial payment, the brokerage firm makes no loan and no interest is paid, as in the case of margin purchases of securities.

There are two kinds of margin in futures trading: initial margin and maintenance margin.

Initial Margin

Initial or original margin is the money deposited for each contract upon the purchase or sale of the contract, usually 10% of the total worth of the contract. The exchanges set initial margin, depending on the volatility of the commodity and of the futures market itself. Brokerage houses usually ask their customers for a slightly higher margin than that set by the exchange.

Example: If an exchange requires initial margin of 10% on its orange juice contracts, a member brokerage firm might require 15%. If the cash price of orange juice is $0.9500 per pound and a contract consists of 15,000 pounds, then the value of the contract is $14,250 (15,000 pounds times $0.95). The brokerage firm will require an initial margin deposit of $2,187.50 (15% of $14,250).

Original margin can be posted in any of the following ways—or in any combination of them:

1. Cash (usually in the form of bank-issued margin certificates).
2. Stock in the clearing corporation.
3. Interest-bearing obligations of the federal government (T-bills, T-bonds, T-notes, and the like).
4. Letters of credit from an approved commercial bank.

Maintenance Margin

Maintenance (or *variation*) *margin* is additional margin required on an established position as a result of a decline in the value of the contract. It is calculated by the exchange clearing house at the end of the trading day. Retail clients are asked by their brokerage houses to put up more margin or have their positions sold out.

Most exchanges set the total amount of margin required in relation to the net short or long position that each member holds in each contract.

Example: A member holds a long position (the buy side) in 15 silver contracts and a short position (the sell side) in 10 silver contracts, and delivery for all the contracts is in the same month. The total margin required is for the net long position of 5 silver contracts.

Some exchanges and many independent clearing corporations seek additional protection by requiring maintenance margin on all long and short positions even when they can be offset by other contracts held by other members.

NORMAL AND INVERTED MARKETS

Refer to Figure 3.1, specifically the settle prices for copper. Notice that the prices for the near months are lower than the months farther out. The market for copper is said to be a *normal,* or *carrying charge,* market—that is, the distant months sell at a premium over near months. The premium is attributed to a carrying charge that is added to the value of the contract and that represents a collective value for insurance, warehousing, and cost of money to "carry" the commodity. The more distant months cost more because they entail greater carrying charges.

In a normal market, the maximum that a distant month can sell over a near month is the total of the carrying charges. If a price included more than these charges, the arbitrageurs would sell the distant month short and take delivery with the nearer, cheaper month, thus locking in a profit whether or not the more distant month's price rose or fell.

An *inverted market* is the opposite of a normal market; that is, the distant months sell at lower prices than near months. In Figure 3.1, the market for corn is inverted, with May contracts trading at a higher price than all others. The implication of an inverted market is that the commodity is in short supply. Buyers are bidding up the price of the near months to the extent that these months' prices more than offset the carrying charges included in the prices of contracts for the distant months.

In an inverted (or "discount") market, each contract that is further out in time trades at a lower price than one closer in. Whereas in a normal market the prices of the further-out contracts are limited by the carrying charges, there is no limit to the amount that a near contract can trade over a more distant contract in an inverted market. Inverted markets usually occur in spurts of extreme bullishness.

MARKET PARTICIPANTS

Those who trade commodities may be categorized as either arbitrageurs, hedgers or speculators.

Today the consumer of commodities, if not as large as, say, General Mills, is considerably larger than the local miller of yesteryear. This consumer-processor must figure out its commodity costs months in advance. Like the farmer in our example, the corporate food processor can fix its commodity costs by hedging—that is, by buying a number of contracts equal to its consumption need. The processor is thereby hedged against an unexpected price rise caused by crop shortages.

The main interest of hedgers is therefore to protect their business against sudden adverse price fluctuations. In traditional agricultural futures, the hedger is usually a producer or processor. Financial futures are traded by large financial institutions, such as banks or insurance companies. Large portfolio managers deal in stock index futures. The speculator may also trade any or all of these futures. *Speculators,* assuming the hedgers' risk, hope to profit through the astute buying and selling of contracts prior to expiration.

The distinction between hedgers and speculators, however, is not always hard and fast. Today's producer/consumers may "lift" (that is, offset) their hedge positions by buying or selling other futures contracts to close their initial purchase or sale. Eliminating the hedge entails risk, even though the large producers have the resources to estimate the size and profit of yearly crops more accurately than most speculators. When they lift their hedge positions, producer/consumers temporarily assume the role and risk of speculators. (As a result, futures exchanges also function as alternate cash marketplaces, because many producers and consumers prefer to deliver or take delivery over risking lifting their hedges at what seems to be a profitable time.)

Both hedgers and speculators benefit the futures marketplace. One of the biggest benefits of hedging is that it results in lower prices for the ultimate consumer. Without hedging, both producers and processors would have to add an extra amount to the price to counterbalance the risk of adverse price change.

Contrary to popular misconception, speculators create neither volatility nor risk in futures markets. In fact, they lessen volatility and *assume* the risk that is already inherent in futures markets and that would otherwise be borne by the producer consumer. Speculators also enhance liquidity by concentrating risk capital at a central location and putting it at the service of producers and consumers.

Arbitrageurs in the market for futures contracts are typically members of the exchange, market participants who know the insides of the market very well. They can also include external investors, who through their particular market insights take advantage of small price discrepancies. Arbitrageurs serve to eliminate price differentials between compatible contracts with similar expiration dates. They also serve to maintain market discipline, so that prices are determined rationally over contract maturities (such as to maintain a carrying charge maximum in a normal market).

In practice, it can be difficult to distinguish between an arbitrageur and a speculator. The main characteristic of an arbitrageur, as opposed to a speculator, is that an arbitrageur in principle assumes no risk positions but primarily tends to make risk-free profits by taking advantage of short-term market inefficiencies, which in itself serves to eliminate market discrepancies. Hence, they serve to make the market more efficient.

LIMITS

Trading on futures exchanges is usually conducted within the restraints of several types of limit:

1. Position limits.
2. Reportable positions.
3. Trading limits.

Position Limit

A *position limit* is the maximum number of contracts a given trader may hold in a commodity. The limit is set by the exchange for the broker, depending on the broker's individual capital structure. In the United States, the Commodity Futures Trading Commission (CFTC) approves the exchange's limits.

Reportable Positions

A *reportable limit* is the number of contracts at which traders must report their total positions by delivery month to the authorized exchange or, in the United States, the CFTC. In the U.S. for most commodities, the reportable limit is 25 contracts, a criterion set by the CFTC. Traders who hold 25 or more contracts, either long or short, are said to be *large traders.*

Both position and reportable limits apply only to large traders. Because of their economic needs, hedgers are not limited in the number of contracts that they may hold at one time. Notice, however, that position limits are considerably higher than reportable positions. If a reportable position is 40 contracts, the position limit may be 400 or even 600, depending on the commodity.

Trading Limit

A *trading limit* is the maximum price movement that an exchange allows for a commodity in one trading session. (Sometimes the term *trading limit* is used to mean *position limit.*)

Example: COMEX gold may move 2,500 points above or below the prior day's settlement.

In a trading session, the market can be "limit up" or "limit down." When the market is *limit up* (or *bid limit*), all participants want to buy, and no one wants to sell. In such a situation, the bids to buy are at the top of the daily allowable limit move, with no offers to sell at that price. In a *limit down* market participants are looking to sell, and no one wants to buy.

The trading limit is established to prevent panic. On stock exchanges, trading may be suspended until catastrophic news has had sufficient time to be consummated. On futures exchanges, there may be a series of limit up or limit down days, but losses are curtailed.

FINANCIAL FUTURES CONTRACTS

Financial futures contracts can typically be separated into three major categories: futures on foreign exchange, interest rate futures, and stock index futures. All financial futures, like commodity futures, are traded by hedgers, speculators, and arbitrageurs. Hedging is conducted primarily by commercial enterprises, such as large industrial businesses and financial institutions seeking to protect themselves against currency and interest rate exposures. Speculators can be specialized financial institutions and other private and institutional investors who try to take advantage of the opportunities for general investments in the futures market. Due to the relatively low margin payments, maintaining positions in the futures market requires less liquidity than do positions in the cash market. Arbitrageurs typically are financial intermediaries, many of which can be members of the futures exchange, who consistently trade with a large volume of both buyers and sellers in the market, and who often, due to specific market knowledge, maintain advisory capacities to external investors.

Background

In the early 1970s the Bretton-Woods Agreement of fixed currency parities was abandoned and as a consequence the U.S. dollar started a free-floating ride that led to volatile foreign exchange rates against the dollar. In response, the Chicago International Monetary Market (IMM), a division of the Chicago Mercantile Exchange, introduced the first financial futures contracts on foreign exchange in 1972.

Over the same period and throughout the 1970s, interest rate policies were liberalized in the United States. As a new school of monetarist economics emerged, monetary policy aims gradually became geared towards managing targeted monetary aggregates as opposed to direct management of the interest rate level. This development and the more erratic foreign exchange rate movements among the major convertible currencies made interest rates more volatile than before and led the way for the introduction of the first interest rate futures contracts on the Chicago Board of Trade (CBOT) in the fall of 1975. The first contracts introduced were the Government National Mortgage Association (GNMA) certificate futures, which essentially were created to further the financing of domestic building activities in the United States and very shortly after U.S. Treasury bill futures contracts were engaged on the futures trading floor.

Since then, financial futures contracts have been developed on several other exchanges within the North American continent—such as the New York Futures Exchange (NYFE), the Kansas City Board of Trade (KCBOT), and the Toronto Stock Exchange (TSE), to mention some. Following several years of successful operation in North America the concept of trading financial futures contracts has gone into a phase of internationalization. In September 1982 the London International Financial Futures Exchange (LIFFE) was inaugurated. The exchange initially introduced three interest futures contracts on three-month pound sterling time deposits, pound sterling long gilts, and Eurodollar three-month time deposits plus foreign currency contracts for all major currencies against U.S. dollars.

Hence the market enabled traders to get direct access to pound sterling interest futures, which in the U.S. market would require engagements in both U.S. dollar interest rate contracts and currency contracts against pound sterling.

Today LIFFE is trading a variety of other contracts, including U.S. T-bonds, Japanese government bonds, German government bonds (Bunds), Italian government bonds (BTP, *Buoni del Tesoro Poliennali*), U.S. dollars, Deutsche marks, Swiss francs, Japanese yen, and FT-SE and Euro Track Index contracts.

Developments of financial futures markets have taken place in Singapore, Hong Kong, and Sydney in cooperation with some of the U.S. and European exchanges, thereby expanding financial futures trading into other time zones. The Singapore International Monetary Exchange (SIMEX) opened for trading in futures contracts in September 1984. The introduction of the financial futures contracts was done in close cooperation with the Chicago Mercantile Exchange. SIMEX offers financial futures contracts in Eurodollars; Deutsche marks and Japanese yen which are all interchangeable with the equivalent futures contracts of the CME. The link between the CME and the SIMEX has opened up for longer trading hours in the futures contracts (close to 24 hours), an issue which becomes an increasingly important consideration to many futures traders. In October 1986, the Sydney Futures Exchange (SFE) similarly joined forces with the LIFFE in trading U.S. Treasury bond and Eurodollar interest rate futures. Financial futures trading is becoming more international due to the improved communication systems, which enable dealings to be carried out in distant overseas markets.

New futures markets continue to be opened. In October 1985 the Tokyo Stock Exchange (TSE) launched a Japanese government bond futures contract and thereby opened up for the first futures contract traded in Japan. During 1986, the French government's attempts to revitalize the financial markets gave birth to the Paris Financial Futures Exchange's (Marché à terme d'instruments financier or MATIF) trading in French government bonds and Treasury bill futures contracts.

Market Developments and Practices

The emergence of many different financial futures exchanges has created a wide variety of financial futures contracts available for trading. Financial futures contracts on interest rates are traded on the GNMA mortgage certificate, the 90-day Treasury bill, Treasury notes, long-term U.S. government bonds, 90-day certificates of deposits, commercial paper, three-month Eurodollar deposits, 90-day pound sterling time deposits pound sterling gilts and Canadian, Australian, New Zealand, Japanese, French, German, Dutch, and Danish government issues.

Financial futures contracts on foreign exchange are, for example, traded in U.S. dollars, Canadian dollars, Mexican pesos, New Zealand dollars, Australian dollars, pounds sterling, German marks, French francs, Swiss francs, European currency units, and Japanese yen.

The introduction of stock index futures contracts began when the Kansas City Board of Trade started trading a Value Line Composite Average Index contract in February 1982. The Chicago Mercantile Exchange introduced the Standard & Poors 500 index contract in April 1982 and in May 1982 the New York Futures Exchange launched a NYSE Composite Index contract. In September 1986, LIFFE introduced a Financial Times–SE 100 ("footsie") share index contract. This development has continued. Stock index contracts are, for example, traded in the Major Market Index (AMEX, CBOT), the NYSE Composite Index (NYSE), the Japanese Stock Oso-50 (OSE), the Hang Seng Index (HKFE), the Dutch Stock Index (EOE), the CAC 40 (MATIF), and the DAX Index (DTB).

There has been a major expansion in the number of futures exchanges in Europe. Virtually every market has seen the introduction or the planning of local futures exchanges dealing in domestic interest rate and stock index contracts. The list of new European futures exchanges include, for example, Garantifonden for futures og optioner (FUTOP) in Copenhagen and the Swiss Option and Futures Exchange (Soffex) in Zürich from 1988, the European Mercantile Exchange (EME) and the

Irish Futures and Options Exchange (IFOX) in Dublin from 1989, the Deutsche Terminsbörse (DTB) in Frankfurt from 1990, the Options Market (OM) in Stockholm and London, the Österreichischen Termin- und Optionsbörse (ÖTOB) in Vienna, the Belgian Futures and Options Exchange (Belfox) in Brussels, and Mercado de Futuros Financieros (Meff) in Barcelona and Madrid.

In terms of trading volume, the most important futures exchanges in Europe has been, in descending order, LIFFE (London), MATIF (Paris), and DTB (Frankfurt). Each of the three exchanges deal in the German Bund contract (a 8½–10-year notional German government bond with 6% coupon) and thus has competed intensively in this contract. To intensify the product focus on the DTB, the Frankfurt-based exchange introduced a medium-term notional bond futures contract (a 3½–5-year notional German government bond with 6% coupon) in October 1991. The contract is often referred to as the *Bobl* future (***B****undes* ***obl****igationen*). A further competitive move in this battle can be a linkup between MATIF and DTB, so that trades in Paris, for example, can use DTB's terminals to trade bund contracts, thereby effectively creating a common bund market out of the two. The DTB might want to establish other similar cross-border links as part of a future expansion strategy.

There has been substantial competition on the type of trading made available on the exchanges, where, for instance, CBOT and LIFFE have been the foremost proponents for the open outcry system. On the other hand, CME and DTB have established electronic trading systems (the CME through the introduction of Globex initially in cooperation with Reuters but today also linked up with CBOT and MATIF). Some exchanges find the open outcry to be the most efficient. They claim that the trading pits are more transparent and consequently are quicker to respond to new market information. In their view the electronic trading systems can be a potential threat to the market liquidity. However, in many cases exchanges (such as LIFFE and MATIF) have accepted the applicability of electronic systems working after normal trading hours. This is often considered a defensive move, but it nevertheless represents an introduction of systems that in principle can be handled outside the exchanges' own time zone and that therefore can extend the global reach of the exchanges. The introduction of electronic trading systems is also a possible way of linking different exchanges—a development we might well see continue in the future. The Options Market (OM) in Stockholm and London, the European Options Exchange (EOE) in Amsterdam, the Swiss Option and Future Exchange (Soffex) in Zürich, and the Österreichischen Termin- und Optionsbörse (ÖTOB) in Vienna have announced a linkup that eventually might enable their contracts to be traded on each others' exchanges. Similarly, the Sydney and Osaka exchanges are considering membership of a Globex listing of their contracts.

There has been a general move on several exchanges to introduce new medium-term contracts based on cash instruments between short-term money market instruments and long-term securities. The aim has been to make contracts available that cover the whole maturity spectrum. Such interest rate contracts have been introduced in underlying U.S. dollar, German mark, Spanish pesetas, and Danish and Swedish krone cash instruments. Some of the most actively traded of these contracts are, for example, the 2- and 5-year U.S. Treasury note futures of the CBOT and the 3½–5-year notional German government bond future (Bobl) of the DTB.

Apart from the standard commodity and financial futures contracts mentioned previously, there have been many efforts to promote new product developments and to extend their present use. Various discussions have taken place regarding contracts on such instruments as commodity price indices, freight rate indices, fertilizer prices, clean air, insurance contracts, among others.

To counterattack the expansion of the OTC-market for derivative instruments, the futures market might see new product expansions. One such move is the CBOT's plan to expand further into the swap market by trading standardized 5- and 10-year interest rate swaps. The posting of collateral (initial and maintenance margin), plus the trade guarantee of the clearing house, might provide the contract with a competitive credit enhancement. As it happens, the CBOT plans to offer the new contracts through a screen-based trading system (Hybrid Instrument Transaction Service, or HITS).

A rationale behind the creation of financial futures contracts on an exchange is that financial commitments are turned into a standard contract, the price of which is determined by the market's demand and supply forces. The conditions on an active exchange are very close to fulfilling the characteristics of the ideal economic state of perfect competition and hence the prices of the financial futures contracts very efficiently reflect the general expectations of the financial markets.

As in the case of commodities exchanges, each of the financial futures exchanges consists of members making the actual deals on the trading floor. The member dealers trade either for own account or for third parties against a commission fee. Memberships are purchased from the exchange, which pretty much functions as a private profit organization. The exchange will carry out a clearing function, or will engage an affiliated clearing agency, in order to settle all trades done by the exchange members during the day. Hence the direct counterpart, when trading financial futures contracts on a certain exchange, is usually the exchange itself or the clearing house and not the membership dealer. In most instances an institution that trades financial futures contracts will have to provide a cash advance of a certain size (as is the case with commodity futures) in order to do the transaction through the exchange. This provides the exchange with a safety margin to cover for potential losses if a counterparty might fail to meet its contractual obligations.

As each financial futures contract is developed to suit the specific conditions prevalent on the exchange on which it is traded, the characteristics of the futures contracts might differ slightly from one exchange to the other. In other words, the same type of financial futures contracts available in different exchanges are often not completely compatible.

Benefits

The development of markets for financial futures contracts not only provides an efficient way of matching economic entities with differing financial exposures, but also enables them through trading of financial futures contracts to ameliorate the financial exposure. The fact that many dealers participate in the markets ensures that the necessary liquidity is always available in the market and that the counterparty risk of the inherent financial obligations is well diversified. The wide variety of financial futures contracts being initiated has created the necessary base for the further development of many other financial services to the institutional market.

The financial futures markets provide the means for institutions to neutralize price risks whether the exposure is brought about by interest rate gaps or a mismatch in foreign exchanges flows. Furthermore, the prices determined on the financial futures markets provide the dealers in the underlying cash markets with a valuable source of information on market trends. Information on exchange statistics and price developments on the major financial futures contracts is available daily in the international newspapers. Figures 3.2 and 3.3 show excerpts from the *Financial Times* and *The Wall Street Journal*.

The *Financial Times* provides information from LIFFE on the trading price at the end of the day (Close), the highest price (High) and the lowest price (Low) quoted, and the closing price of the previous trading day (Prev.). This information is given for each delivery period. Below the price quotations, the London market's estimated trading volume for each futures contract is indicated with the previous trading day's volume added in brackets. Furthermore the previous day's open interests are indicated.

Example: The 20-year 9% notional gilt with March delivery closed at 97–14. It has previously traded within the range 87–26 to 93–31. The pre-

FIGURE 3.2
Quotes on Financial Futures Contracts. (Reprinted by permission of Financial Times.)

LONDON (LIFFE)

20-YEAR 9% NOTIONAL GILT •
£50,000 32nds of 100%

	Close	High	Low	Prev.
Mar	97-14	97-26	96-31	97-09
Jun	97-21			97-16

Estimated volume 48061 (40722)
Previous day's open int. 54817 (52994)

US TREASURY BONDS 8% •
$100,000 32nds of 100%

	Close	High	Low	Prev.
Mar	102-21	103-04	102-17	103-11
Jun	101-19			102-09

Estimated volume 2588 (3360)
Previous day's open int. 4116 (3341)

6% NOTIONAL GERMAN GOVT. BOND •
DM250,000 100ths of 100%

	Close	High	Low	Prev.
Mar	88.16	88.44	88.10	88.39
Jun	88.60	88.90	88.73	88.85

Estimated volume 58553 (76869)
Previous day's open int. 114223 (114729)

6% NOTIONAL LONG TERM JAPANESE GOVT. BOND Y100m 100ths of 100%

	Close	High	Low
Mar	102.67	102.71	102.61
Jun	102.54		

Estimated volume 557 (326)
Traded exclusively on APT

9% NOTIONAL ECU BOND
ECU 200,000 100ths of 100%

	Close	High	Low	Prev.
Mar	103.17	103.39	103.15	103.39
N				
A				

Estimated volume 314 (465)
Previous day's open int. 75 (115)

12% NOTIONAL ITALIAN GOVT. BOND (BTP) •
LIRA 200m 100ths of 100%

	Close	High	Low	Prev.
Mar	98.36	98.57	98.33	98.55
Jun	98.47	98.55	98.55	98.66

Estimated volume 6624 (10319)
Previous day's open int. 17455 (17211)

THREE MONTH STERLING •
£500,000 points of 100%

	Close	High	Low	Prev.
Mar	89.70	89.72	89.59	89.67
Jun	90.07	90.09	89.95	90.01
Sep	90.39	90.40	90.24	90.28
Dec	90.46	90.44	90.35	90.37
Mar	90.50	90.50	90.41	90.44
Jun	90.46	90.46	90.38	90.43

Est. Vol. (inc. figs. not shown) 57918 (66428)
Previous day's open int. 183016 (177598)

FT-SE 100 INDEX •
£25 per full index point

	Close	High	Low	Prev.
Mar	2572.0	2597.0	2557.0	2573.0
Jun	2606.0			2607.0
Sep				

Estimated volume 8778 (10624)
Previous day's open int. 35982 (35014)

FT-SE EUROTRACK 100 INDEX
DM50 per full index point

	Close	High	Low	Prev.
Mar	1131.0			1140.0
Jun				

Estimated volume 0 (0)
Previous day's open int. 137 (137)

• Contracts traded on APT. Closing prices shown.

CHICAGO

U.S. TREASURY BONDS (CBT) 8%
$100,000 32nds of 100%

	Latest	High	Low	Prev.
Mar	102-30	103-05	102-19	102-30
Jun	101-29	102-04	101-18	101-29
Sep	101-03	101-03	100-21	100-30
Dec	100-03	100-04	100-03	100-01
Mar	99-06	99-06	99-06	99-08
Jun	-	-	-	98-17
Sep	-	-	-	97-27
Dec	-	-	-	97-06
Mar	-	-	-	96-18
Jun	-	-	-	96-00

U.S. TREASURY BILLS (IMM)
$1m points of 100%

	Latest	High	Low	Prev.
Mar	96.16	96.16	96.11	96.15
Jun	96.03	96.03	95.96	95.99
Sep	95.75	95.74	95.65	95.69
Dec	95.22	95.22	95.16	95.18
Mar	-	95.00	95.00	-

BRITISH POUND (IMM)
$s per £

	Latest	High	Low	Prev.
Mar	1.7416	1.7466	1.7400	1.7300
Jun	1.7180	1.7200	1.7150	1.7052
Sep	1.6950	1.6980	-	1.6826

SWISS FRANC (IMM)
SFr 125,000 $ per SFr

	Latest	High	Low	Prev.
Mar	-	0.6948	0.6905	0.6872
Jun	-	0.6890	0.6855	0.6815
Sep	-	-	-	0.6767

JAPANESE YEN (IMM)
Y12.5m $ per Y100

	Latest	High	Low	Prev.
Mar	-	0.7802	0.7774	0.7750
Jun	0.7775	0.7787	0.7768	0.7738
Sep	0.7775	0.7780	-	0.7734
Dec	0.7780	0.7780	-	0.7741

DEUTSCHE MARK (IMM)
DM125,000 $ per DM

	Latest	High	Low	Prev.
Mar	0.6132	0.6153	0.6117	0.6095
Jun	0.6060	0.6075	0.6045	0.6020
Sep	-	0.6001	0.6001	0.5956

THREE-MONTH EURODOLLAR (IMM)
$1m points of 100%

	Latest	High	Low	Prev.
Mar	95.75	95.78	95.70	95.75
Jun	95.54	95.57	95.45	95.51
Sep	95.24	95.26	95.12	95.16
Dec	94.64	94.65	94.52	94.57
Mar	94.35	94.37	94.24	94.30
Jun	93.93	93.94	93.86	93.90
Sep	93.54	93.56	93.48	93.52
Dec	93.05	93.08	93.00	93.04

STANDARD & POORS 500 INDEX
$500 times index

	Latest	High	Low	Prev.
Mar	420.90	421.20	420.40	421.60
Jun	422.30	422.60	421.95	423.10
Sep	424.00	-	424.00	424.80

PARIS

7 to 10 YEAR 10% NOTIONAL FRENCH BOND (MATIF) FUTURES

	Open	Sett price	Change	High	Low	Yield	Open Int
March	109.02	108.72	-0.36	109.06	108.68	8.61	140,323
June	109.92	109.68	-0.34	109.92	109.68	8.47	15,725
September	109.94	109.70	-0.34	109.94	109.78	8.47	333

Estimated volume 140,981 Total Open Interest 156,381

THREE-MONTH PIBOR FUTURES (MATIF) (Paris interbank offered rate)

March	90.54	90.47	-0.07	90.55	90.47	9.46	24,413
June	90.95	90.94	-0.01	90.96	90.92	9.05	13,656
September	91.28	91.26	-0.02	91.28	91.24	8.72	7,945
December	91.44	91.46	-	91.47	91.43	8.54	1,002

Estimated volume 21,829 Total Open Interest 47,016

CAC-40 FUTURES (MATIF) Stock Index

January	1885.0	1874.0	-16.0	1893.0	1865.0	-	16,996
February	1900.0	1889.0	-16.0	1908.0	1887.0	-	2,069
March	1914.0	1904.0	-16.0	1922.0	1906.0	-	7,498
June	1931.0	1920.0	-17.0	1937.0	1921.0	-	3,221

Estimated volume 14,353 Total Open Interest 29,784

ECU BOND (MATIF)

March	109.24	109.04	-0.22	109.30	108.98	8.58	6,390

Estimated volume 5,476 Total Open Interest 6,390

OPTION ON LONG-TERM FRENCH BOND (MATIF)

	Calls			Puts		
Strike	March	June	September	March	June	September
106	-	-	-	0.06	-	-
107	1.89	-	-	0.14	0.81	-
108	1.10	-	-	0.38	0.53	-
109	0.53	1.58	-	0.78	-	-
110	0.20	1.07	-	1.45	-	-
111	0.08	0.66	-	-	-	-
112	-	0.40	-	-	-	-
114	-	0.12	0.32	-	-	-
Open Int	130,393	25,574	450	100,785	20,997	250

Estimated volume 28,698 Total Open Interest 278,449

Reported by permission of *Financial Times*.

FIGURE 3.3

Quotes on Financial Futures Contracts. (Reprinted by permission of Wall Street Journal *[Europe],*

Financial Futures

EURODOLLAR (LIFFE)—$1 million; pts of 100%

	Open	High	Low	Settle	Chg	Yield Settle	Yield Chg	Open Interest
Mar	90.76	90.81	90.75	90.75	+ .18	91.41	85.49	6,504
June	90.16	90.23	89.16	89.18	+ .21	90.92	85.66	4,940
Sept	89.64	89.66	89.61	89.61	+ .20	90.37	85.50	2,501
Dec	89.17	89.18	89.15	88.15	+ .21	89.90	88.74	470

Est vol 2,534; vol Fri 7,496; open int 14,517, −42.

STERLING (LIFFE)—£250,000; pts of 100%

	Open	High	Low	Settle	Chg	Yield Settle	Yield Chg	Open Interest
Mar	87.25	87.25	86.88	86.95	− .62	90.86	86.35	2,853
June	88.36	88.44	88.17	88.26	− .42	90.60	86.80	2,100
Sept	88.85	88.85	88.65	88.77	−. .23	90.50	87.10	853
Dec	89.00	89.00	89.00	88.80	− .50	89.75	87.50	455

Est vol 3,318; vol Fri 2,184; open int 6,307, +104.

LONG GILT (LIFFE)—£50,000; pts of 100%

	Open	High	Low	Settle	Chg	Yield Settle	Yield Chg	Open Interest
Mar	103-24	103-31	103-05	103-13	− 1-03	109-21	96-21	4,906
June	103-23	103-23	103-03	103-13	− 0-31	108-03	97-16	456

Est vol 3,321; vol Fri 2,802; open int 5,472, −255.

EURODOLLAR (IMM)—$1 million; pts of 100%

	Open	High	Low	Settle	Chg	Yield Settle	Yield Chg	Open Interest
Mar	90.76	90.80	90.60	90.63	− .08	9.37	+ .08	46,734
June	90.15	90.22	89.95	90.02	− .11	9.98	+ .11	33,368
Sept	89.58	89.65	89.41	89.46	− .10	10.54	+ .10	12,633
Dec	89.11	89.17	88.96	88.99	− .08	11.01	+ .08	5,199
Mr86	88.73	88.77	88.59	88.61	− .06	11.39	+ .06	3,940
June	88.38	88.44	88.25	88.29	− .04	11.71	+ .04	2,798
Sept	88.09	88.14	87.99	88.01	− .02	11.99	+ .02	1,018
Dec	87.78	87.83	87.73	87.74	− .02	12.26	+ .02	232

Est vol 38,479; vol Fri 54,605; open int 105,922, −616.

GNMA 8% (CBT)—$100,000 prncpl; pts. 32nds. of 100%

	Open	High	Low	Settle	Chg	Yield Settle	Yield Chg	Open Interest
Mar	69-14	69-19	69-12	69-17	+ 4	13.251	− .028	3,892
June	68-26	68-29	68-22	68-28	+ 4	13.400	− .029	1,231
Sept	....	....	....	68-08	+ 4	13.545	− .029	211
Dec	....	....	....	67-22	+ 4	13.676	− .029	284
Mr86	....	....	....	67-06	+ 4	13.794	− .030	398
June	....	....	....	66-23	+ 4	13.906	− .030	549

Est vol 600; vol Fri 942; open int 6,627, −113.

TREASURY BONDS (CBT)—$100,000; pts. 32nds of 100%

	Open	High	Low	Settle	Chg	Yield Settle	Yield Chg	Open Interest
Mar	72-09	72-18	71-22	71-26	− 13	11.669	+ .069	137,187
June	71-08	71-16	70-21	70-24	− 14	11.852	+ .076	51,117
Sept	70-14	70-22	69-27	69-29	− 16	12.000	+ .088	9,978
Dec	69-26	70-03	69-07	69-08	− 17	12.118	+ .096	9,281
Mr86	69-08	69-14	68-22	68-22	− 17	12.220	+ .097	7,498
June	68-27	68-30	68-07	68-07	− 17	12.306	+ .097	4,964
Sept	68-07	68-07	67-26	67-26	− 17	12.382	+ .099	2,963
Dec	....	....	....	67-15	− 17	12.446	+ .099	1,313
Mr87	67-30	67-30	67-05	67-05	− 17	12.506	+ .101	865
June	67-06	67-07	66-28	66-28	− 17	12.559	+ .101	1,113
Sept	....	....	....	66-21	− 17	12.601	+ .107	1,173

Est vol 192,000; vol Fri 201,332; open int 227,452, +1470.

TREASURY NOTES (CBT)—$100,000; pts. 32nds of 100%

	Open	High	Low	Settle	Chg	Yield Settle	Yield Chg	Open Interest
Mar	81-10	81-17	80-29	81-01	− 8	11.201	+ .048	28,987
June	80-16	80-22	80-04	80-08	− 8	11.354	+ .049	12,840
Sept	79-29	79-29	79-17	79-20	− 8	11.478	+ .050	1,884
Dec	....	....	....	79-03	− 8	11.584	+ .050	456

Est vol 9,000; vol Fri 12,374; open int 44,278, +1449.

TREASURY BILLS (IMM)—$1 mil.; pts. of 100%

	Open	High	Low	Settle	Chg	Discount Settle	Discount Chg	Open Interest
Mar	91.73	91.78	91.69	91.71	....	8.29	....	20,482
June	91.31	91.39	91.25	91.27	− .02	8.73	+ .02	19,176
Sept	90.82	90.89	90.76	90.77	....	9.23	....	4,177
Dec	90.41	90.46	90.36	90.36	....	9.64	....	1,654
Mr86	....	....	....	90.01	....	9.99	....	1,090
June	89.78	89.79	89.72	89.72	....	10.28	....	970
Sept	89.51	89.53	89.49	89.49	+ .02	10.51	− .02	172

Est vol 10,539; vol Fri 17,915; open int 47,773, +8.

BANK CDs (IMM)—$1 million; pts. of 100%

	Open	High	Low	Settle	Chg	Yield Settle	Yield Chg	Open Interest
Mar	91.06	91.12	90.96	90.99	− .06	9.01	+ .06	4,945
June	90.52	90.56	90.30	90.39	− .09	9.61	+ .09	2,894
Sept	....	....	....	89.86	− .07	10.14	+ .07	3,850
Dec	....	....	....	89.36	− .08	10.64	+ .08	1,278
Mr86	....	....	....	88.97	− .05	11.03	+ .05	182
June	....	....	....	88.65	− .03	11.35	+ .03	98

Est vol 2,075; vol Fri 536; open int 13,267, +74.

Currency Futures

BRITISH POUND (IMM)—25,000 pounds; $ per pound

	Open	High	Low	Settle	Change	Lifetime High	Lifetime Low	Open Interest
Mar	1.1000	1.1005	1.0850	1.0920	− .0035	1.5170	1.0850	19,406
June	1.0900	1.0915	1.0740	1.0825	− .0045	1.3050	1.0740	2,877
Sept	1.0860	1.0870	1.0715	1.0780	− .0045	1.2850	1.0715	264
Dec	1.0845	1.0845	1.0680	1.0760	− .0045	1.2860	1.0680	245

Est vol 8,231; vol Fri 12,207; open int 22,792, +1,188.

CANADIAN DOLLAR (IMM)—100,000 dlrs.; $ per Can $

	Open	High	Low	Settle	Change	Lifetime High	Lifetime Low	Open Interest
Mar	.7466	.7467	.7453	.7465	−.0015	.8050	.7443	8,227
June	.7441	.7443	.7429	.7443	−.0015	.7835	.7429	2,049
Sept		....	....	.7425	−.0016	.7585	.7436	853
Dec	.7419	.7419	.7398	.7416	−.0017	.7568	.7398	192

Est vol 1,503; vol Fri 2,284; open int 11,376, +47.

JAPANESE YEN (IMM) 12.5 million yen; $ per yen (.00)

	Open	High	Low	Settle	Change	Lifetime High	Lifetime Low	Open Interest
Mar	.3845	.3847	.3826	.3839	−.0015	.4695	.3826	17,479
June	.3873	.3875	.3854	.3868	−.0014	.4570	.3854	1,629

Est vol 5,406; vol Fri 9,057; open int 19,216, −414.

SWISS FRANC (IMM)—125,000 francs-$ per franc

	Open	High	Low	Settle	Change	Lifetime High	Lifetime Low	Open Interest
Mar	.3605	.3619	.3584	.3615	+.0001	.5035	.3584	23,986
June	.3638	.3655	.3617	.3650	+.0003	.4900	.3617	1,789

Est vol 17,592; vol Fri 15,322; open int 25,929, +1,585.

W. GERMAN MARK (IMM)—125,000 marks; $ per mark

	Open	High	Low	Settle	Change	Lifetime High	Lifetime Low	Open Interest
Mar	.3078	.3079	.3056	.3070	−.0010	.4110	.3056	37,279
June	.3101	.3101	.3079	.3093	−.0010	.3710	.3079	5,167
Sept	.3119	.3120	.3104	.3118	−.0009	.3560	.3104	466
Dec	.3150	.3150	.3128	.3147	−.0010	.3620	.3128	72

Est vol 20,477; vol Fri 19,562; open int 42,985, +895.

Stock Index Futures

NYSE COMPOSITE FUTURES (NYFE) 500 Times Index

	Open	High	Low	Settle	Change	Lifetime High	Lifetime Low	Open Interest
Mar	106.60	106.65	104.85	105.20	− 1.30	106.85	88.20	9,748
June	108.45	108.50	106.70	107.05	− 1.35	108.80	90.00	1,017
Sept	110.25	110.25	108.60	108.85	− 1.40	110.35	91.35	352

Est vol 14,727; vol Fri 11,097; open int 11,168, −309.

NYSE COMPOSITE STOCK INDEX

	Open	High	Low	Settle	Change	Lifetime High	Lifetime Low	Open Interest
	105.35	105.35	104.30	104.50	− .89	....	....	....

S&P 500 FUTURES INDEX (CME) 500 Times Index

	Open	High	Low	Settle	Change	Lifetime High	Lifetime Low	Open Interest
Mar	183.30	183.45	180.50	180.95	− 2.25	183.80	153.00	55,940
June	186.40	186.45	183.60	184.10	− 2.25	186.90	155.70	2,933
Sept	189.40	189.55	186.90	187.25	− 2.25	189.90	158.10	180

Est vol 64,343; vol Fri 56,455; open int 59,082, +1,697.

S&P 500 STOCK INDEX (Prelim.)

	Open	High	Low	Settle	Change	Lifetime High	Lifetime Low	Open Interest
	181.59	182.18	180.11	180.51	− 1.68	....	....	....

MAJOR MARKET INDEX (CBT) $100 Times Index

	Open	High	Low	Settle	Change	Lifetime High	Lifetime Low	Open Interest
Feb	256 7/8	257	252 3/4	253 1/8	− 3 3/8	257 3/4	235 1/8	8,008
Mar	257 7/8	257 7/8	253 3/8	254	− 3 3/8	258 7/8	236	8,830
Apr	258 1/2	258 1/2	255 1/2	255 1/2	− 3 1/2	*260 1/8	248 1/4	738

Est vol 18,000; vol Fri 16,398; open int 17,655, −38.

MAJOR MARKET INDEX (Prelim.)

	Open	High	Low	Settle	Change	Lifetime High	Lifetime Low	Open Interest
	256.39	256.48	252.78	253.36	− 3.03	....	....	....

KC VALUE LINE FUTURES (KC) 500 Times Index

	Open	High	Low	Settle	Change	Lifetime High	Lifetime Low	Open Interest
Mar	205.00	205.05	200.85	201.30	− 3.35	205.15	168.10	6,952
June	209.10	209.10	204.90	205.30	− 3.55	209.60	170.10	468

Est vol 4,420; vol Fri 3,924; open int 7,433, −319.

KC VALUE LINE COMPOSITE STOCK INDEX

	Open	High	Low	Settle	Change	Lifetime High	Lifetime Low	Open Interest
	199.98	200.05	198.58	198.97	− 1.00	....	....	....

vious day's close was 97–09; so the market is slightly up. The estimated trading volume was 48,061 contracts against the previous day's volume of 52,994 contracts.

The price information from MATIF also provides an opening price (Open) and a closing price (Sett price), with an indication of the day's price change (Change).

The Wall Street Journal provides price information on the major U.S. futures contracts, as well as contracts on LIFFE and MATIF. The price quotation also includes a price change indication (Chg), along with a translation of the price into yield terms indicating both closing price (Settle) and change in yield (Chg).

Example: The 1 million Eurodollar contract (IMM) with March delivery opened the day's trading at a price of 90.76. During the trading day the price varied between 90.80 and 90.60 to close at a low of 90.63, corresponding to a drop of 0.08 from previous day's close. The closing price of 90.63 reflects a yield of 9.37% and an increase in yield from the previous day of 0.08%. Total estimated trading volume in the contract at all delivery months was 38,479 contracts, against the previous day's (FRI—Friday) trading volume of 54,685.

The quotations on the currency future contracts have price intervals for each delivery month on the trading day as well as on a lifetime basis.

4

Types of Contracts

INTEREST RATE FUTURES

An *interest rate futures contract* is a standard agreement that provides the holder with a certain interest-bearing asset at a predetermined price at a future point in time. The contracts are standardized so that each type of future asset is well defined and offered in standard trading units on the exchange. The contracts are usually delivered at predetermined dates in the delivery months of March, June, September, and December[1] (see Table 4.1).

Pricing

The prices on short-term financial futures, such as the 3-month Eurodollar deposits and the 3-month U.S. Treasury bills, are quoted on an index basis. That is the par value of 100.00 minus the annual discount rate of, say, 12.25% making up a quoted price of 87.75. With this pricing system, changes in the interest rate lead to a predictable change in the contract price. Hence the contract values are changed by a fixed minimum price for each basis point (0.01%) change in the discount rate. The minimum

TABLE 4.1
Summary of Some Interest Rate Futures Contracts.

Chicago Board of Trade (CBOT) Commodity (Trading Unit)	*Montreal Exchange (ME) Commodity (Trading Unit)*	*International Monetary Market (IMM) Commodity (Trading Unit)*	*London International Financial Futures Exchange (LIFFE) Commodity (Trading Unit)*
Commercial paper 30-day maturity (US$ 3,000,000)	1-month Canadian banker's acceptance future (C$ 3,000,000)	—	—
Commercial paper 90-day maturity (US$ 1,000,000)	3-month Canadian bankers' acceptance future (C$ 1,000,000)	3-month certificates of deposits (US$ 1,000,000)	3-month sterling deposit (£ stg. 250,000)
—	3-month Canadian bankers' acceptance future (C$ 1,000,000)	3-month Eurodollar deposit (US$ 1,000,000)	3-month Eurodollar deposit (US$ 1,000,000)
GNMA collateralized depository receipt (CDR) (US$ 100,000)	—	3-month U.S. Treasury bills (US$ 1,000,000)	—
—	—	3-month U.S. Treasury bills (US$ 1,000,000)	—
—	—	1-year U.S. Treasury bills (US$ 250,000)	—
2-year U.S. Treasury note future (US$ 200,000)	—	U.S. Treasury notes, 4 years to maturity 7% coupon (US$ 100,000)	—
5-year U.S. Treasury note future (US$ 100,000)	6.5–10-year 9% Canadian government bond future (C$ 100,000)	—	U.S. Treasury bonds, 15 years to maturity, 8% coupon (US$ 100,000)
10-year U.S. Treasury note future (US$ 100,000)	—	—	20-year gilt (£ stg. 50,000)

price change is called a *tick* and is the change in contract value per basis point change in the interest rate. In the case of a 3-month Eurodollar deposit standard contract of US$ 1,000,000, the value of a tick is:

$$\$1,000,000 \times 3/12 \times 0.01/100 = \$25$$

From this, you can see that, if the interest rate increases by 10 basis points (0.1%), the value of one 3-month Eurodollar deposit contract will fall in value by US$ 250.

Given this standard formula for computation, the value a tick can be found for the major short-term interest rate futures contracts.

$$\text{Tick value} = \text{Nominal contract value} \times \frac{\text{Maturity period (days)}}{\text{Year (360 days)}} \times \frac{0.01}{100}$$

Trading Unit			*Tick Value*
30-day U.S. dollar interest rate (CBOT)	US$ 5,000,000 × 30/360 × 0.01/100	=	US$ 41⅔
1-month U.S. dollar LIBOR (IMM)	US$ 3,000,000 × 30/360 × 0.01/100	=	US$ 25
3-month French franc PIBOR (MATIF)	Fr. frc. 5,000,000 × 90/360 × 0.01/100	=	Fr. frc. 125
3-month Eurodollar (LIFFE, IMM)	US$ 1,000,000 × 90/360 × 0.01/100	=	US$ 25
3-month sterling (LIFFE)	£ stg. 500,000 × 90/360 × 0.01/100	=	£ stg. 12½
3-month Euromark (LIFFE)	DM 1,000,000 × 90/360 × 0.01/100	=	DM 25

Turning to financial futures contracts on longer-term securities, the formula for money market instruments just presented no longer applies. Instead, the tick value is calculated based on the smallest possible price change on the underlying assets. In the U.S. and U.K. markets, it has been conceptually determined that the tick value equals 1/32 of a percentage point of the nominal contract value. Hence the tick values can be calculated by means of the following formula:

$$\text{Tick value} = \text{Nominal contract value} \times 1/32 \times 1/100$$

Trading Unit			*Tick Value*
Treasury note (CBOT)	US$ 100,000 × 1/32 × 1/100	=	US$ 31¼
Treasury bond (MCE)	US$ 50,000 × 1/32 × 1/100	=	US$ 15⅝
Long gilt (LIFFE)	£ stg. 50,000 × 1/32 × 1/100	=	£ stg. 15⅝

However, it has increasingly become the norm, specifically inspired by the European contracts, to let basis point changes apply to the tick size of futures contracts also on long-term securities, in which case the following formula applies.

$$\text{Tick value} = \text{Nominal contract value} \times 0.01 \times 1/100$$

Trading Unit			*Tick Value*
Treasury bond (LIFFE)	US$ 100,000 × 0.01 × 1/100	=	US$ 10
German government bond (LIFFE, MATIF, DTB)	DM 250,000 × 0.01 × 1/100	=	DM 25
8–10½-year Italian bond (LIFFE)	Lire 200,000,000 × 0.01 × 1/100	=	Lire 20,000
7–10-year French government bond (MATIF)	Fr. frc. 500,000 × 0.01 × 1/100	=	Fr. frc. 50
Ecu bond (MATIF)	ECU 100,000 × 0.01 × 1/100	=	ECU 10

By convention, the minimum allowable price movement any financial futures contract corresponds to the tick value. Hence the profit or loss incurred from a change in financial futures prices is always calculated by the net change in ticks (plus or minus) multiplied by the tick value. This makes for a very manageable accounting system in the often hectic atmosphere of the exchanges where a handy method of computation is imperative.

Price Limit

During the course of a trading day prices might fluctuate widely or show a strong trend. To prevent extreme volatility and to stabilize the quotation of contract prices, the futures exchanges have introduced the concept of a *price limit,* which is the maximum change in trading prices during any one day. When this limit is reached, the market will be suspended for a period, in some instances until the following business day depending on the exchange.

Margin

Any change in value position caused by price changes will be settled by cash on a day-to-day basis. When a trade is done on the financial futures exchange, the dealer will pay an *initial margin* to the exchange which he eventually will pass on to the client if he is trading on behalf of third party.

The size of the margin varies from contract type to contract type and from exchange to exchange but usually ranges from 2 to 3% for both short-term and long-term financial futures. The rationale behind the initial margin is that the sum total of all cash margins will reduce the immediate risk of default to the exchange's clearing operation if one counterparty cannot fulfill its obligations.

The changes in the value of a trader's position is calculated currently and is settled in cash on a daily basis through a *variation margin*, which then represents the client's profit or loss for that day. The current cash settlement procedure also reduces the potential impact of the inherent counterparty risk. For the customer trading in the financial futures market, the daily cash settlement procedure has cash flow implications that ought to be evaluated when engaging in dealings.

Conversion Factor

The U.S. Treasury bond futures contract has been traded very actively on the Chicago Board of Trade exchange for several years. To transfer the availability of a futures contract carrying the similar characteristics into the European time zone, an equivalent futures contract was introduced on the London International Financial Futures Exchange during 1984.

The problem with the U.S. Treasury bond futures contract, as well as the U.S. Treasury note futures and the sterling gilt contract for that matter, is that the underlying cash markets trade these securities with very different maturity profiles and with different coupons. Therefore no single security acts as a "natural" standard trading unit for a financial futures contract to be offered on the exchange. To circumvent this problem, the exchanges have introduced the concept of a conversion factor whose function is to bring any eligible security into a standard tradeable value.

For the U.S. Treasury bond futures contract, the unit of trading is the par value of a US$ 100,000 notional 15-year U.S. Treasury bond with an 8% coupon. The contract standard determines that an eligible security for delivery under the futures contract is any U.S. Treasury bond that matures at least 15 years from the first day of the contract, and if the security is callable, then the earliest call date must be at least 15 years from the first day of the contract month.

The same principle of eligible securities is applied to some contracts at other exchanges as well, such as LIFFE's 20-year 9% notional gilt futures contract and MATIF's 7–10-year 10% notional French bond futures contract.

Settlement Price

When a futures contract is exchanged between buyer and seller on the exchange, the contract amount involved is the principal amount plus the accrued interest. The principal amount is reached by multiplying the exchange delivery settlement price by a conversion factor:

$$\text{Principal amount} = \text{Exchange delivery settlement price} \times \text{Conversion factor}$$

The *exchange delivery settlement price* (*EDSP*) is determined by the current market price of the contract at a given time on the exchange. The *conversion factor* is simply the par value multiplier, which determines the discount/premium value of a security with different maturity or coupon from the standard trading unit.

Example: A 15-year security with a 7% coupon will be sold at a discount value of 91.44% to give a yield of 8%. For this type of security the conversion factor is 0.9144. Or a 20-year security with a 7% coupon will be sold at a discount value of 90.18% to give a yield of 8%, hence for this type of security the conversion factor is 0.9018.[2]

As these examples show, the conversion factor decreases when the coupon *decreases* and when the maturity *increases*.

The par value conversion factor ensures that all securities eligible for the contract standard will obtain a comparable evaluation. Thus it provides for an efficient way of dealing with contracts on securities of nonhomogenous characteristics.

Comparing Contracts

As already mentioned, each financial futures exchange might well have distinct market procedures which make the price development of two apparently equivalent financial futures contracts hard to compare. A good example is, again, the U.S. Treasury bond futures contract as traded on the Chicago Board of Trade and the London International Financial Futures Exchange:

- The price limit rules on the two exchanges differ. On the Chicago exchange the trading ceases for the remainder of the day unless prices return within the limit, but a progressive scale of price limits is triggered by successive days' excess of the initial price limit. On the London exchange the trading is suspended for an hour if the price limit is reached and then continues without any price limits for the remainder of the day.
- The Chicago exchange has several levels of initial margins, whereas the London exchange only has two initial margins.
- On the Chicago exchange the exchange delivery settlement price is determined by the last trading price before the close of trading on a given trading day, which is 3:00 p.m. (CST). The London exchange determines the exchange delivery settlement price as the average of the contract prices during the minute preceding 3:00 p.m. (London time).

This is to mention but a few of the things that must be taken into consideration when comparing prices at different exchanges and that require detailed procedural knowledge to interpret satisfactorily.

SWAP FUTURES

The Chicago Board of Trade has introduced a new type of interest rate instrument, financial futures contracts on U.S. dollar interest rate swaps. The interest rate swap contract trades the fixed interest rate for a given maturity (based on a generic interest rate swap rate) against the 6-month LIBOR rate (see Table 4.2). Interest rate swaps are quoted in the money and foreign exchange market with a bid and offer rate. The bid rate indicates the fixed rate the bidder is willing to pay for receiving floating rate (LIBOR) whereas the offer rate indicates the fixed rate the bidder is willing to receive for providing floating rate.

TABLE 4.2
Interest Rate Swap Futures Contracts.

The Chicago Board of Trade (CBOT)	
Commodity (Trading Unit)	*Commodity (Trading Unit)*
3-year fixed rate versus 6-month LIBOR (US$ 25,000,000)	5-year fixed rate versus 6-month LIBOR (US$ 25,000,000)

Pricing

The price quotation is indicated as 100 minus the yield reflected in the fixed rate indication of the generic swap. The settlement yield is calculated as the median of the average bid and offer rates of a predetermined set of reference swap dealers.

Example: The swap yield has been calculated from the dealers' quotes to be 8.125%. Then the price is quoted at 91.875 (= 100 – 8.125).

CURRENCY FUTURES

A *currency futures contract* is a standard agreement which provides the holder with a certain amount of foreign currency at a predetermined foreign exchange rate at a future time.

The contracts are standardized so that each contract specifies the same amount of foreign currency. Like interest rate futures, the currency futures contracts are deliverable at specified dates, namely the third Wednesday in March, June, September, and December on the International Monetary Market and on the second Wednesday in the same months on the London International Financial Futures Exchange.

Pricing

Financial futures contracts on currencies are usually quoted in U.S. dollars and cents per unit of the foreign currency as the trading units are determined as a certain amount of the foreign currency (see Table 4.3).

TABLE 4.3
Summary of Some Currency Futures Contracts.

International Monetary Market (IMM) *Commodity (Trading Unit)*	*London International Financial Futures Exchange (LIFFE)* *Commodity (Trading Unit)*
Swiss francs (Sw. frc. 125,000)	Swiss francs (Sw. frc. 125,000)
Mexican pesos (Mx. ps. 1,000,000)	—
German marks (DM 125,000)	German marks (DM 125,000)
Canadian dollars (C$ 100,000)	—
Pound sterling (£ stg. 62,500)	Pound sterling (£ stg. 25,000)
Japanese yen (Y 12,500,000)	Japanese yen (Y 12,500,000)
French francs (Fr. frc. 250,000)	—
Australian dollars (A$ 100,000)	—

Example: A financial futures contract in German marks might be quoted as 0.3185, meaning that the price on the futures exchange for one German mark contract is US$ 39,812.50 = (DM 125,000 × 0.3185 US$/DM).

On the international foreign exchange markets, the exchange rate is normally quoted against the U.S. dollar as the amount of foreign currency per unit of the U.S. dollar, except Commonwealth currencies, which are quoted similarly to the currency futures contracts.

The international foreign exchange market typically quotes the foreign exchange rates against U.S. dollar. However, based on these rates, it is straightforward to calculate rates between any pair of currencies.

Example: The spot rate for the German mark against U.S. dollar is quoted at 3.1250 DM/US$. The spot rate for the Swiss franc is quoted at 2.7800 Sw. frc./US$. Hence, the DM/Sw. frc. cross rate is 1.1241 (= 3.1250/2.7800).

In each domestic market, foreign currencies are often traded on the basis of foreign exchange cross rates. For certain cross rates (X-rates) with particularly high trading activities, it can be worthwhile to establish financial futures contracts on the cross rates. For example, a Chicago Mercantile Exchange (CME) cross-rate contract is:

Deutsche mark/Japanese yen
(DM 125,000 × DM/Y X-rate)

On the International Monetary Market in Chicago the contract sizes have been determined so as to obtain the same tick value of US$ 12.50 for all the currency futures contracts with the exception of the Canadian dollar and the Mexican peso contracts, which have a tick value of US$ 10.00.

The *tick size,* which also indicates the minimum acceptable price fluctuation of the currency contract, is usually denominated in cents per unit of the foreign currency, as is the price of the futures contract. The tick value is calculated by using the following formula:

$$\text{Tick value} = \text{Nominal contract value} \times \text{Tick size}$$

Trading Unit			*Tick Value*
German mark (IMM, LIFFE)	DM 125,000 × 0.01 ¢/DM	=	US$ 12½
Pound sterling (IMM)	£ stg. 62,500 × 0.01 ¢/£ stg.	=	US$ 6¼
Japanese yen (IMM, LIFFE)	Y 12,500,000 × 0.01 ¢/100Y	=	US$ 12½
Australian dollar (IMM)	A$ 100,000 × 0.01 ¢/A$	=	US$ 10

On the London International Financial Futures Exchange, the tick value of all the currency futures contracts traded is also US$ 12.50, except the pound sterling contract, whose tick value is calculated as (£ stg. 25,000 × 0.01 cents/£ stg.) = US$ 2.50. Consequently, this value, which is different from the tick value of the International Monetary Market's pound sterling contract, was calculated at US$ 6¼.

Foreign Exchange Spot Market

The underlying cash market for the currency futures contracts is the foreign exchange spot market where the exchange rate at a given time is determined by the supply and demand forces in play for that currency. In the foreign exchange market, a future foreign exchange rate, also termed the forward rate, can be determined by engaging in money market transactions in the two currencies in question.

Example: U.S. dollars are borrowed and exchanged for German marks in the spot market. The marks are deposited for, say, three months. During that time, the holder of the marks sells the over-the-counter 3-month future foreign exchange contract on German marks at the equilibrium price, against a premium to cover transaction costs.

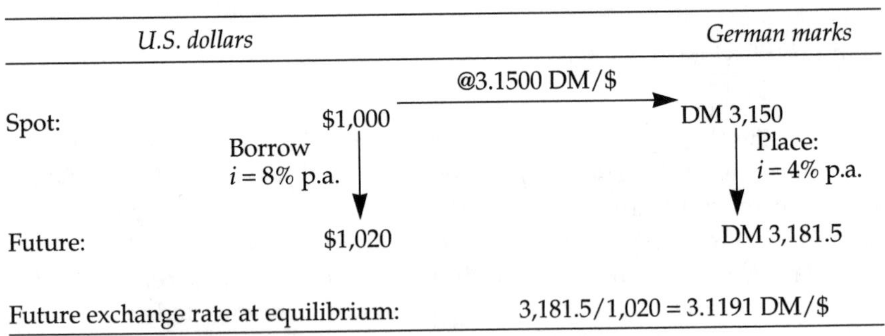

This example focuses on the fact that prices on the currency futures always must tie into the relative interest rates of the currencies traded. If this were not so, risk-free arbitrage would be initiated and would flourish until the prices had adjusted to the equilibrium future price. This illustrates the interest parity theorem which is expressed in its theoretical form by the following formula.[3]

$$F = S \times \frac{1 + i_{f,t}}{1 + i_{\$,t}}$$

where

F = Future foreign exchange price (DM/US$).
S = Spot foreign exchange price (DM/US$).
$i_{f,t}$ = Interest rate in the foreign currency area.
$i_{\$,t}$ = U. S. dollar interest rate.
t = Time period (in our example, three months).

From this example, we can deduce the following basic rules of thumb:

> *The currency of the lower interest rate area will sell at a forward premium in terms of the higher interest currency. Conversely, the currency of the higher interest rate area will sell at a forward discount in terms of the lower interest currency.*

Note, however, that these rules assume a free flow between currencies, which can take place only in unrestricted capital and foreign exchange markets. This also implies that the interest rate parity theorem is valid only for nonregulated and economically stable currency areas. Note also that the real world can deviate slightly from the theory because of internal market procedures of the financial futures exchanges where settlement practices might deviate from those in the underlying cash markets for foreign currency.

INDEX FUTURES

A *stock index futures contract* is a standard agreement that provides the holder with a given index at a predetermined price at a future time. At the Chicago Mercantile Exchange the settlement day is the third Friday of March, June, September, and December.

The stock index futures contract is the third large contract group traded on the financial futures exchanges. The Kansas City Board of Trade introduced the Value Line Average index contract in February 1982 and a variety of exchanges have since then followed suit (see Table 4.4).

TABLE 4.4
Summary of Some Stock Index Futures Contracts.

Chicago Board of Trade (CBOT) *Commodity (Trading Unit)*	*Chicago Mercantile Exchange (CME)* *Commodity (Trading Unit)*	*London International Financial Futures Exchange (LIFFE)* *Commodity (Trading Unit)*
Major Market Index (US$ 500 × index)	Nikkei 225 Stock Index (US$ 5 × index)	FT-SE 100 Index (£ stg. 25 × index)
Standard & Poor's 100 Index (US$ 100 × index)	Standard & Poor's Midcap 400 Index (US$ 500 × index)	FT-SE Eurotrack 100 Index (DM 50 × index)
Standard & Poor's 500 Index (US$ 100 × index)	Standard & Poor's 500 Index (US$ 500 × index)	

Pricing

The prices of the index futures contracts are determined by supply and demand in the market. Like other financial futures, the index contracts are traded on the exchange through general outcry or automated dealing, and an equilibrium market price is reached. The price of the index contract on a given trading day is calculated as the value of an index point multiplied by the index value. The index is determined by the average (or weighted) price movement of a predefined portfolio of stocks.

Example: The underlying portfolio of an index consists of three stocks, and the base year for comparing the price movement is 1980. The index is then calculated as follows:

	1980 No. of Stocks Outstanding	*Price*	*Value*	*1985 No. of Stocks Outstanding*	*Price*	*Value*
Stock 1	100	35	3,500	150	40	6,000
Stock 2	200	25	5,000	200	50	10,000
Stock 3	175	40	7,000	300	20	6,000
Total market value			15,500			22,000

Index value: $22{,}000/15{,}500 = 1.4194$

Settlement value: index point × Index value

US\$ 500 × 1.4194 = US\$ 709.70

The tick value of a financial futures index contract is fixed individually on each exchange to determine the most practical minimum price change in the contract. It is typically indicated as a fraction of an index point.

$$\text{Tick value} = x \times \text{Index point}$$

Trading Unit			*Tick Value*
Major Market Index (MMI)	0.05 × US$ 500	=	US$ 25
Standard & Poor's 500	0.05 × US$ 500	=	US$ 25

Settlement Value

As can be seen, the settlement value is sensitive to the way the index is calculated, which again is a function of the underlying composition of the stock portfolio. Hence there is no guarantee that the various indexes will follow each other over time. Yet, in general, the more diversified and the more comprehensive the underlying stock portfolio is, the better the index will reflect the overall trend of the stock market.[4] The indexes used for the standard index futures contracts are usually well diversified, but due to the different composition of the underlying stock portfolios neither of these indexes fluctuate in a fully correlated manner.[5]

The settlement value of a stock index contract represents the average current value of the market's stocks; there is no directly related cash market for the stock index. As a result, the exchanges have developed a procedure of cash settlement at the maturity of the contracts. In this procedure the buyer and the seller of a specific contract exchange cash through the clearing house at delivery equal to the difference between the settlement value, representing the actual price of the contract at that day, and the price originally agreed to on the futures contract.

COMMODITY FUTURES

Commodity futures contracts deserve a brief mention because these contracts have been traded in the Chicago markets since the latter half of the nineteenth century. The commodity futures markets were created initially to reduce the impact of price fluctuations on producers and users of the commodities, whose availability is very often seasonal. As discussed earlier, commodity futures exchanges are the forerunners for the financial futures markets[6] (see Tables 4.5 and 4.6).

Commodity futures are still very actively traded on several exchanges in North America.[7] A special segment of the commodity futures markets is the futures contracts for precious metals. Due to their durability and "scarcity value," precious metals have always served as a safekeeper in times of economic distress, as well as a means for portfolio in-

TABLE 4.5
Summary of Some Commodity Futures Contracts Traded on the Chicago Mercantile Exchange.

Commodity	*Trading Unit*
Live cattle	40,000 lb.
Feeder cattle	44,000 lb.
Live hogs	30,000 lb.
Pork bellies	38,000 lb.
Fresh white eggs	22,500 doz.
Fuel oil	1,000 barrels
Leaded gasoline	1,000 barrels

TABLE 4.6
Summary of Some Precious Metal Futures Contracts.

Chicago Mercantile Exchange (CME) Commodity (Trading Unit)	*Chicago Board of Trade (CBOT) Commodity (Trading Unit)*	*London Metal Exchange Commodity (Trading Unit)*
Gold futures contract (100 troy oz.)	—	Gold futures contract (10,000 troy oz.)
Silver futures contract (5,000 troy oz.)	Silver futures contract (1,000 troy oz.)	—

vestments and therefore can be traded in conjunction with the financial futures contract. In many ways the price development on the markets for precious metals have close ties to the developments in the real economy. So studying their market developments can give valuable hints to moves in the international economy.

5

Hedging with Financial Futures

The hedger's purpose of trading in the commodity futures markets, as well as in the financial futures markets, is to reduce or eliminate risk. By buying or selling "forward" what is needed or what is in surplus in, say, nine months, you can eliminate or reduce the uncertainty of the price level at the time of delivery, and you can rely on profitability calculations with full or higher certainty—at least as far as prices are concerned.

In the commodity futures market the contracts more often result in the physical delivery of the goods of the contract. This is rarely the case in the financial futures markets. What is special about financial futures is that the commodities traded are financial obligations. Due to the daily mark-to-market (the variation margin), the net gain or net loss will be fully compensated in cash at the time of delivery, which is what most market participants are looking for. Usually, a seller of a futures contract will purchase a similar contract, and a buyer will sell a similar contract on or before the last trading day before delivery. As a result, the position will square out, that is, there will be no delivery of the underlying financial asset. This procedure, often called *closing out,* can be performed at any time during the trading period. Physical delivery of the financial asset of a financial futures contract can take place and does occasionally take place, although it is more the exception than the rule.

What drives the financial futures market is the fact that there is a difference between the future contract price agreed to and the contract price at the time of delivery. The contract price at the time of delivery will usually be equal to the going cash market price.

Example: A market participant sold a contract at a future price of $110, and the actual contract price at the last trading day before delivery is $100. That trader made a profit of $10 by closing out the position.

This principle applies to both speculative participants in the market who expect to incur a long-run profit by taking a position in the market, as well as to hedgers who offset changes in foreign exchange or interest expense by a capital gain or loss on the financial futures contracts.

Example: See Figure 5.1. In March, the actual cash market price for the contract is $95. Our view, as investors, is that the price in nine months, in December, will be $90. Yet the December financial futures contract currently trades at $105 on the futures exchange.

If our view is more correct than the market's indication, we could sell the December futures contract in the expectation of a profit at delivery (futures price of $105 less the expected price of $90 is greater than zero). In June the actual cash market price increases and continues to do so over the remainder of the year to finish at $115 at the time of delivery in December. In this case the investor would incur a loss because the market moved against our expectations (the futures price of $105 less the actual price at delivery of $115 is less than zero). Because the futures

FIGURE 5.1

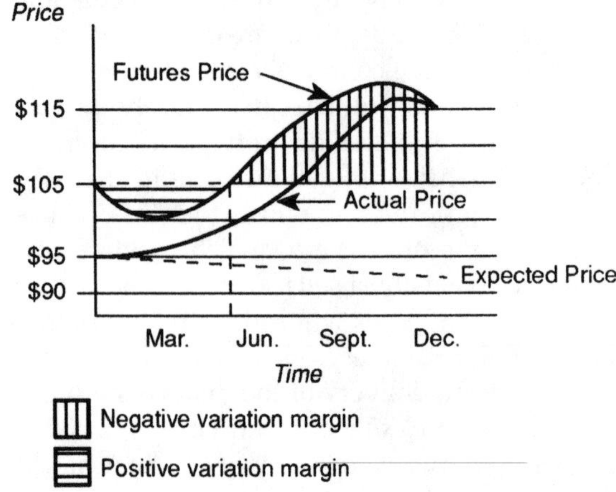

price initially dropped and remained below the futures price we settled for until June ($105) the variation margin is positive and there is a cash inflow on the settlement account. From June onward, the futures price increases, resulting in a negative variation margin and a cash outflow from the settlement account.

Note that the price of the December financial futures contract converges towards the contract price in the underlying cash market to finally be equal at delivery date. This illustrates the phenomenon of *convergence.* In general the closer we get to the delivery date, the less will be the impact of market expectation. This does not mean, however, that one may assume a stable convergence.

This example is presented from an investor's point of view. It could equally well be seen from a hedger's point of view. For example, a buyer of the commodity who fears that the price will increase could then buy a futures contract. In this case he will sell at the higher cash market price against a purchase at the lower futures price which was settled at the purchase of the futures contract. He will thus make a profit (the actual price at delivery less the futures price is greater than zero). This profit would offset the increased cost from the actual purchase of the goods in the cash market. The hedger will end up with a positive variation margin, and the profit would be available in cash in the settlement account at the delivery date.

The actual development in the futures price will only rarely, if ever, follow a smooth movement as indicated by the illustrative example of Figure 5.1. The price development will rather follow erratic intraday and day-to-day movements, reflecting the price risk (volatility) of the underlying cash market instrument. Figure 5.2 provides an example of actual time series of prices on two actively traded interest rate futures contracts.

FIGURE 5.2
Two Actively Traded Interest Rate Futures Contracts.

INTEREST RATE HEDGING

Consider an institution that has a 12-month asset of $20,000,000 on its books at a return of say 12%. To fund this, the institution has acquired a 9-month liability at a rate of 10% p.a. Looking ahead, a liquidity gap of $20,000,000 will, of course, appear during the 3-month period from month 9 to month 12 with funding costs at that time being unknown.

	Balance Sheet	
	Assets	*Liabilities*
3 months	$20,000,000(12%)	$20,000,000(10%)
6 months	$20,000,000(12%)	$20,000,000(10%)
9 months	$20,000,000(12%)	$20,000,000(10%)
12 months	$20,000,000(12%)	(Funding requirement)

Assuming that interest is paid at maturity, the institution must provide interest payments in cash at the end of the 9-month period of:

$$\$20{,}000{,}000 \times 0.10 \times 9/12 = \$1{,}500{,}000$$

That is, the funding requirement in the fourth quarter is not $20,000,000 but $21,500,000—namely principal plus interest on the 9-month loan that has just expired. Hence the breakeven cost of a 3-month loan in the fourth quarter is:

$$\frac{\$20{,}000{,}000(0.12 - 0.10 \times 9/12)}{\$21{,}500{,}000} \times \frac{12}{3} \times 100 = 16\tfrac{3}{4}\%$$

But who knows what will happen over the next nine months?

A less plausible way of closing the interest rate gap would be to obtain a 12-month liability, preferably at a cost below 12% p.a. and acquire a 9-month asset preferably at a return above 10% p.a. The asset and liability positions would be fully matched in maturities, but total footings will have increased from $20,000,000 to $40,000,000, with whatever impact this has on leverage and profitability ratios.

Another possible avenue would be to find a counterparty with exactly the opposite interest rate gapping or an investor who is interested in putting the inverse position on the books—that is, accept a future obligation. This type of search, however, is an arduous process, and why go through it when the financial futures markets deals with financial obligations of exactly this nature? The interest gap can be effectively closed by selling 3-month Eurodollar deposit contracts for delivery nine months hence, preferably at a rate below 16¾% (that is, a contract price in excess of 83.25 = (100 – 16.75)). The financial futures market thus represents an efficient way of accessing counterparties in futures contracts—without affecting the balance sheet.

Short Interest Rate Hedges

Short interest rate hedges generate a profit when interest rates increase above the market's expected future rate, and they are therefore used by borrowers to lock in the future funding cost. The future loan could be an existing loan that is to be rolled over for an extended period, or it could be a completely new loan that is intended to cover expected cash outflows.

Example: In May, a loan of $10,000,000 is to be obtained for a six-month period with three months rollover periods from September this year to February the following year. If the effective borrowing rate is very close to the U.S. domestic certificate of deposit rate, the borrower could lock in the borrowing cost by selling ten 3-month certificate of deposit contracts for delivery both in September and December.

The interest rate was 10% in May and the borrower is worried that interest rates will increase. The 3-month CD contracts for delivery in September and December both trade for a price of 89.00, that is, implying a future interest rate of 11% p.a. By selling the financial futures contracts, the future funding cost will be locked in at the 11%.

In September the 3-month interest rate has increased to 12%, so that a 3-month CD contract is acquired on the futures exchange at a price of 88.00. For each contract sold at the already settled futures price of 89.00, there will be a price gain of 100 ticks. The total capital gain incurred from the sale of futures contracts will count against the increased interest cost on the loan, resulting in a net expense on the loan corresponding to the 11% interest rate.

3-Month Loan September-December	
Price of futures contract	89.00
Cash price of futures contract	88.00
Price gain per contract sold	$1.00 \times 1.00/0.01 = 100$ ticks
Profit per contract sold	100 × $25 = $2,500
Actual interest expense	$300,000
September-December(12%)	
US$ 10,000,000 loan	
Profit from sale of 10 futures contracts	$ 25,000
Net cash expense on loan	$275,000
Corresponding to an effective interest rate of 11.00% p.a.	

In December the 3-month interest rate has increased to 13%, that is, the cash price for the futures contract now amounts to 87.00 leading to a price gain of 200 ticks per futures contract sold. Again the net interest expense on the loan corresponds to an 11% effective interest rate.

3-Month Loan December-February	
Price of futures contract	89.00
Cash price of futures contract	87.00
Price gain per contract sold	$2.00 \times 2.00/0.01 = 200$ ticks
Profit per contract sold	$200 \times \$25 = \$5{,}000$
Actual interest expense	$325,000
September-February(13%)	
US$ 10,000,000 Loan	
Profit from sale of 10 futures contracts	$ 50,000
Net cash expense on loan	$275,000
Corresponding to an effective interest rate of 11.00% p.a.	

The quotes on the futures exchanges will reflect the average interest rate expectation of the market participants themselves. In this example the market expected an interest rate increase from 10% to 11%, and the borrower could fix the future funding cost at the market's future expected interest rate—namely 11%. In this case it turned out to be a wise decision.

In the example, the market expected an increase in the interest rates, and the actual interest rate level turned out to be in excess of the market's expectations. But what happens if the actual interest rate movement turns out to follow a declining trend due to some unforeseeable economic developments?

Example: The actual 3-month CD rate in September has fallen to 10%. The 3-month CD futures contract for September delivery would therefore have a cash price of 90.00, and we would be losing 100 ticks for the sale of each contract.

3-Month Loan September-December	
Price of futures contract sold	89.00
Cash price of futures contract	90.00
Price loss per contract sold	$1.00 \times 1.00/0.01 = 100$ ticks
Loss per contract sold	$100 \times \$25 = \$2{,}500$
Actual interest expense	$250,000
September-December(10%)	
US$ 10,000,000 loan	
Loss from sale of 10 futures contracts	$25,000
Net cash expense on loan	$275,000
Corresponding to an effective interest rate of 11.00% p.a.	

So, no matter what direction the interest rate level takes, the interest rate has been effectively locked in at 11% p.a.

A borrower can fix the future cost of funding by ***selling*** *a suitable number of interest rate futures contracts.*

In the preceding example the funding cost was fully correlated to the CD rate and we therefore obtained a 100% hedge. Such, however, is not always the case. In the example, the time loan periods also corresponded exactly to the maturities of the futures contracts, which made the hedging exercise relatively simple. Yet, often the real world is not so favorable.

Example: In May we foresee that we have to fund ourselves for a six-month period from July to December through a floating rate loan of $10,000,000, with interest payable at the end of each month at the going 1-month CD rate. We would like to hedge the loan against an increase in the interest rate level. As in the previous example, the floating rate loan is hedged through the sale of 20 3-month CD financial futures contracts, of which ten are to be delivered in September and ten are to be delivered in December.

6-Month Loan July-December					
Month	*Principal*	*1-Month CD Rate*	*Interest Amount*	*Futures Settling Account*	*Net Cash Outflow*
July	$10,000,000	11.0% p.a.	$ 91,667	—	$ 91,667
August	$10,091,667	11.5% p.a.	$ 96,712	—	$ 96,712
September	$10,188,379	12.0% p.a.	$101,884	+$25,000	$ 76,884
October	$10,290,263	12.5% p.a.	$107,190	—	$107,190
November	$10,397,453	13.0% p.a.	$112,639	—	$112,639
December	$10,510,092	13.5% p.a.	$118,238	+$50,000	$ 68,238
	$10,246,309	12.25% p.a.	$628,330		$553,330
Corresponding to an average interest rate of 10.8% p.a.					

These calculations imply that, through hedging, the average funding cost was reduced from 12.25% to 10.8% p.a. However, the example also illustrates some of the problems occurring in more complex borrowing situations. As we cannot be sure that the 3-month CD rate will correspond to the average of the 1-month CD rate over the corresponding 3-month period, the future funding cost cannot be locked in 100%, and the timing of the financial futures contracts does not necessarily fit the time schedule of the borrowing program. So in general more skill is required in arranging the appropriate hedging program for a more complex borrowing scheme of the real world. Nevertheless, the following axiom holds true in general:

Institutions can hedge against increasing interest rates by ***selling*** *interest rate futures contracts.*

Long Interest Rate Hedges

Long interest rate hedges generate a profit when interest rates fall below the market's expected future rate. They are therefore used by lenders and investors to lock in the return on future loans or investments.

Example: An institution foresees a cash inflow of US$ 20,000,000 in three months, which it intends to place in 1-year U.S. Treasury bills for a 12-month period. The future return on this investment could be locked in by buying 80 U.S. Treasury bill contracts for delivery in three months. Presently the return on 1-year Treasury bills is 11.50% p.a., but the market expects the rate to fall to 11% in three months (as implied by a futures contract price of 89.00). Fearing that rates might move further down, the institution would like to lock in the future return of 11% p.a. and therefore it buys 80 futures contracts at 89.00.

Three months later, the 1-year U.S. Treasury bill rate has dropped to 10.50%, and so the futures contract now trades at a price of 89.50. The futures contracts, acquired at a price of 89.00, can be sold at a profit.

A 12-Month Investment	
Cash price of futures contract	89.50
Price of futures contract bought	89.00
Price gain per contract bought	$0.50 \times 0.50/0.01 = 50$ ticks
Profit per contract bought	$50 \times \$25 = \$1{,}250$
Actual return	$2,100,000
12 months(10.5%)	
US$ 20,000,000 investment	
Profit from purchase of 80 contracts	$ 100,000
Net return on investment	$2,200,000
Corresponding to an effective interest rate of 11.00% p.a.	

Had the return on 1-year Treasury bills instead remained unchanged at the 11.50% p.a., then the institution would have lost money on the futures contracts because the futures contract bought at a price of 89.00, would sell at 88.50.

A 12-Month Investment	
Cash price of futures contract	88.50
Price of futures contract bought	89.00
Price loss per contract bought	$0.50 \times 0.50/0.01 = 50$ ticks
Loss per contract bought	$50 \times \$25 = \$1{,}250$
Actual return	$2,300,000
12 months(11.5%)	
US$ 20,000,000 investment	
Loss from sale of 80 contracts	$ 100,000
Net return on investment	$2,200,000
Corresponding to an effective interest rate of 11.00% p.a.	

We see that the return on the investment has effectively been fixed at the expected futures rate of 11% p.a. Again we know that this 100% locked-in return is obtained only because the actual return on the Treasury bills was fully correlated to the return of the corresponding futures contracts, based on the assumption that the date of delivery could be completely matched to our timing of the cash inflow. Therefore the best that can be said is:

> *Institutions can hedge against falling interest rates by* ***buying*** *interest rate futures contracts.*

When using a specific market like the 1-year Treasury bill futures contracts, one should understand how the underlying cash market works in order to get a feel for the interest rate development in this market. For instance, intimate knowledge about the Federal Reserve auctioning practice on the 1-year Treasury bills becomes crucial. You might ask what impact will the auction timing (an auction every 28 days) have on interest rate movements, etc.? Hence understanding the related cash market is important in order to stay in touch with what one is trying to hedge and how the hedge itself functions in connection with that specific market.[1]

Hedging Investments in Long-Term Securities

Let's look at the hedging perspective from a long term investor's point of view.

Example: In early January, $10,000,000 has been invested in 15-year 8% coupon U.S. Treasury bonds. At year end, in 12 months, the investor will either sell the securities or have to put the going market value of the securities on the balance sheet, thereby registering an equivalent loss or gain on the income statement for the year. The investor is worried that their initial expectation of an interest rate drop will not hold true so that the year-end discount values of the securities would incur a loss either because the translation values are low or because the actual sale took place at an unfavorable price.

In this case, the investor decides to hedge against an increase in the interest rate level, and the rule of thumb says that this can be done by selling interest futures contracts. So if the investor sold 127 15-year U.S. Treasury bond futures, corresponding to the nominal amount of the investment, it would represent a hedge. The securities were bought at a market rate of 11% p.a., corresponding to a discount purchase price of $78\frac{14}{32}$. The market expects the future Treasury bond rate to be $11\frac{1}{2}$%, that is, the corresponding U.S. Treasury bond futures contracts for December delivery are traded at a price around $75\frac{16}{32}$.

In December the Treasury bond rate turns out to be 12%. The investor therefore gains on the contracts sold at the futures price of $75\frac{16}{32}$ because the current price of the contract in December has dropped to $72\frac{24}{32}$.

12-Month Investment in U.S. Treasury Bonds[2]	
Price of futures contract sold	$75\frac{16}{32}$
Cash price of futures contract	$\underline{72\frac{24}{32}}$
Price gain per contract sold	$2\frac{24}{32} \times 2\frac{24}{32} / \frac{1}{32} = 88$ ticks
Profit per contract sold	88 × \$31.25 = \$2,750
Actual return	\$173,000
\$10,000,000 investment in Treasury bonds	
(Nominal value \$12,700,000)	
Profit from sale of 127 contracts	= \$349,250
Net return on investment	= \$522,250
Corresponding to an effective return of 5.25% p.a.	

If instead the interest rate had dropped to 10½% in December, the investor would lose on the contracts sold at the futures price of $75\frac{16}{32}$ because the current price of the contract in that case would increase to $81\frac{17}{32}$.

12-Month Investment in U.S. Treasury Bonds[3]	
Price of futures contract sold	$75\frac{16}{32}$
Cash price of futures contract	$\underline{81\frac{17}{32}}$
Price loss per contract sold	$6\frac{1}{32} \times 6\frac{1}{32} / \frac{1}{32} = 193$ ticks
Loss per contract sold	193 × \$31.25 = \$6,031.25
Actual return	\$1,262,660.00
\$10,000,000 investment in Treasury bonds	
(Nominal value \$12,700,000)	
Loss from sale of 127 contracts	= \$(765,968.75)
Net return on investment	= \$496,691.25
Corresponds to an effective return of 4.99% p.a.	

The hedge is such that the income from the Treasury bond investment has been adapted to the market's expected future rate of 11.5%.

The reason for the unbalanced gain/loss position relates to the fact that the price change for a given change in the interest rate level is smaller at a higher interest rate level than it is at a lower interest rate level. In the preceding example, note:

- An increase in the interest rate level from 11% to 11.5% on a 14-year 100 nominal security will cause a loss of 2.85 due to a drop in the market price from 79.05 to 76.20.

- Yet a fall in the interest rate from 11% to 10.5% will cause a capital gain of 3.02.

The return on the investment itself over the one-year period is a negligible 5% p.a., which might appear less than satisfactory. Compare this result to the same situation without a hedge, which would bring a return of only 1.75% had the interest rate increased to 12%. So in this context 5% looks reasonable.

The example also illustrates the common characteristic of a futures hedge, namely that it covers for the downside risk but at the same time excludes profit taking from a more favorable interest rate development. In the end whether or not the hedge should be pursued, given the economic outlook, must depend on how strongly the investor feels that the interest rate level will exceed the expected market rate of 11.5%.

Why not sell more contracts to improve the net return on the investment in an increasing interest rate environment? In the first example, where the interest rate increases to 12% in December, the sale of 371 Treasury bond futures contracts, as opposed to the present sale of only 127 contracts, would have brought the investor a net return on the investment of 12% p.a. However, had the interest rate dropped to 10.5%, as in the second example, then the investor would have lost $975,000. So if you buy contracts in excess of the nominal exposure of the long-term investment portfolio to be hedged, a gapping position is opened and a complete hedging position no longer pertains.

The situation could also be presented in a different interest rate environment.

Example: The futures market expects the Treasury bond rate to fall to 10.5% by December, that is, the futures contracts for December delivery are traded at $81\frac{17}{32}$. Yet the investor does not agree, thinking rather that a stable or perhaps a slightly increasing interest rate level is the more likely outcome over the next year. In this situation the investor could lock in the gain from the market expectations by selling 127 Treasury bond futures contracts at the future price of $81\frac{17}{32}$. Let us assume that the investor was right in that the Treasury bond rate in December turned out to be 11.5%, that is, it went through a half-percent increase instead of the expected half-percent reduction. The investor was able to lock in the future rate at 10.5%, despite the adverse rate development in the cash market.

12-Month Investment in U.S. Treasury Bonds	
Price of futures contract sold	$81\frac{17}{32}$
Cash price of futures contract	$\underline{75\frac{16}{32}}$
Price gain per contract sold	$6\frac{1}{32} \times 6\frac{1}{32}/\frac{1}{32} = 193$ ticks
Profit per contract sold	193 × $31.25 = $6,031.25
Actual return	$517,170.00
$10,000,000 investment in Treasury bonds	
(Nominal value $12,700,000)	
Profit from sale of 127 contracts	= $765,968.75
Net return on investment	= $1,283,138.75
Corresponding to an effective return of 12.88% p.a.	

The applicability of a financial futures hedge on a long-term securities portfolio, therefore, very much depends on the prevalent interest rate environment, which must be evaluated thoroughly before engaging in a futures position. Another possibility is to perform a partial hedge to reflect management's uncertain outlook on the future interest rate development.

Example: The view is that there is a 50% chance that the interest rate level will increase by one percentage point and a 50% chance that the interest rate will drop by one percentage point. The investor could then hedge half the investment portfolio against the effect of an interest rate increase by selling only 6 Treasury bond futures contracts. In case the interest rate increases, the portfolio will be partially hedged. If the interest rate drops, the investor will incur a fair share of the upside capital gain associated with the increase in the market price of the securities portfolio.

Including a long-term instrument in a short-term investment portfolio, where the instruments are not to be held to maturity obviously in itself represents an interest rate gapping situation. Here the investor tries to take advantage of an unexpected favorable movement in the interest rate level. In this situation as we have seen, the financial futures can help reduce the loss if the interest moves against the initial outlook, or they can help lock in a gain if the market expectation is bullish.

Hedging New Issues

In North America and overseas on the Eurocurrency markets investment bankers have a long established procedure of underwriting new issues of long-term securities, often termed *bought deals.* At the closing date of the underwriting agreement the investment banker commits to forward a fixed amount of money in return for the securities to be sold in the securities market by the investment banker. Hence the banker carries the full risk of the securities not being sold in the market at the predetermined price.

The underwriter's problem is that the interest rate might increase to a level exceeding what was committed to the borrower at the closing of the underwriting agreement. The securities would then have to be sold in the market at a lower price and would thus bring the underwriter a loss because he already has committed to a future cash payout to the borrower. Usually this risk will be carried throughout a period of a few days to five or six weeks at the worst.

Let's apply the rule of thumb. The risk of increasing interest rates could be hedged through the sale of a suitable number of interest futures contracts.

Example: In August the investment banker has committed an underwriting of US$ 20,000,000 in 15-year 8% coupon Eurobond issue at an interest rate of 10.75%. That is a committed discount price of 79.74.[4] The Treasury bond futures contract for delivery in September is trading at $79\frac{24}{32}$, implying that the market expects the interest rate to stay put. The investment banker would like to lock in this interest rate and does so by selling 200 Treasury bond futures contracts for delivery in September at the going futures price of $79\frac{24}{32}$.

It turns out that in September, when the investment banker is ready to sell the Euro securities, the interest rate actually has increased to 11%—one quarter of a percent up from the August forecast. However, the Treasury bond futures contract, for the same reason, trades at a price around $78\frac{6}{32}$, and the investment banker will make a profit from selling the Treasury bond contracts at the future price of $79\frac{24}{32}$.

1-Month Underwriting Commitment[5]	
Price of futures contract sold	$79\frac{24}{32}$
Cash price of futures contract	$\underline{78\frac{6}{32}}$
Price gain per contract sold	$1\frac{18}{32} \times \frac{18}{32}/\frac{1}{32} = 50$ ticks
Profit per contract sold	$50 \times \$31.25 = \$1,562.50$
Loss from Eurobond issue	= $307,562.71
Profit from sale of 200 contracts	= $312,500.00

As can be seen, the profit from the sale of the Treasury bond futures contracts is approximately equivalent to the loss incurred from the Eurobond issue in our example and the interest rate gap has been effectively closed.

CROSS HEDGING

As implied by the previous examples, a hedge is performed by trading the number of futures contracts that match up to the face value of the financial obligation to be hedged.

Example: Ten US$ 1,000,000 3-month certificate of deposit contracts were sold to hedge a future 3-month loan of US$ 10,000,000.

The general principle adhered to in this process is:

The change in the value of the futures contract should match the change in the interest income/expense of the cash instrument to be hedged.

A special problem occurs when the portfolio to be hedged differs in maturity from the maturity of the futures contract underlying asset.

Example: A 1-month dollar investment is hedged by buying 3-month interest futures. The value of a one-basis-point change in the interest rate on a $1,000,000 1-month investment is $8.33, against the tick value of a 3-month futures contract of $25.00. Therefore financial futures contracts should be bought to match one-third of the principal investment. Conversely, when 3-month futures contracts are used to hedge a 6-month investment, interest contracts should be bought to match twice the principal investment. The value of a one basis point change in the interest rate on a $1,000,000 6-month investment is $50, against the tick value of $25 on the 3-month futures contract.

If there is a maturity mismatch between the futures contract and the cash instrument to be hedged, the number of futures contracts traded should be inversely related to the maturities of the cash instrument and the futures contract.

$$\text{Number of futures contracts traded} = \frac{N}{F} \times \frac{M_c}{M_f}$$

where

N = Nominal value of the cash instrument.
F = Value of the futures contract.
M_c = Maturity of the cash instrument.
M_f = Maturity of the futures contract's underlying asset.

Example: To hedge a 1-month dollar investment of $15,000,000 with 3-month interest futures contracts, buy five contracts:

$$\frac{\$15,000,000}{\$1,000,000} \times \frac{1}{3} = 5$$

In previous examples, one was always able to find a financial futures contract that completely matches the cash instrument to be hedged because they had the same denominations and maturities, and because the interest rates of the two financial instruments were always fully correlated. Obviously this is far from the case at all times. So a method is called for that can tell us, in case no corresponding futures contract exists, how many of the available futures contracts to trade in order to obtain a full hedge.

Example: An investor wants to hedge a portfolio of $20,000,000 Eurobonds with a 7% coupon rate and 20 years to maturity by applying the U.S. Treasury bond futures contract.

We may no longer assume that the interest rate movements of the two dollar-denominated securities are fully correlated. In fact, they *may* be correlated to some extent inasmuch as the two instruments often appeal to the same institutional investors' and the two securities are close substitutes. However, from the investor's point of view there is a major difference between the two—namely, the credit risk. For a domestic U.S. investor a credit to the U.S. Treasury must be considered virtually riskless, whereas a Eurobond represents a loan to an international corporate entity or a sovereign borrower and therefore often represents a slightly higher credit risk. On top of this, changes in the regulatory environment in the U.S. and changes in monetary regulations will also cause a situation in which interest rates do not move in complete unison over time.

For the hedger, it is interesting to know how the two interest rates have developed historically, and to what extent the two time series represent a correlated pattern of movements. This can be investigated by calculating the *regression coefficient.* This is a single number that indicates how much a change in the interest rate of the one security has "induced" an interest rate change in the other security and vice versa.

For a given period, the daily interest rates of the Eurobond and the cheapest deliverable bond[6] under the U.S. Treasury bond futures contract is plotted (see Figure 5.3). In this diagram the development in the Eurobond interest rate is presented as a function of the development in the Treasury bond interest rate.

The regression analysis assumes that a linear relationship can be

FIGURE 5.3
Eurobond and U.S. Treasury Bond Interest Rates.

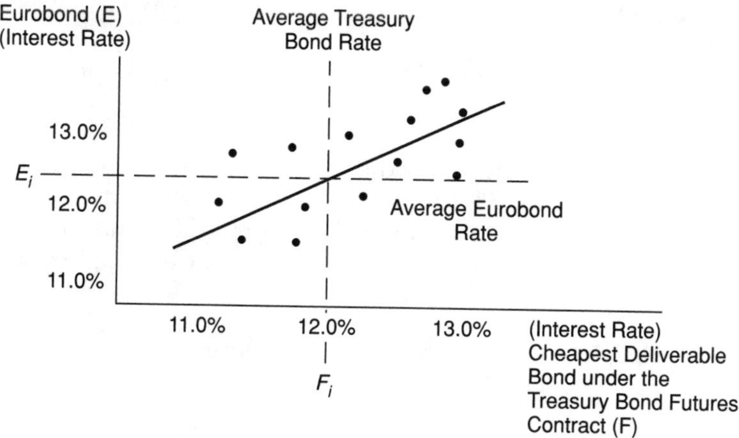

applied to describe the covariation of the two interest rates, and the regression coefficient is calculated by applying the standard formula:[7]

$$b = \frac{\text{sum } (E_i \times F_i)}{\text{sum } (F_i^2)}$$

where

$i = 1, 2, \ldots n$ represent the sample of plotted into the diagram.
E_i, F_i = ith set of observations.
E_i = Eurobond interest rate.
F_i = Treasury bond rate.

Example: Assume that, in our analysis, for different reference periods, the regression coefficient was calculated to be 1.15. In that case, for a one basis point change in the Treasury bond rate, the historical interest rate pattern indicates that there will be a 1.15 basis point change in the Eurobond interest rate. A one basis point change in the yield corresponds to a $10,250 price change on the $20,000,000 Eurobond portfolio and a price change of $11,200 on the corresponding portfolio of notional Treasury bonds.[8]

The relative price change of the two underlying assets is often referred to as the *BPV (basis point value) factor*, because it is established as the relative size of the two contracts' price sensitivity, as measured by the price change on the underlying instruments per basis point change in the interest rate.

BPV factor = **BPV X/BPV Y**

where

BVP X = Change in price of X for a one basis point change in the interest rate.

BVP Y = Change in price of Y for a one basis point change in the interest rate.

Say the cheapest deliverable bond under the Treasury bond futures contract turned out to be the 8% coupon rate bond with 20 years to maturity and that the conversion factor to apply to bring this bond into the standard contract is 0.9010. Then the hedging ratio is calculated by applying the following formula:[9]

$$\text{Hedging ratio} = \text{Regression coefficient} \times \text{BPV factor} \times \text{Conversion factor}$$

$$0.9483 = 115 \times \frac{10,250}{11,200} \times 0.9010$$

where the BPV factor is the Eurobond price change divided by the Treasury bond price change.

With a ratio of 1, we should buy 200 U.S. Treasury bond futures contracts to hedge the investment corresponding to the nominal value of $20,000,000 Eurobonds. Now apply the rule that the change in the value of the futures contracts should match the change in the value of the cash instruments to be hedged: The number of $100,000 Treasury futures contracts to sell is 190 ($20,000,000/$100,000 × 0.9483 = 189.66).

PRICE RELATIONSHIPS

In general a one-basis-point change in the cash market price of the underlying financial instrument should cause an equivalent one-basis-point change in the price of the futures contract. However, this is not always the case, and it becomes less so the further we are from the final delivery date. This is so because the futures price is an indication of the market's expectation of the cash market price of the underlying asset at the delivery date, which, of course, can differ from the current market price.

Nevertheless, there will usually be an impact on the futures price from changes in the cash market price. This relationship is expressed in the *delta value*, which is the incremental change in the futures price as a function of a marginal change in the price of the underlying instrument.

$$\text{Delta value} = \mathbf{dF/dP}$$

where

F = Price of the futures contract.
P = Cash price of the underlying instrument.
d = Derivative (change).

The shorter the period remaining to the delivery date, the more the futures price will correspond to the price movements in the cash market; that is, the delta value moves toward 1 as we get closer to the time of delivery. On the actual delivery date, the delta is usually equal to 1, that is, the futures price corresponds to the cash market price (see Figure 5.4).

FIGURE 5.4
Profit and Loss Profile of a Futures Contract.

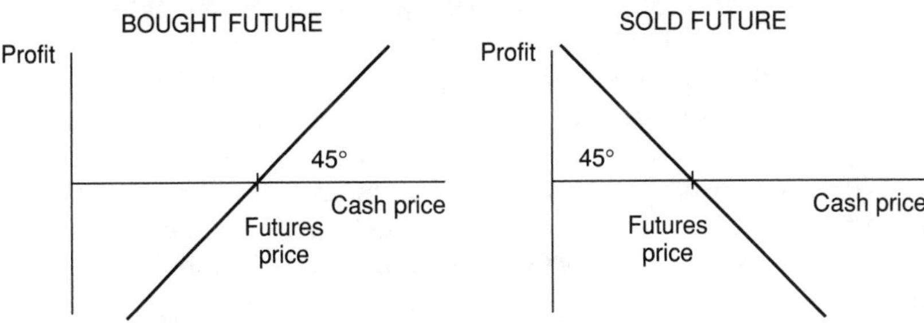

SPREADS

For the astute investor the financial futures market provides a number of investment opportunities. Compared to the cash market, the futures market offers the possibility of investing on a leveraged basis since the futures position only requires payment of initial and variation margins. The simple investment opportunity is to take a view on the future price on the underlying cash instrument or on the future price itself, thereby establishing a so-called *trend position.* Such positions can be closed out at any time before the delivery date if a favorable market situation should occur. But there are other ways to establish positions in the futures market. The same futures contract with different delivery dates can react differently to movements in the underlying cash market. Such a situation enables an investor (speculator) to establish a so-called *spread position* in the contract.

Example: The June and December contracts are quoted with a higher price difference to the cash market price than the September contract. The investor can establish a spread position, for example, by buying 200 September contracts and selling 100 June and 100 December contracts.

The spread technique can be extended from *intramarket spreads,* in the same contract with different delivery dates, to *intercommodity spreads,* involving spread positions between contracts with different maturities in the underlying instruments. For example, a spread position can be established on 3-month sterling contracts versus 20-year gilt contracts. Thereby the investor is taking a view on the development in the interest rate structure (yield curve).

It is also possible to establish an *intermarket spread* between corresponding contracts traded on different exchanges, such as a 15-year 8% notional U.S. Treasury bond traded on both the CBOT and the LIFFE. In Europe it has been quite popular to establish *intercurrency spreads* on different national interest rate instruments, thereby taking advantage of changes in interest rate differentials between currency areas. Typically these positions have been established by selling futures on high-yield assets and concurrently buying futures on assets in a currency with a lower yield. The spread assumes a stable foreign exchange rate development and a strong convergence between the interest rate levels of the two currencies.

When such a position is established the investor should apply an appropriate *hedge ratio,* as discussed previously. This is done to fulfill the general requirement of a spread position, that the amount of assets bought must approximately equal the amount of assets sold.

An investor that buys *a* contracts of future in currency A to create a spread position must sell *b* contracts of future in currency B, as determined by the following calculation:

$$b = \mathbf{N}_A/\mathbf{N}_B \times \text{FX rate } [B/A] \times RC(A,B) \times \text{BPV factor} \times a$$

where

A = Currency A.
B = Currency B.
a = Number of futures contracts of currency A.
b = Number of futures contracts of currency B.
N_A = Contract size on futures contract of currency A.
N_B = Contract size on futures contract of currency B.
$RC(A,B)$ = Regression coefficient between the price movement of the futures contract of currency A and the futures contract of currency B.
BPV factor = BPV A/BPV B.

PORTFOLIO HEDGING

A portfolio can consist of a collective group of either the assets in an investment or the liabilities making up a total loan portfolio. Typically an institution wants to take a longer view of its asset and liability portfolios, often over several years. A net investor, such as a pension fund, can on the basis of the policyholders' claims determine the expected timing of payouts to the policy holders, that is, the average life of the liabilities. Similarly a net borrower, such as a power plant, can determine the expected average life of its assets. The idea behind long-term portfolio hedging is to safeguard the future cash flows of the investment assets established to cover expected liabilities, or conversely to secure the funding costs throughout the productive assets' lifetime.

Portfolio hedging is accomplished by establishing an invested portfolio with a duration of a length equal to the time frame of the liabilities, or conversely to establish a loan portfolio with a duration equal to the life of the assets. The duration indicates the time period throughout which the impact of marginal interest rate movements on the portfolio's cash flows is neutralized.

Hence, under the given circumstances the return on the invested portfolio will be fixed until payments must be made on existing liabilities. Conversely, the funding costs on a loan portfolio have been fixed during the lifetime of the assets that are being funded. The principle is often referred to as *immunization* (see Chapter 2). The duration of a given portfolio of assets (or liabilities) is found simply by adding, on a weighted basis, the duration of the specific investment (or debt) instruments making up the total portfolio.[10] By buying or selling futures contracts into the portfolio, the hedger can adjust the duration of the portfolio accordingly. Hence, a portfolio manager can adjust the duration of a given portfolio through transactions on the futures market.

An increase in the interest rate will reduce the present value of an asset (or a liability), while the reinvestment rate on the current interest income (or the opportunity cost on current interest payments) will increase. A sold futures contract will incur a capital gain when the position is closed toward the delivery date, but will have no impact on the reinvestment rate (or opportunity cost). The capital gain incurred on the futures contract will further reduce the time required for the higher reinvestment rate to compensate for the capital loss on the portfolio, that is, the duration is reduced.

A drop in the interest rate will increase the present value of an asset (or a liability), while the reinvestment rate (or the opportunity cost) will decrease. A bought futures contract will incur a capital loss when the position is closed, but will have no impact on reinvestments (or opportunity costs). The capital loss from the futures contract will further increase the time required for the lower reinvestment rate to compensate for the capital gain on the portfolio. In other words, the duration is increased.

The duration on a portfolio is ***reduced*** *by* ***selling*** *futures contracts.*

The duration on a portfolio is ***increased*** *by* ***buying*** *futures contracts.*

The duration of a portfolio including futures contracts is found by calculating the weighted duration of the cash market instruments and the futures contracts.

$$D = \frac{(D_c \times M_c) + (D_f \times M_f \times d)}{M_c}$$

where

D_c = Duration of the portfolio of cash market instruments.
M_c = Market value of the portfolio of the cash market instrument.
D_f = Duration of the futures contracts.
M_f = Market value of the futures contracts.
d = Delta value of the futures contract (approximately 1).

This formula can be reversed to find the applicable futures position to establish in order to reach a targeted duration for the portfolio in question. This is found by solving the equation for M_f.

$$M = \frac{(D - D_c)M_c}{D_f \times d}$$

As already discussed, the duration measure is a function of the interest rate. Therefore, a portfolio hedge by means of duration measures should be monitored on a current basis to adjust for periodic changes in the interest rate.

CURRENCY HEDGING

Transactions involving the exchange of currencies are usually the ones the net effect of which are registered on the official balance of payments statistics. That is, they are payments for trade transactions involving delivery of goods and services across national borders, capital transactions involving the extension of cross-border credits and debt service payments on outstanding foreign commitments, or settlements relating to short-term currency positions. Within these wide categories of foreign exchange transactions, one could think of a myriad of examples where different institutions would be interested in locking in the future foreign exchange rate. Here we will focus only on a few transactions in order to show how to hedge by using financial futures contracts. The same hedging principles, however, apply to any situation involving the exchange of foreign currencies.

Example: In April an American company has shipped goods for delivery to a corporation in Switzerland, and the price has been settled in Swiss francs. The payment of Swiss francs 10,000,000 is expected in mid-June. The present spot exchange rate is quoted at 2.8852 Sw. frc./US$ (0.3466 US$/Sw. frc.). Given the past U.S. dollar exchange rate development, the American exporter is worried that he will see a weakened Swiss franc in two months, meaning that he will receive at that time fewer dollars for the incoming number of Swiss francs.

The Swiss franc futures contract with delivery in June is quoted on the futures exchange at 0.3400. The American exporter finds this rate attractive because it is higher than his own 2-month forecast for the exchange rate. To lock in this foreign exchange rate, he sells 80 Swiss franc futures contracts for delivery in June. In June it turns out that the exporter's worst guesses were correct, the spot exchange rate has increased to 2.9851 Sw. frc./US$ (0.3350 US$/Sw. frc.). Yet the loss made in the cash exchange market is compensated for by the profit gained on the sale of the futures contracts.

Price of futures contract sold	0.3400
Cash price of futures contract	0.3350
Price gain per contract sold	0.0050 × 0.0050/0.0001 = 50 ticks
Profit per contract sold	50 × $12.50 = $625
Loss on spot sale of Swiss franc	$(50,000)
10,000,000 (0.3350–0.3400)	
Profit from sale of 80 futures contracts	$50,000

Now assume, on the other hand, that the not unlikely event that the exporter's two-month foreign exchange forecast was off the mark as the June spot rate hit 2.8571 Sw. frc./US$ (0.3500 US$/Sw. frc.). Then the exporter would gain on the spot exchange of the Swiss Francs but would correspondingly lose on the sale of the financial futures contracts.

Price of futures contract sold	0.3400
Cash price of futures contract	0.3500
Price loss per contract sold	0.0100 × 0.0100/0.0001 = 100 ticks
Loss per contract sold	100 × $12.50 = $(1,250)
Gain on spot sale of Swiss franc	$100,000
10,000,000 (0.3500–0.3400)	
Loss from sale of 80 futures contracts	$(100,000)

In other words, the future exchange rate has been effectively locked in at the futures market's expected future exchange rate of 0.3400 US$/Sw. frc.

By going through a similar example with the applicable calculations, one can be convinced that an American importer who pays for the import in the exporter's currency can lock in the future exchange rate by buying futures contracts.

Example: An American importer must make a payment of 10,000,000 Swiss francs by mid-June. He would hedge this by buying 80 Swiss franc contracts at the market price of 0.3400. In June the Swiss franc spot rate was 0.3500; so he will have to pay more dollars for the francs on the spot market but will gain from the purchase of the futures contracts.

Price of futures contract	0.3500
Price of futures contract bought	0.3400
Price per contract bought	0.0100 × 0.0100/0.0001 = 100 ticks
Profit per contract bought	100 × $12.50 = $1,250
Loss on spot purchase of Swiss franc 10,000,000 (0.3400–0.3500)	$(100,000)
Profit from purchase of 80 futures contracts	$100,000

The previous examples and calculation exercises lead then to the following rules, which hold true in general:

A U.S. resident who receives payments in a foreign currency hedge by ***selling*** *futures contracts of that currency.*

and

A U.S. resident who makes payments in a foreign currency hedge by ***buying*** *futures contracts of that currency.*

How does such a hedge work in the case of a non-U.S. resident?

Example: A German exporter is exporting to the United States and receives payment in U.S. dollars. In October the exchange rate was quoted at 3.4305 DM/US$ (0.2915 US$/DM). Yet the German exporter is afraid from past experience that this rate might decrease, that is, the DM might strengthen. So he will get less DM in December when his receivable of US$ 5,000,000 comes due. Since the DM futures contract for December delivery is trading at 0.2910, he is willing to lock in this rate by buying 40 German mark contracts for December delivery. In December the exchange rate turned out to be 3.1746 DM/US$ (0.3150 US$/DM), so the German exporter got less DMs for the dollar receivables but instead made an equivalent gain from the purchase of the futures contracts.

Cash price of futures contracts sold	0.3150
Cash price of futures contracts bought	0.2910
Price gain per contract sold	$0.0240 \times 0.0240/0.0001 = 240$ ticks
Profit per contract bought	$240 \times \$12.50 = \$3{,}000$
Loss on spot purchase of DM	$(120,000)
5,000,000 (0.2910–0.3150)	
Profit from 40 contracts bought	$120,000

Had the German resident instead been importing goods from the United States to be paid in U.S. dollars, the dollars payable could be hedged by selling the German mark contracts.

Example: Using the same data as in the previous example, we can perform the following calculation:

Price of futures contracts sold	0.2910
Cash price of futures contracts	0.3150
Price loss per contract sold	$0.0240 \times 0.0240/0.0001 = 240$ ticks
Profit per contract sold	$240 \times \$12.50 = \$3{,}000$
Gain on spot sale of Swiss franc	$120,000
5,000,000 (0.3150–0.2910)	
Loss from sale of 40 German mark futures contracts	$(120,000)

This reasoning enables us to formulate the following rules of thumb:

> *A non-U.S. resident receiving payments in U.S. dollars can hedge by* ***buying*** *futures contracts of the home currency.*

and

> *A non-U.S. resident making payments in U.S. dollars can hedge by* ***selling*** *futures contracts of the home currency.*

CROSS-CURRENCY HEDGING

In a situation in which U.S. dollars are not directly involved, hedging becomes slightly more complicated when using the traditional currency futures contracts.

Example: A French producer is exporting to an English importer. In mid-August the producer has shipped the goods and is expecting pound sterling payments of 5,000,000 when the goods have safely arrived in the United Kingdom in mid-September. In mid-August the pound sterling exchange rate is 1.0668 US$/£ stg., and the French franc exchange rate is 10.4810 Fr. frc./US$ (0.0954 US$/Fr. frc.), thus implying a cross rate of 11.1811 Fr. frc./£ stg. The present market expects the pound to strengthen slightly against the dollar because of an improvement in the international spot price on crude oil. The franc is expected to drop slightly in value against the U.S. dollar, as indicated by the values of the September futures contracts for pounds and French francs of 1.0750 and 0.0952, respectively, implying a cross rate of 11.2920 Fr. frc./£ stg.[11]

Now, the French importer has experienced the volatile foreign exchange markets of the recent past and is worried that the favorable exchange rate development might reverse before receipt of the payments in pounds. However, by selling 200 £ stg. contracts and buying 225 French franc contracts, he can hedge the value of his foreign currency receivables. If the exporter's worries were justified—that is, if the spot exchange cross rate in mid-September turned out to be, for example, 11.1996 Fr. frc./£ stg.—he would receive fewer French francs in the cash spot exchange of the pounds sterling receivables. However, the gains from trading the franc and pound futures contracts will make up for this loss.

Price of £ stg. contract sold	1.0750
Cash price of £ stg. contract	1.0718
Price gain per contract sold	0.0032 × 0.0032/0.0005 = 6 ticks
Profit per £ stg. contract sold	6 × $12.50 = $7,500
Cash price of Fr. frc. contract	0.0957
Price of Fr. frc. contract bought	0.0952
Price gain per Fr. frc. contract bought	0.0005 × 0.0005/0.00005 = 10 ticks
Profit per Fr. frc. contract bought	10 × $12.50 = $125.00
Loss on spot sale of £ stg. against Fr. frc.	$(44,213.40)
(11.2920–11.1996) 5,000,000 × 0.0957	
Profit from sale of 200 £ stg. contracts	$15,000.00
Profit from purchase of 225 Fr. frc. contracts	$28,125.00
Total profit from futures contracts	$43,125.00

In this example, the hedge was very close to being complete but was, however, slightly less advantageous than the straightforward rates indicated. Due to the standard size of the futures contracts, a 100% hedge is rarely possible. In the preceding example 200 £ stg. contracts were sold, thereby perfectly hedging the £ stg. 5,000,000 conversion into U.S. dollars. However, the purchase of 225 Fr. frc. contracts lock in the dollar conversion of Fr. frc. 56,250,000, thus leaving Fr. frc. 210,000 unhedged $(5{,}000{,}000 \times 11.2920 - 56{,}250{,}000)$.

Cross-currency hedging can be formalized in the following rules of thumb:

A non-U.S. resident receiving payments in a foreign currency can hedge by ***selling*** *futures contracts of the foreign currency against dollars and* ***buying*** *futures contracts of the domestic currency against dollars.*

A non-U.S. resident making payments in a foreign currency hedge by ***buying*** *futures contracts of the foreign currency against dollars and* ***selling*** *futures contracts of the domestic currency against dollars.*

INTEREST RATE HEDGING IN OTHER CURRENCIES

Example: At the end of February, a German institution is running a short interest rate gap: It has on its books a 6-month fixed yield German mark asset of DM 10,000,000, which is funded by a 3-month fixed rate German mark liability at 6.4% p.a. On the present day, no suitable short-term future contract on German mark financial instruments seems to be available on appropriate terms. However, one is able to create a German mark interest rate hedge by employing say, 3-month Eurodollar deposit contracts and German mark futures contracts.

The 3-month Eurodollar deposit contract for March delivery is trading at 90.70, implying a 3-month Eurodollar offer rate of 9.3% p.a. The June contract is trading at 90.00, that is, the market expects the 3-month Eurodollar rate to be 10% p.a. three months from now.

The German mark contract for March delivery is trading at 0.3070, thus implying a spot DM exchange rate of 3.257 DM/US$. Since the DM contract for delivery in June is trading at 0.3093, the futures market expects the DM exchange rate to be around 3.2331 DM/US$ by June. By putting the Eurodollar offer rate of 9.3% p.a. into the interest rate parity formula, we see that the corresponding 3-month DM bid rate must be around 6⅜% p.a.

$$
\begin{aligned}
i_{f,t} &= F/S(1+i_{\$,t})-1 \\
&= 3.2331/3.2573\left(1+\frac{0.093}{4}\right)-1 \\
&= 0.0159(=6.36\%\ \text{p.a.})
\end{aligned}
$$

The DM futures contract for September delivery is trading at 0.3118, implying a future spot exchange rate of 3.2072 DM/US$. In other words, the market continues to believe in a strengthening of the mark against the U.S. dollar.

So what we want to accomplish is to:

- Borrow the funds in U.S. dollars at 10% p.a. for three months from June to September.
- Convert the amount into German marks in June at the future rate of 3.2331 DM/US$.
- Convert it back into dollars in September at the future exchange rate of 3.2074 DM/US$.

The expected strengthening of the DM exchange rate from June to September reflects an interest rate differential in favor of the German mark, whose interest rate can be found by applying the interest rate parity theory.

$$
\begin{aligned}
i_{f,t} &= 3.2072/3.2331\left(1+\frac{0.10}{4}\right)-1 \\
&= 0.01679(=6.7\%\ \text{p.a.})
\end{aligned}
$$

So, by adhering to this strategy and given that the future dollar interest rate and the German mark exchange rate can be completely locked in, we have created a future 3-month DM loan at a rate of 6.7% p.a.

We also want to hedge against (1) an increase in the Eurodollar interest rate and (2) a decrease in the German mark exchange rate in June and an increase of it by September.

Example: We accomplish the first hedge by selling three 3-month Eurodollar deposit contracts (10,000,000 × 0.3070/1,000,000 = 3.07). For the second, we buy 80 German mark currency futures contracts for June delivery and sell another 80 for September delivery (10,000,000/125,000 = 80). Now in the cash market the 3-month Eurodollar rate went up to 10⅛% p.a. by June. The German mark exchange rate fell to 3.2279 by June and increased to 3.2410 DM/US$ by September. The whole scenario is laid out in the following table:

	March Actual	Financial Futures (June)	June Actual	Financial Futures (Sept.)	Sept. Actual
Foreign exchange rate (DM/US$)	3.2573	3.2331	3.2279	3.2072	3.2410
DM financial futures price (US$/DM)	0.3070	0.3093	0.3098	0.3118	0.3085
3-month Eurodollar financial futures price	90.70	90.00	89.87	—	—
US$ interest rate (p.a.)	9.30%	10.00%	10⅛%	—	—

We will pay more for the 3-month U.S. dollar loan, get less DM at the June conversion, and have to pay more DM at the September conversion in the cash markets. However, what is lost on the transactions in the cash market is offset by the aggregate profit made on the financial futures trading.

Price of 3-month Eurocurrency futures contract sold	$90.00
Cash price of 3-month Eurocurrency futures contract	$89.87
Price gain per contract sold	$ 0.13 × 0.13/0.01 = 13 ticks
Profit per contract sold	13 × $25 = $325
Cash price of DM futures contract in June	0.3098
Price of DM June futures contract bought	0.3093
Price gain per DM contract bought	0.0005 × 0.0005/0.0001 = 5 ticks
Profit per DM contract sold	5 × $12.50 = $62.50
Price of September DM futures contract sold	0.3118
Cash price of DM futures contract in September	0.3085
Price gain per DM contract sold	0.0033 × 0.0033/0.0001 = 33 ticks
Profit per DM contract sold	33 × $12.50 = $412.50
Loss on increased funding cost	
[10,000,000/3.2279 × (0.00125/4)] =	$968.12
Loss on $-DM conversion in June	
[3,097,990 × (3.2331 – 3.2279)/3.2279] =	$4,990.72
Loss on DM-$ conversion in September	
[3,176,407.87 × (3.2410 – 3.2072)/3.2410)] =	$33,126.38
Total loss from cash market transaction	$39,085.22
Profit from sale of three Eurocurrency contracts	$975.00
Profit from purchase of 80 June DM contracts	$5,000.00
Profit from sale of 80 September DM contracts	$33,000.00
Total profit from financial futures transactions	$38,975.00

Like the cross currency hedge, this hedge is not 100% because the standard size of the financial futures contracts will not allow such a perfect matching of the exposed amounts. Yet the hedge in this case is very close to being complete.

To the extent that applicable currency cross-rate futures contracts are traded, more stable hedges can be established. However, there are only a limited number of actively traded currency cross-rate futures.

HEDGING A STOCK PORTFOLIO

For a portfolio manager the risk attached to holding stocks is primarily linked to stock price fluctuations since the return on a stock is made up by dividend payments and capital gains and losses.

The price fluctuation of a stock is impacted by two distinct risk factors. The *systematic risk* is linked to changes in the interest rate level of the economy as a whole. The other risk factor, often termed the *unsystematic risk,* is stock-specific and relates to the circumstances of the business sector and the specific corporation's financial performance.

The *price variance* of a given stock portfolio is the weighted sum of the covariances among all the individual categories of stocks. As the number of individual categories of stocks increases, the weight attached to each covariance is vastly reduced thus reducing the overall price variance of the stock portfolio. In other words, by increasing the number of stocks added to the stock portfolio, the unsystematic risk can be reduced.[12] This phenomenon is usually termed *risk diversification.*

The systematic risk of a stock portfolio, however, is not reduced through diversification, and traditional portfolio theory gives no answer as how to hedge against this risk factor. Stock index futures contracts, however, provide the means to manage this exposure.

The unsystematic risk factor is often quantified in an expression termed the *beta coefficient,* which provides a standardized measurement of how a specific category of stock fluctuates with the general price movement of the whole stock market. The beta coefficient is found by calculating the price covariance between the category of stock in question and the general stock market. The expression is standardized by dividing by the price variance of the general stock market:

$$\text{Beta}_i = \frac{\text{cov}(P_i, P_m)}{\text{var}(P_m)}$$

where

P = Stock price.
i = A specific category of stock.
m = Total stock market.

Hence a low-risk stock has a beta coefficient close to zero because the covariance with the market is small, and a more risky stock has a coefficient higher than one, showing that it fluctuates with the market but in a more volatile manner. The incorporation of the beta coefficient as a risk measure explaining the average return on a stock is contained in the well known *capital asset pricing model* (*CAPM*). The higher the beta coefficient (risk), the higher is the average return of the stock.

Example: A portfolio manager holds a sample of industrial stock in the investment portfolio with a total market value of US$ 10,000,000. Now, the fear is that the interest rate level in general will increase over the next 3-month period. Yet it is found more opportune to hold the stock investment over the next three months as opposed to liquidating the position up front, provided a proper hedge against a price decrease can be established. Hence the portfolio manager approaches the Chicago Mercantile Exchange to trade in the S&P 500 stock index futures contract.

The 3-month S&P 500 futures index is quoted at 180.95, that is, the value of the futures contract amounts to $90.475 ($500 × 180.95). The beta coefficient of the stock portfolio has been calculated over the past six months to be 1.45, that is, the stock portfolio is more volatile than the general market represented by the Standard & Poors 500 index. To compensate for this excess price volatility, additional index futures contracts should be sold in a ratio of 1.45:1.00. Hence the total number of contracts sold is equal to 160 (1.45 × $10,000,000/$90,475).

If the prices on the stock market decrease, the financial futures sold have been locked in at a higher price. So the loss incurred on the stock portfolio is offset by a capital gain on the index futures position. An element of uncertainty in this type of hedge is that the coefficient calculated for the previous six-month period will not necessarily correspond to the beta coefficient during the three-month period being hedged. However, despite this obstacle, an index futures position will provide the portfolio manager with a reasonable hedge against stock price fluctuations.

BASIS RISKS

As discussed, a precondition for obtaining a full hedge using financial futures contracts is that the financial futures price converts to the cash market price before the delivery date of the futures contract (see Figure

FIGURE 5.5
Convergence of Financial Futures Prices.

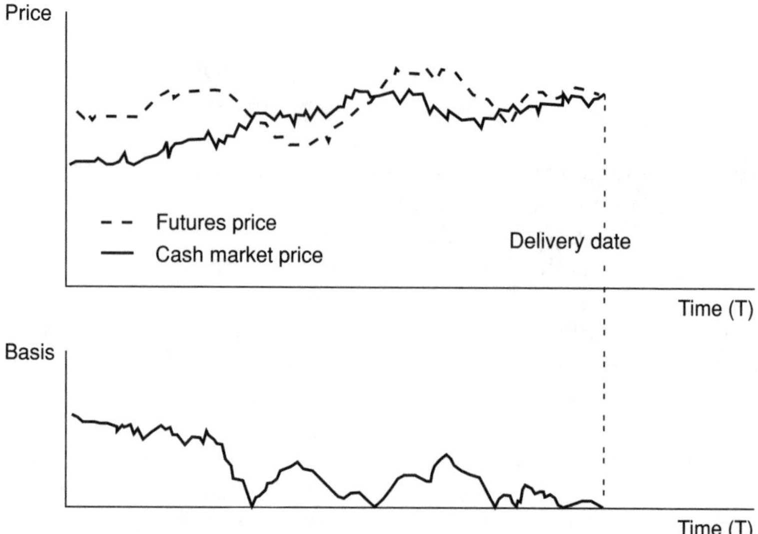

5.5). To discuss this requirement further, we define the *basis* to be the numerical value of the difference between the cash market price and the price of the corresponding financial futures contract:

$$\text{Basis} = |\text{Financial futures price} - \text{Cash market price}|$$

The futures price (P_f) can be expressed as a function of the cash market price of the underlying instrument (P_c) and the time remaining to the delivery date (T). When considering interest rate futures on long-term instruments, the price will also be influenced by the short-term (r_s) and the long-term (r_l) interest rates and by the differential between the two.

$$P_f = g[P_c, T, r_s, r_l (r_l - r_s)]$$

where

g = Functional relationship between the futures price P_f and the explanatory variables P_c, T, r_s, and r_l.

As is apparent, the basis is not always zero and so, to the extent that this is *not* the case, the hedge will be less than perfect. Consequently the outright risk of the position we want to hedge has been converted into a *basis risk* (namely, the risk that the financial futures price will not convert to the cash market price before the delivery date of the financial futures contract) and thus corresponds to the risk of *not* obtaining a full hedge.

To obtain a measure of the size of the basis risk, compare the development of the cash market price and the price of the financial futures contract on the last trading day before delivery of the contract, which is the last price available for closing in the futures position without taking delivery. In general the more closely the two move together over time, the smaller the basis risk is. (See Figure 5.6.) The correlation of the two time series can be quantified statistically by calculating the correlation coefficient as defined in the following standard formula[13]

$$r = \frac{1}{n-1} \text{sum} \frac{X_i - \overline{X}}{S_x} \cdot \frac{Y_i - \overline{Y}}{S_y} = \frac{\text{sum}(X_i - \overline{X})(Y_i - \overline{Y})}{\sqrt{\text{sum}(X_i - \overline{X})^2 \text{sum}(Y_i - \overline{Y})^2}}$$

where $i = 1, 2, \ldots n$ corresponds to each set of observations.

The correlation coefficient measures the average covariation of the two variables X and Y, and the coefficient is put on a standard comparable basis by dividing by the standard deviation of the two variables. Hence the correlation coefficient will always vary between minus one and plus one. If the numerical value is one, there is full correlation between the two variables. As the numerical value moves toward zero, the less significant is the correlation between the two variables. The correlation coefficient is a measure of the *linear* relationship between the two variables being investigated and thus corresponds closely to the linear regression coefficient (b) discussed earlier in the example of cross hedging. This relationship is expressed in the following standard equation:

FIGURE 5.6
Illustration of the Correlation Coefficient and Regression Equation.

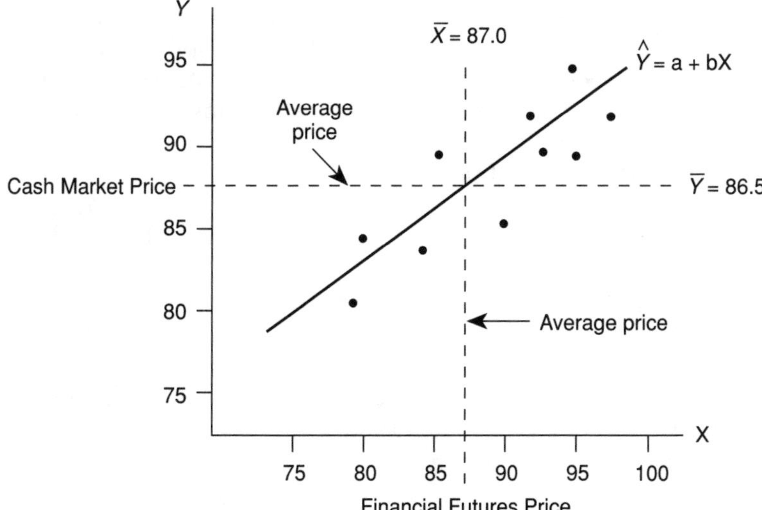

$$r = b\frac{S_x}{S_y} = b\sqrt{\frac{\text{sum }(X_i - \overline{X})}{\text{sum }(Y_i - \overline{Y})^2}}$$

When we want to do cross hedging, we can find out what the potential effectiveness of the hedge is by squaring the correlation coefficient to get the coefficient of determination (R).

$$R = r^2 = \frac{\text{sum}(\hat{Y} - \overline{Y})^2}{\text{sum}(Y_i - \overline{Y})^2} \quad \text{where } \hat{Y}_i = a + bX_i$$

As implied by the formula, the coefficient of determination tells us to what extent the regression analysis explains the variation of the two variables, in that the variation explained by the regression equation is put in relation to the total variation of the variable. Similarly will the coefficient of determination, calculated on the financial futures price on the last trading day and the corresponding cash market price, tell us how potentially effective the financial futures hedge is going to be.

Example: The regression coefficient has been calculated to 0.91. The coefficient of determination is 0.83 (0.91^2). That is, by using the financial futures contract there is a potential that 83% of the outright risk will be hedged.

It is only "potential" because all statistical analysis of this nature is based on historical data. In this analysis we assume that the financial markets in the future will continue to perform as they have in the past, but we have no guarantee that this will be the case. Therefore if one expects market performance to change in the future, that outlook should be incorporated into the evaluation of the statistical coefficients calculated.

The farther away we are from the last trading day of the financial futures contract, the more unpredictable and volatile will be the basis. This is because the financial futures price, by its very nature, is influenced by future expectations on price movements. The interest rate expectation of the market is reflected in the term structure of interest rates in the cash market.

The *term structure* of interest rates in the cash market is derived by plotting the effective yield of different investment alternatives of similar risk at different maturities.

In a *normal market*, the yield curve has a positive slope. Liquidity can be acquired short term at a cheaper rate and can be invested long term at a higher rate, thus earning a positive spread for the mitigater. This is often termed a *positive carry market*. We know that for a given security the capital gain or loss from a change in the interest rate level will be relatively higher for the longer maturity asset. Hence in the neutral situation, when interest rate movements follow a random walk, risk-averse investors would prefer shorter-maturity securities in their portfolios. This would lower the interest rates of shorter-term securities against the longer-term securities and the yield curve would be upward sloping.

When the market expects future interest rates to be higher, the risk-averse investors would be even more inclined to invest short-term and the yield curve would show a steeper positive slope.

When the market expects future interest rates to decline, the capital gain on longer-term securities will be bigger than that of the shorter-term securities. Hence investors are more inclined to invest in longer-term securities which will reduce the interest rate on the longer maturity securities. Hence we will witness a downward sloping yield curve, often termed a *negative carry market.*

We can define two types of changes in the yield curve. One, termed a *horizontal change,* corresponds to a change in the general interest rate level (the change from 1 to 2 in Figure 5.7). This could be caused by a temporary change in liquidity which, through substitution effects, will impose an effect on financial assets of all maturities. The other, called a *vertical change,* relates to a change in the slope of the yield curve (the change from 1 to 3 in the graph). As already discussed, this will be affected by changes in market expectations.

The holder of financial cash market instruments would normally have to fund the investment at the short-term money market rate. At the same time the assets would pay a current coupon at a slightly higher rate under normal circumstances of a positive yield curve. The holder of futures contract, on the other hand, will not incur this net interest gain. So the interest rate futures contract will normally be traded at a discount to the cash market instrument, reflecting the interest rate differential be-

FIGURE 5.7
Term Structure of Interest Rates (Yield Curve).

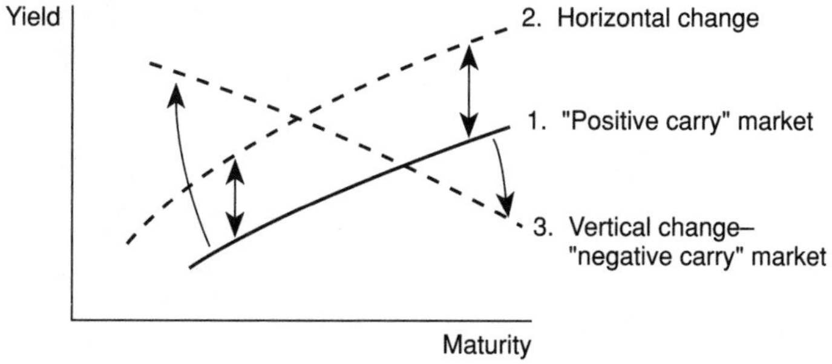

Yield

2. Horizontal change

1. "Positive carry" market

3. Vertical change–
"negative carry" market

Maturity

tween the short-term funding rate and the long-term return on the underlying asset.

A yield curve can also be construed on the financial futures market by plotting the contract prices of financial future contracts on securities of different maturities. The futures yield curve will reflect the market's expectation of the future shape of the cash market term structure of interest rates. As in the cash market, the futures yield curve changes its shape as market conditions and future expectations change.

As the futures price on an interest rate instrument arises as the parity price of 100.00 minus the implied yield, the term structure of futures prices is inversely related to the cash market yield curve.

Once we have taken a position on the futures market we are locked in to the future price of that contract. Until the contract matures the underlying cash market and the financial futures market might go through sharp changes due to changes in market conditions and market expectations (see Figure 5.8). Under these circumstances, one might take the view that it pays off to close in the futures position before the last trading day of the futures contract. However, if one decides to do so, do not forget that the hedge is eliminated for the period remaining to the maturity of the contract and that the cash market might still move against you.

In general we see that a change in the basis of interest rate futures contracts is determined by changes in the yield curve on the cash market and by changes in the term structure of interest rates in the financial futures market. The farther we are away from the last trading day of the financial futures contract, the higher the volatility of the basis. Conversely, the closer we get to the maturity date of the financial futures contract, the more the futures market will convert toward the cash market and the less will be the impact of market expectations.

FIGURE 5.8
Term Structure of Futures Prices.

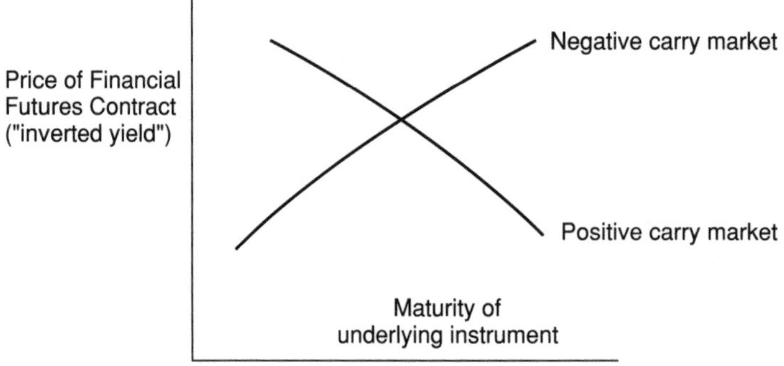

CONCLUSION

The application of financial futures contracts for hedging purposes requires substantial planning. Initially the open position to hedge must be properly identified and an appropriate hedging program established in accordance with the management board's view on the size of the exposure risk that is acceptable to the institution. Once the hedging program is implemented it is essential that a central function in the financial controls department monitor the development of the hedge and tie it into the planning strategy of future hedging programs to be implemented.

When planning a hedging program, one should pay attention to the timing of the cash flows on the settlement account at the futures exchange clearing house and the underlying income stream to be hedged. The potential cash implication appearing from the principle of the daily mark to market should be investigated in the planning phase of the hedging program. An intimate knowledge of the mechanics of the financial futures market entered into will always put the hedger in a stronger position, and an understanding of the underlying market forces in the financial futures markets will enable the hedger to take advantage of favorable market conditions that might develop.

An essential precondition for successful hedging through the financial futures markets is that the income or loss incurred from the futures contract position by the tax authorities is treated in the same way as is the income flows it is hedging. Consequently, it is very important to investigate the current tax treatment of income and losses emanating from financial futures trading. For the management board and for financial analysts in general another interesting and important area of concern is the accounting treatment of financial futures contracts.

Usually financial futures contracts are not recorded on the balance sheet before actual delivery of contracts, and unrealized gains and losses are not registered on the profit and loss account. However, it has been suggested that open financial futures positions be valued at the difference between the entered contract price and the current price of closing out at the date the accounts are settled. Hence the unrealized profit or loss would be registered on the profit and loss account. If the correlation between the hedged asset or liability and the financial futures contract is very high, the conditions for a perfect hedge are present. In this case it appears reasonable that the unrealized gains and losses also be recorded on the profit and loss account. However, there are no uniform rules regarding the accounting treatment of financial futures contracts in different countries and consultation with local auditors is strongly recommended before engaging in financial futures trading.

When using financial futures contracts for hedging purposes, one should realize that it does *not* guarantee a full hedge. Also the financial futures market provides the hedger with a limited time horizon. Financial futures contracts can usually be traded for delivery only up to twelve months ahead. This obviously limits the time horizon of a financial futures hedge. If the open position to hedge has a maturity exceeding the twelve-month period, the whole period of the gap cannot be closed through this type of hedging technique. However, accessing the financial futures markets usually enables the institution to hedge within the coming accounting year, which to many institutions is sufficient.

The financial futures markets, as witnessed in this chapter's examples, offer many hedging applications. The financial futures exchanges are efficient markets that can be accessed by making only a minimal initial payment, and that can provide institutions with a variety of off-balance-sheet hedging opportunities.

III

OPTIONS AND OTC FINANCIAL SERVICES

6

The Option Contract

Options were first introduced on the international stock exchanges, and stock options have been quoted on these exchanges for many years. On the other hand, the currency and interest rate options are by comparison relatively new inventions introduced by the futures and options exchanges in the early 1980s. For this reason the original theory on options was developed against a background of stock options. This theory has since been adapted to the analysis of currency and interest rate options. To get a feel for the chronological development of the options markets and the initial theory on options, this chapter will take a discussion of the market for stock options as its starting point.

Today, options are actively bought and sold on a number of exchanges in the United States and in Europe, as well as in the over-the-counter market. In addition to stock options, there are options on indexes, debt instruments, and foreign currencies. To get an idea of the scope of options trading, buy a copy of *The Wall Street Journal*, the *New York Times*, or the *Financial Times*, and turn to the section containing options quotations. Notice how many different individual options series, with different expiration months and exercise prices, can be connected on one underlying security.

STOCK OPTIONS

The *stock option* has been a common feature of the major stock exchanges in North America and Europe for several decades. However, an organized trading floor for standardized stock options was first introduced in the United States in April 1973 through the creation of the Chicago Board of Options Exchange (CBOE). Several other markets have since then developed into the major stock exchanges in North America and Europe.

An *option* is the right, but not the obligation, to purchase or sell a stated number of shares at a specified price (the *exercise price*) within a predetermined period. The option to purchase stock is known as a *call option* in that it gives the holder the right to *buy* the underlying security. A *put option* entails the right to sell the security. Either type of option can be traded on the market or exercised by the holder.

Let us begin by defining the basic components of an option contract (see Table 6.1).

1. The *underlying security* is the stock that the option holder is entitled to buy or sell.
2. The *expiration date* is the date after which the contract is worthless.

TABLE 6.1
Basic Components of a Stock Option Contract.

Component	*Example*
Underlying stock	100 shares (to be adjusted as necessary for stock dividends or splits)
Expiration month	Three fixed cycles: 1. January/April/July/October 2. February/May/August/November 3. March/June/September/December For example, in January options may be written for expiration only in April, July, or October. In May, they may be written only for August, November, and February. For certain very active stocks, three nearly monthly expiration dates are permitted. For example, in March, options may be written for April and May, as well as for March itself.
Expiration day	The option must be exercised by 5:30 p.m. New York time, on the Friday before the third Saturday of the expiration month. If not offset or exercised by this time, it expires worthless.
Strike price	• 2½ points up to $25 per share. • 5-point intervals above $25, such as 35–40–45. • 10-point intervals above $200.

3. The *strike (or exercise) price* is the specified price at which an option contract may be exercised.

Options are usually exercisable into 100 shares of their underlying related stock, the normal round lot unit of trading.

Example: An "MP Feb 40 call" is a call option that gives the owner:

- The right to *buy* (it's a call).
- One hundred shares of MetPath Lines (MP) stock (the underlying and, in this case, fictitious stock).
- At $40 per share (40, the strike price).
- By the third Friday in February (Feb., the expiration date).

Example: An "MP Feb 40 put" is a put option that entitles the owner to *sell* 100 shares of MetPath stock at $40 per share by the third Friday in February.

If either the put or the call is not *exercised* (that is, bought or sold) by the expiration date, then it expires worthless.

OPTIONS CLEARING HOUSE

Perhaps as great an innovation as the standardized contract is the Options Clearing house. The Options Clearing house has the following three primary functions:

1. After payment of the cost of the option to the original seller, the Options Clearing house assumes the opposite side of each options transaction—that is, the clearing house issues and guarantees each option contract. The cost of an option is referred to as the *premium*.
2. The Options Clearing house clears all trades in listed options.
3. The Options Clearing house assigns exercise notices.

By acting as the issuer of each option contract, the clearing house ultimately steps between the original buyer and seller. Once the order is executed, the Option Clearing house *clears* it. At that point, the original buyer and seller have no further responsibility to each other. Their relationships are now with the Option Clearing house: If buyers choose to exercise, they rely on the clearing organization, not on the sellers, for performance. Thus, the Option Clearing house guarantees performance to all participants.

The Option Clearing house also handles the assignment of options exercise notices submitted by buyers. Although most writers and holders close their positions with offsetting purchases or sales by selling or covering their options, a writer should not be surprised to be notified that some holder has exercised his or her option and that the writer has been assigned the obligation of delivering stock (which is known as being a *call writer*) or purchasing it (being a *put writer*). Holders of calls may elect to *buy* the stock at the strike price, and put holders may choose to *sell* it at the strike price. In either case, option holders simply notify their brokerage firm. The firm in turn notifies the Option Clearing house, which then assigns an exercise notice to an Option Clearing house member brokerage firm that has options writers identical to the one exercised. The assignment obligation is then assigned to one of those option writers—almost always to the oldest options first (FIFO—first in, first out).

The Options Clearing house takes it from there. For every buyer of a given option, there must be a writer on its books. The Option Clearing house finds a member firm in its records that has written an option and assigns it as the firm against which the option is to be exercised. The selection is usually made at random. Upon receipt of the exercise notice, the firm must assign the exercise notice to one of its customers who has written such an option. That customer then has to honor the exercise notice and deliver or purchase the stock depending on whether it is a call or a put option, as the case may be.

TRADING OPTIONS

Short and Long

Option investors are said to "open" or "close" their positions. Buying an option is an *opening* (or *initial*) *transaction* by which the holder takes a *long* open position. Writing an option is also an opening transaction in which the seller is considered to create an open *short* option position. A *closing transaction* reduces (or closes) an open option position. A closing purchaser reduces (or closes) a prior opening sale, and a closing sale closes a previous opening purchase.

Going long or short is an indicator of investors' expectations. Those who buy calls (long) or sell puts (short) are generally regarded as bullish. They will profit if the underlying stock's price rises. By writing calls or buying puts, investors present themselves as bearish. They expect the stock's value to decline and will profit if it does so.

Writers

Option writers have one basic aim: to earn income. A writer may be classified as "covered" or "uncovered" (naked). To illustrate this point, let's examine the following:

1. Covered call writing.
2. Naked call writing.
3. Put writing.

Covered Call Writing. An option is *covered* when the writer owns enough of the underlying stock to meet the requirements of the contract if it is exercised. In such a case, a covered call writer is not required to pay any initial margin costs. A writer is also covered by owning another call of the same class that has a lower strike price.

Example: Investor Smith writes an MP May 35 call, which represents 100 shares of MetPath. Because Smith owns 100 shares of MP, the call is covered.

The covered call writer, by pocketing the premium, gives up the right to any increase in the value of the stock beyond the strike price. Call writers are usually neutral to bearish on the stock. At the same time, they retain the risk that their stock might decline in price.

Example: If MetPath is trading at $30 a share when Smith writes his Mar 30 call as a covered writer, the contract is at parity.

If MetPath stock declines to a price below $30, the option holder will not exercise. The premium income Smith receives for selling the call will offset, or cushion, Smith's stock portfolio loss up to the amount received.

If MetPath increases in value to $35 per share before expiration, then Smith (assuming the probability of his being exercised against) has limited his share of this increase to the premium.

Naked Call Writing. When the option writer does not own shares of the underlying stock to meet the requirements of the exercise notice, the contract is said to be *uncovered,* or *naked.*

Example: Smith writes an MP 30 call, but he does not own 100 shares of MetPath. The call is naked, or uncovered. Because it is the equivalent of a short sale, Smith must pay initial margin as collateral.

Writers of naked calls face the possibility of a theoretically unlimited loss. As the market price of the underlying stock increases beyond the options strike price, the writer's loss grows.

Example: MetPath's stock increases to a price above $30 (to $34 per share, for example) just before expiration, and Smith receives an exercise notice from his broker. He is forced to buy 100 shares of MetPath in the open market at its current price of $34 and deliver it to the option exercising holder at $30, for a loss of $4 per share, which is only partially offset by the premium income.

Put Writing

The risk to a put writer is that the price of the underlying stock will decline. Put writers are generally bullish on the security.

Example: Smith sells an MP Mar 40 put for 2 ($200) when MetPath stock is trading at $40. Because the put is at the money and because (for this example) MetPath is not considered to be a volatile stock, the premium represents pure time value.

Over the next few weeks, during the life of the option, MetPath declines to $32, and Smith gets an exercise notice. He must buy the stock from the holder at $40 per share even though its market value is only $32. Only the $2 premium eases some of the $8 loss ($40 less $32).

Note. All these examples illustrate events that can make writing an option unprofitable. Needless to say, whenever the market moves in the direction that writers expect, they see their contracts expire worthless to the holders—and they keep the premiums.

Buyers

People and institutions buy options for a number of reasons. Some need to hedge a position or otherwise manage their risk by locking in a stock's appreciation in value or protecting a position in some other way. Others are speculators who are trading simply in the pursuit of profit.

Advantages

Buying options has two main benefits:

1. Limited loss.
2. Great leverage.

The potential loss that an option holder faces is limited to the premium paid. If the underlying stock does not move as expected, the holder simply lets the contract expire and tries again.

Perhaps the greater benefit of the two, however, is *leverage:* By buying options, an option holder can control a great deal more stock than by buying the stock outright.

Example: Smith and Phelps have $3,000 each to invest. Phelps buys 100 shares of MetPath now trading at $30 ($3,000 total). She controls 100 shares. Smith buys 10 MP Mar 30 calls ($3,000 total). He controls 1,000 shares (10 contracts, 100 shares each).

Over the next 60 days, MetPath stock rises to $33. Phelps enjoys a $300 increase in the value of her stock. Smith, if he exercises his calls, can collect a gross profit of $3,000. He buys 1,000 shares at the strike price of 30 ($30,000) and resells them right away at 33 ($33,000).

Option holders thus use their funds to purchase the *right* to buy or sell a security, not the security itself. Because the option costs less than the underlying stock, a holder can control a great deal more shares than in an outright purchase of the stock.

Drawbacks

Owners of stock might be a "little wrong" about their purchases; that is, if the stock does not increase in value as expected, they can wait a little longer if they still feel confident about their purchase.

Not so with options, which are wasting assets. To enjoy a profit, option buyers must be right about three things:

1. Price direction.
2. Magnitude.
3. Timing.

Direction: They must forecast whether a stock's price is going up or down and by how much. Then they must purchase an appropriate put or call—in, at, or out of the money.

Magnitude: They must also be sure that the price will move far enough in the right direction to make the option profitable.

Timing: Finally, they must be certain that the price will move before expiration.

If any of these forecasts is wrong, the investment may be rendered worthless at expiration.

Example: With Phelps holding her 100 shares and Smith his 10 MP calls, MetPath stock falls by 5 points to 25. At expiration the options are still deep out of money.

Phelps gets the bad news and decides to hold the stock for another 60 days.

Smith takes a short-term capital loss of $3,000.

So, although one of the benefits of buying options is that all you can lose is the premium, one of the drawbacks is that you *can* lose all of the premium if you are not right on all three points.

MARGIN

Investors may borrow money, referred to as *margin*, from their brokerage firms to purchase stock. Options, however, cannot be purchased on margin. With options, *margin* is the money or stock that the naked (uncovered) call writer must deliver to the brokerage firm and that assures the writer's performance. Because option holders must pay premiums in full, they do not come under any margin requirements.

How much collateral a writer has to put up is set by Regulation T in the United States, but the brokerage firms often require even more than the exchanges do.

Outside the United States the margin requirements are typically fixed by the individual exchanges. However, the exchanges themselves and their practices will usually be under the scrutiny of the regulatory authorities of the host country.

READING OPTIONS QUOTATIONS

Figure 6.1 shows an excerpt from the options section of *The Wall Street Journal*'s financial news, and Figure 6.2 similarly gives some examples of stock options from the *Financial Times*.

Underlying Stock

In Figure 6.1 and 6.2, the first column lists the underlying stocks in alphabetical order. Below the name of each company is the day's closing price on the exchange on which the stock is traded. The closing price is repeated for each option series traded on the stock.

Strike Price

In Figure 6.1, the second column lists the strike prices. Notice how they occur in multiples of 5—and, in some cases, in multiples of 2½ on the U.S. quotes. The multiples on London-based quotes are somewhat larger (see Figure 6.2), but as a percentage of the actual stock price the multiples are of a comparable size. Note also how the strike prices approximate the closing price of the underlying stock.

FIGURE 6.1

Quotes on Stock Options. (Reprinted by permission of Wall Street Journal *[Europe], © Dow Jones & Company, Inc., March 5, 1986. All rights reserved.)*

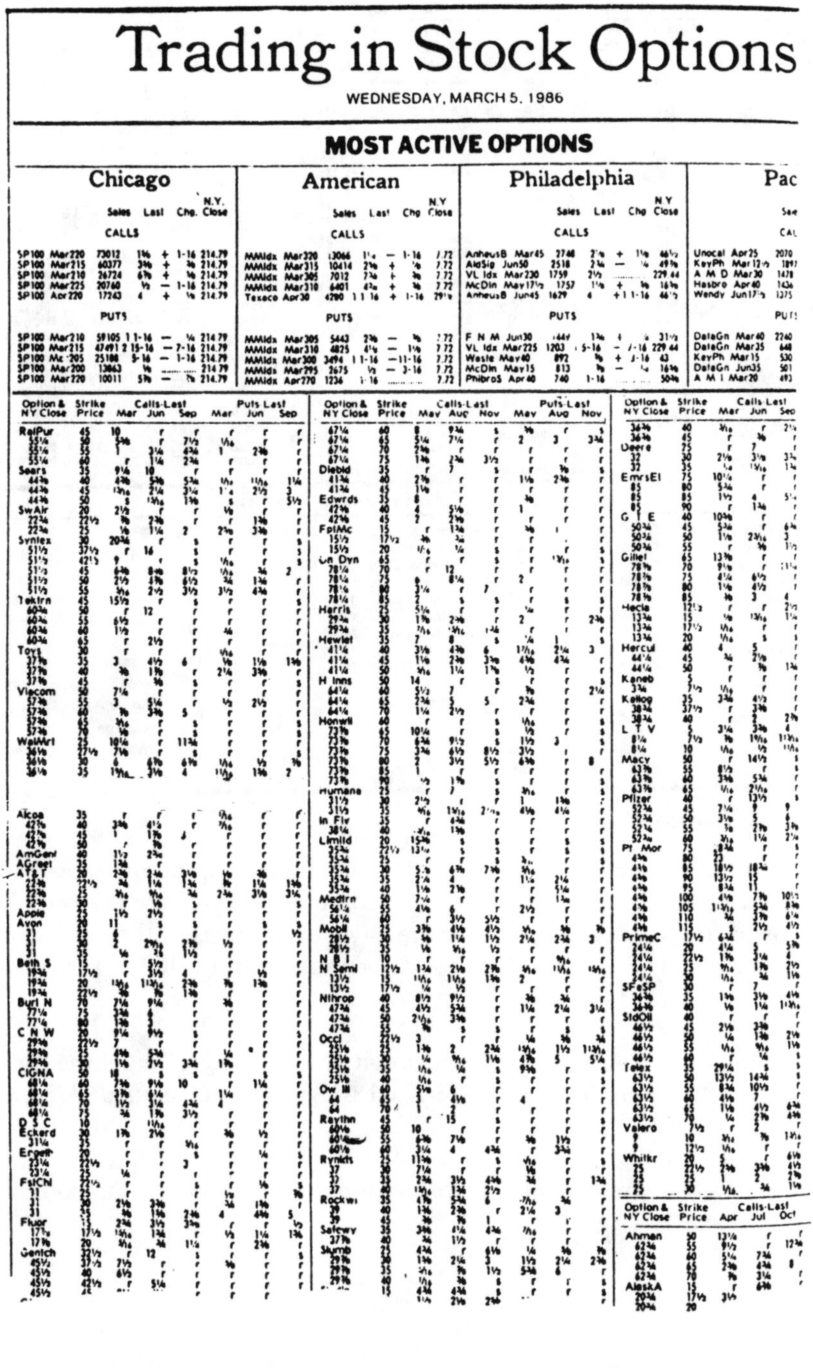

Trading in Stock Options

WEDNESDAY, MARCH 5, 1986

MOST ACTIVE OPTIONS

Chicago

	Sales	Last	Chg.	N.Y. Close
CALLS				
SP100 Mar220	73012	1⅛	+ 1-16	214.79
SP100 Mar215	60377	3⅜	+ ⅜	214.79
SP100 Mar210	26724	6⅞	+ ⅜	214.79
SP100 Mar225	20760	½	− 1-16	214.79
SP100 Apr220	17243	4	+ ⅛	214.79
PUTS				
SP100 Mar210	59105	1 1-16	− ¼	214.79
SP100 Mar215	47491	2 15-16	− 7-16	214.79
SP100 Mar205	25188	5-16	− 1-16	214.79
SP100 Mar200	13863	⅛	......	214.79
SP100 Mar220	10011	5⅞	− ⅞	214.79

American

	Sales	Last	Chg	N.Y. Close
CALLS				
MMIdx Mar320	13066	1¼	− 1-16	7.72
MMIdx Mar315	10414	2⅞	+ ⅛	7.72
MMIdx Mar305	7012	7¾	+ ⅜	7.72
MMIdx Mar310	6401	4¾	+ ⅜	7.72
Texaco Apr30	4290	1 1-16	+ 1-16	29⅛
PUTS				
MMIdx Mar305	5443	2⅜	− ⅜	7.72
MMIdx Mar310	4825	4¼	− 1⅛	7.72
MMIdx Mar300	3494	1 1-16	−11-16	7.72
MMIdx Mar295	2675	½	− 3-16	7.72
MMIdx Apr270	1236	1-16	......	7.72

Philadelphia

	Sales	Last	Chg	N.Y. Close
CALLS				
AnheusB Mar45	2748	2⅛	+ 1⅛	46½
AldSig Jun50	2518	2¼	− ¼	49⅞
VL Idx Mar230	1759	2½	......	229.44
McDln May17½	1757	1⅛	+ ⅜	16⅞
AnheusB Jun45	1629	4	+1 1-16	46½
PUTS				
F N M Jun30	1449	1¾	+ ¼	31½
VL Idx Mar225	1203	5-16	− 7-16	229.44
Waste May40	892	⅜	+ 3-16	43
McDln May15	813	⅜	− ¼	16⅞
PhibroS Apr40	740	1-16	......	50⅜

Pac

	Sa
CAL	
Unocal Apr25	2070
KeyPh Mar12½	1897
A M D Mar30	1478
Hasbro Apr40	1436
Wendy Jun17½	1375
PUT	
DataGn Mar40	2260
DataGn Mar35	648
KeyPh Mar15	530
DataGn Jun35	501
A M I Mar20	493

Option & NY Close	Strike Price	Calls-Last Mar	Calls-Last Jun	Calls-Last Sep	Puts Last Mar	Puts Last Jun	Puts Last Sep
RalPur	45	10	r	r	r	r	r
55⅛	50	5⅜	r	7½	1/16	r	r
55⅛	55	1	3¼	4¾	1	2⅜	r
55⅛	60	r	1¼	2¾	r	r	r
Sears	35	9⅛	10	r	r	r	r
44⅞	40	4⅞	5⅜	5¾	1/16	11/16	1¼
44⅞	45	13/16	2¼	3¼	1¼	2½	3
44⅞	50	s	13/16	1⅜	s	r	5½
SwAir	20	2½	r	r	⅛	r	r
22¾	22½	⅜	2⅜	r	r	1⅜	r
22¾	25	⅛	1¼	2	2⅜	3⅜	r
Syntex	30	20¾	r	s	r	r	s
51½	37½	r	16	s	r	r	s
51½	42½	9	r	s	1/16	r	s
51½	45	6⅜	8⅜	8½	1/16	¾	2
51½	50	2½	4⅞	6½	¾	1¾	r
51½	55	3/16	2½	3½	3½	4¾	r
Tektrn	45	15½	r	s	r	r	s
60¾	50	r	12	r	r	r	r
60¾	55	6½	r	r	r	r	r
60¾	60	1½	r	r	⅛	r	r
60¾	65	r	2½	r	r	r	r
Toys	30	r	r	r	1/16	r	r
37⅞	35	3	4½	6	⅛	1⅛	1⅜
37⅞	40	⅜	1⅞	r	2¼	3⅜	r
37⅞	45	r	⅜	s	r	r	s
Viacom	50	7¼	r	r	r	r	r
57⅜	55	3	5¼	r	½	2½	r
57⅜	60	⅞	3⅜	5	r	r	r
57⅜	65	3/16	r	s	r	r	s
57⅜	70	⅛	r	s	r	r	s
WalMrt	25	10⅛	r	11¾	r	r	r
36⅛	27½	7⅛	r	s	r	r	s
36⅛	30	6	6⅞	6⅞	1/16	½	⅜
36⅛	35	1 9/16	3⅛	4	11/16	1⅜	2
Alcoa	35	r	r	r	1/16	r	r
42⅞	40	3⅜	4½	r	7/16	r	r
42⅞	45	1	1⅞	[illegible]	r	r	r
42⅞	50	r	⅞	r	r	r	r
AmGenl	40	1½	2¾	r	r	r	r
AGreet	35	1⅜	r	r	r	r	r
A T & T	20	[illegible]	[illegible]	[illegible]	r	r	r
22⅛	22½	[illegible]	[illegible]	[illegible]	r	1⅛	1⅜
22⅛	25	⅜	¾	r	2⅜	3⅛	3¼
22⅛	[illegible]	r	r	r	r	r	r
Apple	[illegible]	1½	2½	r	r	r	r
Avon	[illegible]	11	r	r	r	r	r
31	[illegible]	[illegible]	[illegible]	[illegible]	[illegible]	[illegible]	[illegible]
31	[illegible]	2	[illegible]	[illegible]	[illegible]	[illegible]	[illegible]
31	[illegible]	[illegible]	[illegible]	[illegible]	[illegible]	[illegible]	[illegible]
Beth S	15	[illegible]	[illegible]	[illegible]	[illegible]	[illegible]	[illegible]
19⅝	17½	[illegible]	[illegible]	[illegible]	[illegible]	[illegible]	[illegible]
19⅝	20	[illegible]	[illegible]	[illegible]	[illegible]	[illegible]	[illegible]
19⅝	22½	[illegible]	[illegible]	[illegible]	[illegible]	[illegible]	[illegible]
Burl N	70	[illegible]	[illegible]	[illegible]	[illegible]	[illegible]	[illegible]
77¼	75	[illegible]	[illegible]	[illegible]	[illegible]	[illegible]	[illegible]
77¼	80	[illegible]	[illegible]	[illegible]	[illegible]	[illegible]	[illegible]
C N W	[illegible]	[illegible]	[illegible]	[illegible]	[illegible]	[illegible]	[illegible]
29⅝	[illegible]	[illegible]	[illegible]	[illegible]	[illegible]	[illegible]	[illegible]
29⅝	25	[illegible]	[illegible]	[illegible]	[illegible]	[illegible]	[illegible]
29⅝	30	[illegible]	[illegible]	[illegible]	[illegible]	[illegible]	[illegible]
CIGNA	50	10	[illegible]	[illegible]	[illegible]	[illegible]	[illegible]
68¼	60	[illegible]	[illegible]	10	[illegible]	[illegible]	[illegible]
68¼	65	[illegible]	[illegible]	[illegible]	[illegible]	[illegible]	[illegible]
68¼	70	[illegible]	[illegible]	[illegible]	4	[illegible]	[illegible]
68¼	75	[illegible]	[illegible]	[illegible]	[illegible]	[illegible]	[illegible]
D S C	10	[illegible]	[illegible]	[illegible]	[illegible]	[illegible]	[illegible]
Eckerd	30	[illegible]	[illegible]	[illegible]	[illegible]	[illegible]	[illegible]
31¼	35	[illegible]	[illegible]	[illegible]	[illegible]	[illegible]	[illegible]
[illegible]	20	[illegible]	[illegible]	[illegible]	[illegible]	[illegible]	[illegible]
23¼	[illegible]	[illegible]	[illegible]	[illegible]	[illegible]	[illegible]	[illegible]
23¼	25	[illegible]	[illegible]	[illegible]	[illegible]	[illegible]	[illegible]
FstChi	[illegible]	[illegible]	[illegible]	[illegible]	[illegible]	[illegible]	[illegible]
31	25	[illegible]	[illegible]	[illegible]	[illegible]	[illegible]	[illegible]
31	30	[illegible]	[illegible]	[illegible]	[illegible]	[illegible]	[illegible]
31	35	[illegible]	[illegible]	[illegible]	[illegible]	[illegible]	[illegible]
Fluor	15	[illegible]	[illegible]	[illegible]	[illegible]	[illegible]	[illegible]
17⅛	17½	[illegible]	[illegible]	[illegible]	[illegible]	[illegible]	[illegible]
17⅛	20	[illegible]	[illegible]	[illegible]	[illegible]	[illegible]	[illegible]
Genich	[illegible]	[illegible]	12	[illegible]	[illegible]	[illegible]	[illegible]
45½	37½	7½	[illegible]	[illegible]	[illegible]	[illegible]	[illegible]
45½	40	6½	[illegible]	[illegible]	[illegible]	[illegible]	[illegible]
45½	42½	r	5¼	[illegible]	[illegible]	[illegible]	[illegible]
45½	[illegible]	[illegible]	[illegible]	[illegible]	[illegible]	[illegible]	[illegible]

Option & NY Close	Strike Price	Calls-Last May	Calls-Last Aug	Calls-Last Nov	Puts-Last May	Puts-Last Aug	Puts-Last Nov
67¼	60	8	9¾	s	⅜	r	s
67¼	65	5¼	7¼	r	2	3	3¾
67¼	70	2⅜	r	r	r	r	r
67¼	75	1⅜	2¾	3½	r	r	r
Diebld	35	r	7	s	r	⅜	s
41¾	40	2⅞	r	r	1⅛	2⅜	r
41¾	45	1⅛	r	r	r	r	r
Edwrds	35	8	r	r	⅜	r	r
42⅜	40	4	5⅛	r	1	r	r
42⅜	45	2	2⅞	r	r	r	r
FptMc	15	r	1¾	r	⅜	1	r
15½	17½	⅜	¾	r	r	[illegible]	r
15½	20	1/16	¼	s	r	r	s
Gn Dyn	65	r	r	s	r	13/16	s
78¼	70	r	12	r	r	r	r
78¼	75	8	8¼	r	2	r	r
78¼	80	3¼	r	7	r	r	r
78¼	85	2	s	s	r	s	s
Harris	25	5¼	r	r	¼	r	r
29¾	30	1⅜	2⅜	r	2	r	2⅜
29¾	35	7/16	13/16	1¼	r	r	r
Hewlet	35	7	8	s	¼	1	s
41¼	40	3⅛	4⅜	6	1 7/16	2¼	3
41¼	45	1⅛	2⅜	3⅜	4⅜	4¾	r
41¼	50	5/16	1¼	1⅞	½	r	r
H Inns	50	14	r	s	r	r	s
64¼	60	5½	7	r	⅜	r	2¼
64¼	65	2¾	5	5	2¾	r	r
64¼	70	1¼	2½	r	r	r	r
Honwll	60	r	r	s	1/16	r	s
73⅜	65	10¼	r	s	½	r	s
73⅜	70	6¾	9½	s	1½	3	s
73⅜	75	3¾	6½	8½	3½	r	r
73⅜	80	2	3½	5½	6⅜	r	8
73⅜	85	1	r	r	r	r	r
73⅜	90	½	1⅞	s	r	r	s
Humana	25	r	7	s	3/16	r	s
31½	30	2½	r	r	1	1⅜	r
31½	35	9/16	1 5/16	2 1/16	4⅛	4¼	r
In Flv	35	r	4¾	r	r	r	r
38¼	40	3/16	1⅜	r	r	r	r
Limitd	20	15⅜	s	s	r	s	s
35¾	22½	13¼	s	s	r	s	s
35¾	25	r	r	s	¾	r	s
35¾	30	5⅞	6⅞	7⅜	3/16	r	r
35¾	35	2¼	4	r	1⅛	2¼	r
35¾	40	1⅛	2⅞	r	r	5¼	r
Medtrn	50	7¼	r	r	r	1¾	r
56¼	55	4⅛	6	r	2½	r	r
56¼	60	r	3½	5½	r	r	r
Mobil	25	3⅜	4⅛	4½	1/16	⅜	⅜
28½	30	⅜	1¼	1½	2¼	2¾	3
28½	35	⅛	5/16	½	r	r	r
N B I	10	r	r	r	r	9/16	r
N Semi	12½	1¾	2⅛	2⅜	3/16	11/16	15/16
13½	15	11/16	1 1/16	1⅜	2	r	r
13½	17½	¼	½	r	r	r	r
Nthrop	40	8½	9½	r	⅜	¾	r
47¾	45	4½	5¾	r	1¼	2¼	3¼
47¾	50	2 1/16	3⅜	r	r	r	r
47¾	55	⅜	s	s	r	s	s
Occi	22½	3	r	r	⅛	⅜	¾
25⅛	25	1⅜	2	2¾	15/16	1½	1 13/16
25⅛	30	¼	9/16	1⅛	4⅞	5	5¼
25⅛	35	1/16	¼	s	9⅜	r	s
25⅛	40	1/16	r	s	r	r	s
Ow Ill	60	5⅛	6	r	r	r	r
64	65	3	4⅛	r	4	r	r
64	70	1	2	r	r	r	r
Raythn	45	r	15	s	r	r	s
60⅛	50	10	r	r	r	r	r
60⅛	55	6⅜	7⅛	r	⅜	1½	r
60⅛	60	3¼	4	4¾	r	3¾	r
Rynlds	25	11⅞	r	s	1/16	r	s
37	30	7¼	r	r	⅛	r	r
37	35	2¾	3½	4⅜	¾	r	1¾
37	40	15/16	1⅜	2½	r	r	r
Rockwl	35	4⅞	5¾	6	7/16	¾	r
39	40	1⅜	2⅜	r	2¼	3	r
39	45	⅜	⅜	1	r	r	r
Safewy	35	3⅜	4¼	4¾	7/16	r	r
37⅞	40	¾	1½	r	r	r	r
Slumb	25	4¾	r	6⅛	¼	⅜	⅜
29⅞	30	1⅜	2¼	3	1½	2¼	2⅜
29⅞	35	5/16	⅜	1½	5¾	6	r
29⅞	40	1/16	⅜	s	r	r	s
[illegible]	15	4¾	4¾	s	r	r	s
[illegible]	[illegible]	1¼	2⅛	2⅜	[illegible]	[illegible]	r

Option & NY Close	Strike Price	Calls-Last Mar	Calls-Last Jun	Calls-Last Sep
36⅞	40	3/16	r	2⅛
36⅞	45	r	⅜	r
Deere	75	r	7	r
32	30	2⅛	3⅛	3¾
32	35	¼	15/16	1¾
EmrsEl	75	10¼	r	r
85	80	5¾	r	r
85	85	1½	4	5¼
85	90	r	1¾	r
G T E	40	10⅜	r	r
50¾	45	5¾	r	6¾
50¾	50	1⅛	2 3/16	3
50¾	55	r	⅜	1½
Gillet	65	13⅞	r	r
78⅞	70	9⅛	r	11¼
78⅞	75	4¼	6½	r
78⅞	80	1⅛	4½	r
78⅞	85	⅜	3	4
Hecla	12½	r	r	2½
13¾	15	⅛	13/16	1¼
13¾	17½	1/16	r	r
13¾	20	1/16	s	s
Hercul	40	4	5	r
44¼	45	¾	2⅛	r
44¼	50	r	⅜	1¾
Kaneb	5	r	r	r
3¾	7½	1/16	r	r
Kellog	35	3¾	4½	r
38¾	37½	r	3⅜	r
38¾	40	r	2	2⅞
L T V	5	3¼	3⅜	4
8¼	7½	⅞	1 9/16	1 13/16
8¼	10	1/16	½	11/16
Macy	50	r	14½	s
63⅞	55	8½	r	s
63⅞	60	3⅜	5¾	r
63⅞	65	1/16	2 1/16	r
Pfizer	40	r	13½	s
52¾	45	7¼	9	9
52¾	50	3⅛	5	6
52¾	55	⅞	2⅞	3⅞
52¾	60	3/16	1¼	2¼
Pt Mor	75	28¾	r	s
4⅞	80	23	r	r
4⅞	85	18½	18¾	r
4⅞	90	13½	15	r
4⅞	95	8¾	11	r
4⅞	100	4⅛	7⅞	10½
4⅞	105	1 13/16	5¾	8⅜
4⅞	110	¾	3⅞	6¼
4⅞	115	s	2½	4½
PrimeC	17½	6¾	r	s
24¼	20	4¼	5	5⅜
24¼	22½	1⅞	3¼	4
24¼	25	9/16	1⅜	2½
24¼	30	1/16	¾	1⅛
SFeSP	30	r	7	r
36⅜	35	1⅜	3⅛	4⅛
36⅜	40	⅛	1¼	1 13/16
StdOil	40	r	r	r
46½	45	2⅛	3⅜	r
46½	50	¼	1⅜	2⅛
46½	55	1/16	9/16	1⅛
46½	60	r	¼	s
Telex	35	29¼	s	s
63½	50	13½	14¾	s
63½	55	8¾	10½	r
63½	60	4⅛	7	r
63½	65	1⅛	4½	6¾
63½	70	¼	2⅞	4⅜
Valero	7½	r	2	r
9	10	3/16	⅜	1 3/16
9	12½	1/16	r	r
Whitkr	20	5	r	6⅛
25	22½	2⅜	3⅜	4½
25	25	1	2	2⅞
25	30	1/16	¾	1⅛

Option & NY Close	Strike Price	Calls-Last Apr	Calls-Last Jul	Calls-Last Oct
Ahmen	50	13¼	r	r
62¾	55	9½	r	12¾
62¾	60	5¼	7¾	r
62¾	65	2⅜	4¾	8
62¾	70	⅞	3¼	r
AlaskA	15	r	6⅜	r
20¾	17½	3½		
20¾	20			

FIGURE 6.2

Quotes on Stock Options. (Reprinted by permission of Financial Times.)

LONDON TRADED OPTIONS

Option		Calls Jan	Calls Apr	Calls Jul	Puts Jan	Puts Apr	Puts Jul
Alld Lyons	600	44½	70½	80½	1¼	14½	24½
(*645)	650	8½	39½	50½	10½	33½	47½
ASDA	34	1½	5½	-	1	4½	-
(*35)	40	-	-	5¼	-	-	9½
Brit. Airways	220	28	37	40½	½	3¾	7½
(*248)	240	9	22	27½	3	10	14½
SmKl Beecham A	900	28½	65½	88½	3½	29½	37½
(*922)	950	6½	41½	63½	30½	53½	60½
Boots	420	17½	36½	43	¼	8	14½
(*437)	460	½	13½	20	23	26	31
B.P.	280	12½	20½	25½	1	8	11½
(*292)	300	1¾	10	15½	9½	17½	21½
British Steel	70	7	10¾	12¼	¼	2½	4¾
(*77)	80	1	4¾	6¾	4	7	9
Bass	1050	37½	73½	95½	1¼	20½	30½
(*1084)	1100	-	45½	70½	-	37½	51½
C & Wire	600	14½	41	54½	4	20	32½
(*612)	650	-	18½	32½	-	48	59
Courtaulds	500	13½	38	46	3¾	16	23
(*509)	550	½	15	24	41	42	48
Com. Union	460	8½	22	32½	3½	22	27½
(*464)	500	½	7	15½	35½	49½	51½
Fisons	360	6½	22	33	7	21½	23
(*361)	390	1	13	21	30	38	41

Option		Calls Feb	Calls May	Calls Aug	Puts Feb	Puts May	Puts Aug
BTR	420	11½	22	30	9½	21	24½
(*420)	460	1½	7½	-	40	47½	-
Brit. Telecom	300	25	37	43	2¾	5¼	9
(*322)	330	6	18	24½	12½	16½	20½
Cadbury Sch	420	38	47½	59½	5	14½	21
(*449)	460	13½	27½	39½	20	33½	38½
Eastern Elec	220	-	-	23	-	-	12½
(*226)	230	5½	14½	-	9½	12½	-
Guinness	525	18½	32	-	12	22½	-
(*531)	550	7	21½	32	24	34½	37½
GEC	180	16	22	25	1	3¾	6
(*194)	200	3¾	9¾	12	8	10½	14
Hanson	200	17½	25	28	1	3¼	5¾
(*216)	220	4¼	12¼	14¾	7¼	10¾	14
LASMO	240	17½	24	30½	6¾	16½	21
(*249)	260	6½	14½	22	17½	30½	31½
Lucas Inds	110	10½	15	18	2	5	6
(*118)	120	4¼	9	12½	4	9	11½
P. & O.	420	40	47½	53½	3½	16	21
(*453)	460	14	22½	33½	16½	35½	40½
Pilkington	140	7	14½	15½	6	11	15½
(*140)	160	2¼	7	-	20	22½	-
Prudential	220	18½	21½	26½	1¾	8½	10

Option		Calls Mar	Calls Jun	Calls Sep	Puts Mar	Puts Jun	Puts Sep
Midland Bk	220	18	27	32½	11½	17½	22
(*224)	240	10	17½	-	22	28	-
National Power	130	10½	16½	18½	3½	5	8
(*139)	140	5	10½	12	7¾	9	12½
Reuters	1050	61½	98	123	33½	53½	65
(*1068)	1100	35½	71½	99	60	80	90
R. Royce	130	10¼	12	16¼	6	8	10
(*136)	140	5¼	7¼	11	11½	13½	15½
Scottish Power	90	12	16	17½	1¼	2¼	5¼
(*100)	100	5	10	10	4½	6½	10½
Sears	90	10	12½	14½	2¼	5¼	7
(*97)	100	4½	7¼	9	6	10½	12½
Forte	220	18½	22½	27	3¼	9½	12½
(*231)	240	6½	12½	16½	12	19½	22
Thorn EMI	800	34½	60½	64	18½	27½	37½
(*806)	850	13½	34½	-	47½	49½	-
TSB	120	10½	13½	14½	4	5¼	8
(*128)	130	4¼	9½	10	9	11½	13½
Vaal Reefs	60	11	14	14	1¼	4	5
(*$67)	70	4	8	10	6	9	11
Wellcome	1000	68½	106	135	35½	55½	61½
(*1019)	1050	43½	83½	110	60½	78½	79½

TRADITIONAL OPTION 3-month call rates

■ INDUSTRIALS	p	Charter Cons.	42	Ladbroke	19	Sears	8½	**■ OILS**	
Allied-Lyons	50	Comm Union	34	Legal & Gen	30	SmKl Bchm A	70	Aviva Pet	1½
Amstrad	4	Courtaulds	40	Lex Service	16	TI	41	BP	30
Astec (BSR)	5	Eurotunnel	40	Lloyds Bank	24	TSB	9	Burmah Castrol	38
BAT Inds	48	FKI	5	Lonhro	18	Tesco	15½	Conroy Pet	4
BOC	49	FNFC	5	Lucas Inds	11	Thorn EMI	59½	Gaelic Res	½
BTR	33	Forte	20	Marks Spencer	22	T & N	10½	Premier Cons	4
Barclays	24	GKN	24	Midland Bank	17	Unilever	78	Shell	41
Blue Circle	18	Gen Accident	37	NatWest Bank	21	Vickers	13½	Tuskar Res	1½
Boots	33	GEC	15	P & O Dfd	35	Wellcome	80	**■ MINES**	
Bowater	54	Glaxo	64	Racal Elect	4½	**■ PROPERTY**		RTZ	38
Brit Aerospace	18	Grand Met	70	RHM	20	Brit Land	20½		
British Steel	5	GRE	11	Rank Org	47	Land Sec.	36		
Brit Telecom	25	Hanson	15	Ratners	6	MEPC	33		
Cadburys	34	ICI	88	Reed Intl	42	Mountleigh	3		

Calls and Puts

The next six columns in Figure 6.1 reflect the current expiration cycles for calls and puts. The figures under these column headings are the premiums as of the close of business for the days. In most cases, they reflect a value (such as U.S. dollars) that has to be multiplied by 100 to arrive at the currency cost of the option.

Example: The Alcoa Jan 25 call closed at 4¼, or \$4.25. To get the dollar total of the premium, multiply by 100: \$4.25 times 100 equals \$425 for the total cost of the call.

The letter symbols in the price columns are explained at the bottom of the newspaper page:

- *r* means "restricted."
- *s* means "no option offered."
- *o* means "old."

Example: Look at a few of the entries in Figure 6.1.

- The Alcoa Mar 40 call has an intrinsic value of 2⅞ (stock price of 42⅞ less the strike price of 40). Yet its last trade was at 3⅝. The ¾ point is time value.
- The AT&T Jun 22½ put is ⅛ point in the money (strike price of 22½ less stock price of 22⅜). Its premium of 1¼ point is almost purely time value. The AT&T June 30 put is not traded (r), and the September is not even offered (s).

Volume and Open Interest

At the bottom of all the listings for each U.S.-based exchange are tabulations of volume and open interest for puts and calls.

- *Volume* is the total number of contracts, puts or calls, trading on the exchange for the day.
- *Open interest* is the total number of open positions at the close of trading, which have not been closed either by exercise or covering purchases.

PRICING

A number of factors affect the purchase price (the premium) of an option. They are the following:

1. The relationship of the market price of the underlying stock to the options strike price.
2. The time remaining to the expiration date (that is, the life of the option).
3. The volatility of the underlying stock.
4. Interest rates.
5. Cash dividends on the underlying stock.

Market Price of the Underlying Stock

The relationship between the stock's current market price and the option's strike price determines whether or not the option has an actual value, which is referred to as the *intrinsic value*. This relationship also establishes whether the option is either in the money or out of the money. An option is said to be *in-the-money* if it can be exercised profitably. A call is in-the-money if the stock is selling at a price higher than the strike price.

Example: An MP 40 call is in-the-money because MetPath stock is trading at 41⅛. The call holder may exercise the option, buy 100 shares of MetPath at 40, and resell it profitably at 41⅛. An MP 45 call, with the stock at 41⅛, has no intrinsic value and is at the same time out of the money. No holder of MP 45 would exercise and pay $45 per share for a stock currently at 41⅛.

A put is in-the-money if the stock is trading below the strike price.

Example: An MP 45 put is in-the-money because the stock is at 41⅛. The holder of the put may exercise the option and sell the 100 shares of MP stock at $45 per share. At the same time, an MP 40 put is out-of-the-money. With the stock at 41⅛, no holder of MP 40 would exercise, which would require the holder to sell 100 shares of MetPath at $40 per share.

Example: In the case of the MP 40 call, the intrinsic value is 1⅛ (41⅛ less 40), or $1.125. For a standard 100-share contract, the intrinsic value is $112.50 ($1.125 times 100).

The intrinsic value of the put is 4⅞ (45 less 41⅛), which amounts to $487.50 ($4.875 times 100).

An option is said to be *at-the-money* if the stock's market price is equal to the strike price.

Example: Assume that MetPath stock is currently trading at $40 per share. Any MP option—put or call—with a strike price of 40 is at the money.

An at-the-money option is said to have no intrinsic value. Were it to be exercised, it would yield no profit.

An option is *out-of-the-money* if exercising it would result in a loss. A call is out-of-the-money when the stock's price is lower than the strike price.

Example: Assume that MetPath is trading at 39½. An MP 40 call is out-of-the-money by ½ point, or $50 ($40 less $39.50 equals $0.50 times 100).

For a put to be out-of-the-money, the strike has to be lower than the stock's price.

Example: An MP 40 put is out-of-the-money when MetPath stock is trading at 41. The out-of-the-money amount is $100 ($41 less $40 equals $1 times 100).

Out-of-the-money options have zero intrinsic value, but cannot have a negative value.

An options premium is said to be at *parity* when it is trading at a dollar amount equal to its intrinsic value alone, without any additional charge for time value or volatility.

Example: An MP Mar 40 call is at parity when the market price of MetPath stock is 43 and the option premium is $3.

Life of the Option (Time Value)

An option is a security with a limited and relatively short life span. If it is not exercised, liquidated, or covered by the expiration date, it ceases to exist. It becomes worthless. As a result, an option is considered a *wasting asset.* As the day of expiration nears, the contract is worth less and less because of the diminishing time of its life span.

Time value is often reflected in the current price of an option, or the premium, as an amount in excess of the option's intrinsic value.

Example: An MP Feb 40 call, with MetPath trading at 43, is in the money by 3 points ($300). That is, its intrinsic value is $3. Yet in early December the premium is $5. The difference of $2 between the call's intrinsic value ($3) and the actual trading price ($5) is the call's time value.

By mid-January, with MetPath still trading at 43, the February call is selling for $4. Its premium is lower, even though the intrinsic value is unchanged. The time value has decreased as the expiration date has approached.

Time value plays more of a role in what are known as "American" options, as opposed to "European" options. An *American option* may be exercised at any time up to expiration; all U.S.-listed stock options are of this kind. A *European option* may be exercised only *at* expiration.

Time value theoretically follows a fairly predictable pattern during the life of an option, decreasing as time passes.

Experience has shown that investors are almost always willing to pay more than the intrinsic value of an option. Because an option represents a right and not an obligation, it can never have a value below zero. So, for a *call:*[1]

$$\text{Call premium} > \text{Intrinsic value of call} \geqq 0$$

where

$$\text{Intrinsic value of call} = (\text{Stock price} - \text{Exercise price}) \times \text{Number of shares}$$

This relationship is often illustrated graphically as in Figure 6.3.

FIGURE 6.3
Relationship of Market Price to Theoretical Value for a Call Option.

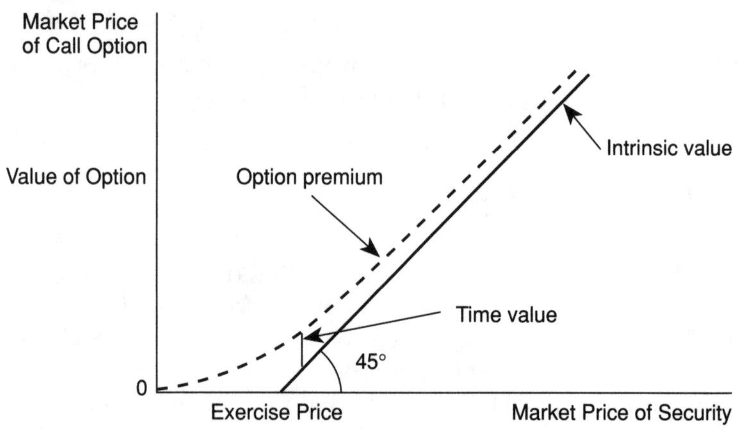

Why is an investor willing to pay more than the intrinsic value? The reason has to do with the very nature of an option: It provides the holder with a future chance to make money by exercising the contract under favorable conditions. If the price of the underlying stock historically has shown a positively sloping trendline, then the likelihood of making a future profit is increased. Similarly, if the price movements of the underlying stock are volatile, then the chance of finding an opportune moment to make more money through exercise is enhanced. Hence the price of the call is also a function of the price variance of the underlying stock, as illustrated in Figure 6.4.

The longer the time to maturity, the higher is the chance that the investor can exercise the call at an optimal profit. So in general the longer the time to maturity, the higher will be the market price of the option. Conversely, the closer we get to the maturity date, the closer the price of the contract will get to the contract's intrinsic value.

Volatility of the Underlying Stock

When the underlying stock is considered *volatile*—that is, capable of dramatic and rapid price changes—the premium tends to be higher than for nonvolatile stocks.

FIGURE 6.4
Price as a Function of Time.

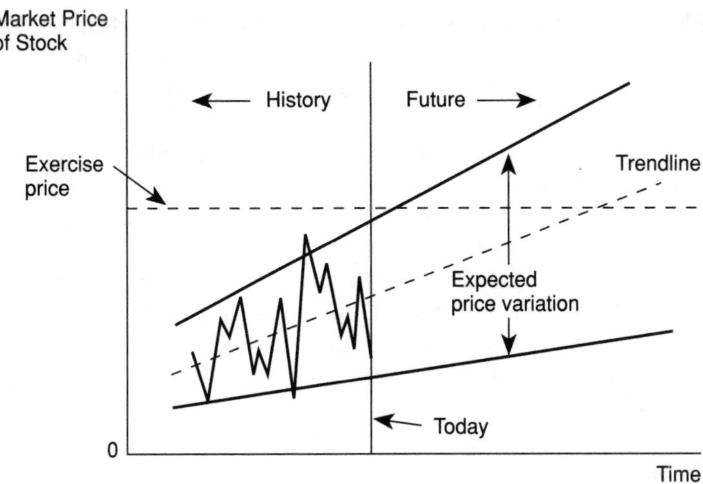

Example: An MP Feb 40 call is selling for \$5, with \$3 of that premium consisting of intrinsic value. The other \$2 is considered pure time value because MetPath historically moves no more than ⅛ to ¼ point at a time.

Laser Hi-Tech (a fictitious stock), on the other hand, is a growing firm whose stock can move 2 to 5 points in a morning or afternoon of trading. For this reason, it is considered to be a highly volatile stock. Given a \$3 intrinsic value and a "reasonable" \$2 worth of time value, Hi-Tech calls should be selling for \$5. Instead, they are selling for \$6.50.

The rationale for the added \$1.50 premium value is that a volatile stock is very likely to move into the money more quickly than a more stable stock. Of course, a volatile stock could also move far out of the money. It is for this reason that options are said to be instruments to transfer the underlying stocks' volatility to themselves.

Interest Rate Level

It can be argued that the market price of the option relates to the interest rate level. If the market price of the call option is fully correlated with the market price of the underlying stock, then a fully hedged (riskless) investment can be made in the stock by concurrently writing a suitable number of call options on that stock.

If the price of the stock increases, the investor will incur a capital gain on the long position in the stock but will lose money on the short position in the call option because he is obliged to sell at the exercise price even if the market price is higher. Conversely, if the market price of the stock falls, the investor will incur a loss on the long position in the stock, but there will be no exercise of the option, the value of which will be zero. The investor who sold the call option can retain the full premium paid by the option buyer.

Given that the price of the call is determined efficiently no matter what the stock price does, the investor will end up with a return on the investment equal to what can be termed a risk-free rate. Hence the argument is that, when the risk-free rate increases, so will the price of the call, whereas a decrease in the risk-free rate induces a lower price on the option.

The argument therefore is that, if the risk-free part of the return from a stock portfolio increases, then the investor will be willing to pay more for the option to purchase the stock at a given price. This is not intuitively clear because an increase in the general interest rate level would normally cause the stock prices to drop, thus reducing the value of the call option. However, the following theoretical example might clarify the argument.

Example: Initially we invest in a zero dividend stock with a value of $100. Assume that only two events are possible:

1. The stock price can increase to $105.
2. The stock price can decrease to $95.

Also assume that probabilities can be attached to each event. Because the stock doesn't pay a dividend, the return on the investment relates solely to an increase in the market value of the stock. For this reason we assume that there is a likelihood of 60% that the stock price will increase and only a 40% chance that the stock price will decrease (see Figure 6.5).

The expected value of the investment at the end of the period is

FIGURE 6.5

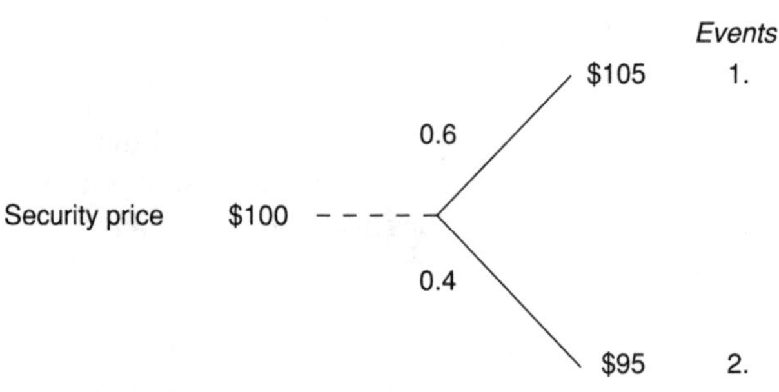

(0.6 × \$105) + 0.4 × \$95) = \$101, amounting to a 1% return on the investment during the period.

To hedge this investment, a certain number of at-the-money call options must be written in the same stock. The number to issue can be found by dividing the maximum fluctuation of the stock price by the fluctuation in the price of the option during the period:

$$\text{Number of contracts} = \frac{\$105 - \$95}{\$5 - \$0} = \frac{10}{5} = 2$$

So two contracts are issued with an exercise price of \$100. In situation 1, the investor will incur a capital gain of \$5 on the stock portfolio. On the other hand, the two options will be exercised at a total cost of \$10 (\$2 × \$5), leaving the investor with an end-of-period net worth position of \$95 (\$100 – \$5).

Let us further assume that the riskless rate in this period amounts to 0.50%. We can then calculate the price of the option that secures the risk-free return on the fully hedged investment. The net worth position at the beginning of the period equals the initial investment minus the price incurred from the sale of the contract, and the initial net worth position plus the risk-free return should equal the end-of-period net worth position. Hence:

$$(\$100 - 2w)\ 1.0050 = 95$$

$$\text{Option Price } (w) = \frac{100.50 - 95}{1.0050} \quad / 2 = \$2.7363$$

Initial net worth position $100 - 2 \times 2.7363 = 94.5274$

We see that the return on the investment exactly equals the risk-free return:

$$\frac{95 - 94.5274}{94.5274} \times 100 = .50\%$$

If the market price of the option differs from the equilibrium price, investors would be able to increase the return above the risk-free rate through positioning. Such transactions would force the equilibrium price back into place.[2]

If we assume an increase in the risk-free rate from 0.50% to 0.75%, we can recalculate the new option price using the same principle:

$$(\$100 - 2w) \quad 1.0075 = 95$$

$$w = \frac{100.75 - 95}{1.0075} \quad / 2 = \$2.8536$$

Initial net worth position: $\$100 - 2 \times 2.8536 = 94.2928$.

Again it is seen that the return on the investment equals the risk-free return:

$$\frac{95-94.2928}{94.2928}\times 100 = 0.75\%$$

An increase in the risk-free rate from 0.50% to 0.75% per period hence will induce an increase in the price of the call option from $2.7363 to $2.8536, given that the options are efficiently priced.

Cash Dividend Rate

Another determinant of the stock option price is the cash dividend rate of the underlying stock, which can be particularly influential on high-yield stocks. The relationship has to do with the fact that stock prices vary with the dividend payment dates. The stock price increases as the dividend payment date approaches, and the ex-dividend stock price is usually reduced by the amount of the cash dividend payout. In general the larger the stock dividend is, the lower will be the option price. This is so because, if the market price increases as the dividend date approaches, then the intrinsic value of a call option in-the-money will decrease correspondingly.

Black-Scholes Formula[3]

All these factors can be summarized in a single expression:

$$C = g(P, E, s^2, T, r_f)$$

where g indicates a relationship function and

C = Price of the call option.
P = Market price of the underlying stock.
E = Exercise price of the option.
s^2 = Annual price variance of the underlying stock.
T = Time to expiration date (as percentage of a year).
r_f = The risk-free rate.

The mathematical relationship among these variables has been approximated by Black and Scholes under simplified assumptions in the following formula for the price of a European-type option, which is used both by professional option traders as well as by researchers to explore the developments in the market prices of call options. The experience with the pricing model vis-à-vis stock options has concluded that it usually estimates the true option price with a satisfactory accuracy.

$$C = P \cdot N(X_1) - e^{-r}f^{T} \cdot E \cdot N(X_2)$$
$$X_1 = (\ln P / E) + [r_f + (s^2 / 2) \cdot T)] / (s \cdot \sqrt{T})$$
$$X_2 = (\ln P / E) + [r_f - (s^2 / 2) \cdot T)] / (s \cdot \sqrt{T})$$

where

$\ln$ = Natural logarithm.
$e = 2.71828$
$N_{(\cdot)}$ = Cumulative normal probability of a normally distributed variable with a mean value of 0 and a standard deviation of 1.

The Black and Scholes formula assumes that:

- There are no transaction costs or taxes.
- No dividends are being paid on the stocks before maturity date.
- The price development follows a log normal distribution, that is, the compounded rate of return is normally distributed.
- There is a constant volatility on the price movements.
- The interest rate is unchanged.
- There is continuous trading in the stock.

In most cases, all of these assumptions cannot be fulfilled in real life situations. In practice, however, the theoretical calculations on stock option premiums have usually turned out to be accurate enough.

Often when using the model to calculate theoretical option premiums, the analyst will have to make assumptions about the future volatility of the financial instrument.

Example: An institution is about to write call options on a stock, and considers at which minimum price (premium) they should be issued. A statistical analysis shows a volatility of 9% over the past 6 months. However, the minimum premium required in the offering is adjusted upwards to reflect the expected market volatility.

The Black and Scholes formula assumes that no dividend payments take place during the period until the option's expiry date. However, this is not always the case and therefore the option premium should be adjusted accordingly. This is usually done by subtracting the expected dividend payment from the premium.

Example: An institution issues European call options on MetPath's stock at a strike price of $40 per share with expiry in May ("MP May 40 calls"). The theoretical value of the call option, which allows the holder to buy 100 MP shares at $40 per share, is calculated to be $410. Since a dividend of $1.50 a share has been announced for payment at the end of April, the actual call premium is fixed at $260 [= 410 – (100 × 1.50)].

Conversely, the theoretical Black and Scholes model is often used to indicate the *implied volatility* of a given option premium being quoted in the market. This can often help an investor decide whether an option appears to be priced too high or too low in the market.

Example: The AT&T Sept. 23 call option is quoted at a premium of 1⅛. This corresponds to an implied volatility of around 10%. However, an investor expects the volatility to increase to 19% over the coming month. She is therefore willing to buy the AT&T call options at the going price, because she considers the contracts to be cheap, and because she expects the premiums on that contract to increase in the near future.

The Black and Scholes formula assumes that the rate of return on the security is normally distributed. This assumption is violated specifically when the price movements include a few extreme jumps, as are known, for example, in the stock market from time to time.

With regard to bond option contracts as opposed to stock option contracts, the other Black and Scholes model's assumptions become slightly more critical, such as the assumption of constant volatility throughout the life of the option and the assumption of a constant interest rate level. We know that by the very nature of the securities market, bond prices instantly move inversely to current changes in the interest rate level. Also, it often turns out, for example, that out-of-the-money options on bonds have a higher implied volatility than at-the-money options. Therefore, option contracts with the same maturity but with different strike prices can have different implied volatilities. This phenomenon can be illustrated graphically by the so-called *smile curve,* which sets out the implied volatility for similar contracts with different strike prices (Figure 6.6). The differences in implied volatility can from time to time provide an opportunity to establish *volatility spreads,* in which the investor will buy contracts with a relatively low implied volatility and sell similar option contracts with a relatively high implied volatility.

The preceding price discussion relates to the European type of option, but all the arguments apply as well to the American type of option. In general an American option is worth more than a European option because it provides the holder with a wider possibility of exercising the option at the opportune moment. Consequently, an American option will trade at a higher price than the equivalent European option.

FIGURE 6.6
"Smile Curves" (Volatility Spreads).

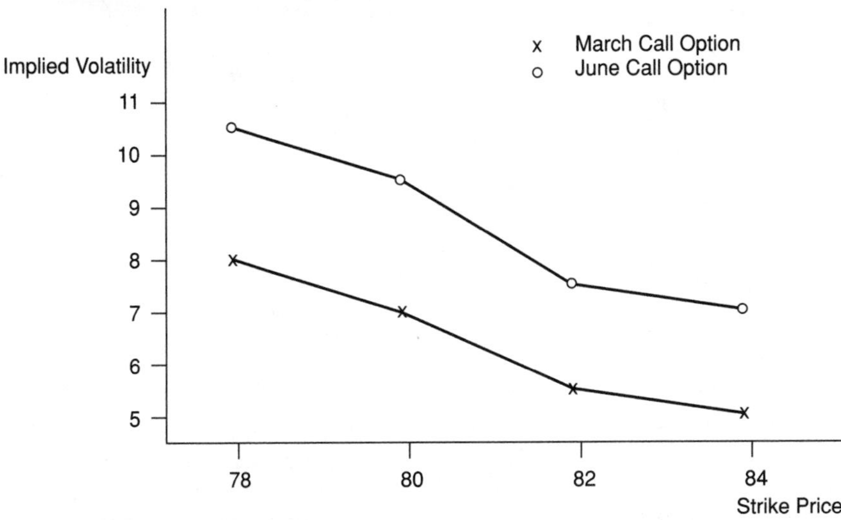

Pricing Puts

Similarly the price of a stock put option can be found. The intrinsic value of the put is equal to the difference between the current market price and the exercise price of the underlying security times the number of securities the put entitles the holder to sell. The put holder will make a profit if the going market price of the security is lower than the exercise price. Because the put represents an option and not an obligation, it cannot have a negative value.

$$\text{Put premium} > \text{Intrinsic value of put} \geqq 0$$

where

$$\text{Intrinsic value of put} = (\text{Exercise price} - \text{Stock price}) \times \text{Number of shares}$$

This relationship is illustrated in Figure 6.7.

For the same reasons as in the case of calls, the market price of a put option exceeds that of its theoretical value. Although the Black-Scholes option pricing model applies only to call options, it can be adapted to the put option case due to the inherent relationship between a call and a put option.

A risk-free arbitrage position can be created by buying the stock, buying a put option, and simultaneously selling a call option with the same exercise price as the put option. This transaction is often termed *conversion*.

FIGURE 6.7

Relationship of Market Value to Theoretical Value for a Put Option.

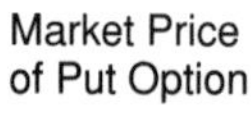

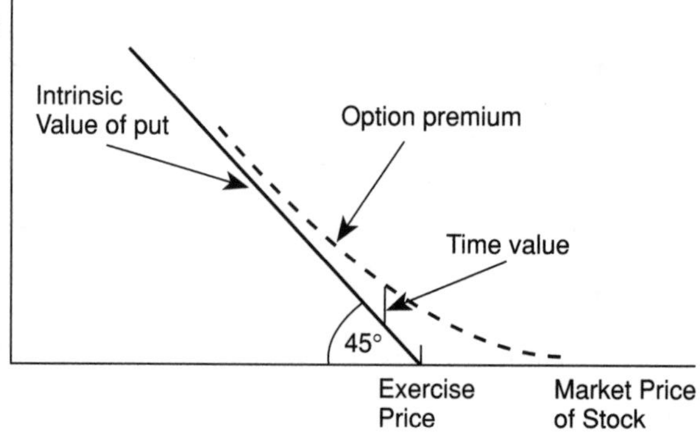

If the stock price increases, the capital gain on the portfolio outweighs the loss from the holder's exercise of the call option. If the stock price decreases, the gain from exercising the put option will outweigh the loss incurred on the stock portfolio. Hence it describes a risk-free transaction.

What is interesting in this context is that this conversion process also describes the relationship between the call premium and the put premium prevailing in an efficient option market.[4] The cost equation of the zero risk position is established in the following way:

1. *Establish Zero-Risk Position:*

Position	*Payments*
Buy stock	Pay stock price [–]
Buy put option	Pay put premium [–]
Write call option	Receive call premium [+]

2. *Unwinding Zero-Risk Position:*

Position	*Payments*
Sell stock	Receive exercise price [+]
	Funding cost of position [–]

Total Payment Equation:

Stock price + Put premium – Call premium = Exercise price – Funding cost

or

Put premium = Call premium – Funding costs of position

when

Exercise price = Initial stock price

FIGURE 6.8

The Option Premium as a Function of the Maturity.

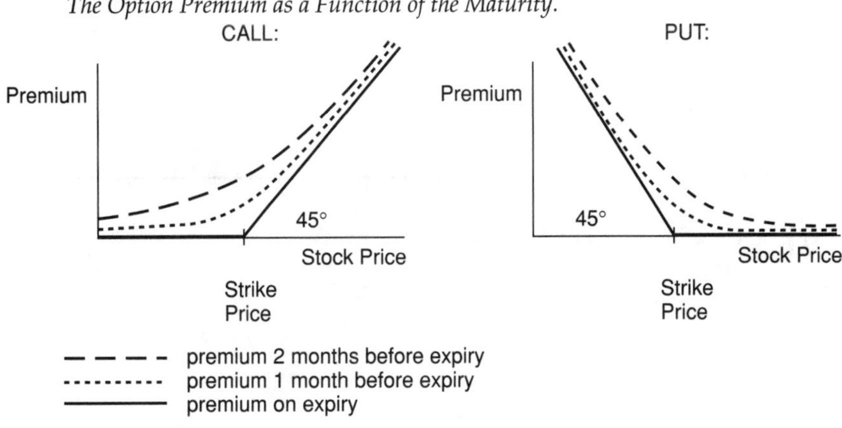

Due to the close relationship between the premium on puts and calls, the put premium will depend on the price variation of the underlying stock and the time to the expiration date in the same way as discussed in the case of a call option. That is, the larger the price variation of the stock and the longer the time remaining until the option's expiry date, the higher will be the theoretical value of the put option. A higher volatility in the underlying asset's price induces higher call and put premiums on option contracts on that asset. These relationships are illustrated in Figures 6.8 and 6.9.

FIGURE 6.9

The Option Premium as a Function of the Volatility.

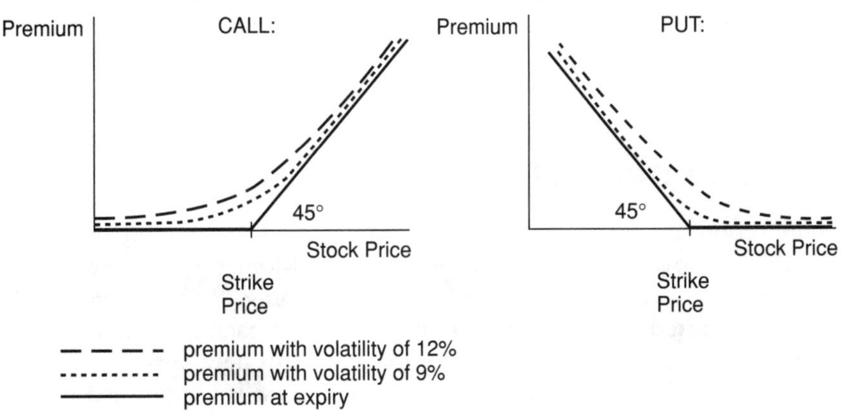

7

Types of Contracts

For many years, options trading remained within the equities marketplace. The early 1980s, however, saw options trading begin on other "underlying interests," particularly:

- Foreign currencies.
- Interest rate (debt) instruments.
- Stock indexes.

See Table 7.1.

CURRENCY OPTIONS

Option contracts on foreign currencies were first introduced in North America in November 1982, at which time the Montreal Exchange (ME) introduced a Canadian dollar option on the trading floor. The Montreal Exchange started trading Canadian stock options back in 1975, and this market was used as a model in the introduction of new option contracts in the early 1980s. The success of the Canadian dollar option led to the

TABLE 7.1
Comparison of Types of Options.

Option	*Underlying Interest*	*Contract Size*	*Exercise and Settlement*	*Strike Price*	*Premiums*
Equity (listed)	Stocks	100 shares	Writer buys or sells stock at stock price	In dollars or other local currency	In points
Foreign currencies	Pound, yen, mark, franc, etc.	Varies by currency	Writer buys or sells currency at strike price. Delivery made in country of origin.	U.S. cents per unit of foreign currency (except for Japanese yen)	U.S. cents per unit of foreign currency (except for yen)
Debt	Treasury securities	*Bonds & notes:* $100,000 in principal *Bills:* $1 million in principal	Writer buys or sells security at strike price	*Bonds & notes:* par value *Bills:* discount rate	Points & 32nds
Index	Stock Indexes	Multiplier	Writer makes cash payment to holder	In dollars or other local currency	In points

introduction of currency options on pounds sterling, German marks, Swiss francs, and Japanese yen. Subsequently the Montreal Exchange has changed its business strategy, and today the exchange only trades option contracts on Canadian debt instruments. The European Options Exchange also started trading Dutch guilder option contracts against U.S. dollars to follow the success of the already established currency options.

In December 1982 the Philadelphia Stock Exchange (PHLX) introduced a pound sterling option contract, which was followed by option contracts in other major international currencies—German marks, Swiss francs, Canadian dollars, Japanese yen, Australian dollars, French francs, and ECUs. Other currencies, such as the Belgian franc, the Dutch guilder, and the Italian lira, have been considered for future introduction on the exchange. However, the German mark contract accounts for approximately ⅔ of the turnover on the exchange, followed by the Japanese yen counting for around ⅙ of the turnover. Hence, the market interest for contracts in other European currencies historically has been relatively limited.

Partly induced by the success of the introduction of currency options, the Chicago Mercantile Exchange decided to introduce an option on the German mark futures contract of the same exchange during January 1984. Option contracts in pound sterling, Swiss francs, Japanese yen, Canadian dollars, and Australian dollars followed. The German mark option has turned out to be very successful and, instead of taking away trade volume from the already established exchanges, the publicity of the new option seemed to stimulate options trading activities in general. One explanation is that the new option contract provided the vast number of futures traders on the Chicago Mercantile Exchange with a suitable instrument to hedge their futures positions, an exercise that apparently was found more applicable with an option geared directly toward the futures contract of the exchange. At the same time it represented a new investment opportunity in an option contract available directly on that busy exchange.

During June 1985 LIFFE introduced its first currency option based on its financial futures contract in pound sterling with a trading unit of £ stg. 25,000.

In November 1985 the European Options Exchange (EOE) in Amsterdam successfully introduced the first option contract in the European currency unit. Several other exchanges have since introduced ECU options. In October 1985 the European Options Exchange introduced the first *cross-currency* option contract, a Dutch guilder/pound sterling contract with a trading unit of £ stg. 10,000 and consequently quoted in guilders per pound sterling. However, the pound sterling cross currency contract is no longer being traded on the EOE, but other exchanges are looking to establish active cross-currency option contracts. In November 1991 the Philadelphia Stock Exchange commenced trading a cross-currency option on German marks against Japanese yen (two of the most actively traded foreign currencies next to the U.S. dollar), and other cross-currency option contracts are planned for listing. Similarly, the Chicago Mercantile Exchange is looking into the listing of pound sterling/German mark, German mark/Japanese yen, and German mark/Swiss franc cross-rate options. A further development of the market for exchange-traded currency options is the introduction of *long-term* option contracts. Hence, the Philadelphia Stock Exchange, for one, is proposing to offer 18-, 24-, 30-, and 36-month European currency option contracts, which would help extend the applicability of exchange-traded currency options (see Table 7.2).

Contract Size

The option contracts introduced on the Montreal Exchange, the European Options Exchange, and the Philadelphia Stock Exchange were

TABLE 7.2
Trading Units for Some Currency and Cross-Currency Option Contracts.

European Options Exchange	*Philadelphia Stock Exchange*	*Chicago Mercantile Exchange Option Contracts*	*Chicago Mercantile Exchange Financial Futures*	*London International Financial Futures Exchange Option Contracts*	*London International Financial Futures Exchange Financial Futures*
		Currency Options:			
—	Swiss franc (US$ 62,500)	Swiss franc (Sw. frc. 125,000)	Swiss franc (Sw. frc. 125,000)	—	Swiss franc (Sw. frc. 125,000)
—	Pound sterling (£ stg.31,250)	Pound sterling (£ stg. 62,500)	Pound sterling (£ stg. 62,500)	Pound sterling (£ stg. 25,000)	Pound sterling (£ stg. 25,000)
—	German mark (DM 62,500)	German mark (DM 125,000)	German mark (DM 125,000)	German mark , (US$ 50,000)	German mark (US$ 50,000 & DM 125,000)
—	Japanese yen (¥ 6,250,000)	—	Japanese yen (¥ 12,500,000)		Japanese yen (¥ 12,500,000)
—	Canadian dollar (C$ 50,000)	—	Canadian dollar (C$ 100,000)	—	—
Dutch guilder (US$ 10,000) (US$ 100,000)	—	—	—	—	—
—	French franc (Fr. frc. 250,000)	—	—	—	—
—	European currency (ECU 62,500)	—	European currency (ECU 125,000)	—	—
—	Australian dollar (A$ 50,000)	—	Australian dollar (A$ 100,000)	—	—
		Cross-Currency Options:			
	German mark/ Japanese yen (DM 1,000,000)		German mark/ Japanese yen (DM 125,000)		

based on delivery of physical commodities, whereas options traded on the Chicago Mercantile Exchange and the London International Financial Futures Exchange were based on the delivery of the corresponding financial futures contract. Because the futures contracts also provide the physical delivery of the underlying currency, if required, the general features of the option contracts are very similar.

The contract size varied from one exchange to the other, but they were all initially related to the size of the corresponding financial futures contracts on the Chicago Mercantile Exchange. The contract size of the options on the Montreal Exchange at their initial introduction was one-fifth the size of the corresponding futures contracts on the Chicago Mercantile Exchange, whereas the contract size on the Philadelphia Stock Exchange was half the size of the CME contracts. Since the initial introduction of currency option contracts, the contract size has in several cases been changed and adapted to better serve the market requirements.

During 1984 the Montreal Exchange carried out a market study to determine the optimal trading units for the option contracts traded on the exchange. As a result of this investigation the Montreal Exchange terminated the trading of the old contract denominations in December 1984 and instead implemented new trading units of C$ 50,000 and £ stg. 100,000 on the two commonwealth currencies and trading units of US$ 100,000 on the other currencies—German marks, Japanese yen, and Swiss francs. This meant that the currency options would have a quotation similar to that prevailing in the foreign exchange markets. The Dutch guilder contracts of the European Options Exchange follow the same principle of denomination and have trading units of US$ 10,000 and US$ 100,000. In early 1987, the London International Financial Futures Exchange also adopted the principle to follow the foreign exchange market quotation by introducing option contracts in pounds sterling and German marks with £25,000 and US$ 50,000 denominations on the two contracts.

Quotations

Currency option quotes are usually indicated in cents or dollars per unit of the contract amount of foreign currency.

Example: The PHLX £ stg. June call option may be quoted at 0.45¢/£, and the premium is found by multiplying the contract amount by the option quote:

$$£31,250 \times 0.0045\ \$/£ = \$140.625$$

Since the trading unit of the Dutch guilder contract on the EOE is quoted in U.S. dollars, the option contract in this case is quoted in Dutch guilders (Hfl) and cents per U.S. dollar.

Example: If the Dutch guilder contract is quoted at 2.20 ¢/US$, the premium is found to be Hfl 220 (0.0220 × 10,000). Hence the option quotes on the EOE Dutch guilder contracts correspond to the foreign exchange rate denominations prevalent in the interbank market.

The German mark/Japanese yen cross-currency option on the Philadelphia Stock Exchange and the Chicago Mercantile Exchange is denominated in units of DM 1,000,000 and DM 125,000, respectively, and is consequently quoted in yen per DM.

Example: The German mark/Japanese yen PHLX June (strike 79) call is quoted at 1.07. Then the premium per contract is found as ¥1,070,000 (= 1.07 × 1,000,000).

The cross-rate options are settled in the trading currency rather than in the U.S. dollar. An investor who wants to convert the investment into U.S. dollars must be aware of the possible simultaneous movements in both the currencies in the cross rate.

Example: An investor buys a DM/¥ X-rate option (strike 80) and pays the premium by converting U.S. dollars into yen. Toward the expiry date, the German mark has strengthened relative to the yen (or the yen has weakened relative to the mark), and hence the option can be closed at a net profit in yen, which is to be converted back into U.S. dollars. However, if the yen has weakened significantly against the dollar, the profit might be turned into a loss when measured in U.S. dollars.

Price quotations on currency option contracts can be found in the major international newspapers. *The Wall Street Journal* brings daily quotations on the currency options of the Philadelphia Stock Exchange and the currency future options of the Chicago Mercantile Exchange-IMM (see Figure 7.1). The *Financial Times* brings daily quotations on the £/$ currency options traded on the Philadelphia Stock Exchange (see Figure 7.2). The quotations are presented in different ways, but they all contain the same basic information.

The Wall Street Journal presents the foreign exchange rate in cents per unit of the foreign currency, with the exercise price indicated by the addition to the "big figure." The closing prices on calls and puts are given for the different exercise (strike) prices traded on the exchanges with contract maturities presented horizontally. The quotes are given as cents per unit of foreign currency. A summary statistic indicates the total number of contracts traded during the day (volume) on each exchange and gives the total number of open call and put option quotes made during the business day (open interest).

Pricing

The values of foreign currency options rise and fall in reaction to the values of the underlying foreign currency.

FIGURE 7.1

Quotes on Currency Option Contracts. (Reprinted by permission of *The Wall Street Journal,* Europe.)

OPTIONS

PHILADELPHIA EXCHANGE

Option & Underlying		Strike Price	Calls—Last Mar	Calls—Last Apr	Calls—Last Jun	Puts—Last Mar	Puts—Last Apr	Puts—Last Jun
50,000 Australian Dollars-cents per unit.								
ADollr.....		74	r	r	r	0.21	r	r
75.73	....	75	r	r	r	0.42	r	r
75.73	....	76	0.37	r	r	0.86	r	r
75.73	....	77	0.19	r	r	r	r	r
31,250 British Pounds-cents per unit.								
BPound ..		165	r	r	r	0.30	1.00	r
175.54	..	167½	r	r	r	0.44	r	r
175.54	..	170	4.80	r	r	1.10	2.05	r
175.54	..	172½	3.16	r	r	1.70	r	r
175.54	..	175	2.05	r	4.20	3.15	r	7.00
175.54	..	177½	1.13	r	3.13	r	r	r
175.54	..	180	0.59	r	r	r	r	r
175.54	..	182½	0.35	r	r	r	r	r
175.54	..	187½	0.10	r	r	r	r	r
50,000 Canadian Dollars-cents per unit.								
CDollr.....		83½	r	r	r	0.18	r	r
84.33	....	84	0.72	r	r	r	r	r
84.33	....	85	0.17	r	r	r	r	r
84.33	....	85½	r	r	r	1.30	r	r
84.33	....	86½	r	r	r	2.13	r	r
84.33	....	87	r	r	r	2.57	r	r
250,000 French Francs-10ths of a cent per unit.								
FFranc....		17¾	r	r	r	r	3.98	r
178.92	...	18	1.60	r	r	r	r	r
178.92	...	18¾	r	r	1.58	r	r	r
178.92	...	19¼	r	r	0.88	r	r	r
1,000,000 GermanMark-JapaneseYen cross.								
GMk-JYn	.	78	r	r	r	1.15	r	r
94.62	....	79	r	r	1.07	r	r	r
94.62	....	81	r	r	r	3.46	r	r
62,500 German Marks-European Style.								
DMark		57	r	r	r	r	0.32	r
60.85	....	60	r	r	r	0.85	r	r
60.85	....	60½	r	r	s	r	1.65	s
60.85	....	61½	r	r	s	r	2.29	s
60.85	....	62½	0.27	r	s	r	r	s
60.85	....	63	r	r	r	2.98	r	r
60.85	....	64	0.10	r	r	r	r	r
62,500 German Marks-cents per unit.								
DMark		55	r	r	r	r	r	0.43
60.85	....	56	r	r	r	r	r	0.52
60.85	....	57	r	r	r	0.11	r	0.80
60.85	....	58	r	r	r	0.16	0.57	1.13
60.85	....	58½	r	r	s	r	0.61	s
60.85	....	59	r	r	r	0.38	0.76	1.44
60.85	....	59½	r	r	s	0.66	1.15	s
60.85	....	60	1.04	1.37	1.90	0.64	1.14	1.95
60.85	....	60½	1.00	1.13	s	0.82	r	s
60.85	....	61	0.80	1.07	1.41	1.36	1.67	2.60
60.85	....	61½	r	0.85	s	r	r	s
60.85	....	62	0.42	0.59	0.96	1.84	r	3.42
60.85	....	62½	0.30	0.54	s	r	r	s
60.85	....	63	0.20	0.34	0.81	2.55	r	r
60.85	....	64	0.08	0.23	0.49	r	r	4.98
60.85	....	65	r	r	0.34	r	r	r
60.85	....	68	r	r	0.12	r	r	r
6,250,000 Japanese Yen-100ths of a cent per unit.								
JYen......		74½	r	r	s	0.07	r	s
78.01	....	75	r	r	r	r	0.30	r
78.01	....	76	r	r	r	0.25	0.52	1.03
78.01	....	76½	r	r	s	0.33	r	s
78.01	....	77	r	r	r	r	0.84	1.41
78.01	....	77½	0.74	r	s	0.72	r	s
78.01	....	78	r	r	1.40	0.68	r	1.88
78.01	....	78½	0.37	0.68	s	r	r	s

CURRENCY

JAPANESE YEN (IMM)

12,500,000 yen; cents per 100 yen

Strike Price	Calls—Settle Mar	Calls—Settle Apr	Calls—Settle May	Puts—Settle Mar	Puts—Settle Apr	Puts—Settle May
7650	1.34	....	....	0.20	0.60	....
7700	0.97	....	....	0.33	0.79	1.11
7750	0.66	1.02	....	0.52	1.02	....
7800	0.44	0.80	1.12	0.80	1.30	1.61
7850	0.28	0.61	....	1.14	1.60	1.92
7900	0.18	0.46	0.76	1.56	1.94	2.25

Est. vol. 8,766;
Wed vol. 2,784 calls; 3,001 puts
Op. int. Wed 54,622 calls; 59,264 puts

DEUTSCHEMARK (IMM)

125,000 marks; cents per mark

Strike Price	Calls—Settle Mar	Calls—Settle Apr	Calls—Settle May	Puts—Settle Mar	Puts—Settle Apr	Puts—Settle May
5950	1.40	1.32	....	0.37	1.07	....
6000	1.07	1.07	1.43	0.53	1.32	1.67
6050	0.79	0.86	....	0.75	1.60	....
6100	0.56	0.69	1.04	1.02	1.93	2.27
6150	0.39	0.55	0.87	1.35	2.29	2.60
6200	0.26	0.43	0.72	1.72	2.66	....

Est. vol. 27,004;
Wed vol. 7,486 calls; 8,474 puts
Op. int. Wed 95,572 calls; 101,972 puts

CANADIAN DOLLAR (IMM)

100,000 Can.$, cents per Can.$

Strike Price	Calls—Settle Mar	Calls—Settle Apr	Calls—Settle May	Puts—Settle Mar	Puts—Settle Apr	Puts—Settle May
8350	0.90	0.71	....	0.12	0.57	....
8400	0.54	0.47	0.70	0.25	0.83	....
8450	0.27	0.29	....	0.49	1.15	....
8500	0.12	....	....	0.84	1.53	....
8550	0.04	....	....	1.26	1.95	....
8600	0.01	0.05	....	1.73	2.41	....

Est. vol. 1,043;
Wed vol. 500 calls; 315 puts
Op. int. Wed 10,354 calls; 16,935 puts

BRITISH POUND (IMM)

62,500 pounds; cents per pound

Strike Price	Calls—Settle Mar	Calls—Settle Apr	Calls—Settle May	Puts—Settle Mar	Puts—Settle Apr	Puts—Settle May
1700	5.02	4.40	....	0.54	2.54	....
1725	3.18	3.20	....	1.20	3.72	....
1750	1.80	2.22	....	2.32	5.20	6.10
1775	0.88	1.42	....	3.92	6.90	....
1800	0.40	0.90	1.68	5.92	8.88	....
1825	0.18	0.56	....	8.16	11.02	....

Est. vol. 4,306;
Wed vol. 930 calls; 926 puts
Op. int. Wed 12,467 calls; 12,760 puts

SWISS FRANC (IMM)

125,000 francs; cents per franc

Strike Price	Calls—Settle Mar	Calls—Settle Apr	Calls—Settle May	Puts—Settle Mar	Puts—Settle Apr	Puts—Settle May
6600	1.52	1.62	....	0.42	1.07	....
6650	1.18	1.38	....	0.58	1.31	....
6700	0.91	1.14	....	0.81	1.58	1.98
6750	0.68	....	....	1.08	1.88	....
6800	0.49	0.78	....	1.39	2.21	....
6850	0.35	0.62	....	1.74	2.55	....

Est. vol. 2,887;
Wed vol. 2,195 calls; 1,767 puts
Op. int. Wed 15,102 calls; 16,943 puts

U.S. DOLLAR INDEX (FINEX)

500 times index

Strike Price	Calls—Settle Mar	Calls—Settle Apr	Calls—Settle May	Puts—Settle Mar	Puts—Settle Apr	Puts—Settle May
88	2.03	3.46	....	0.33	0.46	....
89	1.34	....	....	0.64	0.73	....

FIGURE 7.2
Quotes on Currency Option Contracts. (Reprinted by permission of *Financial Times.*)

PHILADELPHIA SE £/$ OPTIONS
£31,250 (cents per £1)

Strike Price	Calls Apr	Calls May	Calls Jun	Calls Sep	Puts Apr	Puts May	Puts Jun	Puts Sep
1.350	9.52	9.50	9.60	9.95	0.07	0.33	0.71	1.95
1.375	7.24	7.41	7.61	8.24	0.21	0.68	1.20	2.65
1.400	5.12	5.49	5.88	6.75	0.56	1.25	1.90	3.57
1.425	3.28	3.84	4.35	5.40	1.20	2.09	2.80	4.68
1.450	1.84	2.58	3.09	4.25	2.28	3.21	4.02	6.00
1.475	1.00	1.63	2.18	3.30	3.82	4.75	5.54	7.50
1.500	0.46	0.97	1.46	2.56	5.77	6.57	7.30	9.13

Previous day's open int: Calls 521,224 Puts 411,807 (All currencies)
Previous day's volume: Calls 22,172 Puts 12,889 (All currencies)

1. As the currency's price rises, call premiums go up and put premiums go down.
2. As the currency's price declines, so do call prices, whereas put prices increase.

Example: Ultrabank (a fictitious firm) has a call option and a put option on the British pound, each with a strike price of $1.40. The call entitles the bank to buy $1 million worth of pounds at $1.40 each; the put gives it the right to sell $1 million worth of pounds at $1.40. The pound is presently trading at $1.40.

Then the value of the pound decreases to, say, $1.35—that is, the pound *weakens* with respect to the U.S. dollar. In this case, the call goes out-of-the-money, and the put takes on an intrinsic value of $0.05.

If the pound gets *stronger*—that is, if its price rises to $1.50—then the call assumes an intrinsic value of $0.10, and the put goes out-of-the-money.

Currency option prices (premiums) are calculated in U.S. dollars insofar as the contract amount is denominated in the foreign currency and the exercise price is quoted in dollars per unit of the foreign currency. (When the contract amount is denominated in U.S. dollars, the exercise price is quoted in units of the foreign currency per U.S. dollar and the option premiums are calculated in the foreign currency amount.)

In the case of an option to buy a foreign currency (or to buy dollars against a foreign currency), the premium denotes the amount of dollars (or foreign currency) that the market is willing to pay for the right to buy the contract amount of foreign currency (or dollars) at the agreed-upon exercise price.

In the case of an option to sell a foreign currency (or to sell dollars against a foreign currency), the premium denotes the amount of dollars (or foreign currency) that the market is willing to pay for the right to sell the contract amount of foreign currency (or U.S. dollars) at the agreed-upon exercise price.

Expiration Dates

The currency options are usually deliverable with monthly maturities. The expiration months correspond to the delivery months on the financial futures exchanges. Within the months of maturity, however, there are certain differences among exchanges on the exact day of expiration, as well as on the last trading day. As in the financial futures market, option traders will pay an initial margin to clear the option trade through the exchange clearing house, although only option writers are required to pay margin, the size of which varies with the type of option strategy. The higher the potential risk of the position, the higher will be the initial margin, and, if rates move against the position holder, additional margins will be required.

Trading Limits

To regulate and stabilize the trading activities on the exchanges, certain rules are established with regard to exercise price intervals, minimum change in the option quotes (tick size), and, from time to time, limits. On all the exchanges with dollar-denominated trading units, the tick size is 0.01 cents ($.0001), which on the Chicago Mercantile Exchange, German mark option contracts have a tick value of $12.50 (DM 125,000 × 0.0001 $/DM), equivalent to the tick value of the corresponding financial futures contract. The tick value indicates the minimum change in the option premium. Due to the differing contract sizes the corresponding tick value on the Philadelphia Stock Exchange German mark option is $6.25 (DM 62,500 × 0.0001 $/DM).

The exceptions to the tick size of 0.01 cents are the pound sterling option contract with a tick size of 0.02 cents and the Japanese yen option contract with a tick size of 0.0001 cents. The tick values following the Chicago Mercantile financial futures denomination are $12.50 (£ 62,500 × 0.0002 $/£) and $12.50 (¥ 12,500,000 × 0.000001 $/¥), respectively, thereby bringing about the same tick value for all contracts traded on each exchange.

As in the financial futures markets, an option position can be liquidated without actual delivery of the underlying commodity by incurring an offsetting option trade. If, for instance, a call option is bought and it turns out that the option price stays very far above its theoretical value as it gets closer to maturity, the option holder may sell the call option and thereby offset the initial purchase of the option. The excess price advantage can be taken as profit before the maturity of the contract.

INTEREST RATE OPTIONS

Option contracts on debt instruments are quite similar to stock option contracts. Interest rate or debt options differ from stock options in that their values respond much more quickly to changes in interest rates. When prevailing interest rates are on the rise, new issues of debt generally have increased yields. Old debt issues with lower yields lose value in the marketplace, as their prices drop. So the value of a debt instrument varies inversely with interest rates. That is, bond prices generally go down when interest rates are up, and they rise when interest rates are down.

Interest rates also affect, of course, the prices of debt options. Specifically:

- When rates increase, the market prices of the lower-yielding underlying instruments drop, call prices go down, and put prices go up.
- When rates decrease, underlying prices advance, call prices rise, and put prices drop.

Debt options are becoming increasingly popular and new instruments continue to be developed.

Specifically the emergence of futures and options exchanges in Europe has paved the way for an introduction of a wide variety of option contracts on domestic market interest rate instruments. Similarly, for example, the Montreal Exchange has now concentrated all option trading on Canadian-dollar-denominated debt instruments. Fairly early in the 1980s, a row of short-term deposit contracts were introduced in the major Eurocurrencies including the U.S. dollar, pound sterling, and German mark.

The debt options are often tied into an underlying futures contract. For example, the 15-year U.S. Treasury bond futures contract of the Chicago Board of Trade is an actively traded financial futures contract. Tied to this is a U.S. Treasury bond future option contract.

Quotes on the Treasury bond option are made in $\frac{1}{64}$ intervals, equivalent to half the tick size of the underlying Treasury bond futures contract.

Example: A quote of 1-07 on the Treasury bond option indicates that the option premium is equal to $1\frac{7}{64}$ percentage points of the contract amount, that is, US\$ 100,000 × 71/64 × .01 = \$1,109.375. The minimum change in the option premium is indicated by the tick size of 1/64, which is equivalent to \$15.625 (\$100,000 × 1/64 × 0.01).

U.S. Treasury options are traded on the Chicago Board Options Exchange, the Chicago Mercantile Exchange and the London International Financial Futures Exchange.

The development in interest rate option contracts has been dominated by the introduction of contracts based on leading government bonds, including Canadian government bonds, long gilts, German, French, and Italian government bonds, just to mention the most actively traded. Most of the national futures and option exchanges established throughout Europe trade their own domestic interest rate option contracts (see Table 7.3).

TABLE 7.3
Trading Units for Some North American and European Debt Option Contracts.

Chicago Board of Trade (CBOT)	*International Monetary Market (IMM)*	*Montreal Exchange (ME)*	*London International Financial Futures Exchange (LIFFE)*	*Marché à Térme International de France (MATIF)*	*Deutsche Terminsbörse (DT)*
Treasury bonds (US\$ 100,000)	Treasury bills (US\$ 1,000,000)	10-year Canadian (C\$ 100,000)	Treasury bonds (US\$ 100,000)	Long-term French government bond (Fr. frc. 500,000)	8.5–10-year German government bond (DM 250,000)
Treasury notes (US\$ 100,000)			Long gilt (£ stg. 50,000)	Long-term German government bond (DM 250,000)	4–5-year German government bond (DM 250,000)
	Eurodollar time deposit (US\$ 1,000,000)		Short-term sterling deposit (£ stg. 500,000)		
	One-month US\$ LIBOR (US\$ 3,000,000)		Long-term German government bond (DM 250,000)		
			Euromark deposit (DM 1,000,000)		

FIGURE 7.3

Quotes on Interest Rate Option Contracts. (Reprinted by permission of *The Wall Street Journal*, Europe.)

INTEREST RATES

T-BONDS (CBT)
$100,000; points and 64ths of 100%

Strike	Calls—Settle			Puts—Settle		
Price	Mar	Jun	Sep	Mar	Jun	Sep
96	4-00	3-38	3-38	c1	0-46	1-48
98	2-00	2-17	2-32	0-01	1-23	2-40
100	0-12	1-17	1-42	0-12	2-23	3-50
102	c6	0-42	1-07	2-00	3-46	5-08
104	c3	0-20	0-44	4-00	5-23	....
106	c1	0-09	0-28	6-00	7-11	8-26

Est. vol. 80,000;
Wed vol. 77,917 calls; 67,853 puts
Op. int. Wed 436,255 calls; 299,888 puts

T-NOTES (CBT)
$100,000; points and 64ths of 100%

Strike	Calls—Settle			Puts—Settle		
Price	Mar	Jun	Sep	Mar	Jun	Sep
101	2-06	2-02	....	0-01	0-63	....
102	1-07	1-30	....	0-02	1-26	....
103	0-13	1-01	....	0-07	1-61	....
104	0-01	0-44	....	0-60	2-39	....
105	0-01	0-29	....	1-58	3-23	....
106	0-01	0-18	....	2-58	4-12	....

Est. vol. 20,000;
Wed vol. 5,860 calls; 6,333 puts
Op. int. Wed 49,987 calls; 55,115 puts

MUNICIPAL BOND INDEX (CBT)
$100,000; pts. & 64ths of 100%

Strike	Calls—Settle			Puts—Settle		
Price	Mar	Jun	Sep	Mar	Jun	Sep
92	....	....	....	0-06	....	....
93	1-15	1-20	....	0-09	0-61	....
94	0-35	....	....	0-25	1-32	....
95	0-12	0-39	....	1-06	2-11	....
96	0-03	0-26	....	1-61	2-62	....
97	0-02	....	....	2-58	....	....

Est. vol. 0;
Wed vol. 0 calls; 0 puts
Op. int. Wed 7,272 calls; 7,321 puts

5 YR TREAS NOTES (CBT)
$100,000; points and 64ths of 100%

Strike	Calls—Settle			Puts—Settle		
Price	Mar	Jun	Sep	Mar	Jun	Sep
10300	1-43	....	....	0-01	0-40	....
10350	1-11	1-00	....	0-01	0-52	....
10400	0-43	0-46	....	0-04	1-02	....
10450	0-16	0-35	....	0-23	....	....
10500	0-02	0-24	....	0-53	1— 43	....
10550	0-01	0-17	....	1-21	....	....

Est. vol. 1,600;
Wed vol. 245 calls; 1,249 puts
Op. int. Wed 11,841 calls; 10,703 puts

EURODOLLAR (IMM)
$ million; pts. of 100%

Strike	Calls—Settle			Puts—Settle		
Price	Mar	Jun	Sep	Mar	Jun	Sep
9525	0.51	0.39	0.27	.0004	0.10	0.34
9550	0.27	0.23	0.17	0.01	0.18	0.48
9575	0.07	0.12	0.09	0.06	0.32	0.65
9600	0.02	0.06	0.05	0.26	0.51	0.85
9625	0.01	0.03	0.03	0.50	0.72	1.08
9650	.0004	0.01	0.02	0.74	....	....

Est. vol. 27,358;
Wed vol. 14,646 calls; 22,311 puts
Op. int. Wed 387,833 calls; 497,890 puts

LIBOR – 1 Mo. (IMM)
$3 million; pts. of 100%

Strike	Calls—Settle			Puts—Settle		
Price	Mar	Apr	May	Mar	Apr	May
9525	0.51	....	....	.0004	....	....
9550	0.27	0.33	0.30	0.01	0.04	0.08
9575	0.07	0.15	0.15	0.06	0.11	0.18
9600	0.01	0.05	0.07	0.25	0.26	0.35
9625	.0004	0.02	0.03	0.49	0.48	0.56
9650	....	....	....	....	....	....

Est. vol. 955;
Wed vol. 90 calls; 0 puts
Op. int. Wed 3,089 calls; 1,489 puts

TREASURY BILLS (IMM)
$1 million; pts. of 100%

Strike	Calls—Settle			Puts—Settle		
Price	Mar	Jun	Sep	Mar	Jun	Sep
9550	0.57	0.51	0.36	.0004	0.03	....
9575	0.32	0.32	....	.0004	0.09	....
9600	0.07	0.15	0.12	.0004	0.17	0.42
9625	.0004	0.07	0.05	0.18	0.34	0.61
9650	.0004	0.02	....	....	0.53	....
9675	....	....	....	....	....	....

Est. vol. 151;
Wed vol. 0 calls; 3 puts
Op. int. Wed 2,835 calls; 1,843 puts

EURODOLLAR (LIFFE)
$1 million; pts. of 100%

Strike	Calls—Settle			Puts—Settle		
Price	Mar	Jun	Sep	Mar	Jun	Sep
9525	0.52	0.42	0.29	0.00	0.11	0.35
9550	0.28	0.25	0.18	0.01	0.19	0.49
9575	0.09	0.13	0.11	0.07	0.32	0.67
9600	0.02	0.07	0.06	0.25	0.51	0.87
9625	0.01	0.03	0.03	0.49	0.72	1.09
9650	0.00	0.01	0.01	0.73	0.95	1.32

Est. vol. Thur, 1000 calls; 0 puts
Op. int. Wed , 6,130 calls; 8,703 puts

LONG GILT (LIFFE)
£50,000; 64ths of 100%

Strike	Calls—Settle			Puts—Settle		
Price	Mar	Jun	....	Mar	Jun	....
95	2-54	3-36	....	0-00	0-26	....
96	1-54	2-50	....	0-00	0-40	....
97	0-55	2-06	....	0-01	0-60	....
98	0-06	1-34	....	0-16	1-24	....
99	0-01	1-05	....	1-11	1-59	....
100	0-00	0-47	....	2-10	2-37	....

Est. vol. Thur, 1,400 calls; 940 puts
Op. int. Wed, 54,662 calls; 36,858 puts

LONG-TERM FRENCH BOND (MATIF)
FFr. 500,000; pts of 100%

Strike	Calls—Settle			Puts—Settle		
Pr.	Mar	Jun	Sep	Mar	Jun	Sep
106	....	....	....	....	0.10	....
107	0.86	....	....	0.03	0.22	....
108	0.14	....	....	0.31	0.45	....
109	0.01	0.98	....	1.16	0.79	....
110	....	0.53	....	....	1.35	....
111	....	0.27	....	....	....	....
112	....	0.12	....	....	....	....

Vol. 17,083; Calls:11,027; Puts:6,056;
Open Interest 369,571

SHORT STERLING OPTIONS (LIFFE)
£500,000; pts of100%

Strike	Call—Settle		Put—Settle	
Price	Mar-c	Jun-c	Mar-p	Jun-p
8900	.	.	.	0.04
8925	.	.	0.01	.
8950	0.40	. .	0.03	0.10
8975	0.18	.	0.07	0.16
9000	0.06	0.38	0.20	0.25
9025	0.02	0.25	0.39	0.35
9050	.	0.16	.	.

Est. vol. 5,980; Calls: 3,322; Puts: 2,658
Open Interest; Calls: 100,786; Puts: 56,397

The major option contracts on interest rate instruments are quoted daily in *The Wall Street Journal* and the *Financial Times* (see Figures 7.3 and 7.4).

FIGURE 7.4

Quotes on Financial Futures Option Contracts. (Reprinted by permission of *Financial Times.*)

FINANCIAL FUTURES AND OPTIONS

LIFFE LONG GILT FUTURES OPTIONS
£50,000 64ths of 100%

Strike Price	Calls-settlements Mar	Calls-settlements Jun	Puts-settlements Mar	Puts-settlements Jun
94	3-34	4-11	0-06	0-33
95	2-39	3-25	0-11	0-47
96	1-51	2-45	0-23	1-03
97	1-08	2-07	0-44	1-29
98	0-41	1-39	1-13	1-61
99	0-22	1-13	1-58	2-35
100	0-11	0-57	2-47	3-15
101	0-06	0-41	3-42	3-63

Estimated volume total, Calls 3142 Puts 2907
Previous day's open int. Calls 29874 Puts 23758

LIFFE US TREASURY BOND FUTURES OPTIONS
$100,000 64ths of 100%

Strike Price	Calls-settlements Mar	Calls-settlements Jun	Puts-settlements Mar	Puts-settlements Jun
99	3-53	3-48	0-11	1-10
100	2-62	3-07	0-20	1-33
101	2-13	2-34	0-35	1-60
102	1-36	2-02	0-58	2-28
103	1-03	1-38	1-25	3-00
104	0-42	1-15	2-00	3-41
105	0-25	0-61	2-47	4-23
106	0-15	0-47	3-37	5-09

Estimated volume total, Calls 254 Puts 704
Previous day's open int. Calls 1166 Puts 1252

LIFFE BUND FUTURES OPTIONS
DM250,000 points of 100%

Strike Price	Calls-settlements Mar	Calls-settlements Jun	Puts-settlements Mar	Puts-settlements Jun
8650	1.71	2.30	0.05	0.20
8700	1.26	1.90	0.10	0.30
8750	0.87	1.53	0.21	0.43
8800	0.54	1.21	0.38	0.61
8850	0.31	0.93	0.65	0.83
8900	0.16	0.70	1.00	1.10
8950	0.08	0.51	1.42	1.41
9000	0.04	0.37	1.88	1.77

Estimated volume total, Calls 5493 Puts 3265
Previous day's open int. Calls 138212 Puts 68782

LIFFE EUROMARK OPTIONS
DM1m points of 100%

Strike Price	Calls-settlements Mar	Calls-settlements Jun	Puts-settlements Mar	Puts-settlements Jun
8975	0.93	1.41	0	0.01
9000	0.68	1.16	0	0.01
9025	0.44	0.93	0.01	0.03
9050	0.22	0.70	0.04	0.05
9075	0.08	0.50	0.15	0.10
9100	0.03	0.32	0.35	0.17
9125	0.01	0.19	0.58	0.29
9150	0	0.11	0.82	0.46

Estimated volume total, Calls 3301 Puts 1195
Previous day's open int. Calls 57048 Puts 29798

LIFFE ITALIAN GOVT. BOND (BTP) FUTURES OPTIONS **Lira 200m 100ths of 100%**

Strike Price	Calls-settlements Mar	Calls-settlements Jun	Puts-settlements Mar	Puts-settlements Jun
9650	1.90	2.28	0.04	0.31
9700	1.44	1.90	0.08	0.43
9750	1.03	1.56	0.17	0.59
9800	0.68	1.26	0.32	0.79
9850	0.41	0.99	0.55	1.02
9900	0.22	0.77	0.86	1.30
9950	0.11	0.58	1.25	1.61
10000	0.05	0.43	1.69	1.96

Estimated volume total, Calls 408 Puts 35
Previous day's open int. Calls 4719 Puts 2053

LIFFE SHORT STERLING OPTIONS
£500,000 points of 100%

Strike Price	Calls-settlements Mar	Calls-settlements Jun	Puts-settlements Mar	Puts-settlements Jun
8875	0.96	1.36	0.01	0.04
8900	0.73	1.14	0.03	0.07
8925	0.51	0.93	0.06	0.11
8950	0.31	0.73	0.11	0.16
8975	0.17	0.55	0.22	0.23
9000	0.08	0.41	0.38	0.34
9025	0.04	0.29	0.59	0.47
9050	0.01	0.20	0.81	0.63

Estimated volume total, Calls 20053 Puts 5197
Previous day's open int. Calls 79642 Puts 40872

STOCK INDEX OPTIONS

The introduction of the Standard & Poors 500 Stock Index future on the Chicago Mercantile Exchange and the introduction of the NYSE Composite Index future on the New York Futures Exchange during 1982 subsequently led both the exchanges to introduce option contracts on the two stock index futures.

Several other North American index options are traded on the exchanges including other stock index options like the NYSE Double Index contract, the AMEX Major Market Index contract, and the Value Line Index option of the Kansas City Board.

In conjunction with the introduction of the FT-SE 100 index futures contract, the London International Financial Futures Exchange also offered an option on the index future, and this initial index has been expanded with option contracts on the Euro FT-SE Stock Index and the FT-SE Eurotrack 100 Stock Index. Over the past years most of the many national futures and options exchanges established across Europe have introduced their own option contracts based on leading domestic stock indexes. The European Options Exchange in Amsterdam offers three stock index contracts based on the Dutch TOPS Index, the Eurotop 100

Index, and the EOE Stock Index. The Deutsche Terminsbörse in Frankfurt offers an option contract on the DAX Index (Deutsche Aktienindex), and the Paris-based Options Exchange (MONEP) offers an option contract on the CAC-40 Index.

The maturity of the index option contracts has in certain cases been extended, and these contracts have been introduced under the name of *LEAPS*. These contracts are being traded on the Chicago Board Options Exchange on the S&P 500 Index and the S&P 100 Index contracts. The LEAP contracts extend the expiry date of the option contracts up to two years, hence widening the applicability of the contracts.

The Chicago Board Options Exchange also trades the so-called *CAPS* on the S&P 100 and the S&P 500 Index contracts. The CAP contracts have limited upside potential (for call options) or limited downside potential (for put options), and consequently the contract premiums are somewhat lower. The CAP contracts resemble the limited bull and bear spreads that can be pursued in a double option strategy based on standard option contracts. The difference is that the CAP contracts are standardized, while the double option strategy is more flexible. Furthermore, the CAP contract is settled at the moment when the upper or lower limit of the contract is reached, whereas a double option strategy has greater flexibility regarding the closing and settlement of the position. The double option strategies are discussed further in Chapter 9.

Underlying Interest

An index option differs from all others in that it has no one underlying security. Instead, the underlying interest consists of an *index,* which is a measure of the value of a group of stocks. The New York Stock Exchange and Standard & Poors, for example, publish two such indexes—the value of the index, which is expressed as a dollar figure in the case of a U.S.-based index, serves as the "price" of the underlying interest.

The value of the index is also relative. When an index is first published, it is assigned an arbitrary *base value*. For example, on the first day of recording the index, the value may be established at 100 (the base value). From that day forward, all index values are expressed in terms of the 100 base value. (Other base values can be used, of course). If the index declines on the next day, its value will be something less than 100. Should it advance, the value will be greater than 100.

The Multiplier

The link between the index value and the option's value is the *multiplier,* which does not change. To arrive at the dollar value of either the strike price or the underlying index value, multiply it by the multiplier.

Example: The OEX Index has a multiplier (not a base value) of 100. An OEX June 95 call has a strike price (expressed as a dollar value) of $9,500 ($95 strike price times the multiplier of 100).

Settlement

Index options are unusual in that settlement consists solely of a cash payment. No securities are involved. For either a put or a call, the writer is obligated to pay the holder the intrinsic value, which is the cash difference between the strike price and the index value.

Example: With the OEX index at 80, Barnes exercises his OEX Mar 89 put, which is 9 points in-the-money (strike price of $89 less index value of $80 equals intrinsic value of $9). The assigned writer must pay Barnes $900 (intrinsic value of $9 times the OEX multiplier of 100).

Example: With the OEX index at 95, Barnes exercises his OEX June 90 call, which is 5 points in the money ($95 index value less $90 strike price). The assigned writer must pay Barnes $500 ($5 intrinsic value times the multiplier of 100).

Quotations

The option index quotes are represented as a multiplicand to the contract amount.

Example: The Standard & Poors 500 Stock Index option is quoted at 5.55, and the option premium is equal to $2,775 ($500 times 5.55).

The option indexes are quoted daily in *The Wall Street Journal,* as shown in Figure 7.5.

A variety of stock index option contracts have been developed over the recent years, such as those based on the S&P 500, the NYSE Composite, and the FT-SE 100 stock indexes—a development that continues on a global basis. The Chicago Mercantile Exchange (CME) and the Chicago Board Options Exchange (CBOT) are looking into ways of establishing futures and options trading on an index of international securities, which should become increasingly interesting for many institutional investors. Other types of index contracts have been established over the years. Index contracts are currently being traded in areas such as oil and gas prices and future freight rates, and various exchanges have been planning to introduce trading of a commodity price index option, to mention but a few of the innovations in the market for index futures and options contracts.

FIGURE 7.5
Quotes on Stock Index Option Contracts. (Reprinted by permission of *The Wall Street Journal*, Europe.)

INDEX TRADING

Thursday, February 20, 1992

OPTIONS

Chicago Board

S&P 100 INDEX-$100 times index

Strike Price	Calls—Last Feb	Mar	Apr	Puts—Last Feb	Mar	Apr
330	....	....	....	1/16	....	....
335	....	....	....	....	¼	....
340	....	46½	....	....	5/16	1
345	....	....	....	....	7/16	....
350	36	....	....	....	⅝	1 13/16
355	32	32½	....	1/16	13/16	2⅛
360	27	27¼	....	1/16	1 1/16	2⅝
365	21	22⅞	24⅛	1/16	1 7/16	3¼
370	16⅞	18	21⅛	⅛	1 15/16	4¼
375	11⅞	14⅜	14½	⅛	2¾	5⅜
380	7⅛	10¾	14	5/16	3⅞	7⅛
385	2⅝	7½	10⅜	15/16	5¾	8½
390	½	4¾	7¾	3⅝	8⅛	10¾
395	1/16	2¾	5	8⅜	11½	14⅞
400	1/16	1 9/16	3⅜	....	15½	17¼
405	1/16	13/16	2 5/16	19½	19¼	22½
410	....	7/16	1½	....	24½	....

Total call volume 224,406 Total call open int. 420,423
Total put volume 203,680 Total put open int. 528,844
The index: High 386.90; Low 381.12; Close 386.78, +5.66

S&P 500 INDEX-$100 times index

Strike Price	Calls—Last Feb	Mar	Apr	Puts—Last Feb	Mar	Apr
325	....	84⅜	....	....	1/16	....
360	50	50⅝	....	....	5/16	....
370	....	....	....	....	½	....
375	....	....	....	....	⅝	....
380	....	33	....	....	15/16	....
385	....	....	....	....	1	....
390	....	21¾	....	....	1 9/16	3⅛
395	18	20	22	1/16	1⅞	4
400	13⅛	16	18¾	3/16	2⅝	5
405	8⅞	12¼	....	⅜	3⅝	6⅝
410	3⅝	8⅞	11⅝	¾	5⅜	8
415	1	5¾	8⅝	2⅞	7½	10
420	⅛	3⅝	6⅜	7	10	12½
425	....	2 5/16	....	12	13¾	16
430	....	1⅛	2¾	....	17¾	....
435	....	....	1¾	....	....	....
440	....	7/16	....	....	....	....
450	....	⅛	....	....	....	....

Total call volume 38,359 Total call open int. 391,491
Total put volume 41,051 Total put open int. 550,033
The index: High 413.90; Low 408.26; Close 414.90, +5.64

LEAPS-S&P 100 INDEX

Strike Price	Calls—Last Dec 92	Dec 93	Puts—Last Dec 92	Dec 93
27½	....	....	⅛	....
35	....	....	1⅛	....
37½	....	....	2	....
40	1¾	3⅜	3	....

Total call volume 10 Total call open int. 32,136
Total put volume 81 Total put open int. 122,811
The index: High 38.69; Low 38.11; Close 38.68, +0.57

LEAPS-S&P 500 INDEX

Strike Price	Calls—Last Dec 92	Dec 93	Puts—Last Dec 92	Dec 93
30	....	....	....	⅝
40	....	....	1¾	2⅝

Total call volume 0 Total call open int. 30,741
Total put volume 80 Total put open int. 95,615
The index: High 41.39; Low 40.83; Close 41.39, +0.56

CAPS-S&P 100 INDEX

Strike Price	Calls—Last Feb 92	Apr 92	Puts—Last Feb 92	Apr 92
360	....	....	....	2½
380	5⅝	15½	....	7¼

Total call volume 4 Total call open int. 1,544
Total put volume 17 Total put open int. 5,664
The index: High 386.90; Low 381.12; Close 386.78, +5.66

CAPS-S&P 500 INDEX

Strike Price	Calls—Last Mar 92	Jun 92	Puts—Last Mar 92	Jun 92
430	....	....	17½	....

Total call volume 0 Total call open int. 216
Total put volume 51 Total put open int. 4,839
The index: High 413.90; Low 408.26; Close 413.90, +5.64

Pacific Exchange

FINANCIAL NEWS COMPOSITE INDEX

Strike Price	Calls—Last Feb	Mar	Apr	Puts—Last Feb	Mar	Apr
260	....	28⅜	....	....	....	....
265	....	22¾	....	....	....	....
270	....	17⅞	....	....	....	....
280	7⅞	10⅛	....	1/16	2	....
285	3½	5½	....	⅝	3⅜	....
290	....	3¾	....	....	....	....

Total call volume 370 Total call open int. 2,121
Total put volume 145 Total put open int. 1,520
The index: High 288.47; Low 283.65; Close 288.28, +4.63

N.Y. Stock Exchange

NYSE INDEX OPTIONS

Strike Price	Calls—Last Feb	Mar	Apr	Puts—Last Feb	Mar	Apr
210	....	....	....	....	....	1¼
215	....	....	....	....	13/16	....
220	....	....	....	....	1 9/16	....
225	2 11/16	....	....	....	....	....
230	1/16	....	....	1½	5⅛	5⅞
235	....	....	....	....	9⅜	....
240	....	....	....	11½	....	....

Total call volume 50 Total call open int. 1,068
Total put volume 282 Total put open int. 1,807
The index: High 228.60; Low 225.74; Close 228.60, +2.75

Philadelphia Exchange

GOLD/SILVER INDEX

Strike Price	Calls—Last Feb	Mar	Apr	Puts—Last Feb	Mar	Apr
80	2⅞	....	....	....	....	....
85	3/16	....	....	....	....	....
105	....	....	⅜	....	....	....

Total call volume 61 Total call open int. 1,500
Total put volume 0 Total put open int. 1,175
The index: High 83.68; Low 82.49; Close 83.68, +0.57

VALUE LINE INDEX OPTIONS

Strike Price	Calls—Last Feb	Mar	Apr	Puts—Last Feb	Mar	Apr
315	47	....	....	....	....	....
330	32½	....	....	....	....	....
345	17	....	....	1/16	....	....
350	11¾	....	....	....	....	....
355	6⅝	....	....	⅛	3	....
360	2⅛	7⅛	10	9/16	....	....
365	5/16	4½	....	3⅜	6¾	....
380	....	½	....	....	....	....

Total call volume 1,026 Total call open int. 9,667
Total put volume 334 Total put open int. 6,402
The index: High 361.84; Low 357.93; Close 361.81, +3.88

UTILITIES INDEX

Strike Price	Calls—Last Feb	Mar	Apr	Puts—Last Feb	Mar	Apr
255	....	....	1⅞	5⅞	....	....

Total call volume 4 Total call open int. 1,952
Total put volume 7 Total put open int. 8,640
The index: High 249.44; Low 248.38; Close 249.44, +1.39

London Traded Options

FT-SE 100 SHARE INDEX

Strike Price	Call—Settle Feb	Mar	Apr	May	Put—Settle Feb	Mar	Apr	May
2200	357	368	383	397	0.5	3.5	9	15
2250	307	320	336	351	0.5	5	13	21
2300	257	272	290	308	1	8	17	25
2350	207	225	247	267	1.5	11	23	34
2400	157	180	206	226	2.5	15	32	42
2450	107	138	167	188	3.5	24	43	55
2500	61	100	130	154	9	35	56	71
2550	24	67	98	125	24	54	76	90
2600	6	41	72	96	58	82	103	114
2650	1.5	23	52	74	108	118	134	142
2700	0.5	12	35	55	158	160	170	175
2750	0.5	6	22	39	208	209	211	216
2800	0.5	2.5	15	28	258	258	260	260

Volume 6,624; Calls:2,211; Puts:4,413
Open Interest 101,146

European Options Exchange

Dutch Stock Index

Strike Price	Call-Last Feb	Mar	Apr	Put-Last Feb	Mar	Apr
290	13.30	15.50	17.00	0.10	0.50	1.50
295	8.00	11.00	13.00	0.10	1.40	2.50
300	3.20	7.00	9.00	0.20	2.50	3.80
305	0.40	4.50	6.20	2.00	4.40	6.30
310	0.10	2.10	4.10	7.50	7.30	9.00

Total call volume 9,413 Total call open int. 68,965
Total put volume 3,588 Total put open int. 95,593
The index: High 303,03; Low 300,35; Close 303,03, +3,94

8

Profitability Patterns

In Chapter 5, it was discussed how future foreign exchange rates and interest rates could be locked in by positioning in the appropriate financial futures contracts. Neglecting the basis risk, this means that the rates are fixed once and for all, making future financial variables certain, to the benefit of the business planner. The benefits of selling U.S. dollars against German marks at 3.6550 when the actual spot exchange rate has moved down to 3.2550 are easy to see. Not as easy to accept, however, is a locked-in exchange rate of 3.6550 when rates have moved to a level of 3.8550 DM/US$ because the upside potential of the gain is eliminated. Options, as opposed to futures contracts, close the downside risk while leaving open the upside potential for gains on favorable rate movements. This is one reason for the options markets' increasing role in hedging applications.

Another important determinant in an uncertain business environment is the fact that the decision maker often does not know if a future transaction will actually occur. To provide a committed offer the potential foreign exchange or interest rate risks should still be hedged. Under these circumstances options appear to be an ideal solution, because buyers of options can exercise the option at their choice, but are not committed to do so if the situation does not require doing so.

FIGURE 8.1
Profitability Pattern of a Call Option.

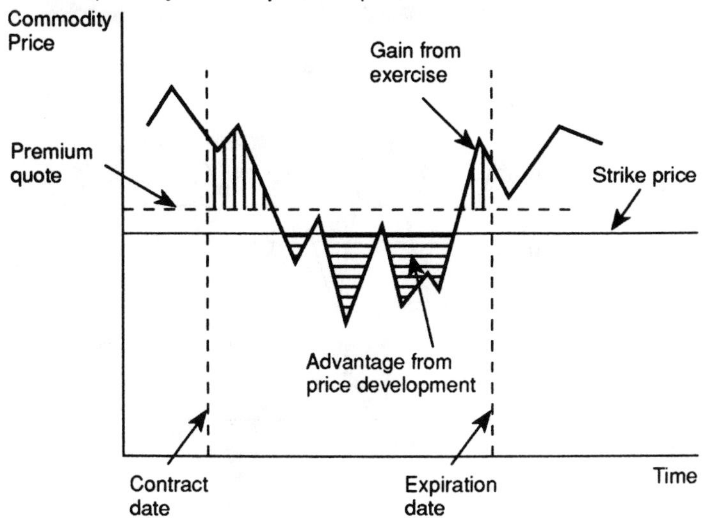

The profitability pattern of options is illustrated in Figure 8.1. A call option will be profitable for the holder if the market price of the underlying commodity increases above the strike price including the premium quote. If the market price drops below the strike price, the option holder will not exercise the option but will take full advantage of the favorable development in the commodity price.

A put option will be profitable if the market price of the underlying commodity falls below the strike price minus the premium quote (see Figure 8.2). If the market price increases above the strike price, the option holder will not exercise the option but will take full advantage of the favorable price development.

PROFIT AND LOSS PROFILES

A *call option* provides the holder with the right, but not the obligation, to purchase an asset at the strike (or exercise) price during a specified period. The buyer pays the premium up front for that right. Conversely, the seller (or writer) of a call option is obliged to sell the asset to the holder against receipt of the up-front premium. Figure 8.3 provides a graphic presentation of the profit and loss profiles for the buyer's and seller's positions in a call option contract.

FIGURE 8.2
Profitability Pattern of a Put Option.

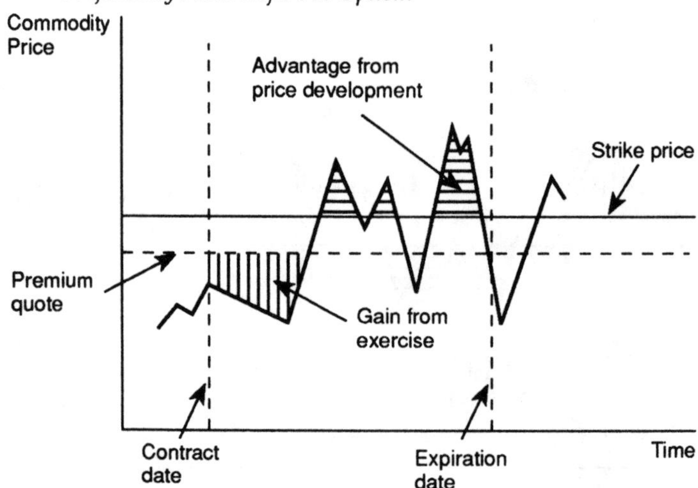

A *put option* provides the holder with the right, but not an obligation, to sell an asset at the exercise price during a specified period. The option buyer pays the premium up front. Conversely, the put option writer is obliged to buy the asset from the holder against receipt of the premium up front (see Figure 8.4).

As shown in Chapter 6, the *intrinsic value* of the option is determined solely by the current market price of the underlying asset and the strike price of the option contract. The *time value* is a function of several factors, with time to maturity playing a major role: the shorter the time to

FIGURE 8.3
Profit and Loss Profiles: Call.

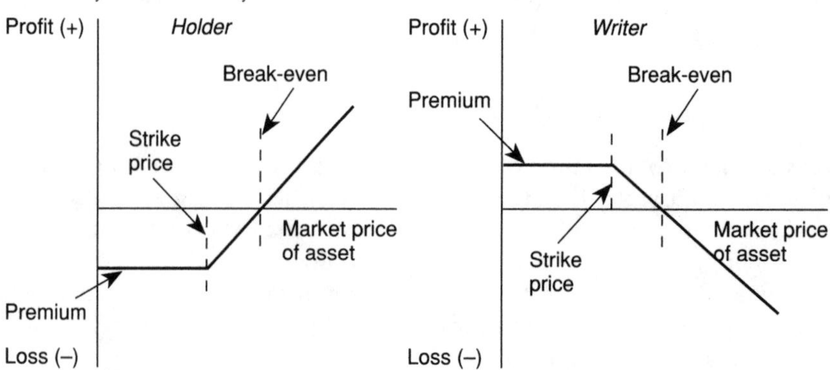

FIGURE 8.4
Profit and Loss Profiles: Put.

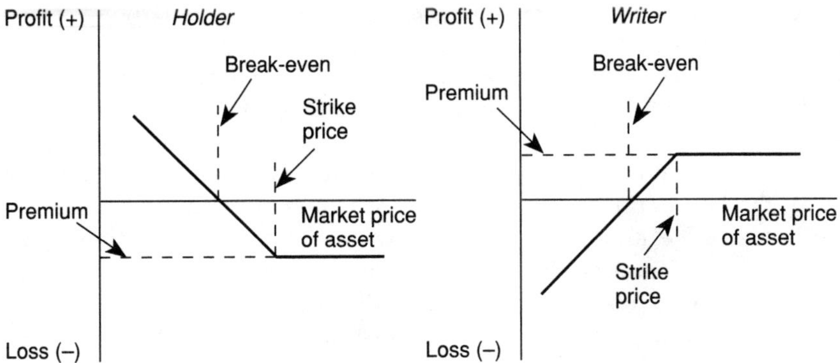

maturity, the smaller the time value. At the expiration date the time value is zero and the option premium is equal only to the intrinsic value. The time value of the option is at its maximum value when the market price of the asset is close to the strike price.

An option may be "at," "out of," or "in" the money. An option is deemed *at the money* when the current market price of the asset equals the strike price of the contract. A call option whose strike price is above the current market price of the underlying asset is *out of the money,* as is a put option whose exercise price is below the current market price of the asset. There is no benefit for the option holder in exercising the option because the intrinsic value is zero. A call option whose strike price is below the current market price of the underlying asset is *in the money,* as is a put option whose strike price is above the going market price of the asset. Exercising the option is beneficial to the holder since the intrinsic value is positive (see Table 8.1).

TABLE 8.1

At the Money	Time value is at maximum. Strike price = Market price
Out of the Money	Intrinsic value is zero. Call: Strike price > Market price Put: Strike price < Market price
In the Money	Intrinsic value is positive. Call: Strike price < Market price Put: Strike price > Market price

Whether an option is in, at, or out of the money at the time of purchase influences the profit and loss profile of an option. If the strike price of a call is lower than the current market price of the underlying asset, the contract is in the money, and the option premium will be high: It is beneficial to exercise the option right away because the intrinsic value is positive, or to sell the option in the market. If the strike price is higher than the current market price, the call is out of the money, the intrinsic value is zero, and the option premium is relatively low. Variations in the size of the option premium will have a corresponding impact on the option holder's break-even points, as shown in Figure 8.5. The higher the call option premium is, the higher the market price (break-even price) must be before the option is beneficial to the holder.[1]

When writing a call option, one must determine which strike price to choose for a given market price of the underlying commodity. The choice of options with different strike prices is illustrated in Figure 8.6. When the strike price is higher than the current market price, the option premium will be low. And when the strike price is lower than the current market price, the option premium will increase in value as the option's intrinsic value increases.

FIGURE 8.5
Profit and Loss Profile of a Call Option.

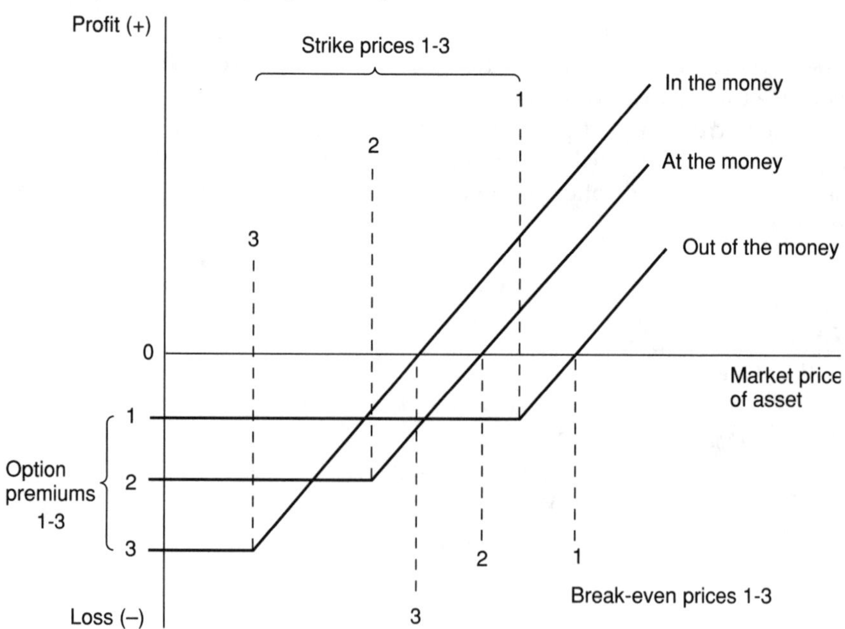

FIGURE 8.6
Break-Even Points for a Call Option at Different Strike Prices.

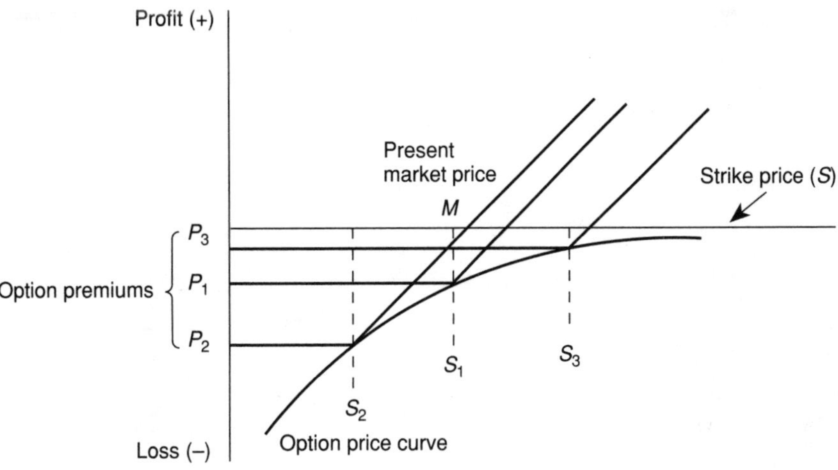

As the graph makes apparent, the higher the strike price ($S_3 > M$), the higher will be the break-even point, while the option premium gets lower (P_3). Reducing the strike price ($S_2 < M$) reduces the break-even point, but it can never get lower than the actual market value of the commodity. At the same time the option premium increases (P_2). Hence for a given market price:

1. The maximum break-even point is infinitely high, for which an infinitely small premium is paid.
2. The minimum break-even point is the current market price, for which an infinitely large premium can be paid.

Assuming that the future market price moves at random, we can conclude from this that choosing too low a strike price will become far too expensive, and choosing too high a strike price hardly has any benefits if the premium is very low.

A similar set of circumstances applies to a put option, whose choice of a strike price is represented in Figure 8.7. If the strike price is lower than the current market price the option premium is low, and when the strike price exceeds the current market price the option premium increases corresponding to the increased intrinsic value of the put option.

As is apparent, the lower the strike price is, the lower will be the break-even point, and the option premium will decrease at the same time. By increasing the strike price ($S_3 > M$), the break-even point is in-

FIGURE 8.7
Break-Even Points for a Put Option with Different Strike Prices.

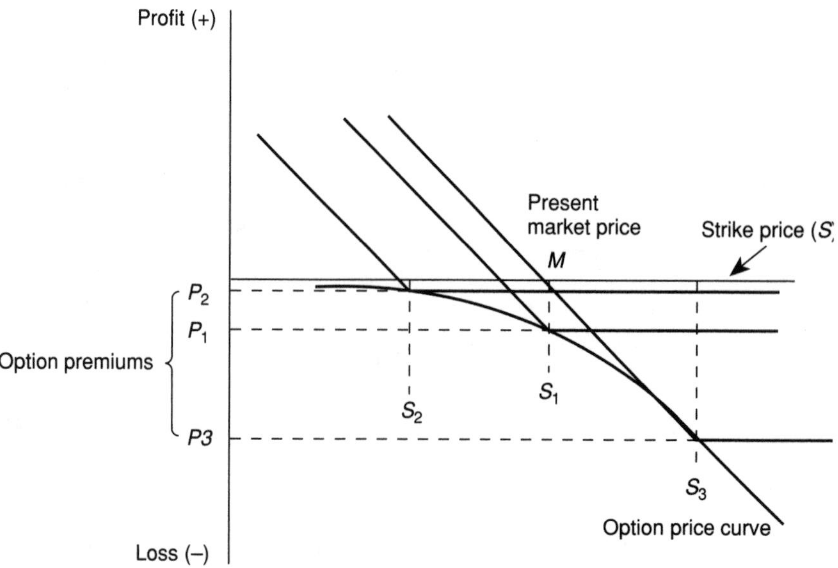

creased, but it can never exceed the current market price; however, the option premium increases (P_3). Hence for a given market price:

1. The minimum break-even point is infinitely low, for which an infinitely small premium is paid.
2. The maximum break-even point is the current market price, for which an infinitely large premium can be paid.

As a general rule the optimum strike price to choose for an option buyer is a slightly out-of-the-money option, because the premium is relatively low and the upside potential for gain is high. If a highly in-the-money option is chosen, the premium will be relatively high, due to the high intrinsic value of the option and the relatively limited upside potential for a gain.

The investor who has to choose the appropriate strike price of a given call or put option should take into consideration several factors, such as:

- The expected price change of the underlying asset.
- The probability that an expected price trend will materialize.
- The size of the premium (either the premium income for the option writer or the maximum loss for the option buyer).

- The maturity of the option (compared to the time horizon of the expected price development).

The investor who expects the price to increase should consider buying call options or writing put options. The investor who expects the price to drop should consider buying put options or writing call options. The certainty of the investor's market view should play a major role in the investment decision.

The premium of a bought in-the-money option will react relatively quickly to price changes in the underlying asset. If the future price development is volatile, then the risk of losing the up-front premium is fairly high. Conversely, an option writer who is uncertain of the future price trend should be very careful, because the potential loss of an unfavorable price development is in principle unlimited.

It is also important for an option holder for the expected price development to occur within the lifetime of the option; otherwise the option expires worthless. A fulfilment of an expected trend after expiry date avails the option buyer little. Conversely, an option writer can take advantage of the expected timing of events before and after the option's expiry.

DELTA

The *delta* (or hedge-ratio) of an option indicates the amount by which the option premium changes when the market price of the underlying asset moves by one point.

$$\textbf{Delta} = \frac{dg(\cdot)}{dP}\left(\frac{\textbf{Change in premium}}{\textbf{Change in price}}\right)$$

The delta is not a constant but changes continuously as the market price of the asset changes. The graph showing the call option premium as a function of the market price of the underlying asset in Figure 8.8 illustrates that the delta factor is equivalent to the slope of the tangent to the option price curve. As shown in the figure, the delta factor is defined as the differential coefficient of the option price curve [$g(\cdot)$], with respect to the market price of the asset (P). The delta factor of an option at the money (2) is close to 0.5. The more the option gets in the money (3), the closer the delta factor gets to 1, showing that the option premium curve approximates the intrinsic value line. The further out of the money (1) the option is, the closer the delta factor gets to zero.

If we apply the previously discussed Black-Scholes call option pric-

FIGURE 8.8
Call Option Premium and Delta Factor.

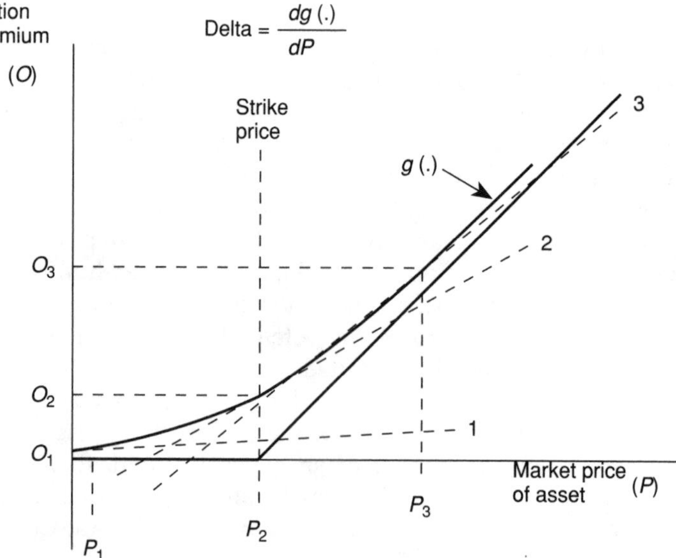

ing model (discussed in Chapter 6) to describe the option price curve $[g(\cdot)]$, the delta factor is determined by one of the arguments of the formula:[2]

If

$$g(\cdot) = P \cdot N(x_1) - (e^{-r}f^{\cdot T}) \cdot E \cdot N(x_2)[\text{Black-Scholes}]$$

where

$$x_1 = \ln(P/E) + (r_g + s^2/2) \cdot T))/(s \cdot T)$$

then

$$\text{Delta} = N(x_1)$$

This provides us with a formula to calculate the theoretical delta values.

The delta factor provides us with analytical information on the shape of the option premium curve, and it can prove useful when determining the optimal option choice.

The changing delta values for a call and a put option at a given market price are illustrated graphically in Figure 8.9.

For a given market price, the delta of a *call option* would be close to 1 when the strike price is much lower than the market price (in the money) because the option price curve will be close to the intrinsic value of the call option. When the strike price is equal to the market price, then

FIGURE 8.9
Changing Delta Values for a Call and a Put Option at a Given Market Price.

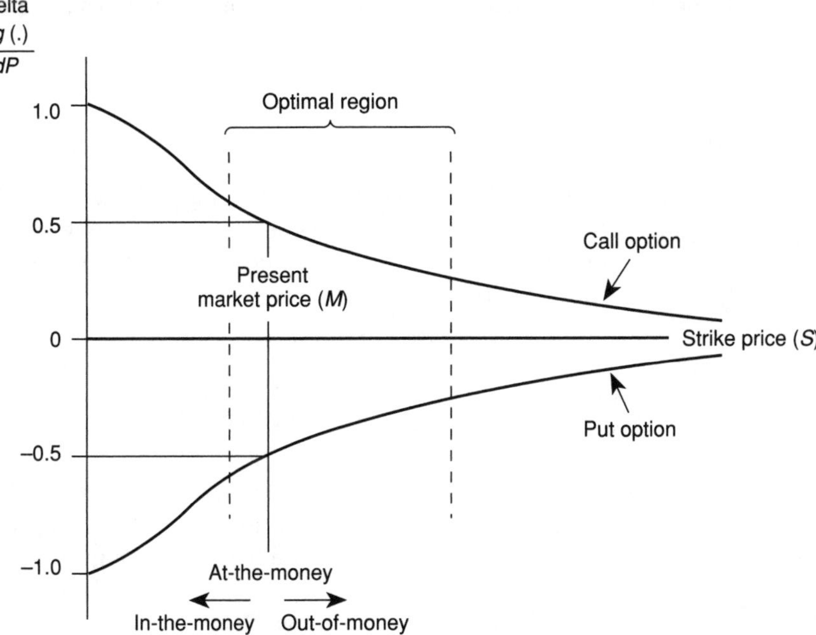

the delta will be close to 0.5 and will converge toward zero as the strike price increases over the market price (out of the money).

For a given market price, the delta of a put option would be close to –1 when the strike price is much higher than the market price (in the money) because the option price curve will be close to the intrinsic value of the put option. When the strike price is equal to the current market price (at the money), then the delta is close to –0.5 and will converge toward zero as the strike price falls below the market price (out of the money).

If the optimum option contract is the slightly out-of-the-money contract, then the delta value of the call option is slightly below 0.5 and the delta value of put option is slightly above –0.5, and the delta value of put option is slightly above –0.5 in the optimal region.

Option contracts can be used to establish a *delta hedge.* The delta, or *hedge,* ratio indicates the proportion of option contracts to trade to hedge an asset portfolio, or rather it indicates the number of units of the underlying asset being hedged by one option contract.

Example: A portfolio of 1,300 Met Path shares is to be delta-hedged through the purchase of MP Feb 40 put options with a delta of 0.65. Since each put option is exercisable into 100 shares, the investor buys 200 put option contracts [= 1,300/(100 × 0.65)].

GAMMA

The *gamma* of an option indicates the marginal change of the option's delta when the market price of the underlying asset moves by one point. The gamma then denotes the second differential coefficient of the option price curve, with respect to the market price of the asset.

$$\text{Gamma} = \frac{dg(\cdot)}{dP^2}\left(\frac{\dfrac{\text{Change in premium}}{\text{Change in price}}}{\text{Change in price}}\right)^1$$

Hence the gamma is equivalent to the slope of the delta curve and indicates the stability of the delta value. The lower the gamma, the less price sensitive is the delta (and consequently the delta hedge). See Figure 8.10.

Since the delta value is a function of the market price of the underlying asset, the delta changes over the course of the option's lifetime. Consequently, a delta hedge must be modified on a current basis to reflect the new delta values. The gamma measures how stable the delta value of a given option contract is and therefore provides a relative measure of how frequently a delta hedge should be adjusted. See Figure 8.11. As seen in this figure, the option will typically have the highest gamma value when it is at the money, that is, out of the money or in the money options provide for more stable delta hedges.

FIGURE 8.10

Gamma as a Function of the Option Premium (Call Option).

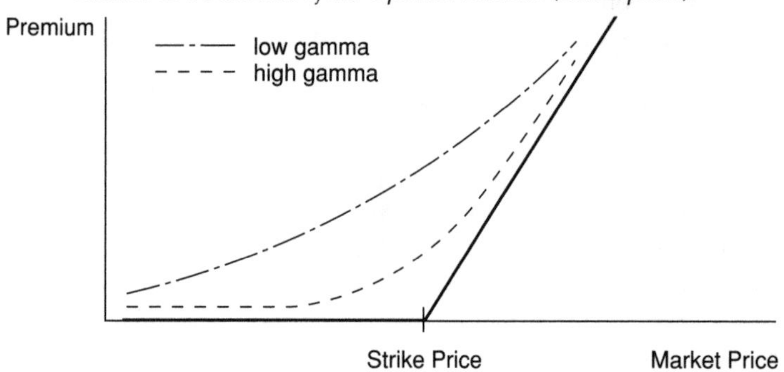

FIGURE 8.11
Delta and Gamma Values of a Call and Put Option.

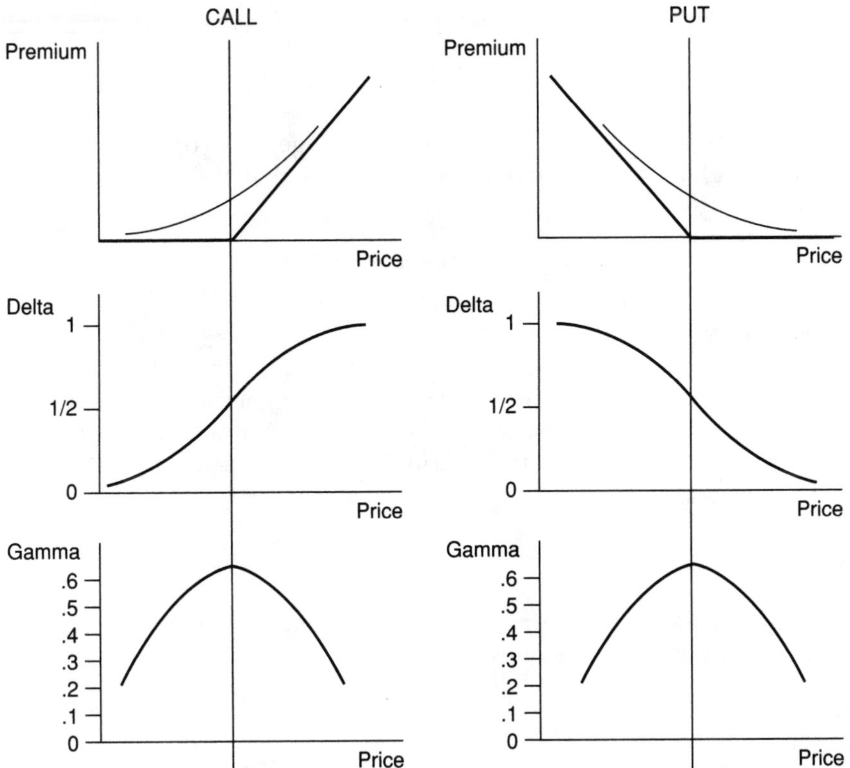

As discussed earlier, the option premium is a function of the time to the option's expiry date, the volatility of the price of the underlying asset, and the interest rate level.

THETA

The *theta* of an option indicates how much the option premium changes if and when the time to maturity is reduced by one day with no simultaneous change in the market price of the underlying asset.

$$\textbf{Theta} = \frac{\textbf{Change in premium}}{\textbf{Change in time}}$$

The theta value will typically be negative. That is, the time value is reduced toward the option's expiry date, and the relative loss of time value will increase as the time to maturity decreases. Theta tells the investor how quickly the option loses its value over time.

ETA

The *eta* (or *vega*) of an option indicates the change in the option premium when the volatility of the underlying asset price changes by a percentage point.

$$\text{Eta} = \frac{\text{Change in premium}}{\text{Change in volatility}}$$

The eta value is typically positive. That is, the higher the volatility of the price development of the underlying asset, the higher is the option premium. Eta can indicate the relative sensitivity of different option contracts and can be used to analyze various volatility spreads.

RHO

The *rho* indicates the marginal change in the option premium when the interest rate is changed by one basis point.

$$\text{Rho} = \frac{\text{Change in premium}}{\text{Change in interest rate}}$$

Hence the rho value provides a measure for the isolated interest rate sensitivity of a given option contract.

9

Hedging with Option Contracts

Futures contracts enable the hedger to lock in the future prices of underlying assets or liabilities within the maturity spectrum of the contracts being traded in the market, typically for periods of 3, 6, 9, 12 months forward and sometimes up to 24–36 months. Disregarding the potential basis risk, futures contracts make it possible to eliminate price uncertainties in the short- to medium-term perspective.

Option contracts, as opposed to futures contracts, do not lock in the future prices of underlying assets or liabilities, but rather provide an upper or a lower limit on a future unfavorable price development. Hence the hedger is protected against a potentially risky price change, but at the same time maintains the full gain, if the price development turns favorable. Some examples will point to the possible use of option contracts for hedging purposes.

HEDGING A SHORT CURRENCY POSITION

Example: A U.S.-based company is negotiating an important contract in May to be executed within two months and is therefore committed to give a firm pricing offer immediately. To meet the deadline on the offer, machinery worth 1,000,000 Swiss francs must be imported from a Swiss manufacturer to be at the production plant in the United States during the month of October. The Swiss manufacturer has promised to ship the machinery in September against cash payment.

To hedge the potential payment of Sw. frc. 1,000,000 in September, the U.S. company can buy Swiss franc call options up to the contract amount of Sw. frcs. 1,000,000. Assuming that the company approaches the Philadelphia Stock Exchange to buy the options, it would purchase 16 call option contracts of Sw. frcs. 62,500 each.

On this day in May, the Swiss franc foreign exchange rate is quoted at 2.0513 Sw. frc./US$ (0.4875 US$/Sw. frc.). In the present situation the company wants to hedge against a potential strengthening of the franc, which would cause them to pay more U.S. dollars for the import in September. The September call options are quoted as follows:

Strike Price ($/Sw. frc.)	*Quote ($/Sw. frc.)*	*Call Premium*
0.4800	0.0248	$1,550 (in the money)
*0.5000	0.0151	$ 943.50 (out of the money)

The company decides to buy the out-of-the-money call option because it is close to being at the money and the front-end call premium is considerably lower than that of the in-the-money contract. Hence for the purchase of 16 Swiss franc (50) call option contracts, the company will pay up front US$ 15,100 (16×943.50).[1]

The U.S. company wins the bid for the project and orders the machine from the Swiss manufacturer. In the coming period the expectation of a strengthening franc in general is proven correct, but there has been some exchange rate volatility. To assess the potential gain and loss position, calculations are made to get a feel for the sensitivity to the exchange rate movements:

Exchange Rate (US$/Sw. frc.)	*Profit/(Loss)*
0.4800	$(15,100)
0.4900	$(15,100)
0.5000	$(15,100)
0.5100	$(5,100)
0.5200	$ 4,900
0.5300	$ 14,000
0.5400	$ 24,900
0.5500	$ 34,900

In view of the fact that a change from the present exchange rate of 0.4875 US$/Sw. frc. to the break-even rate of 0.5150 constitutes only a 5% change in the foreign exchange rate, the premium of US$ 15,100 is considered reasonable by the company. The profit and loss profile is presented graphically in Figure 9.1.

The use of currency option contracts is a highly relevant possibility in this case, because the company knows the maximum cost of its hedge position, namely US$ 15,100. Should the underlying commercial transaction be lost in a competitive bidding, then the option position can be maintained without incurring further cost. The option contract simultaneously represents a potential gain from a favorable price development. Had the company instead hedged the currency exposure by the use of futures contracts, then it would be exposed to a new open position if the

FIGURE 9.1
Profit and Loss Profile of 16 Sw. frc. (50) Call Options.

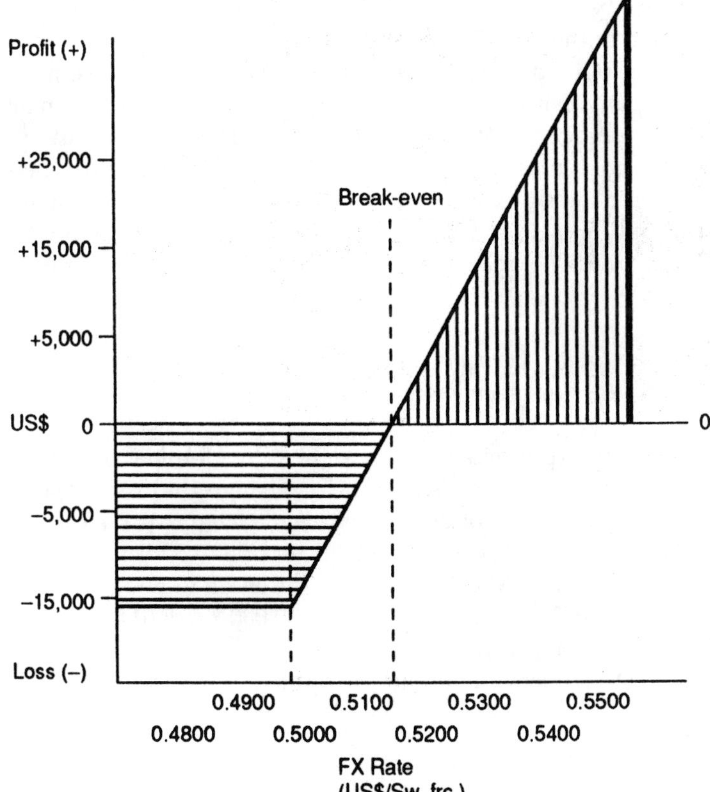

commercial transaction did not materialize. This new open position would then have to be reversed or covered at an unknown cost reflecting the prevailing market conditions at the time of closure.

The short Swiss franc position could also have been covered by the sale of 16 Swiss franc put options, which would incur a front-end premium to the company as a writer. However, this does not constitute a perfect hedge, because the option to sell francs to the writer lies solely with the holder of the put option, and if the exchange rate moves against the put option writer the potential loss can be excessively high.

HEDGING A LONG CURRENCY POSITION

Example: During August a German company is bidding for delivery of equipment in December to a U.S.-based manufacturing company. The value of the equipment amounts to US$ 2,000,000 to be received upon delivery of the equipment. Because the exporting company will have receivables in U.S. dollars, the worry is that the dollar will weaken against the German mark, because such a development will reduce the export earnings measured in the domestic currency.

To hedge the potential receivables of US$ 2,000,000 in December, the German company can buy U.S. dollar put options against German marks up to the contract amount of US$ 2,000,000. This kind of put option provides the holder with the right to sell U.S. dollars against German marks at a predetermined exchange rate. This is equivalent to holding a mark call option against U.S. dollars, since it provides the holder with the right to buy DM against US$ at a predetermined foreign exchange rate.

> A ***call*** *option of currency* (*x*) *against currency* (*y*) *is equivalent to a* ***put*** *option of currency* (*y*) *against currency* (*x*).

So the German exporter approaches the Philadelphia Stock Exchange to buy the option contracts. On this exchange the mark option contracts have a denomination of DM 62,500 each. Given that the foreign exchange rate in August was around 3.2669 DM/US$ (0.3061 US$/DM), we see that the number of DM call options to purchase to hedge the full contract amount of US$ 2,000,000 is 104.5 [($2,000,000 / 0.3061) / 62,500]. Hence 105 DM call option contracts are bought on the exchange.

Suppose the December call options are quoted as follows:

Strike Price	*Quote (¢/DM)*	*Call Premium*
0.3000	1.34	$837.50 (in the money)
0.3100	0.86	$537.50 (at the money)
*0.3200	0.46	$287.50 (out of the money)
0.3300	0.26	$162.50 (out of the money)
0.3400	0.13	$ 81.25 (out of the money)

The company decides to buy the out-of-the-money call option with strike price 32. Hence for the purchase of 105 DM (32) call option contracts, the company will pay up front US$ 30, 187.50 (105 × 287.5) or DM 98,619.73 (30,187.50/0.3061). To assess the option position the company carries out a profit and loss analysis reflecting the consequences of different developments in the foreign exchange rate:

Exchange Rate (US$/DM)	*Profit/(Loss)*
0.3100	DM (98,619.73)
0.3200	DM (98,619.73)
0.3300	DM 100,243.91
0.3400	DM 287,409.68
0.3500	DM 463,880.27
0.3600	DM 630,546.94

The exchange rate sensitivity analysis is presented graphically in the profit and loss profile in Figure 9.2. As shown there, the profit and loss profile of the call options this time does not follow a completely straight line. This relates to the fact that the dollar gain when converted into marks is impacted by the increasing US$/DM exchange rate. To get the profit and loss profile of the put options, we simply revert the foreign exchange rate denomination from US$/DM to DM/US$ as marked along the horizontal axis in Figure 9.2 (see Figure 9.3).

The long U.S. dollar position could also be covered by writing 105 dollar call options against receipt of a front-end option premium. Since the option to exercise lies solely with the holder of the call option, writing DM put options represents an imperfect hedge.

CROSS-CURRENCY HEDGE

Example: A French company is exporting goods to a UK-based sales company. Receivables of £ stg. 1,500,000 are expected in six months. To hedge the French franc value of the future pound sterling receivables, the

FIGURE 9.2

Profit and Loss Profile of 105 DM (33) Call Options.

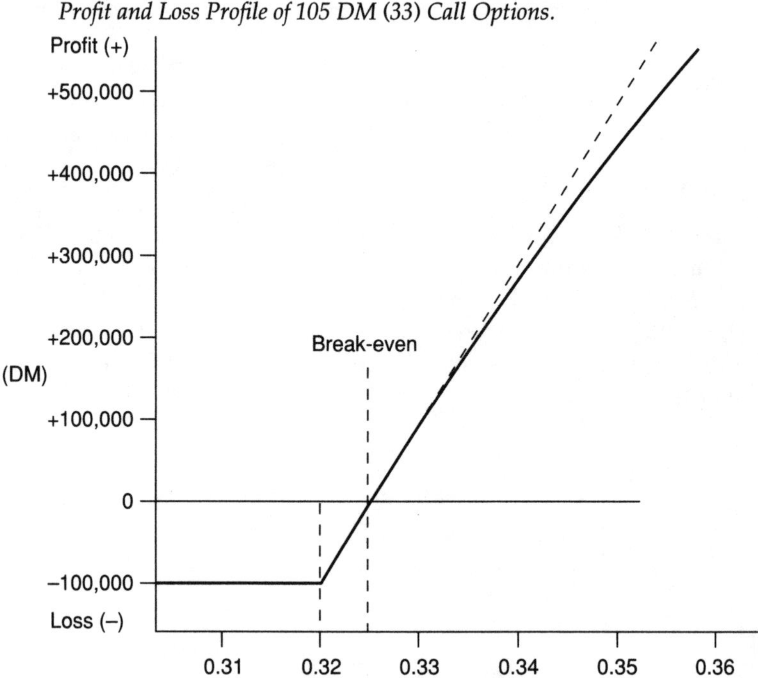

French exporter would like to buy pound put options against French francs in an amount equivalent to the face value of the export order.

Because no option exchange market exists for pounds sterling against French francs, the French exporter must follow another route—namely, buying pound put options against U.S. dollars—for example, on the Philadelphia Stock Exchange—and at the same time buying franc call options against U.S. dollars. Thus the exporter (the option holder) has the right to sell pound sterling against U.S. dollars at a predetermined exchange rate, and concurrently maintains the right to buy French francs against U.S. dollars at a predetermined rate.

The six-month pound sterling put option is quoted as follows:

Strike Price (U.S.$/£ stg.)	*Quote (¢/£ stg.)*	*Put Premium*
*1.05	2.20	$ 687.50
1.10	4.30	$1,343.75
1.15	7.40	$2,312.50
1.20	12.00	$3,750.00

FX Rate: 1.0971 US$/£ stg.

FIGURE 9.3
Profit and Loss Profile of 105 DM (3.03) Put Options.

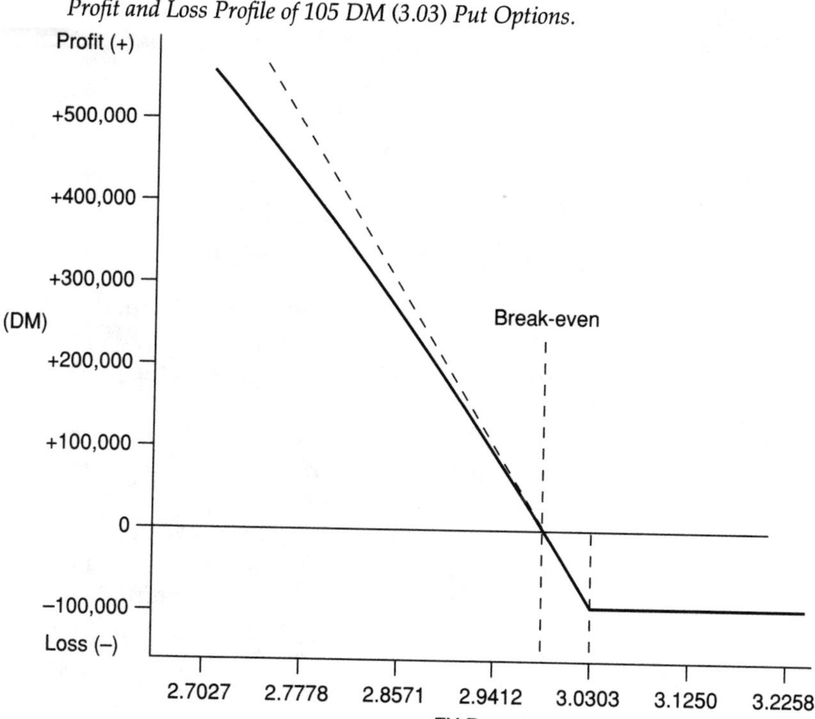

The 6-month French franc call option is quoted as follows:

Strike Price (US$/Fr. frc.)	*Quote (¢/Fr. frc.)*	*Call Premium*
*0.105	0.50	$1,250
FX rate: 0.1063 US$/Fr. frc.		

The French exporter decides to purchase 48 £ stg. (105) put options (1,500,000 / 31,250) and to buy 60 French franc (0.105) call options ([(1,500,000 × 1.05) / 0.105] /250,000). This should correspond to the purchase of 48 pound sterling put options against French francs with a strike price of 10.0 Fr. frc./£ stg. at a per-contract premium of US$ 2,250 ($687.50 + $1,250 × 60/48), that is, a total up-front premium of US$ 108,000 (Fr. frc. 1,015,992.47).

A profit and loss analysis on the 48 pound sterling put options against French franc was carried out:

Exchange Rate (Fr. frc./£ stg.)	*Profit/(Loss)in Fr. frcs.*
8.00	1,984,007.53
8.50	1,234,007.53
9.00	484,007.53
9.50	(265,992.47)
10.00	(1,015,992.47)
10.50	(1,015,992.47)

FX rate: 10.32 Fr. frc./£ stg. (1.0971/0.1063)

The profit and loss profile of the French franc/pound sterling hedge is illustrated in Figure 9.4.

Due to the double front-end premium to be paid on the pound sterling put options and the French franc call options, this type of hedge is expensive. This expense is also reflected in the low break-even exchange rate, which corresponds to a change in the Fr. frc./£ stg. exchange rate of around 10%.

Keep in mind, however, that the Fr. frc./£ stg. exchange rate can represent a whole scenario of foreign exchange rate movements of franc and pound against the U.S. dollar. Since there is no obligation to exercise

FIGURE 9.4
Profit and Loss Profile of 48 Pound stg. Put Options Against Fr. frc.

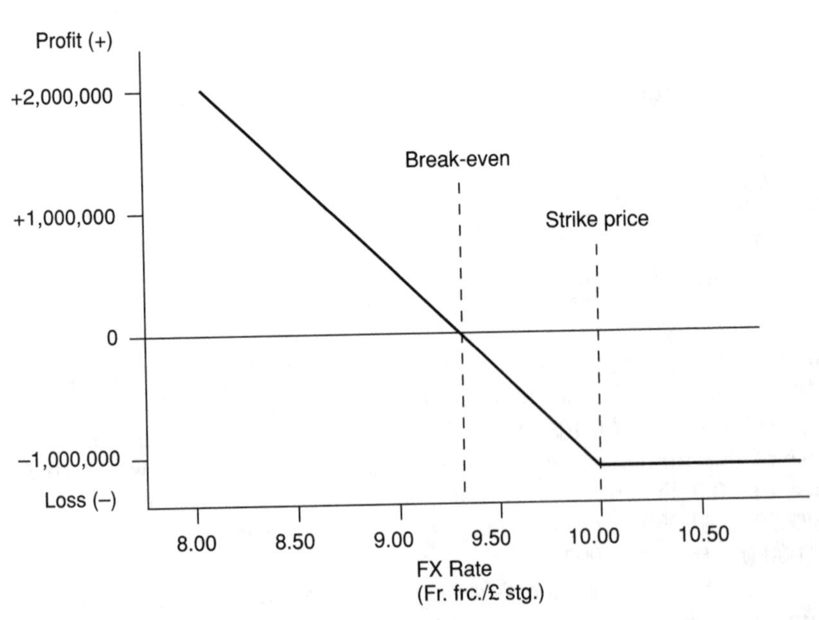

both options simultaneously, various scenarios will provide a better profit and loss profile than presented. The calculations here assume that the US$/£ stg. and the US$/Fr. frc. change simultaneously in opposite directions and thus represent the "worst" exchange rate scenario. In actuality, the hedge is somewhat more complicated to analyze because each of the two currency options should be looked upon independently and then analyzed vis-à-vis all the possible future cross currency exchange rate scenarios.

Looking first at the pound option, the purchase of 48 pound 31,250 put option contracts requires an initial premium of US$ 33,000 (48 × $687.50). The corresponding profit and loss analysis for different foreign exchange rate developments is as follows.

Exchange Rate (US$/£ stg.)	*Profit/Loss*
1.05	(33,000)
1.00	42,000
0.95	117,000
0.90	192,000
0.85	267,000
FX rate: 1.0971 US$/£ stg.	

Turning to the French franc option, the purchase of 60 Fr. franc 250,000 call option contracts results in an initial premium of US$ 75,000 (60 × $1,250). The profit and loss analysis for different future foreign exchange rates is as follows.

Exchange Rate (US$/Fr. frc.)	*Profit/Loss*
0.105	(75,000)
0.110	0
0.115	75,000
0.120	150,000
0.125	225,000
FX rate: 0.1063 US$/Fr. frc.	

The two options' profit and loss profiles are illustrated in Figures 9.5 and 9.6. The combination of the two profiles are presented in Figure 9.7, with the cross-currency exchange rate corresponding to 10.00 Fr. frc./£ stg.

The next step would be to analyze the potential Fr. frc./£ stg. foreign exchange rate development. What is interesting is to look at the locked-in foreign exchange rate of 10.00 Fr. frc./£ stg., made up of the

FIGURE 9.5
Profit and Loss Profile of 48 £ stg. Put Options.

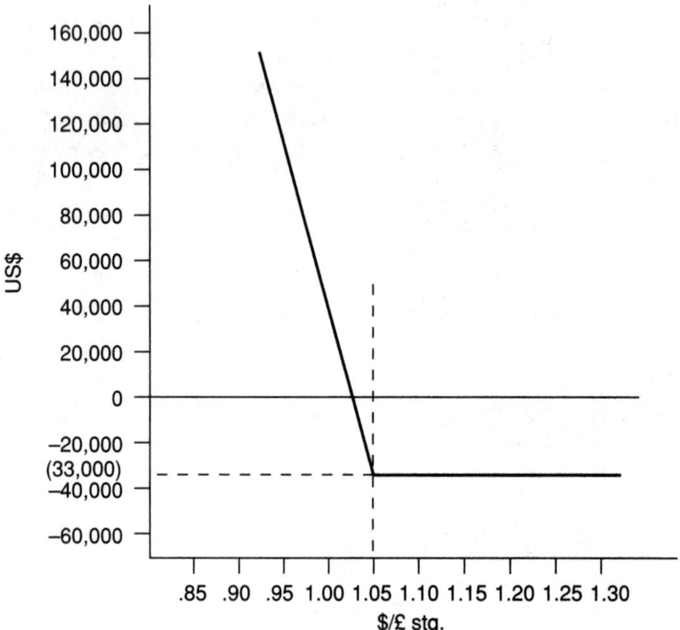

FIGURE 9.6
Profit and Loss Profile of 60 Fr. frc. Call Options.

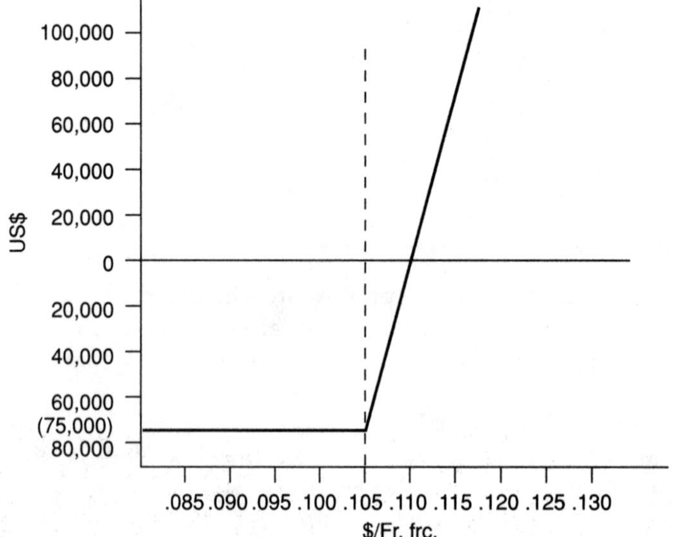

FIGURE 9.7
Combination of the Two Profiles—Cross-Currency Exchange Rate 10.00 Fr. frc./£ stg.

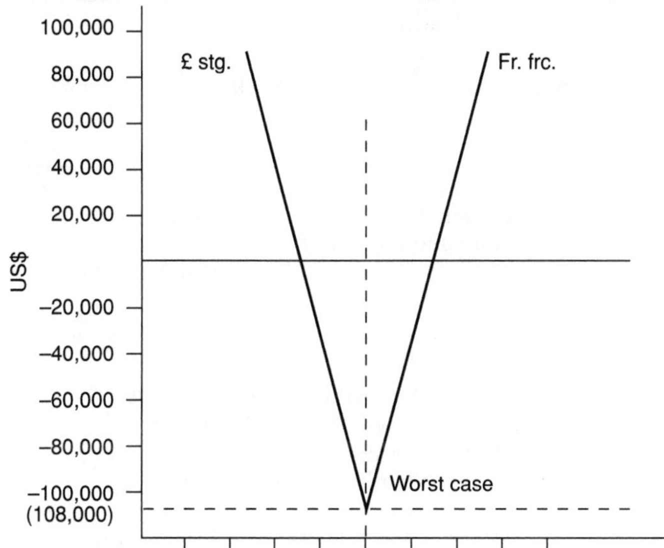

combined strike prices of the pound put option and the franc call option. and potential deviations from this exchange rate, whether resulting in a higher or a lower rate.

To simplify further analysis, let x represent the US\$/£ stg. exchange rate and y, the US\$/Fr. frc. rate. At the combined strike price, the relationship could be expressed in a simple manner as follows:

$$x/y = 10$$

or

$$y = 1/10 \times x$$

In a graphical form, this relationship appears as shown in Figure 9.8. All combinations of the US\$/£ stg. and the US\$/Fr. frc. rates that corre-

FIGURE 9.8
Relationship of US\$/£ stg. to US\$/Fr. frc. exchange rate.

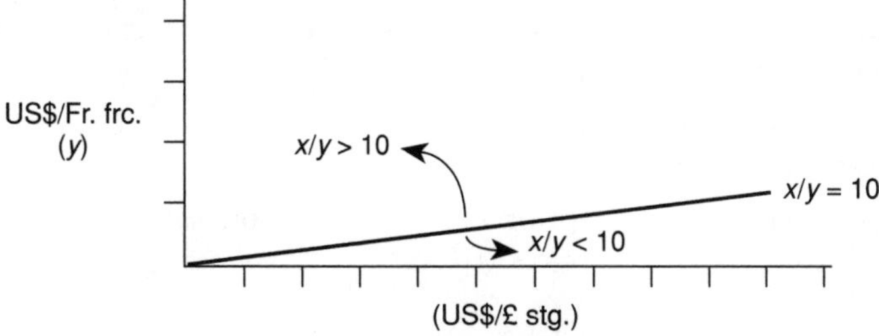

spond to a cross currency rate of Fr. frc./£ stg. of 10.00 are contained on the straight line. Exchange rate combinations leading to a cross currency rate in excess of 10.00 Fr. frc./£ stg. are contained above the straight line, and exchange rate combinations leading to a cross currency rate below 10.00 Fr. frc./£ stg. are contained below the straight line.

The various foreign exchange rate scenarios can then be listed as follows:

I. Fr. frc./£ stg. = 10.00	Profit and loss profile illustrated by the combined profit and loss profiles of theUS$/£ stg. put options and the US$/Fr. frc. call options. The "worst case" is the combined premium payout of US$ 108,000.
II. Fr. frc./£ stg. > 10.00	1. $/£ stg. increases and $/Fr. frc. decreases, flat cost line of US$ 108,000.
	2. $/£ stg. increases faster than $/Fr. frc. profit curve will follow $/Fr. frc. profit profile.
	3. $/Fr. frc. decreases faster than $/£ stg. profit curve will follow the $/£ stg. profile.
III. Fr. frc./£ stg. < 10.00	1. $/£ stg. decreases and $/Fr. frc. increases, combined gains of $/£ stg. and $/Fr. frc. profit profiles.
	2. $/£ stg. decreases faster than $/Fr. frc., gain will follow $/£ stg. profit profile.
	3. $/Fr. frc. increases faster than $/£ stg., gain will follow $/Fr. frc. profit profile.

This listing illustrates the complexity of cross currency hedging using traditional currency options against U.S. dollars. It also explains why it can be an advantage to develop cross currency option contracts like the German mark/Japanese yen cross-currency option contract on the PLHX.

Double Option Strategies

Before demonstrating the use of double option strategies for hedging, let us take a closer look at the "brokers' language" for various types of hedging strategies.

- A *bullish* option strategy is based on the expectation of an increase in the price of the underlying commodity.
- Conversely, a *bearish* option strategy assumes a decrease in the price of the underlying commodity.
- In a *vertical* option strategy, the option contracts have the same expiration dates but differing strike prices.

- Conversely, in a *horizontal* option strategy (often termed a *calendar spread*) the option contracts have the same strike price but differing expiration dates. Hereby the option trader can take advantage of the time development of the option premium and the price of the underlying commodity.

Vertical Bull Spread

A *vertical bull spread* can be established to hedge a *short* position in the underlying commodity. In the single option strategy, a short exposure is hedged by buying a call option. If an increase in the price of the underlying commodity is expected (a bullish market), the likelihood that a put with a lower strike price will be exercised is relatively low. So the hedger concurrently writes a put option against receipt of the option premium. The profit and loss profile of a vertical bull spread—that is, the combination of profiles of the put option and the call option—is illustrated in Figure 9.9.

Vertical Bear Spread

A *vertical bear spread* can be established to hedge a *long* exposure of the underlying commodity. In the single option strategy, a long exposure is hedged by buying a put option. However, since expectations point to a decrease in the price of the underlying commodity (a bearish market), the likelihood that a call option with a higher strike price will be exercised is limited. So the hedger concurrently writes a call option against receipt of the option premium. The profit and loss profile of a vertical bear spread can be illustrated graphically by combining the profit and loss profiles of the put and call options (see Figure 9.10).

The hedging strategies discussed so far are summarized in Table 9.1.

Straddle

A *straddle* position is established by buying a call option and a put option with the same strike prices. This option position gives the holder the right to buy the underlying commodity at a predetermined price, which is an advantage if the commodity's price escalates. Simultaneously the holder has the right to sell the commodity at a predetermined price, which is an advantage if the commodity's price collapses. Hence buying a straddle position will be advantageous when the price development is very volatile but with no distinct trend. The profit and loss profile of the straddle position, shown in Figure 9.11, is obtained by combining the profit and loss profiles of the call and put options.

Strangle

A *strangle* position is similar to the straddle position in that it entails the simultaneous purchase of a call and a put option, but the two options

FIGURE 9.9
The Profit and Loss Profile of a Vertical Bull Spread.

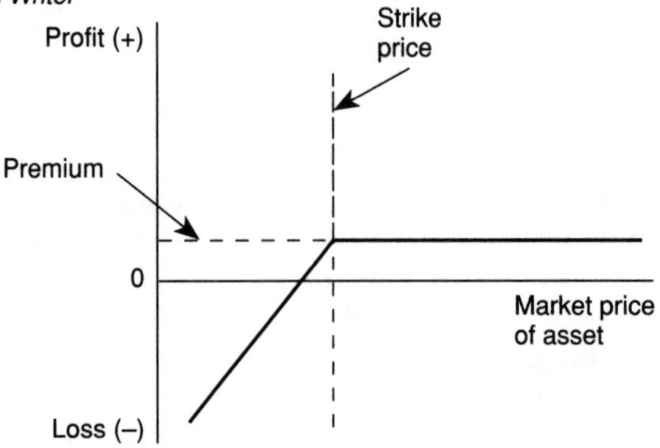

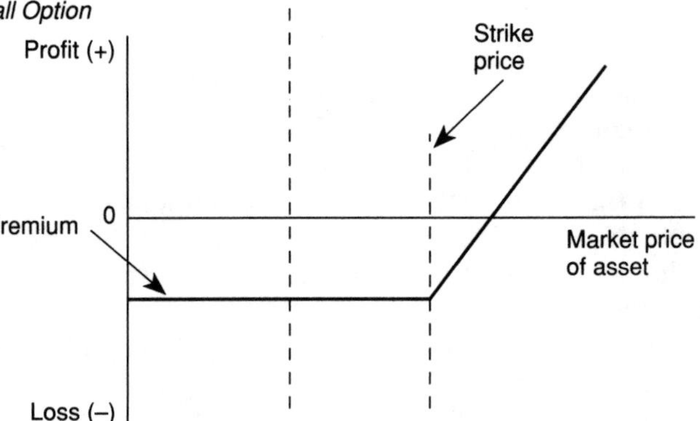

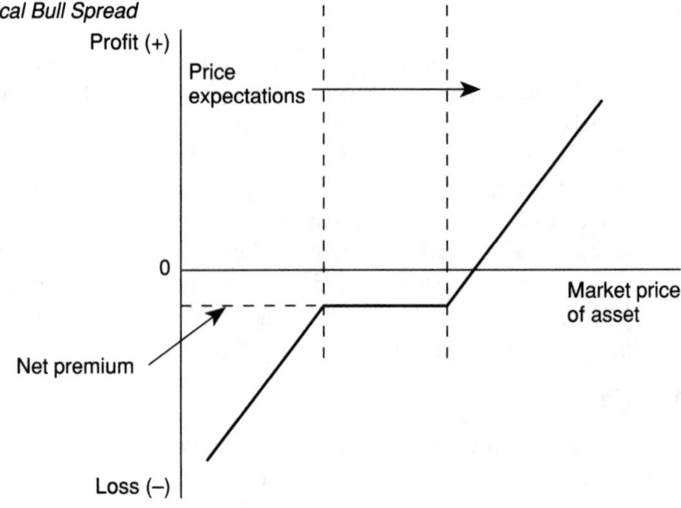

FIGURE 9.10
Profit and Loss Profile of a Vertical Bear Spread

1. *Holder of a Put Option*

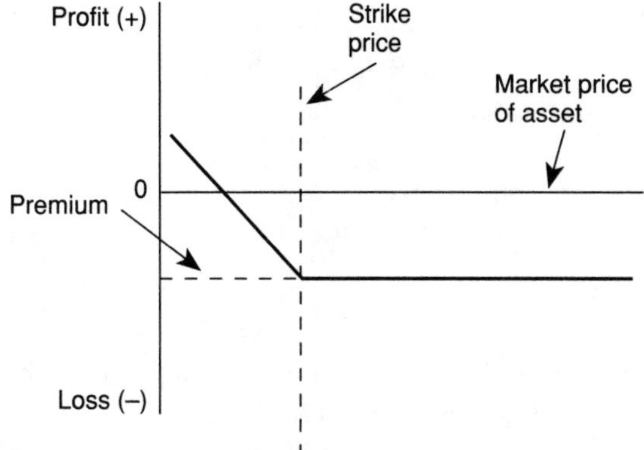

2. *Call Option Writer*

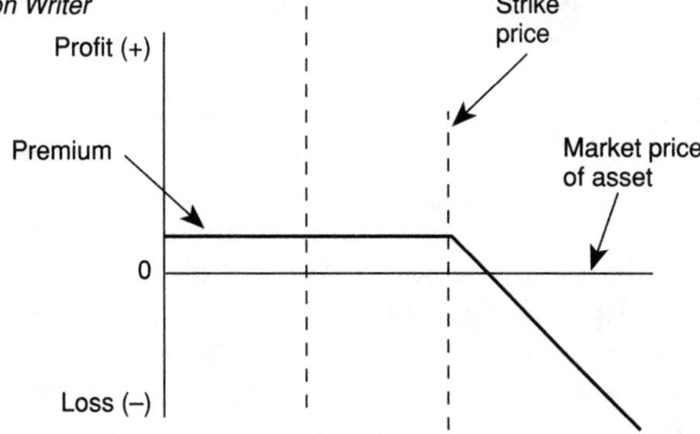

3. *Vertical Bear Spread*

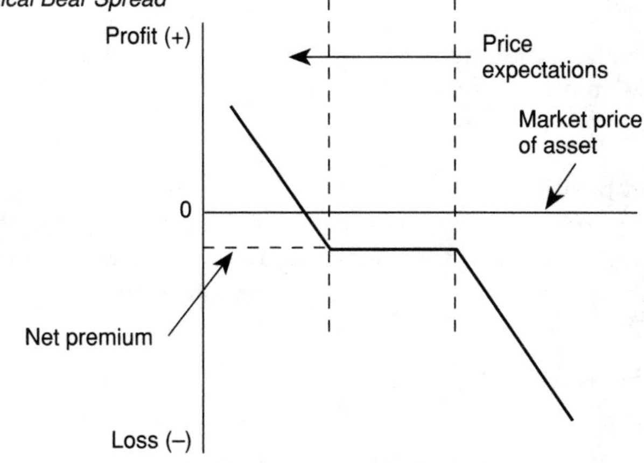

TABLE 9.1
Option Hedging Strategies.

Single Option Strategies:	
• Long position	Buy put option, or sell call option.
• Short position	Buy call option, or sell put option.
Double Option Strategies:	
• Long position	Buy put option and write a call (put strike price < call strike price).
• Short position	Buy call option and write a put (call strike price > put strike price).

have *different* strike prices. The two option contracts would be bought at out-of-the-money strike prices to reduce the double premium cost, so that the strike price of the put option will be less than the strike price of the call option. The profit and loss profile of a strangle position is shown in Figure 9.12.

Butterfly

A *butterfly spread* position entails three strike prices. It is a combination of a bull spread and a bear spread, in which the bull spread utilizes the lower two strike prices and the bear spread utilizes the two higher strike prices. With the bull and the bear spreads created as discussed previously, Figure 9.13 presents the profit and loss profile of the butterfly spread. As shown in that graph, the butterfly spread takes the view of a volatile price development. Yet the position has both a limited risk and a limited profit potential as compared to the straddle position.

Ratio Spreads

Ratio spreads occur when the underlying contracts are traded in different quantities, that is, in different ratios to each other.

Ratio Call Spread

A *ratio call spread* position is established by purchasing a call option and selling two call options (ratio = 2) at a higher strike price. This position is relevant for institutions taking the view that prices will rise but not to extreme heights or at least not within the immediate future. Figure 9.14 shows the profit and loss profile of the position.

Ratio Put Spread

A *ratio put spread* position is established by purchasing a put option and selling two put options (ratio = 2) at a lower strike price. This position is relevant for institutions expecting that prices will drop, but not immedi-

FIGURE 9.11

Profit and Loss Profile of a Straddle.

1. *Holder of Call Option*

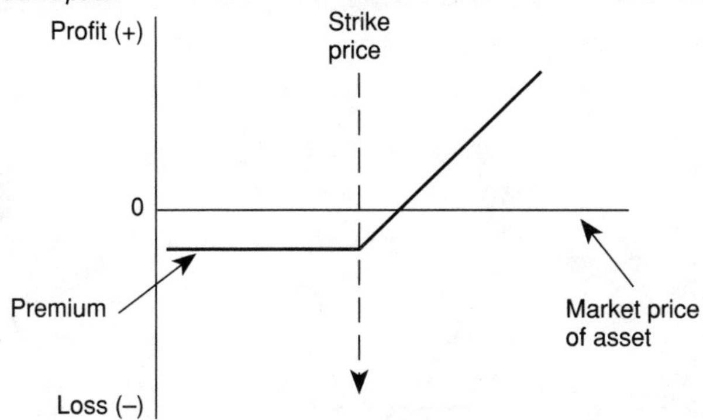

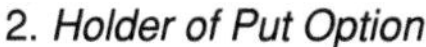
2. *Holder of Put Option*

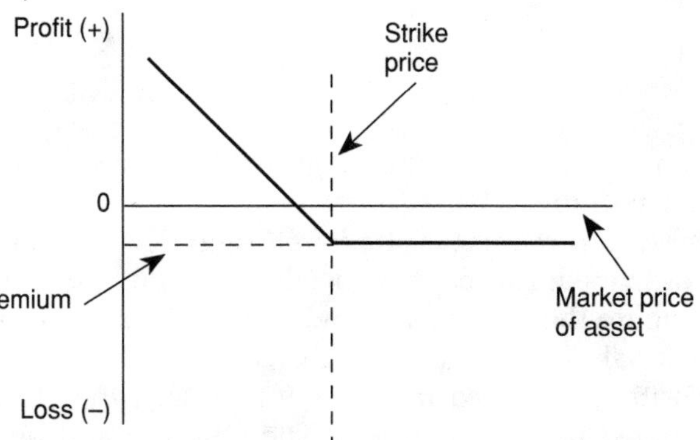

3. *Holder of Straddle*

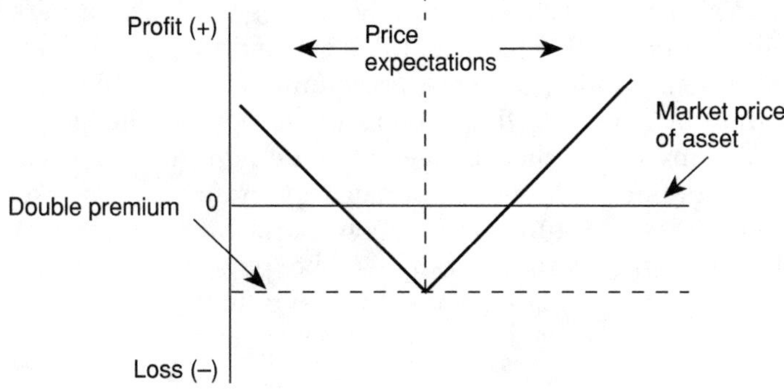

FIGURE 9.12
Profit and Loss Profile of a Strangle.

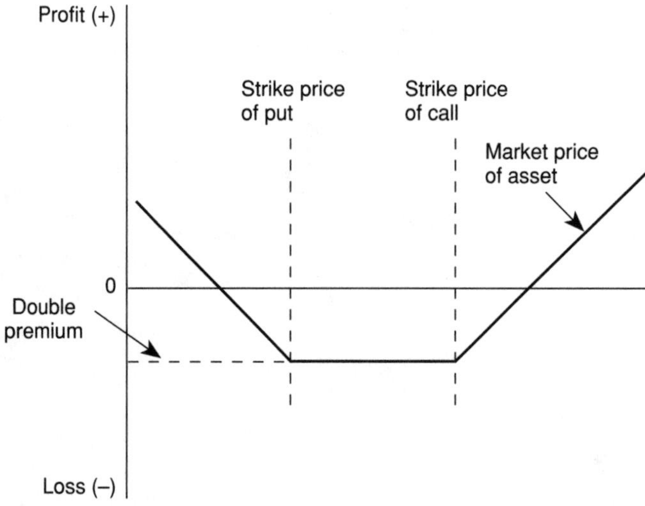

ately and not by a large amount. Figure 9.15 shows the profit and loss profile of the position.

Similarly, for example, a straddle position, or any of the other positions just described, can be ratioed whenever the different option contracts making up the position are traded at different ratios to each other. The ratio can take any positive number. A ratio of 1 corresponds to the straddle position described in Figure 9.11, where the call and put contracts are traded in equal numbers. The ratio call and put spreads can take different shapes depending on the choice of ratio, which can take any number, also being different from the number 2 chosen in the examples of Figures 9.14 and 9.15, such as 1.7, 2.3, 4, and so on.

These option position strategies are summarized in Table 9.2.

The straddle and butterfly positions often represent hedged investment transactions rather than hedges of underlying cash transactions. These hedged option positions are pursued by professional market participants who use the futures and option markets for investment purposes. However, the positions can also be pursued by commercial hedgers, where the underlying transaction exposure is incorporated as one of the elements of the hedge position (see Appendix II).

Example: A U.S.-based exporter expecting the receipt of German mark payments has a natural underlying long position in German marks represented by the straight upward sloping profit and loss line (cash position) in Figure 9.16. By buying at-the-money put option contracts, the

FIGURE 9.13
Profit and Loss Profile of a Butterfly Spread.

1. *Bull Spread*

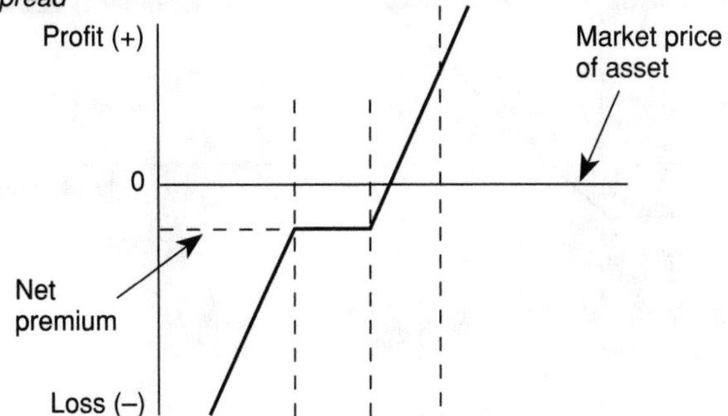

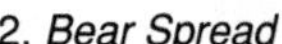

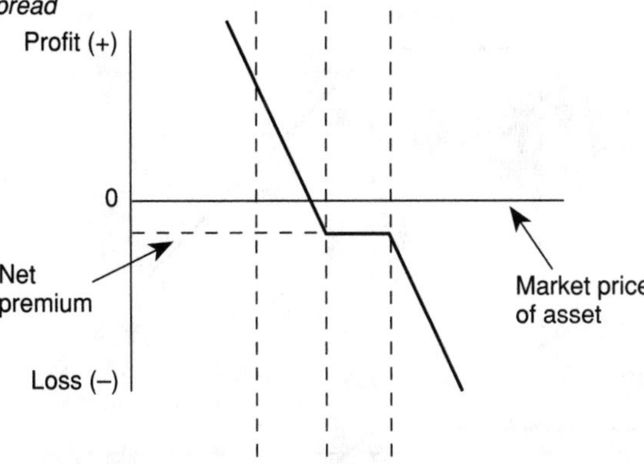

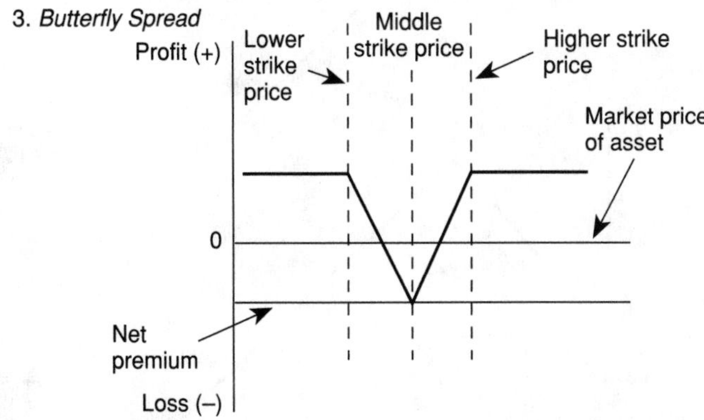

FIGURE 9.14
Profit and Loss Profile of Ratio Call Spread.

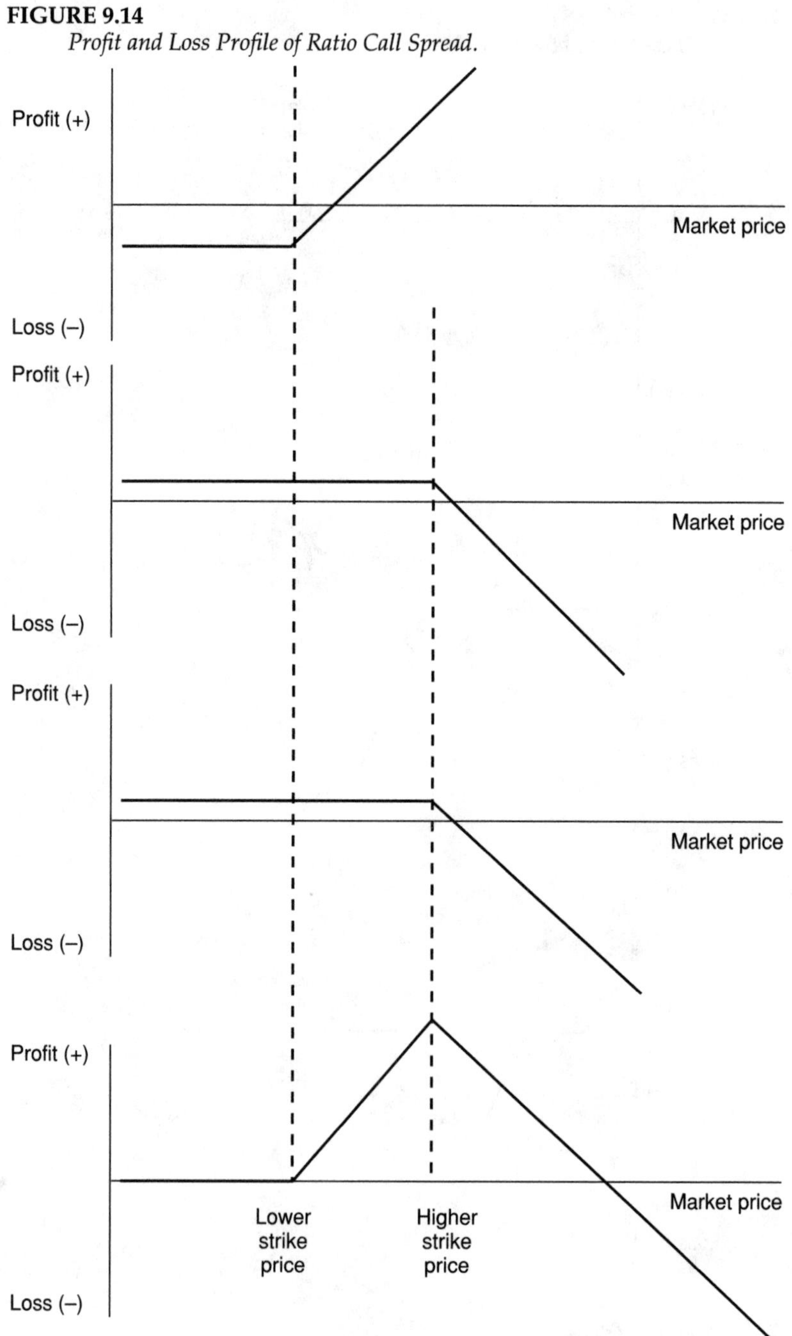

FIGURE 9.15
Profit and Loss Profile of Ratio Put Spread.

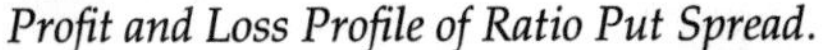

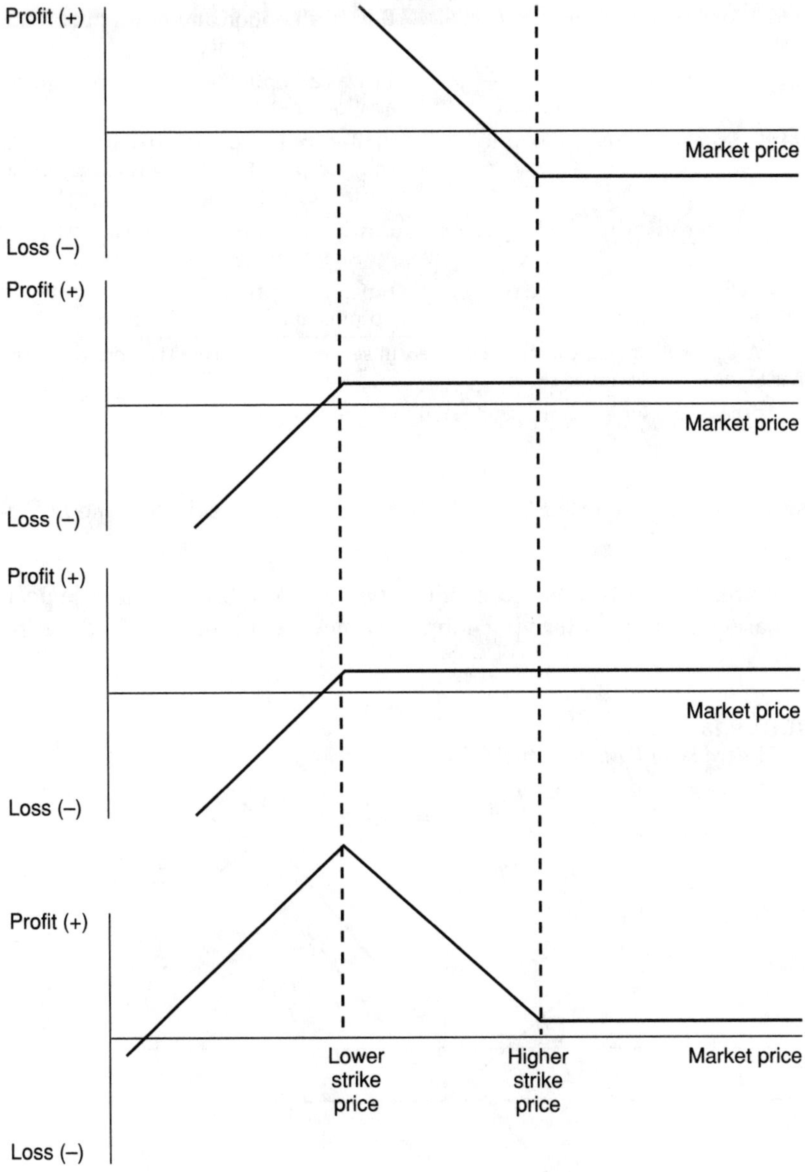

TABLE 9.2
Option Position Strategies.

Straddle (one strike price):	Buy a call option and buy a put option at same strike price.
Strangle (two strike prices):	Buy a call option and buy a put option at a lower strike price.
Butterfly Spread* (three strike prices):	Write a put at lower strike price, buy a call and put at middle strike price, and write a call at a higher strike price.
Ratio Call Spread** (two strike prices):	Buy a call option and sell two call options at a higher strike price.
Ratio Put Spread** (two strike prices):	Buy a put option and sell two put options at a lower strike price.

* A butterfly spread can be established in several other ways: This formula corresponds to the examples discussed.

** These ratio spreads correspond to ratio = 2. The ratio can also take any other number.

position can be converted to a bought call option. (The dotted line in Figure 9.16.)

Example: The U.S.-based exporter wants to establish a strangle position based on the underlying long currency position. This is done by

FIGURE 9.16
Hedged Long Position (Bought Call).

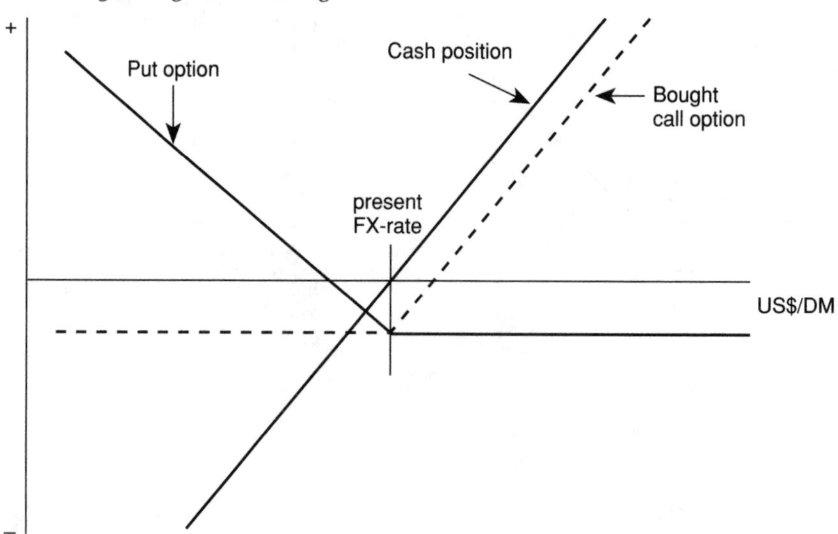

FIGURE 9.17
Hedged Long Position (Strangle).

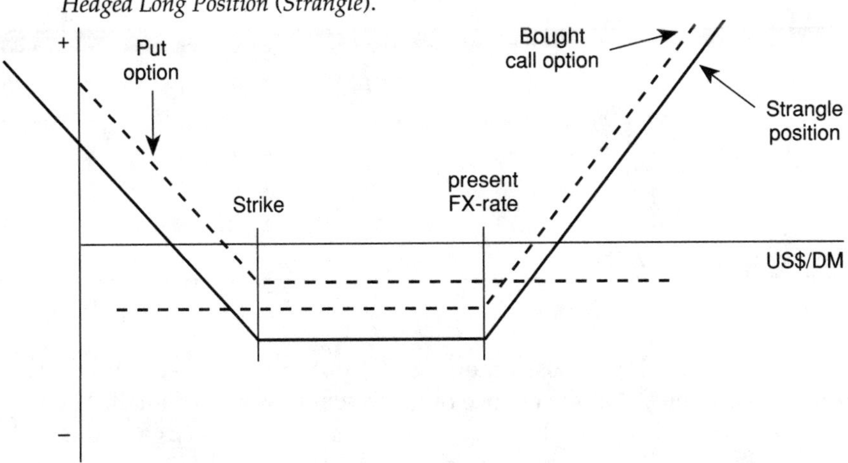

buying out-of-the-money put options, which, combined with the bought call option position, establishes a strangle position (see Figure 9.17).

Hedging a Short Currency Position Using Two Options

A Scandinavian institutional investor presently holds a securities portfolio in U.S. dollars, representing a total value of $10,000,000. The institution has taken the view that the German mark will strengthen against the U.S. dollar over the next year and therefore finds it opportune to switch the portfolio from dollar-denominated securities to mark-denominated securities. For various reasons the investor cannot switch the portfolio for three months. Applying a single option strategy to hedge the foreign exchange gap, the institution would buy DM call options in an amount equivalent to the total value of the portfolio. However, due to a very strong view that the mark will strengthen against the U.S. dollar, it simultaneously sells an equivalent number of DM put options at a lower strike price. The front-end premium income from the sale of the DM put options will count against the front-end premium to be paid for the purchase of the call options, thereby reducing the net premium for the hedge. At the same time, the likelihood that the put holder will exercise the options is considered very small, and so the downside risk is evaluated as being marginal.

Example: The three-month DM call and put options were quoted as follows on the Philadelphia Stock Exchange:

Strike Price (US$/DM)	*Quotes (US¢/DM)* Calls	Puts	*Premium* Calls	Puts
*0.29	2.57	0.26	$1,606.25	$ 162.50
0.30	1.34	0.54	$ 837.50	$ 337.50
0.31	0.86	1.00	$ 537.50	$ 625.00
*0.32	0.46	1.70	$ 287.50	$1,062.50
0.33	0.26	2.50	$ 162.50	$1,562.50
0.34	0.13	3.30	$ 81.25	$2,062.50

FX rate: 0.3061 US$/DM.

The institution chooses the DM (29) put option because it is so far out-of-the-money that the chance of exercise is reasonably small. The DM (32) call option is chosen because it gives a reasonable hedge in the bullish market. Hence the institution decides to buy 523 DM (32) call options [($10,000,000/0.3061)/62,500] and to write 523 DM (29) put options. Thus the institution will pay an up-front premium for the call options of US$ 150,362.50 (523 × $287.50) and will receive and up-front premium from writing the put options of US$ 84,987.50 (523 × 162.50). The net premium payout of US$ 65,375 is less than half the cost of the single option strategy.

To monitor the option position's sensitivity to changes in the foreign exchange rate, a calculation is carried out:

Exchange Rate (US$/DM)	*Calls*	*Puts*	*Bull Spread*
0.28	(150,362.50)	(241,887.50)	$(392,250)
0.29	(150,362.50)	84,987.50	$(65,375)
0.30	(150,362.50)	84,987.50	$(65,375)
0.31	(150,362.50)	84,987.50	$(65,375)
0.32	(150,362.50)	84,987.50	$(65,375)
0.33	162,147.50	84,987.50	$ 247,135
0.34	472,517.50	84,987.50	$ 557,505
0.35	787,287.50	84,987.50	$ 872,275

With this data, constructing a graphical presentation of the profit and loss profile is easy (see Figure 9.18). As shown in the graph, the institution has obtained a hedge against a strengthening of the mark against the U.S. dollar for a limited fee. Yet there is a downside loss potential, however small the likelihood might be for it to materialize.[2]

FIGURE 9.18

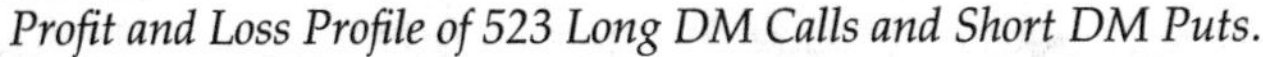

Profit and Loss Profile of 523 Long DM Calls and Short DM Puts.

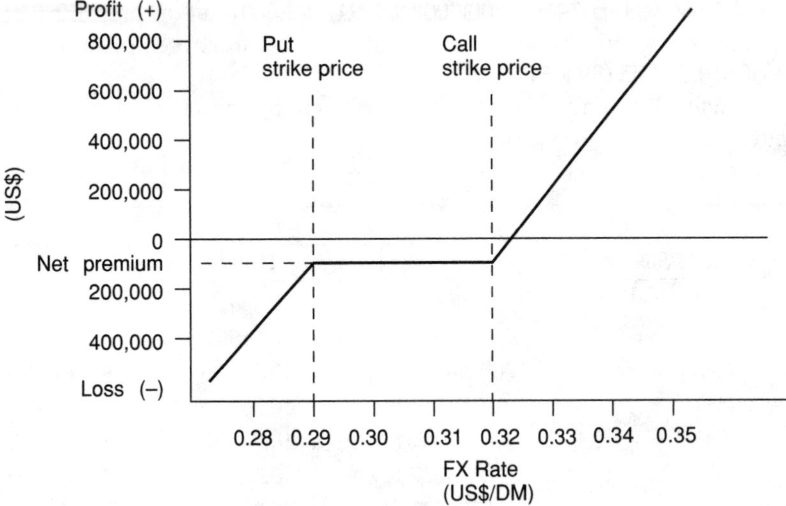

Hedging a Long Currency Position Using Two Options

An international trading company is expecting Swiss franc receivables to hit its Euro Swiss franc account in three months. It plans to use these receivables for a US$ 2,000,000 payment also due at this time. The company has a strong belief that the franc will weaken against the U.S. dollar and consequently would like to hedge this exposure. Applying the single option strategy, the company would buy a number of Swiss franc put options corresponding to the total amount of the dollar payment. Because their view is very strong that the franc will weaken against the U.S. dollar, the company also decides to write an equivalent number of Swiss franc call options.

Example: The 3-month Sw. frc. put and call options are quoted as follows on the Philadelphia Stock Exchange:

	Quotes (US¢/Sw. frc.)		*Premium*	
Strike Price (US$/Sw. frc.)	*Puts*	*Calls*	*Puts*	*Calls*
* 0.36	0.31	1.17	$ 193.75	$731.25
0.37	0.54	0.72	$ 337.50	$450.00
0.38	0.88	0.48	$ 550.00	$300.00
* 0.39	1.55	0.19	$ 968.75	$118.75
0.40	2.26	1.12	$1,412.50	$ 75.00

FX rate: 0.3594 US$/Sw. frc.

The company decides to buy the at-the-money Sw. frc. (36) put option and to write the out-of-the-money Sw. frc. (39) call option. Hence the company buys 89 puts [(2,000,000/0.3594)/62,500)] at a premium of $17,243.75 (89 × $193.75), and it writes 89 calls against receipt of a premium of $10,568.75 (89 × $118.75).

A sensitivity analysis on the foreign exchange fluctuation was carried out (see also Figure 9.19):

	Profit/(Loss)		
Exchange Rate ($/Sw. frc.)	*Puts*	*Calls*	*Bear Spread*
0.34	93,868.25	10,568.75	$ 104,437
0.35	38,266.25	10,568.75	$ 48,835
0.36	(17,243.75)	10,568.75	$ (6,675)
0.37	(17,243.75)	10,568.75	$ (6,675)
0.38	(17,243.75)	10,568.75	$ (6,675)
0.39	(17,243.75)	10,568.75	$ (6,675)
0.40	(17,243.75)	(45,056.25)	$ (62,300)
0.41	(17,243.75)	(100,681.25)	$ (117,925)

HEDGING A FUTURE SHORT INTEREST POSITION

A U.S.-based corporate entity is planning to raise funding in U.S. dollars some time over the coming months. However, the cost of funding is not known in advance and consequently the corporation is interested in hedging against an increase in the general interest rate level. How can this be done by accessing the options market? The European 3-month Eurodollar deposit option on the Philadelphia Board of Trade (PBOT), the Chicago Mercantile Exchange (CME), and the London International Financial Futures Exchange (LIFFE), for example, provide access to U.S. dollar interest rate option contracts.

Alternatively, by turning to the Chicago Board of Trade, the IMM, or LIFFE Treasury bond options market, the corporation can obtain an option position that hedges against an increase in long-term interest rates, as reflected in the Treasury bond yield. Suppose that the U.S. dollar loan is expected to materialize in December, that is, in four months. Then the potential borrower can buy a suitable number of December put options, which will give the holder the right to sell the Treasury bonds at a predetermined price. If the interest rate level increases—that is, if Trea-

FIGURE 9.19
Profit and Loss Profile of 89 Long Sw. frc. Puts and 89 Short Sw. frc. Calls.

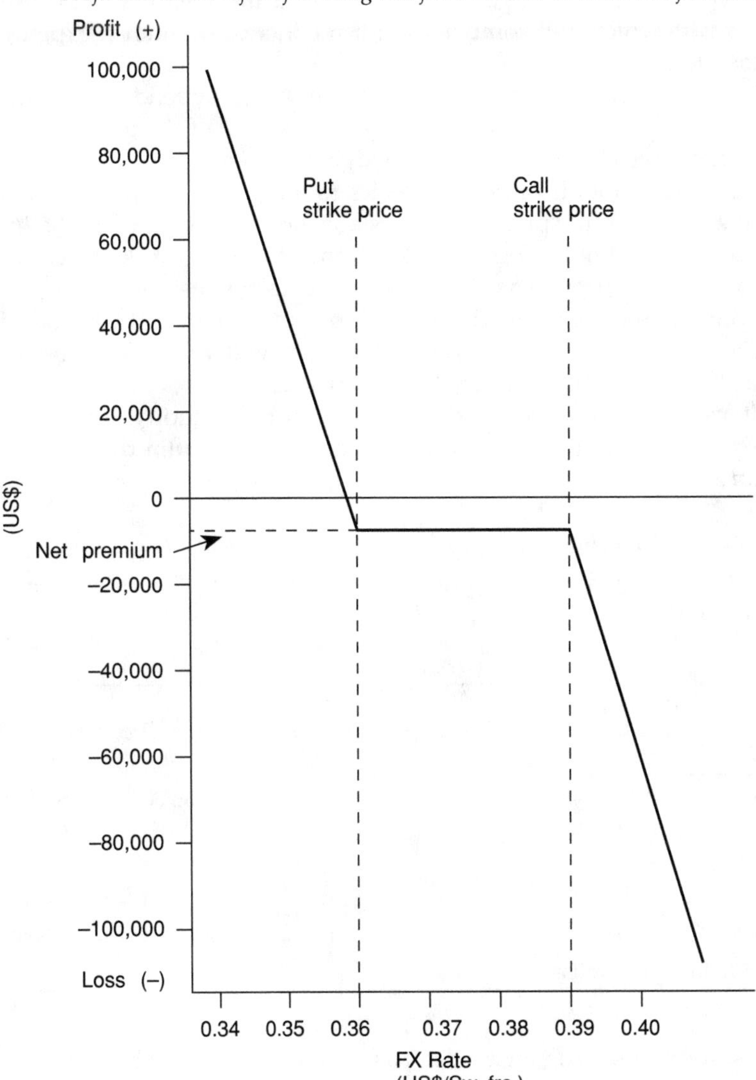

sury bond prices drop by more than the market expectation indicates—then the option holder will gain from exercising the Treasury bond put options, a gain which will compensate for the increased interest expense on the loan to be obtained.

The number of put option contracts to buy will depend on the correlation between the bond prices and the interest rate of the type of loan to be obtained (see Chapter 5 on cross hedging).

By applying double option strategies to this hedging situation, it is seen that a vertical bull spread can be established that will hedge the interest rate level within a certain band determined by the strike prices of the call write and put purchase involved in the hedge position.

Given that the borrowing is planned to take place over the Eurodollar market, the Eurodollar contracts obviously will represent a better hedging alternative than Treasury bond contracts.

Alternatively, let us look at an investor of net liquidity who is expecting to hold U.S. dollar assets in the Euromarket within the foreseeable future.

Example: The following option quotes on the LIFFE U.S.$ 1,000,000 3-month Eurodollar deposit contract are prevailing for December delivery, four months hence:

Strike Price	*Implied Market Rate (%)*	*Quotes (pct. of 100%)*		*Premium*	
		Calls	*Puts*	*Calls*	*Puts*
91.00	9.00	1.37	0.01	$13,700	$ 100
91.50	8.50	0.91	0.05	$ 9,100	$ 500
*92.50	8.00	0.50	0.14	$ 5,000	$1,400
*92.50	7.50	0.22	0.36	$ 2,200	$3,600
93.00	7.00	0.06	0.70	$ 600	$7,000

Current 3-month Eurodollar deposit rate: 7.75% p.a.

The investor can hedge against a decrease in the interest rate by buying a suitable number of interest rate futures contracts. Similarly the position could be hedged by buying a suitable number of call option contracts, which will allow the holder to buy an equivalent number of interest rate futures contracts at a predetermined price at the expiry date. In this case a minimum interest rate will be guaranteed, whereas there is no upward limit on the potential gain from a possible increase in the interest rate level.

Say the investor is expecting to make a US$ 1,000,000 3-month Eurodollar deposit maturing in December the return of which should be guaranteed. The hedger could then buy one call option contract at a strike price of, say, 92.50 which is slightly out of the money and hence carries a lower premium. The profit and loss calculation of this call option hedge would look as follows:

Futures Price	*Implied Market Rate (%)*	*Option Premium*	*Exercise (Yes/No)*	*Gain*	*Net Gain*	*Effective Rate (%)*
90.00	10.00	$2,200	N	—	$(2,200)	9.12
90.50	9.50	$2,200	N	—	$(2,200)	8.62
91.00	9.00	$2,200	N	—	$(2,200)	8.12
91.50	8.50	$2,200	N	—	$(2,200)	7.62
92.00	8.00	$2,200	N	—	$(2,200)	7.12
92.50	7.50	$2,200	N	—	$(2,200)	6.62
93.00	7.00	$2,200	Y	$1,250	$(950)	6.62
93.50	6.50	$2,200	Y	$2,500	$ 300	6.62
94.00	6.00	$2,200	Y	$3,750	$1,550	6.62
94.50	5.50	$2,200	Y	$5,000	$2,800	6.62

The gain from exercising the option when it is in the money is calculated as the number of ticks gained multiplied by the tick value of the underlying futures contract. If the futures price at expiration gets toward 93.00, the price gain from exercising the option will correspond to 50 ticks. When multiplied by the tick value of $25 for the 3-month Eurodollar futures contract, the 50-tick amount gives $1,250 (50 × $25).

In pursuing this hedge, the investor has effectively secured a minimum rate of interest on the deposit of 6.62% p.a., whereas there is no limit on the upward potential for interest return.

Example: Consider another situation, where a borrower is to obtain funding of US$ 1,000,000 fixed to the 3-month LIBID and would like to hedge the interest payment for the three-month period from December. This could be obtained by buying a put option contract at a strike price of, say, 92.00 which is slightly out of the money and hence carries a lower premium. The profit and loss calculation of this put option hedge is as follows:

Futures Price	*Implied Market Rate (%)*	*Option Premium*	*Exercise (Yes/No)*	*Gain*	*Net Gain*	*Effective Rate (%)*
90.00	10.00	$1,400	Y	$5,000	$3,600	8.56
90.50	9.50	$1,400	Y	$3,750	$2,350	8.56
91.00	9.00	$1,400	Y	$2,500	$1,100	8.56
91.50	8.50	$1,400	Y	$1,250	$(150)	8.56
92.00	8.00	$1,400	N	—	$(1,400)	8.56
92.50	7.50	$1,400	N	—	$(1,400)	8.06
93.00	7.00	$1,400	N	—	$(1,400)	7.56
93.50	6.50	$1,400	N	—	$(1,400)	7.06
94.00	6.00	$1,400	N	—	$(1,400)	6.56
94.50	5.50	$1,400	N	—	$(1,400)	6.06

By engaging in this hedge, the borrower has guaranteed a maximum funding rate of 8.56% p.a. whereas there is no downward limit on gains from a decreasing interest rate level.

Let us turn back to the investor and take the view that the interest rate level is very likely to fall and that the likelihood of an increase above 8% p.a. is marginal. In this situation the hedger could buy the call option with strike price 92.50 to guarantee a minimum return and simultaneously write a put option at a strike price of 92.00, corresponding to the 8.00% limit. In this case the premium income from the put write will reduce the net premium payout on the position. The investor has established a vertical bull spread in the interest rate option contracts, which covers for an increase in the interest futures price but which concurrently takes a position on the downside movement of the futures price. So it does not represent a complete hedge.

The profit and loss calculation of the vertical bull spread is obtained by combining the profit and loss profiles of the preceding call and put options (see also Figure 9.20).

			Net Gain		
Futures Price	*Implied Market Rate (%)*	*Net Premium*	*Call Buy*	*Put Write*	*Spread*
90.00	10.00	$800	($2,200)	($3,600)	($5,800)
90.50	9.50	$800	($2,200)	($2,350)	($4,550)
91.00	9.00	$800	($2,200)	($1,100)	($3,300)
91.50	8.50	$800	($2,200)	$ 150	($2,050)
92.00	8.00	$800	($2,200)	$1,400	($ 800)

Futures Price	Implied Market Rate (%)	Net Premium	Net Gain: Call Buy	Net Gain: Put Write	Net Gain: Spread
92.50	7.50	$800	($2,200)	$1,400	($ 800)
93.00	7.00	$800	($ 950)	$1,400	$ 450
93.50	6.50	$800	$ 300	$1,400	$1,700
94.00	6.00	$800	$1,550	$1,400	$2,950
94.50	5.50	$800	$2,800	$1,400	$4,200

This is to say that, if the 3-month Eurodollar deposit rate increases above 8.00% p.a., the position holder will lose money because he will have to honor the put option. If the interest rate falls below 7.5% p.a., however, he will gain from exercising the call options (see Figure 9.21).

A borrower could establish a vertical bear spread. First, he would buy a put option, which would require payouts by the option writer in case the interest rate falls below the level indicated by the call option.

FIGURE 9.20
Profit and Loss Profile of a Vertical Bull Spread.

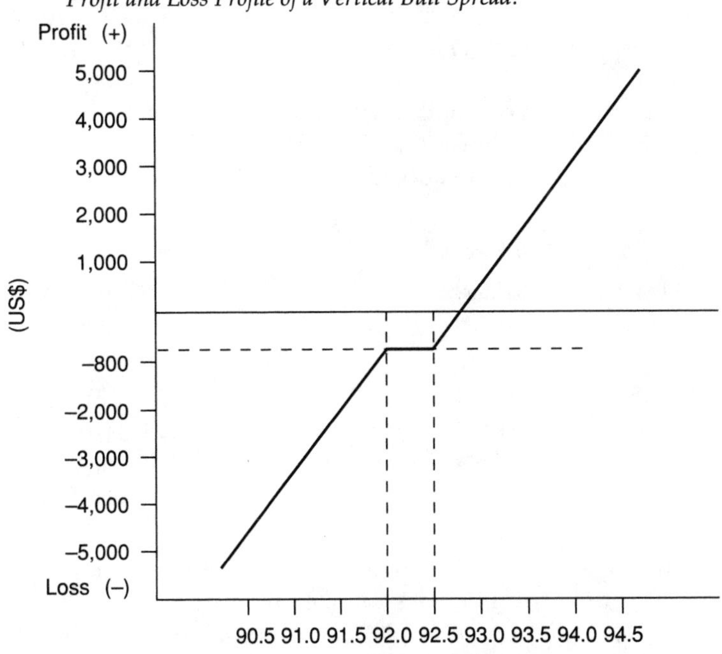

FIGURE 9.21
Profit and Loss Profile of a Vertical Bear Spread.

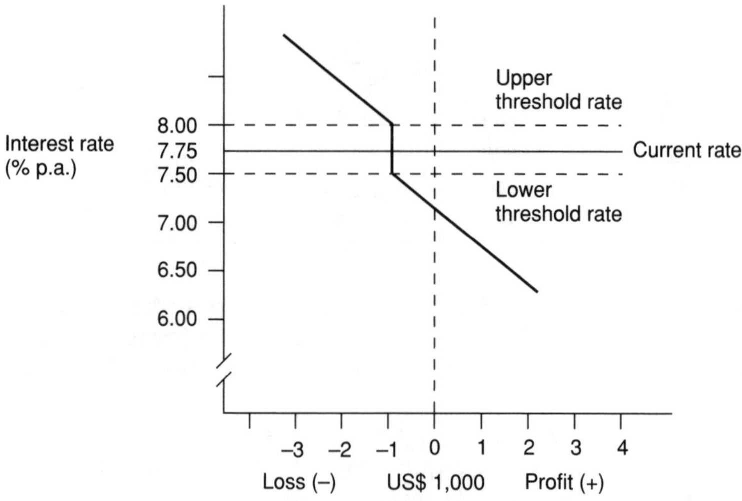

HEDGING A SHORT STOCK POSITION

Example: A portfolio manager is expecting funds of US$ 10,000,000 in three months. The funds are scheduled to be invested in a well diversified portfolio of corporate stocks. However, the fear is that stock prices in general will rise in the near future. This can be hedged by buying a suitable number of stock index call options, such as the S&P 500 index option contract on the Chicago Mercantile Exchange.

The 3-month call options are quoted as follows:

Strike Price	*Quote*	*Call Premium*	*Stock Index*	*Profit/(Loss)*
170	15.00	$7,500	175	$(299,700)
175	11.20	$5,600	180	$(299,700)
180	8.00	$4,000	185	$(299,700)
*185	5.55	$2,775	190	$(29,700)
190	3.65	$1,825	195	$ 240,300
195	2.35	$1,175	200	$ 510,300
			205	$ 780,300

The portfolio manager decides to purchase the out-of-the-money contract with a strike price of 185. The number of contracts purchased amounts to 108 [10,000,000 / (185 × 500)], and the premium to pay up front equals $299,700 (108 × $2,775) (see Figure 9.22).

FIGURE 9.22

Profit and Loss Profile of 108 S&P Stock Index Call Options.

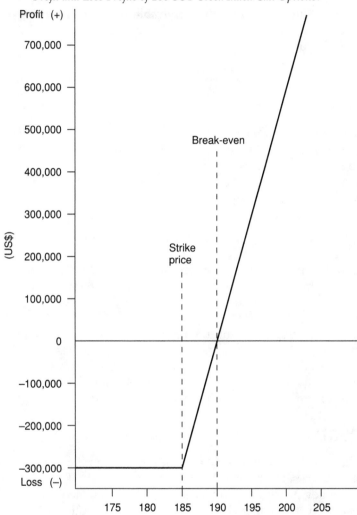

PORTFOLIO HEDGING

As already discussed, portfolio hedging often attempts to modify the invested portfolio to make it resemble a zero-coupon bond. The zero-coupon bond should correspond to the average life of the liabilities; that is, the duration of the invested portfolio is made to match the duration of the institution's financial obligations.

Assuming that the option contracts are based on underlying futures contracts, the analysis initially centers around the options' underlying asset, the futures contract. Hence, the applicable number of futures or option contracts to trade to adjust the duration of the portfolio is determined by the following formula.

$$n = \frac{D_z - D_p}{D_f} \times \frac{P}{F}$$

where

n = Number of futures contracts.
D_z = Duration of the applicable zero-coupon bond.
D_p = Duration of the invested portfolio.
D_f = Duration of the futures contract.
P = Value of the invested portfolio.
F = Price of the futures contract.

Hence, the n denotes the number of futures or option contracts on the future to be traded to adapt the duration of the invested portfolio to the duration of the relevant zero-coupon bond.[3] A positive n indicates the number of futures contracts or call option contracts to buy. A negative n indicates the number of futures contracts to sell or put option contracts to buy.

The indicated number of futures or option contracts apply to a long-term hedge of the invested portfolio where the contracts are held until maturity. In other situations, such as when it is difficult to determine a meaningful average life of the institution's liabilities, the investor might want to engage in a current or permanent delta hedge.

DELTA HEDGING

As already discussed, the option's delta indicates the number of units of the underlying asset being hedged by one option contract. If, for example, an at-the-money put option with a delta of ½ is used to hedge the underlying asset, then the hedger should acquire two put options. Hence, when the asset price drops by one point, the two put options incur a gain of one point. This delta hedge de facto establishes a long straddle position, which can be illustrated by the profit and loss profile of the position at the option contracts' expiry date (see Figure 9.23).

When using put option contracts with delta values different from ½, the hedged position will represent *ratioed,* or *skewed,* straddle positions (see Figure 9.24).

The characteristic feature of a straddle position, as discussed, is that it generates a profit if the price of the underlying asset is volatile. If the

FIGURE 9.23
Delta Hedge of Long Asset Position.

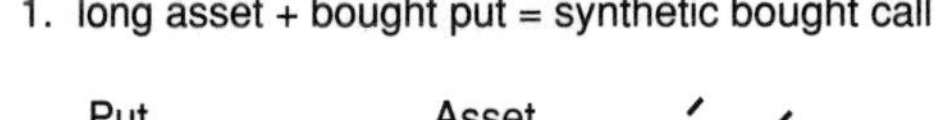

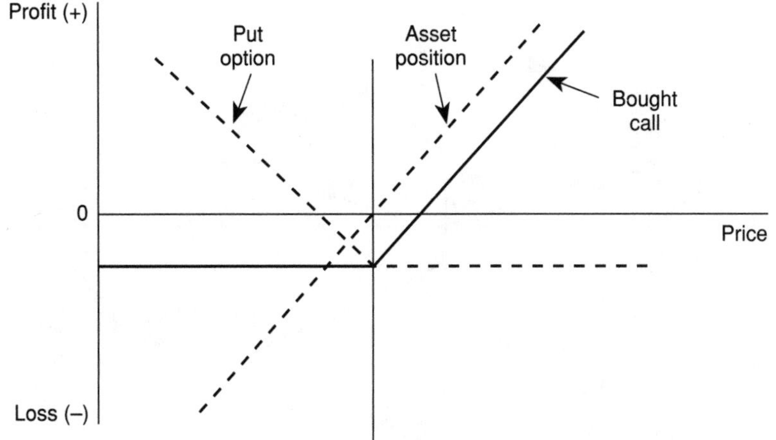

2. synthetic call + bought put = bought straddle
1 asset position + 1 put option = 1 bought call
1 bought call + 1 put option = 1 straddle

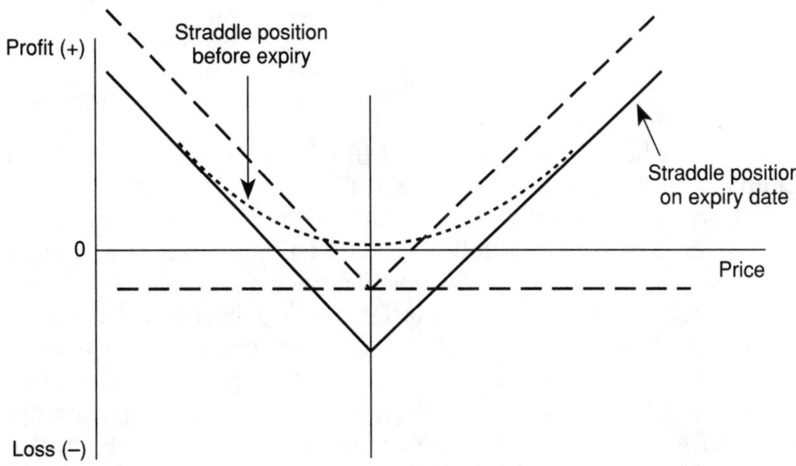

asset price increases, the hedger will buy more put options that are cheaper, because the put is more out of the money. Conversely, the hedger sells the now more expensive puts when the asset price decreases. So, when a delta hedge is maintained on a current basis, income is generated by buying cheap puts and selling more expensive puts. This is often referred to as *gamma scalping*.

FIGURE 9.24
Delta Hedge—Ratioed Straddle Positions.

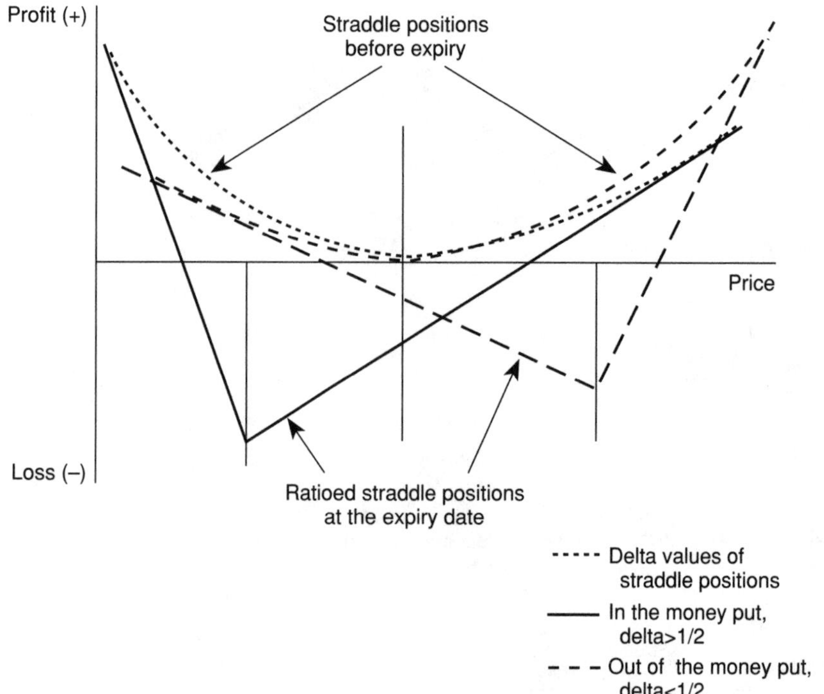

Example: A hedger has bought 20 MP February 40 put options at a premium of US$ 3.85 per option contract. The price of the MetPath share increases and the delta of the MP February 40 put option increases from –0.65 to –0.35. Hence, the portfolio of 1,300 MetPath shares is no longer delta neutral. The delta value of the position has increased by 6 [= (0.65 – 0.35) × 20] from 0. To adjust the portfolio to a delta neutral position, the hedger buys another 17 MP February 40 put option contracts {= [1,300/(100 × 0.35)] –20} at a premium of US$ 2.15 per option contract.

Subsequently the share price drops and the delta of the put option decreases to –0.85. The delta value of the position has consequently dropped by 18.5 [= (0.85 – 0.35) × 37] from 0. Hence the hedger sells 22 MP February 40 put option contracts {= 37 – [1,300/(100 × 0.85]} at a premium of US$ 4.87 per option contract. The current hedging transactions are:

- Bought 20 contracts at US$ 3.85.
- Bought 17 contracts at US$ 2.15.
- Sold 22 contracts at US$ 4.87.

A hedger that wants to manage and maintain a delta hedge on a current basis must be sufficiently professional to take advantage of the current premium changes on the put contracts and thereby generate a profit before the option contract loses its time value on the expiry date. A hedger who only wants to establish an initial delta hedge without maintaining it thereafter, however, must have a market view of high volatility for it to pay off.

CONCLUSION

As in the case of financial futures, the development of each option hedge must be closely monitored. One reason for such diligence is that it provides a full overview of the institution's collective hedging activities vis-à-vis the risk profile endorsed by the management board. Another is that it establishes a tracking mechanism that enables the financial management to learn from previous experience. Again it is important to know the specific trading practices of the option exchanges involved. Transaction costs, such as brokerage fees and margin requirements, can turn out to be important factors and must be fully understood.

Option contracts are interesting for hedging purposes because, unlike financial futures, they offset or minimize the downside risk, while leaving open the upside potential for gains. Double option strategies all take a view on price movements and therefore carry an element of downside risk, which should be carefully scrutinized. Single option strategies, however, provide holders with complete hedges.

For most institutions the taxation and reporting aspects are essential. In general the net premium on an uncovered option position is considered an investment, which will lead to capital gains or losses at maturity. If the option position is linked to an asset for hedging purposes, the cost of the hedge is considered part of the cost of trading the asset. However, tax laws change, as do reporting requirements, so consultation with local auditors is always recommended.

The option exchanges provide the financial world with liquid and efficient markets for a wide variety of option positions, which have a whole range of hedging applications. A disadvantage of exchange-traded options is that they are traded in standard sizes which will not always completely match the requirements of the hedger's position. Also, the limited maturity of option contracts sometimes restricts their usage. Nevertheless, a vast number of participants on the options exchange are investors who, through relatively small initial capital investments, can position themselves at an overall profit and thereby they become indispensable counterparts to the hedgers approaching the same markets.

10

Forward Agreements

In response to the continued expansion of the futures and options exchanges, international commercial banks and investment banks have developed a wide spectrum of financial services delivered directly to the client over-the-counter (OTC), as opposed to dealings on the exchanges. Usually the OTC services are tailor-made to the specific situation of the client and thereby break free of the restrictions imposed by standardized exchange-traded contracts. However, the financial institution offering the OTC services themselves hedge part of their net positions on the futures and options exchanges, and therefore the emergence of exchange-traded futures and options contracts have been an encouragement and, to some extent, a prerequisite for the development of OTC hedging services.

An international currency forward market has existed for many years. Today it represents a major trading arena, together with spot foreign exchange dealings in the treasury departments of banks and corporations around the world. Interest rate forwards, on the other hand, have developed in the wake of the expanded trading in interest rate contracts on the futures exchanges over recent years.

CURRENCY FORWARDS

Example: If an institution needed to create a forward cover for the purchase of, say, US$ 1,000,000 against Swiss francs in six months, it would buy US$ 1,000,000 spot against Swiss francs. The franc amount used for the dollar purchase would be borrowed at the 6-month money market rate, and the dollar amount would be deposited at the going 6-month U.S. dollar money market rate. The dollar interest received on the deposit will, at the end of the 6-month period, be converted into francs, and the receipts will be included in the Swiss francs payable against the loan plus interest (see Figure 10.1).

The following market rates are prevailing:

Spot foreign exchange rate	2,0000 Sw. frc./US$
Six-month Eurodollar rate	12.00% p.a.
Six-month Euro Swiss franc rate	7.00% p.a.

The forward foreign exchange rate, also called the *outright rate,* is equal to 1.9500 Sw. frc./US$.[1] The difference between the spot and forward rate is 0.0500, which is often termed the *swap.* The swap value is a function of the interest rate differential between the U.S. dollar and the Swiss franc, as shown in the following formula:

$$\text{Swap} = \frac{\text{Spot exchange rate} \times \text{Interest rate differential} \times \text{Number of days}}{360}$$

The calculation of the interest rate differential depends on the denomination of the foreign exchange rate. Here the foreign exchange rate is de-

FIGURE 10.1
Diagram of a Forward Currency Arrangement.

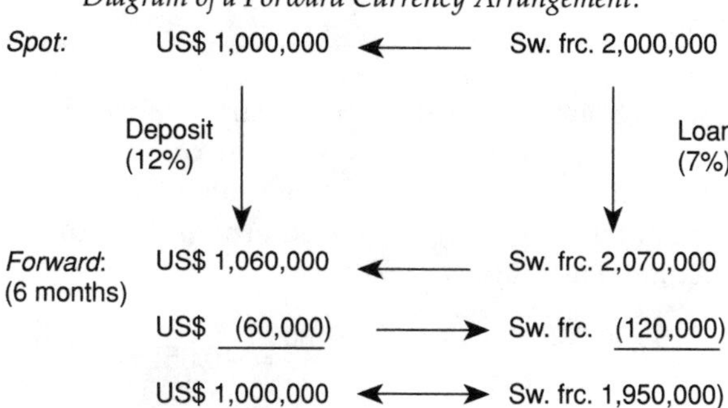

nominated as Sw. frc./US$, so that the interest rate differential is calculated as the Swiss franc interest rate minus the U.S. dollar interest rate, that is:

$$\text{Swap} = \frac{2.0000 \times (0.07 - 0.12) \times 180}{360} = -0.0500$$

The minus indicates that the dollar is bought forward at a discount.

Spot rate	2.0000 Sw. frc./US$
Swap	–0.0500 Sw. frc./US$
Outright rate	1.9500 Sw. frc./US$

In general the following rule of thumb applies:[2]

*The currency of the **higher** interest rate is always traded forward at a **discount.***

The banking system as a whole will manage its net open forward position by engaging in cover transactions in the Euromarket. So the swap calculation in the forward market generally will follow the interest rate differential approach that was just described and that is in accordance with the interest rate parity theory discussed in Chapter 4.

The preceding example was slightly simplified because it did not take into consideration that foreign exchange and interbank interest rates are quoted with two-way *bid* and *offer* prices.

Example:

	Bid	*Offer*
Spot foreign exchange rate (Sw. frc./US$)	1.9990	2.0010
6-month Euro U.S. dollar rate (% p.a.)	11⅞	12⅛
6-month Euro Swiss franc rate (% p.a.)	6⅞	7⅛

In the case of a forward purchase (bid) of U.S. dollars against Swiss francs, the dollars are bought spot at the offered rate of 2.0010 Sw. frc./US$. Francs are borrowed at the interbank offered rate of 12⅛%, and the equivalent dollar amount is deposited at the interbank bid rate of 6⅞%. The swap bid is calculated as follows:

$$\text{Swap (bid)} \frac{2.0010 \times (0.06875 - 0.12125) \times 180}{360} = -0.0525$$

Conversely, in the case of a forward sale (offer) of U.S. dollars against Swiss francs, dollars are sold spot at the bid rate of 1.9990 Sw. frc./US$. Francs are deposited at the interbank bid rate of 1⅞%, and the equivalent dollar amount is borrowed at the interbank offered rate of 7⅛%. The swap offered is calculated as follows:

$$\text{Swap (offer)} = \frac{1.9990 \times (0.07125 - 0.11875) \times 180}{360} = -0.0475$$

Consequently, the two-way forward foreign exchange quote is 0.0525/0.0475 (Sw. frc./US$).

By convention the negative sign is omitted, but we can see that it is at a discount because the bid swap quote is higher than the offer swap quote. Hence the outright rate is found as follows:

	Bid	*Offer*
Spot rate (Sw. frc./US$)	1.9990	2.0010
Swap (Sw. frc./US$)	0.0525	0.0475
Outright rate (Sw. frc./US$)	1.9465	1.9555

When an institutional client asks for a forward quote with a commercial bank, usually a spread will be subtracted from the bid quote and added to the offer quote. The spread compensates the bank for the transaction costs and the counterparty risk engaged in when closing the forward agreement.

Like financial futures in currencies, the forward agreement locks in the future exchange rate, but it also eliminates the basis risk inherent in any financial futures position. And, since markets in currency forwards exist in a wide variety of cross currencies, they have wider applications than do currency futures contracts.

PAR FORWARDS

Par forward is the typical term for a *flat rate forward* currency agreement. The par forward puts together a series of traditional forward currency agreements at different future dates and settles these forward agreements at the same forward foreign exchange rate. Hence, a flat rate forward enables a company to cover a series of exposures in the same currency at different future dates at the same forward rate.

Example: A French corporation making international sales has regular receivables in U.S. dollars over the coming two years. The forward foreign exchange rate converting U.S. dollars into French francs will gradually increase, reflecting that the U.S. dollar interest rate is lower than the French franc interest rate (see Figure 10.2).

FIGURE 10.2
Flat Rate Forward Currency Agreement.

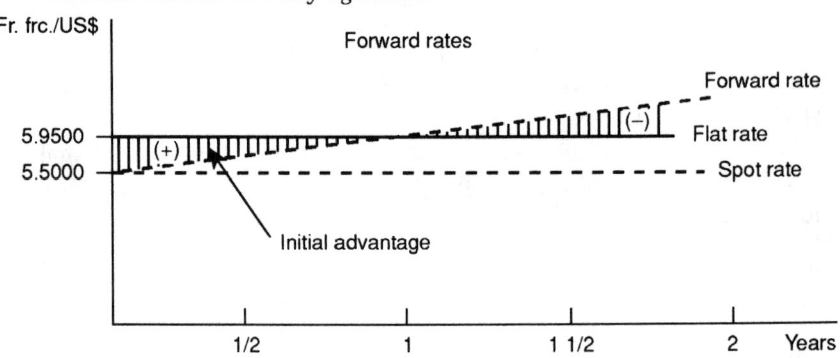

Hence the French corporation will get more and more French francs for the U.S. dollar receivables from the 6, 12, 18, and 24 months' forward rates. By incurring a flat rate forward, the exporter books the receivables at the same forward rate for the entire two-year period. At the same time, the par forward represents a cash flow advantage to the hedger, because the receivables initially are converted at a relatively higher forward foreign exchange rate.

> *When **selling** a **lower interest rate** currency or when **buying** a **higher interest rate** currency a flat rate forward provides an initial **cash flow advantage.***

Such features can, for example, be applied to move earnings from export receivables forward to earlier accounting periods in the income statement.

INTEREST RATE FORWARDS

Most developed financial markets today have an active market in domestic-currency-denominated *forward rate agreements* (*FRAs*). Hence many international banks offer FRAs in all the major currencies. Through the use of FRAs, an institutional borrower or lender can fix the future interest rate on loans and deposits for periods of up to several years, with the maximum maturity depending on the depth of the FRA market of the currency in question. As discussed in Chapter 5, the institution offering a forward rate agreement can cover the transaction through an opposite position in the cash market.

Example: We want to create a forward rate for a $1,000,000 3-month loan in three months' time (forward forward loan). So we would borrow $1,000,000 for six months and deposit the amount for three months.

The following interbank rates prevail on the money market:

	Bid	*Offer*
3 months (% p.a.)	10⅜	10⅝
6 months (% p.a.)	11⅞	12⅛

We would borrow enough 6-month dollars at 12⅛% so as to leave us with $1,000,000 after three months at a 3-month deposit rate of 10⅜% (see Figure 10.3). The break-even interest rate for the 3-month loan in three months is found to be 13.52% p.a. [($1,033,810.54 − $1,000,000)/ $1,000,000 × 360/90 × 100].

Conversely, if we want to create a forward rate for a $1,000,000 3-month deposit (forward forward deposit) in three months, we would borrow a dollar amount at 10⅝%, which after three months is to be repaid by $1,000,000. The dollar amount would be deposited for six months at 11⅞% (see Figure 10.4). The break-even rate on the three-month deposit in three months is calculated as 12.78% [($1,031,963.47 − $1,000,000)/$1,000,000 × 360/90 × 100].

Another avenue for the intermediary offering forward interest rates is to cover the position directly in the financial futures market. In this

FIGURE 10.3
Interest Rate Forward Arrangement (Asset Hedge).

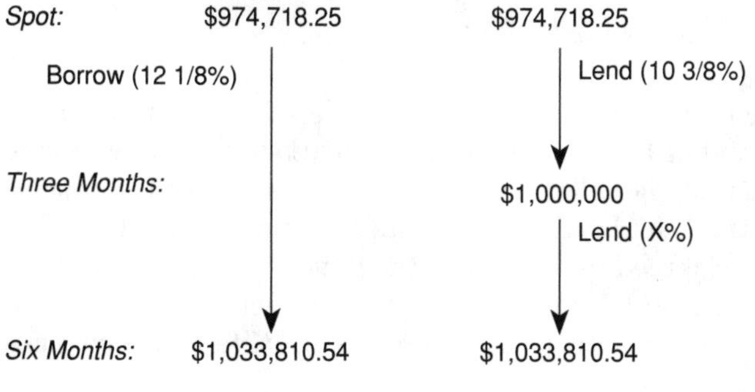

Spot: $974,718.25 $974,718.25
Borrow (12 1/8%) Lend (10 3/8%)
Three Months: $1,000,000
Lend (X%)
Six Months: $1,033,810.54 $1,033,810.54

FIGURE 10.4
Interest Rate Forward Agreement (Liability Hedge).

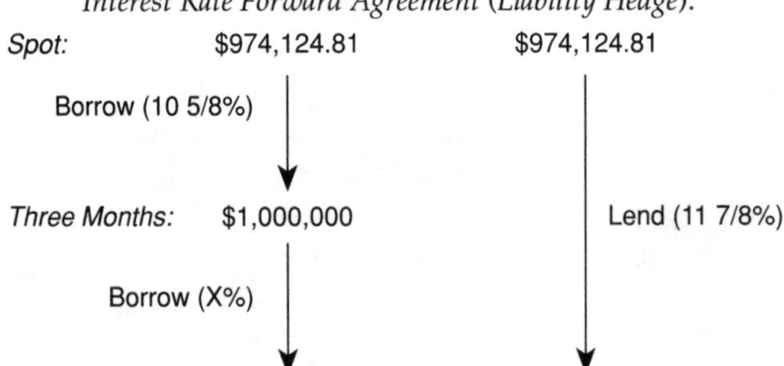

case the institution offering the forward rate assumes the basis risk of the futures position prevailing over the course of the forward period.

FORWARD RATE AGREEMENTS

A *forward rate agreement* (*FRA*) is a confirmed agreement between two counterparties to periodically exchange interest rate differentials on an agreed interest rate basis (the *reference rate*) on a predetermined currency amount over a given period of time. The FRAs are often offered with two-way bid and offer prices in the interbank market.

	Bid	*Offer*
3-month rate in 3 months' time:	10.56	10.70

When the FRAs are sold to counterparties outside the interbank market, the bank will typically add a margin or charge an up-front fee to cover handling cost and management of counterparty risk.

*The **buyer** of an FRA agrees to a future **borrowing rate.***

*The **seller** of an FRA agrees to a future **lending rate.***

The reference rate of an FRA is usually the applicable money market rate for the period of the agreement. If the market rate moves above the agreed forward rate, the seller will compensate the buyer with the interest rate differential calculated on the contract amount. If the market rate moves below the agreed forward rate, the buyer will compensate the seller with the interest rate differential on the contract amount. It is an advantage of the FRA that only the interest rate differential changes hands, whereas nothing happens to the principal. Hence, the FRA can be considered an off-balance-sheet instrument as opposed to forward forward transactions, which typically will require full balance sheet disclosure.

FRAs could in principle cover any broken amount and any future time period. However, a standard market practice confines the use of FRAs to multiples of full millions and in full monthly periods, such as the following:

Interest Period	*and*	*Settlement Date*
1 month	in	1 month
1 month	in	2 months
1 month	in	3 months
3 months	in	1 month
3 months	in	2 months
3 months	in	3 months
3 months	in	6 months
3 months	in	9 months
3 months	in	12 months
6 months	in	3 months
6 months	in	6 months
6 months	in	12 months
6 months	in	18 months
6 months	in	24 months

Table 10.1 provides a comparison of financial futures contracts with forward agreements offered in the OTC-market.

The FRA is settled between the two counterparties, the *buyer* and the *seller*, who thereby are able to hedge against interest rate movements. Typically a bank active in the interbank market will act either as buyer or seller with institutional clients. A buyer obtains protection from an increase in the interest rate above the agreed rate, and thus can secure a maximum borrowing rate. A seller obtains protection from a drop in the interest rate below the agreed rate, and thus can secure a minimum lending or investment rate.

The forward rate agreement is settled on the first day of the interest period. The *settlement amount* is determined as the difference between the market rate (the reference rate of the agreement) and the agreed forward rate for the interest period. The buyer will receive the difference in interest amounts from the seller if the reference rate exceeds the agreed forward rate. The seller will receive the difference in the interest amount from the buyer if the reference rate is below the agreed forward rate.

TABLE 10.1
Comparing Exchange Futures Contracts with OTC Forward Agreements.

Futures Exchange	*OTC Forwards*
Trading is done on a trading floor consisting of buyers and sellers of contracts and contract prices are determined by open outcry.	Banks give two-sided quotes and deals are closed over the phone.
Brokers who are members of the exchanges trade for their own accounts and on behalf of third parties.	Transactions are done directly between banks and institutional clients.
Market participants are unknown to each other, and settlement is done through the exchange clearing house.	Participants are known to each other, and the deal implies acceptance of counterparty risks among the participants.
All participants pay initial margin, and cash settlement is done by marking-to-market on a daily basis. The exchange brokers charge third parties a brokerage fee to cover handling costs.	No margin is required, but counterparty risk is carried by changing a spread around the two-sided forward price.
Actual delivery of the underlying goods is possible, but only rarely takes place.	Most trades result in delivery.
Contracts have standard amount and standard maturities.	Contract amounts and maturity dates are flexible, but at times requirements are made for the minimum size of contract amount. Maturities often exceed those of the futures exchanges.
Most currency futures are quoted against U.S. dollars and only for major currencies. Interest rate futures exist only in U.S. dollars and pound sterling.	In principle, quotes can be given for any cross currency exchange rate and foreign currency interest rate.
A futures position imposes a "basis risk" on the position holder.	There is no basis risk to the buyer of a forward agreement, which is assumed by the institution offering the forward agreement.

The settlement amount is calculated as follows:

$$SA = \frac{(MR - FR) \times T \times A}{(360 \times 100) + (MR \times T)}$$

where

SA = Settlement amount.
MR = Market rate (reference rate).

FR = Agreed forward rate.
T = Number of days in the interest period.
A = Contract amount of the agreement.

A positive settlement amount (MR > FR) denotes that the seller pays to the buyer. A negative settlement amount (MR < FR) denotes that the buyer pays to the seller.

If the FRA is covering periods exceeding one year, the formula for calculating the settlement rate is extended as follows:

$$SA_1 = \frac{(MR - FR) \times T_1 \times A}{36{,}000 + (MR \times T_1)}$$

$$SA_2 = \frac{(MR - FR) \times T_2 \times A}{36{,}000 + (MR \times T_2)}$$

$$\vdots \qquad \vdots$$

$$SA_n = \frac{(MR - FR) \times T_n \times A}{36{,}000 + (MR \times T_n)}$$

where
SA_n = Settlement amount in year n.
T_n = Number of days in year n.

then

$$SA = \sum_{x=1,2,\ldots,n} \frac{SA_x}{(1 + T_{x-1}/36{,}000 \times MR) \times (1 + T_{x-2}/36{,}000 \times MR) \times \ldots (1 + T_1/36{,}000 \times MR)}$$

As already discussed, the forward rates are determined by the discounted forward break-even rate, which makes up the alternative hedge or arbitrage opportunity to the FRA market.

Example: A 3-month deposit in three months' time is created by placing the amount for six months at the 6-month money market bid rate of 8.50% p.a., and borrowing the amount for three months at the 3-month money market offer rate of 8.90% p.a.

Conversely, a 3-month loan in three months' time is created by borrowing the amount for six months at the 6-month money market offer rate of 8.65% p.a., and placing the amount for three months at the 3-month money market bid rate of 8.75% p.a. (see Figure 10.5).

Money Market Rates

	Bid	*Offer*
3 months	8.75	8.90
6 months	8.50	8.65

FIGURE 10.5
Forward Forward Placement and Loan Arrangement.

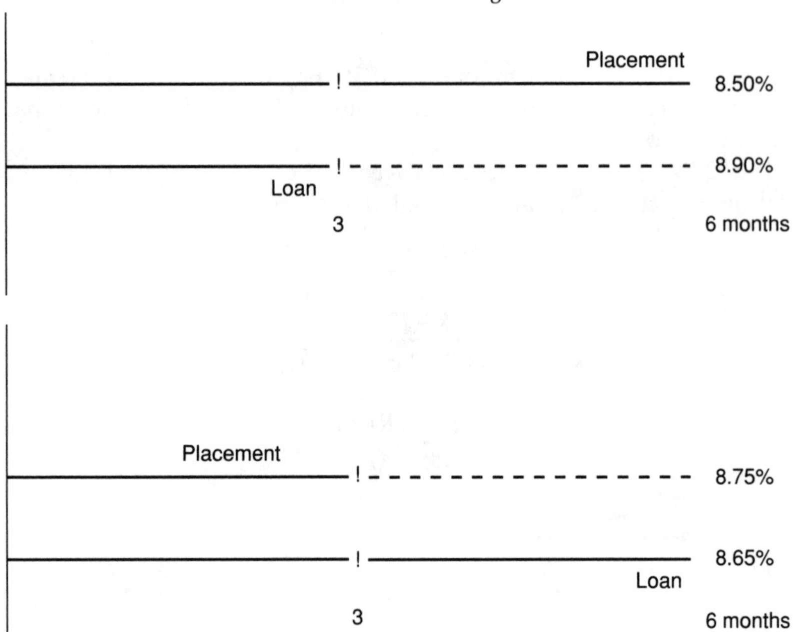

The FRA bid and offer rates are then calculated in the following way:

FRA bid rate :

$$\frac{[(8.5\times180/360\times100-8.90\times90/100\times360)\times360\times100]}{90}=8.1\%$$

FRA offer rate :

$$\frac{[(8.65\times180/360\times100-8.75\times90/360\times100)\times360\times100]}{90}=8.55\%$$

The general formula for calculating the forward rate can be presented in the following way.

$$FR=\frac{(RL\times TL)-(RS\times TS)}{(TL-TS)}$$

where

FR = Forward rate.
RL = Interest rate of the longer period.

RS = Interest rate of the shorter period.
TL = Number of days in the longer period.
TS = Number of days in the shorter period.

Since the difference in interest amounts for the whole interest period is paid in the beginning of the interest period, the settlement rate is the forward rate discounted back to the first day of the interest period.

$$\text{Discounted settlement rate (DSR)} = FR \times \frac{1}{1+(RS \times TS)/36{,}000}$$

$$\text{DSR (bid)} = 8.1 \times 1/[1+(8.9 \times 90)/36{,}000] = 7.92\%$$

$$\text{DSR (offer)} = 8.55 \times 1/[1+(8.75 \times 90)/36{,}000] = 8.37$$

FORWARD SPREAD AGREEMENT

A *forward spread agreement* (FSA) is a confirmed agreement between two counterparties to periodically exchange interest rate differentials on a predetermined interest rate spread between two currencies.

Example: A financial institution is funding a 3-year, 6-month LIBOR-based German-mark–denominated loan with U.S.-dollar, 6-month LIBOR borrowing in the Euromarket. To hedge against a reduction in the spread between the 6-month German mark LIBOR and the 6-month U.S.-dollar LIBOR, the hedger could buy U.S. dollar FRAs and sell German mark FRAs. Alternatively, the hedger could buy a 6-month US$/DM LIBOR interest rate forward spread agreement in the OTC market, which effectively locks in the future 6-month LIBOR spread between the German mark and the U.S. dollar for a three-year period (see Figure 10.6).

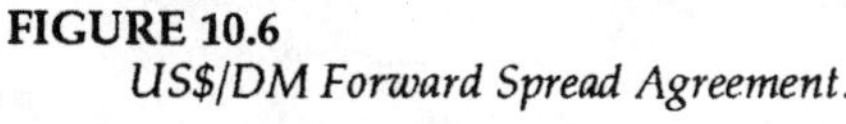

FIGURE 10.6
US$/DM Forward Spread Agreement.

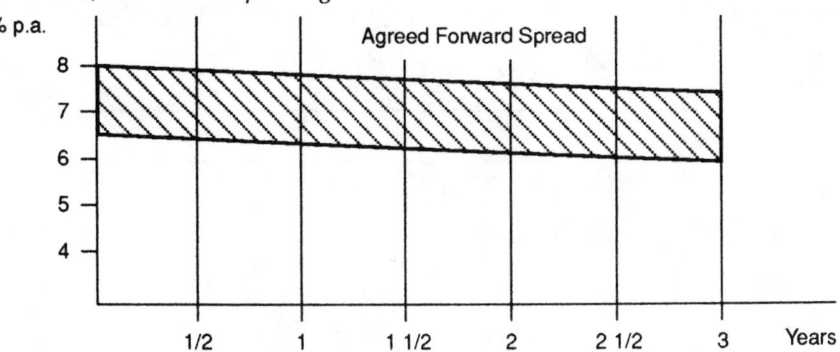

HEDGING WITH FRAs

By buying FRAs, a borrower can hedge the future funding costs. An investor can hedge the future return by selling FRAs. The borrower has, in effect, locked in the future funding cost against the payment of a front-end fee. This position is illustrated in Figure 10.7. The investor has locked in the future return against payment of a front-end fee. This position is illustrated in Figure 10.8.

Hence, the institution buying a forward rate agreement can fix the forward interest rate on any loan or deposit without going through the administrative procedures involved in managing a financial futures hedge and without incurring any risk. The amount and maturity of a forward rate agreement are usually more flexible than financial futures where the contract is tied into the fixed maturity dates and standard sizes of the futures exchange.

Example 1: A construction company needs capital of $1,000,000 for a six-month period in four months to carry out a project. To lock in the future cost of capital required to complete the project, the company *buys* a forward rate agreement guaranteeing that the $1,000,000 can be borrowed for six months within four months time at a rate of, say, 12⅜% p.a. The company pays a fixed fee of perhaps ¼% p.a. during the ten months of the forward rate agreement to obtain the forward obligation from the bank. Hereby the risk associated with the future financing cost is eliminated, and the company can carry out a feasibility study with full certainty, at least as far as funding costs are concerned.

FIGURE 10.7
Bought FRA Position (Borrower).

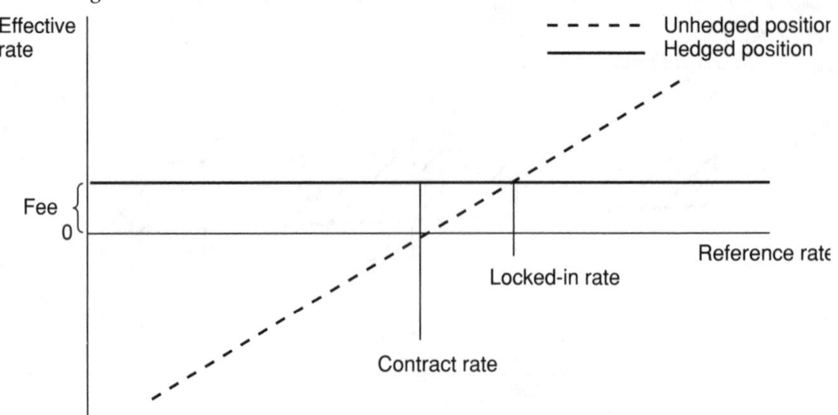

FIGURE 10.8
Sold FRA Position (Investor).

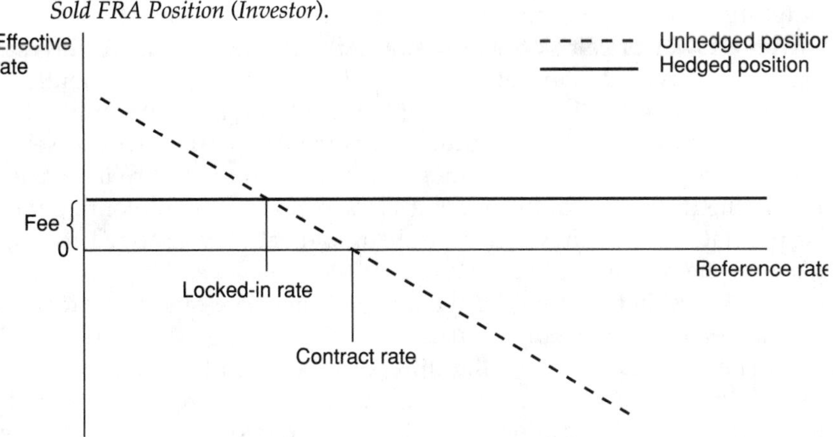

Example 2: An international trading company periodically raises funds through issuance of bankers' acceptances (BAs). Traditionally there has been an interest rate advantage of ⅝% on bankers' acceptance financing as compared to direct bank financing. In one month the company will have a financing requirement of $3,000,000 for two months, but management is worried that interest rates will increase. The company then *buys* from the bank a forward rate agreement which secures the borrowing of $3,000,000 in the Euro interbank market for two months in one month's time at a cost of, say, 12½% p.a.

At the time of drawdown the ⅝% advantage remains. The company therefore decides not to draw the funds from the bank, but rather to fund itself through the issuance of banker's acceptances. The forward rate agreement is cancelled and a cancellation fee is calculated by marking-to-market. Let's say that the interbank offer rate has increased to 13½% p.a. The rate has then increased by 1% as compared to the forward rate fixed at 12½% p.a. The cancellation fee is calculated as the p.a. interest differential between the forward rate and the new spot rate prevailing at the date of drawdown.

In this case the cancellation fee is in favor of the company, which will be credited the interest amount of 1% p.a. (that is, $5,000) on $3,000,000 for the two-month loan period. The company will issue banker's acceptances and raise funds at the new market rate of 12⅞% p.a. (13½% – ⅝%). The company pays the bank a commission of ¼% p.a. during the three-month period of the forward rate agreement. Hence by engaging in the forward rate agreement, the company has secured a future funding cost at an all-in rate of 12⅛% p.a., which is 1⅜% p.a. below the going interbank offered rate.

Example 3: An institutional investor periodically places idle dollar liquidity in short-term commercial paper because this type of investment carries a lower price risk than do, say, U.S. Treasury bonds. An investor expects to have idle liquidity of US$ 5,000,000 during a two-month period in one month's time, but fears that the interest rate level might drop in the meantime. To fix the future investment rate, the investor sells a forward rate agreement to a bank, which locks in the future investment rate in the Euro interbank market at 11½% p.a. for the two-month period. At the date of drawdown, the interbank bid rate has dropped to 10½% p.a. and the commercial paper rate is at the same level. The investor decides to invest in the commercial paper and therefore cancels the forward rate agreement by marking-to-market.

The cancellation fee is the difference between the forward rate of 11½% p.a. and the spot rate of 10½% p.a. The bank therefore pays the interest amount of 1% p.a. on $5,000,000 for the two-month period to the investor. The investor pays a commission of perhaps ¼% p.a. to the bank during the three-month period of the forward agreement. So the investment in commercial paper is done at an all-in rate of 11⅛% p.a. In case the commercial paper rate had dropped more than the interbank bid rate, the investor could choose to deliver the funds directly to the bank to secure the fixed return of 11⅛% p.a.

The forward rate agreement locks in the future interest rate, that is, it provides a complete hedge against the downside risk. Yet it does not leave open the upside potential for gains from a favorable development in interest rates.

Case: Interest Rate Forward Contract: Project Finance, Delay Start/Stepped Structure, Interest Rate Gapping

A construction company, the St. Louis Constructers, Inc., had just been awarded a US$ 15,000,000 contract in December 1985 for a major real estate development project in a St. Louis suburban area, as part of the municipal urban development plan to commence in May 1986. The project was to be a forerunner for several other development projects, to be commenced upon the initial project's completion. To be awarded the first contract meant a "foot in the door" when future bids were to be solicited.

The initial construction project was scheduled for completion over an 18-month period thus requiring a stepped-up financing scheme throughout the construction period. The municipality would make gradual and partial downpayment as construction work was satisfactorily completed. Hence a 10% advance payment would be paid as the construction work commenced in May, around 20% of the total contract price would be paid after six months in November, and another 20% would be due for payment after 12 months in May 1987. The remaining 50% would be paid upon satisfactory completion of the work after 18 months, scheduled for November 1987.

According to William Sorensen, the Financial Controller of the St. Louis Constructers, Inc.:

> We had been awarded the contract in very hard competition, and partially in a situation where we wanted to utilize some excess capacity built up in similar works which we had just completed. Obviously we made our bid on very competitive terms with a view to the future construction works which could flow to us if we were awarded the first construction project.

Because St. Louis Constructers had to invest money in the initial mobilization of equipment and construction workers, they foresaw some heavy drawdowns on the variable rate overdraft facilities made available by their major banks. The interest rate volatility made the future interest expense an unknown factor in the company's calculations. As William Sorensen put it:

> The interest rate uncertainty provided us with a bit of a headache when making our cash projections. You see, we were willing to consider the new project at a "break-even" price or a slight profit but obviously wouldn't like to lose money on it if we could avoid it. Fortunately, in discussing this issue with one of our banks, they suggested that we engage in interest rate contracts in order to fix the future interest rate.

In mid-December 1985 the short-term interbank offered rate (one to three months) had moved down to around 8% p.a. from a level well beyond 10% earlier in the year. This meant that the St. Louis Contractors could fund themselves presently at a rate of 8.50–8.75% p.a. Looking at the cash flow analysis a funding rate of 8.75% would result in an overall profit to St. Louis Constructers of around $110,000 on the total construction project. However, assuming instead a funding rate of 12% throughout the period of April 1986–November 1987, this profit figure would turn into a loss of around $122,600 (see Table 10.2).

Now it just so happened that the market was bullish in December 1985 and future interest rates in general were expected to drop. So St. Louis Constructers could lock in the future rates at rather favorable terms against a 0.25% p.a. fee, payable to the bank throughout the period of the forward contracts.

TABLE 10.2
Liquidity Forecast.

Date	*Incremental Investment Need ($1,000)*	*Current Working Capital Need ($1,000)*	*Down-payments ($1,000)*	*Expected Cumulative Overdraft ($3,000)*	*Interest Expense (US$ at) 8% p.a.*	*12% p.a.*
Apr. 86	1,000	100	1,100	1,100	7,333	11,000
May 86	1,000	425	1,500	1,025	6,833	10,250
June 86	1,000	425		2,450	16,333	24,500
July 86	1,000	400		3,850	25,667	38,500
Aug. 86		300		4,150	27,667	41,500
Sept. 86		325		4,475	29,833	44,750
Oct. 86	1,500	325		6,300	42,000	63,000
Nov. 86	500	335	3,000	4,135	27,567	41,350
Dec. 86		355		4,490	29,933	44,900
Jan. 87		355		4,845	32,300	48,450
Feb. 87		360		5,205	34,700	52,050
Mar. 87		360		5,565	37,100	55,650
Apr. 87	1,000	400		7,215	48,100	72,150
May 87		345	3,000	4,560	30,400	45,600
June 87		345		4,905	32,700	49,050
July 87		345		5,250	35,000	52,500
Aug. 87		355		5,605	37,367	56,050
Sept. 87		400		6,005	40,033	60,050
Oct. 87		380		6,385	42,567	63,850
Nov. 87		350	7,500	−765	−5,100	−7,650
Dec. 87		275		−490	−3,267	−4,900
Total	7,000	7,260	15,000		575,060	862,600

TABLE 10.3
Forward Rate Contracts.

Period	*Locked-In Rate*	*Amount*
2nd quarter 1986	8.50% p.a.	$2,500,000
3rd quarter 1986	8.60% p.a.	$4,500,000
4th quarter 1986	8.75% p.a.	$4,500,000
1st quarter 1987	9.00% p.a.	$5,500,000
2nd quarter 1987	9.00% p.a.	$5,000,000
3rd quarter 1987	9.25% p.a.	$6,000,000

By engaging in these interest rate forward contracts (Table 10.3), the average all-in funding cost could be locked in at a rate below 9.25% p.a. and thus guarantee a profit of around $80,000 on the project, everything else being equal.

William Sorensen commented on it this way:

> We considered it worthwhile to fix a maximum interest rate under the given circumstances. Despite a general expectation of dropping interest rates, we found the chance that the interest rate would increase again to be so significant that we decided to eliminate the risk of an increase in the rate and instead concentrate our efforts on our real business, namely to manage and monitor the construction development and avoid any potential cost overruns during the construction period.

11

Currency Option Agreements

In the foreign exchange forward market, a "pseudo-option" has existed for many years. This traditional "option" in the forward market gives the buyer of a forward agreement the right to choose the time of exercise of the forward agreement before the maturity date. However, because the "option" *must* be exercised before or on the maturity date, it does not constitute a true option. A *true option* provides the holder with the right but *not* the obligation to exercise before maturity. In principle it is similar to a forward agreement, but it does not oblige the option holder to exercise the forward transaction.

Parallel to the development of exchange-traded option contracts, an over-the-counter (OTC) market has been created by the major international banks, merchant banks, and brokerage houses, providing tailor-made currency options to institutional clients.

CURRENCY OPTIONS

True options in the OTC market take many shapes, adapted to the specific hedging requirements of institutional clients. Option quotes can usually be obtained for all major currencies against U.S. dollars, and most international currencies are quoted. In addition, cross currencies will be quoted on request, which is a clear advantage compared to hedging with option exchange contracts.

Expiration Dates

OTC options normally have maturities of up to one year, but maturities are often longer. The final maturity date is flexible and can be fixed or broken (or irregular) dates, as opposed to exchange-traded options.

The expiration date of an option agreement is the last day on which it can be exercised and usually corresponds to the spot date of the underlying currency. In spot foreign exchange deals, settlement takes place two days after the spot transactions, except transactions in U.S. dollars against Canadian dollars and Mexican pesos, which settle the following day.

Example: A Swiss franc call option, written for value on May 17, has an expiration date of May 15. Most banks require to be informed by the option holder before a certain deadline on the expiration date in order to execute the option.

Contract Size

Usually the size of the option agreement entails a minimum requirement, often about US$ 1,000,000. For smaller transactions, the costs are too high to make it worthwhile. Above the minimum requirement, the amount is flexible. It can be set at broken amounts at the buyer's choice to match a specific position.

Strike Price

The strike price is chosen by the option buyer and quotes are given to match the request of the client. The exchange-traded option terminology also pertains to the OTC market. Although the holder of a European option can exercise only at the expiration date, he can lock in profits prior to expiration by engaging in an offsetting forward agreement. Hence it can be argued that the strike price of a European option should be based on the outright rate. The holder of an American option can exercise the option at any time up to the expiration date, and profit can be locked in prior to expiration either by engaging in an offsetting forward agreement or by accessing the foreign exchange spot market. So it can be argued that the strike price of an American option should be based on the foreign exchange spot rate. Whether one or the other principle is used does not matter, as long as the market participants among themselves agree on the practice and terminology of the deal.

This is especially true of an at-the-money strike price. Whether it is defined as the current spot price or as the forward rate, be sure to obtain agreement on the definition of the at-the-money strike price, when requesting option quotes, in order to avoid confusion and misinterpretation of competitive bids.

Premium

Quotes are usually given for American-type options as well as for European-type options. Since the American option is slightly more expensive than the European, it usually pays to clarify whether the flexibility of the American option brings additional benefits to the option buyer in a given hedging situation.

Usually the option premium is paid up front and is quoted as a percentage of the currency amount of the option agreement, with the calculation of the currency amount based on the current spot exchange rate.

However, under special circumstances the premium can be paid in arrears. For example, the premium for the *limited option* is not paid until the contract's expiration date. In this case the option holder *must* act on the option on the expiration date. If the option is profitable, the option holder will exercise the option and pay the premium as the percentage calculated on the currency amount. The currency amount is determined by using the strike price of the option agreement. If the option is unprof-

TABLE 11.1
Types of Options.

True Option:

—A right to buy or sell a currency before a future date at a predetermined price.
—No obligation to exercise.
—Amount in excess of $1,000,000 is flexible.
—Maturity date is flexible.
—Strike price at buyer's choice.
—Premium payable up front.

Limited Option:

—Same as true option, but premium payable on maturity date.

Option-on-an-Option:

—A right to buy an option before a future date at a predetermined premium.
—Buyer selects terms of future option.
—Bank quotes premium payable up front.

itable, the option holder will not exercise the option but will pay the premium on the currency amount calculated from the current spot price prevailing at the expiration date. The feature of the delayed payment of premium has cash implications for the option buyer, who will pay the premium at the time that, for example, a foreign currency receivable will materialize.

Often financial managers have an aversion against paying a front-end fee for something whose outcome is unknown. For this reason traditional forward contracts are often adhered to because they provide the contract buyer with full certainty about the future foreign exchange rate, even though this might not be an optimal hedging solution for the specific situation. Most users of forward contracts do not make comparative calculations between the forward contract and the comparable option contract at the maturity date to analyze whether the hedging decision was optimal. Although previous decisions represent "sunk cost," which cannot be reversed, such analysis might bring about more knowledge so as to determine the optimal hedging technique to pursue in similar future situations.

Paying the option premium at the option's expiration date makes it easier for the option buyer to see the advantage of the option purchase. The profitability of the option is then a straightforward calculation.

Example: An American company is expecting a receivable of DM 2,500,000 in three months and has bought a German mark limited put option against U.S. dollars with an at-the-money strike price of 2.5000 DM/US$ at a premium of 3%. After the three-month period, the spot rate has gone to 2.3500 DM/US$ and so the option is not exercised. If nevertheless the put option is exercised at the strike price, the German mark receivables would bring the company $1,000,000. Conversely, if the mark receivables were sold on the spot market at the current foreign exchange rate, they would bring the company $1,063,829.79.

Because the option puts no limitation on the upside potential for price gains, the company earns $63,829.78 more than if it had engaged in a forward agreement at a forward rate of 2.5000 DM/US$. On expiration date, the company pays a 3% premium of $31,914.89 (0.03 × $1,063,829.79). The net gain from the favorable exchange rate development amounts to $31,914.89 ($63,829.78 − $31,914.89), when compared to the situation where the future German mark receivables had been covered by a forward contract at the same future foreign exchange rate.

Option-on-an-Option Agreement

A further development on the OTC option market is the creation of the *option-on-an-option agreement.* The holder of an option-on-an-option has the right to purchase an option at or before a certain future date at a predetermined premium. The buyer determines the characteristics of the option to purchase in the future, and the bank will quote a premium to be paid up front or in arrears. The option-on-an-option can be advantageous, for example, to a construction company negotiating a future contract that might require hedging of foreign currency flows.

Option Writer's Risks

When writing options, financial institutions have to hedge considerable option positions day by day. The option writer has two inherent risks to cover: an unfavorable development in the *forward rate* and an unfavorable development in the *spot rate.*

Example: Refer to the first example on the Swiss franc forward rate in Chapter 10. Assume that a 3-month Swiss franc European call option has been written at a strike price of 1.9500 Sw. frc./US$ (0.5128 US$/Sw. frc.). If the U.S. dollar interest rate increases by 1% and the Swiss franc interest rate decreases by 1%, then the swap is calculated as –0.0700 and the new outright rate amounts to 1.9300 Sw. frc./US$ (0.5181 US$/Sw. frc.). In this situation a holder of a European option could sell francs forward at 0.5181 US$/Sw. frc. and exercise the call option at 0.5128 US$/Sw. frc., thereby realizing a gain of 53 points (*pips*—in foreign exchange jargon).

The chance of exercise would also increase in the case of a continued strengthening of the Swiss franc spot exchange rate toward the expiration date. The option position could be closed by the option writer by buying francs *forward* and selling them spot against the dollar.

Example: A 3-month Swiss franc American call option has been written at a strike price of 2.0000 Sw. frc./US$ (0.500 US$/Sw. frc.). If the franc's spot foreign exchange rate starts to strengthen against the U.S. dollar, the chance that the option holder will exercise increases. This open position can be closed by the option writer by buying francs *spot* against the dollar.

The decisions on *when* to close the call option gap, *how* to close it (either through the spot purchase of the currency or through the purchase of the currency forward), and the timing of the transactions is very much based on subjective evaluations of the future foreign exchange rate as a part of the overall foreign exchange position management of the financial institution. Similar exposure management applies to the put options written by the institution. Consider that hedged options that are out-of-the-money also represent a position to the option writer. Hence the option position must be hedged and unhedged in response to the current change in the foreign exchange rate.

Applying Black-Scholes

From the preceding discussion, we deduce that the call option premium on an in-the-money American option must exceed the difference between the spot rate and the exercise price. Otherwise the option holder can exercise the option at a profit right after purchase.

Similarly, the call option premium on a European or an American option must exceed the difference between the forward exchange rate and the exercise price. If not, the option holder can lock in a future profit right after purchase by selling the currency forward and exercising the option at expiration date (see Table 11.2).

So, as also discussed in Chapter 6, the option price depends on:

1. The current spot foreign exchange rate.
2. The forward foreign exchange rate.
3. The strike price.
4. The maturity date of the option agreement.
5. The volatility of the foreign exchange rate.

These relationships are formalized in the Black-Scholes formula, which can be applied to approximate the "efficient" call option premium.

Buying a call option and writing a put option on a currency at the same strike price (*conversion*) corresponds to buying a forward agreement for the purchase of the currency in question. In an efficient market the cost of acquiring an amount of the future currency either way must be equal in size. Otherwise arbitrage transactions would generate profits.

The cost of the currency acquired through the option position (or through a forward agreement) is calculated as follows:

Forward rate = Exercise price + Call premium – Put premium
+ Interest on net premium

TABLE 11.2

European	
Call Option Premium ≥	(Forward foreign exchange rate – exercise price)* ≥ 0
American	
Call Option Premium ≥	(Spot foreign exchange rate – exercise price) ≥ 0

* Discounted to present value at current money market rate.

that is,

Call premium = Put premium + (Forward rate – Exercise price)
– Interest on net premium

(The "Forward rate" and "Exercise price" are discounted to present value at current money market rate.)

From the equation we can establish a relationship between the call option premium and the put option premium that enables us to utilize the Black-Scholes formula also to calculate the put option premium.[1]

The Role of Volatility

In view of the inherent risk associated with the management of an option position, another approach has been to look at the option agreement as an "insurance policy" which protects the option holder against adverse and volatile changes in the foreign exchange rate. Seen in this perspective, the option premium becomes an "insurance premium," covering the cost of a likely loss on the option position in the future. To analyze the future loss structure and to assess the potential risk associated with a given option agreement, statistical simulation analysis can be applied.

In this analysis the foreign exchange rate volatility plays an important role. The volatility calculation can be based on the change in the foreign exchange rate within regular intervals during a given period. There is no general agreement on which time intervals to use or on which periods to analyze. The fact of the matter is that all statistical analysis is based on historical data. However updated these might be, what really matters is the expected exchange rate volatility over the future period of the option agreement.

So judgement is again called for when determining the appropriate exchange rate volatility figure for a given option agreement.

Example: Let's calculate the foreign exchange rate volatility of the German mark exchange rate against the U.S. dollar in monthly intervals over the past 12 months (see Table 11.3).

Notice an increase in the exchange rate volatility over the latter half of the year. If the expectation is that this pattern will remain over the coming months, we should use the annualized monthly change of 15.76% for our calculations.

Example: The spot foreign exchange rate is 2.9500 DM/US$ and we are about to quote for a 3-month European call option with strike price of 2.9000 DM/US$. Assuming a future annual change of 15.76% in the exchange rate, we expect that the exchange rate might increase or decrease

TABLE 11.3
Calculating Foreign Exchange Rate Volatility (Example).

Date	*Rate (DM/US$)*	*Pct. Change*	*Pct. Change Squared*	*Pct. Change Squared*
Sept. 28	2.7500			
Oct. 31	2.6300	– 4.36%	19.01	
Nov. 30	2.5875	– 1.62%	2.62	
Dec. 31	2.7300	+ 0.55%	0.30	
Jan. 31	2.7005	– 1.08%	1.17	
Feb. 28	2.6400	– 2.24%	5.02	
Mar. 29	2.5908	– 1.86%	3.46	
Apr. 30	2.6705	+ 3.08%	9.49	9.49
May 31	2.7900	+ 4.47%	19.98	19.98
June 28	2.9803	+ 6.82%	46.51	46.51
July 31	3.1515	+ 5.74%	32.95	32.95
Aug. 30	3.1008	– 1.61%	2.59	2.59
Sept. 30	2.9900	– 3.57%	12.74	12.74
Sum total			155.84	124.26
Monthly average (pct. variance)			12.99	20.71
Square root (pct. standard deviation)			3.60	4.55
Annualized pct. change		$\sqrt{12} \times 3.60 =$	12.47%	
Annualized pct. change		$\sqrt{12} \times 4.55 =$		15.76%

by 7.88% (15.76%/$\sqrt{4}$) over the coming three-month period. If the foreign exchange rate develops at random, we assign a 50% likelihood that the foreign exchange rate will increase and a 50% likelihood that it will drop (see Figure 11.1).

The option holder will exercise the call option only if the foreign exchange rate drops below the strike price. The option writer's potential payout on this call option can be calculated as 0.50 (0.0000) + .50 (2.9000 – 2.71754) = 0.09123. Given that the three-month interest rate presently is 12% p.a., the present value of the potential payout is 0.0886 (0.09123/1.03), which as a percentage of the spot price amounts to 3.0% (0.0886/0.0295).

This then corresponds to the up-front premium required to cover the future potential payouts of the call option.

Figure 11.2 presents the up-front premium required for shorter sequences, such as months.

Example: The monthly change in the foreign exchange rate is 4.55% (15.76/$\sqrt{12}$). In the first month there is a 50% likelihood that the foreign

FIGURE 11.1
Graph to Determine Foreign Exchange Rate Volatility.

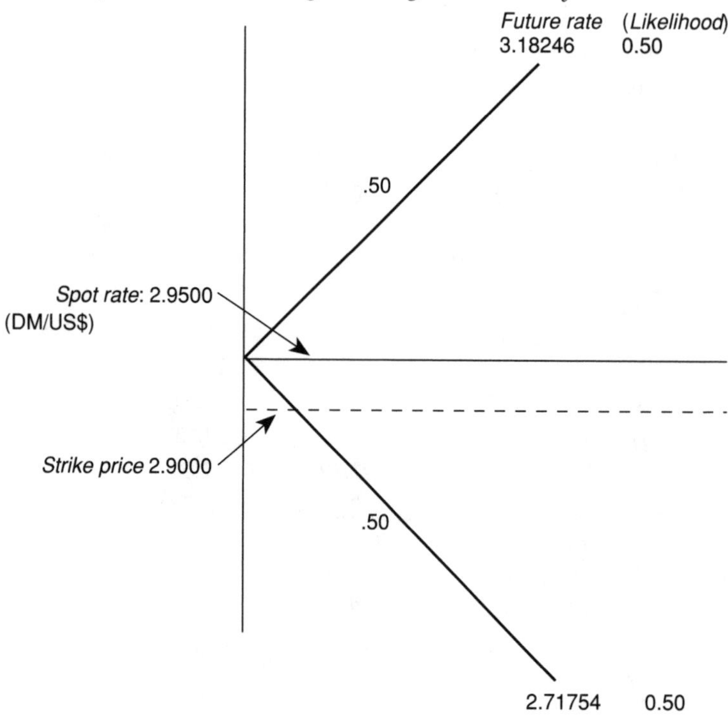

exchange rate increases to 3.0842 and a 50% likelihood that the foreign exchange rate decreases to 2.8158. And so on.

For the three-month period, each month's outcome has assigned a 50% likelihood of occurrence. Figure 11.2 shows that the future rate of 3.3526 can only occur in one way, with three events happening successively in each month. The likelihood of the rate being 3.3526 after three months is therefore calculated as 12.5% [= 0.50 × 0.50 × 0.50]. The foreign exchange rate of 3.0842 can arise in three ways during the three-month period. It can increase to 3.0842 in the first month, increase again to 3.2184 in the second month, and then drop to 3.0842 in the third month. Or it can rise to 3.0842, drop to 2.9500, and then increase to 3.0842. Or it can drop to 2.8158 and then increase to 2.9500 and 3.0842. The likelihood of the rate being 3.0842 after three months is therefore calculated as 37.5% [= 3 × 12.5%]. Similarly the likelihood of the rate being 2.8158 after three months is found to be 37.5%, and for the rate 2.5474 to be 12.5%.

If the spot foreign exchange rate ends up above 2.9000 DM/US$, the option will not be exercised. This will happen only if the foreign ex-

FIGURE 11.2
Up-Front Premiums for Monthly Periods.

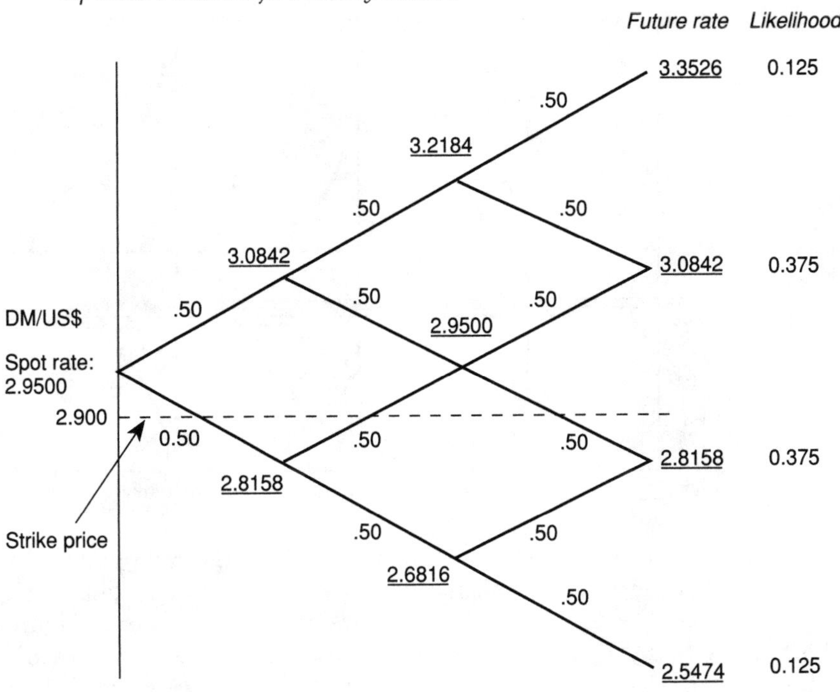

change rate falls below the strike price. Hence the potential payout on the call option is calculated as:

$$\begin{array}{l} +0.125\ (0.000) \\ +0.375\ (0.000) \\ +0.375\ (2.9000 - 2.8158) \\ \underline{+0.125\ (2.9000 - 2.5474)} \\ +0.07565 \end{array}$$

The present value amounts to 0.0734 (0.07565/1.03) which as a percentage of the spot price makes up 2.5%.

The smaller we make the time intervals, the more interactions will be performed and the closer we will get to determining the option premium—which adequately reflects the risk attached to writing the option. The more interactions we perform, the more the statistical distribution of the resulting future foreign exchange rate will approach the normal distribution (see Figure 11.3). The mean value will then be equal to the initial spot exchange rate and a standard deviation equal to the one previously determined to reflect the future volatility of the exchange rate.

FIGURE 11.3

Graph of Normally Distributed Foreign Exchange Rate Development.

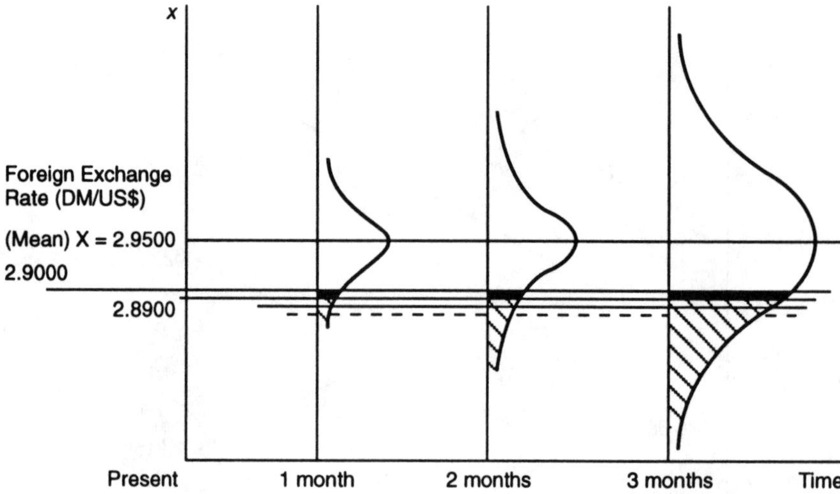

This value can be used in a further analysis of the call option. The likelihood that the foreign exchange rate will fall within a certain interval, such as between 2.8900 and 2.9000 DM/US$ (the black area in Figure 11.3), can be found by applying a tabularized cumulative normal distribution. This likelihood is then multiplied by the cost of exercise, to find the expected cost of the exchange rate falling inside this interval. This is performed for all similar intervals (n) below the strike price between 2.8800 and 2.8900, 2.8700 and 2.8800, and so forth (the shaded area in Figure 11.3). The costs of falling within each interval are then added together to give the total expected cost of the call option with a strike price of 2.9000 DM/US$.

$$\text{Cost of call option} = \sum P\,[((y - 0.01 \times n) < x < (y - 0.01\,(n-1))) \times (0.01 \times n)] \quad \text{for all } n$$

where

P = Likelihood of event.
x = Variable foreign exchange rate (DM/US$).
y = Strike price of 2.9000 DM/US$
n = 1, 2, 3, 4, 5, …, sufficiently large number.
0.01 = Determined to be the appropriate interval size.
$(0.01 \times n)$ = Cost of exercise in that specific interval.

To analyze an American option we have to monitor the development of the current spot exchange rate through each iteration. By calculating the intrinsic value of the call option at each iteration, we can determine the value of the option if it is exercised before final maturity. This value is compared to the calculation of the option value if exercised at expiration. Whichever is the higher of these two values will represent the cost of the option, which then becomes the option premium to charge by the option writer.

Several option pricing models, based on this line of thought, have been developed over the years. Although most of these require a very high level of mathematical sophistication, none of them presents a perfect solution to the option pricing dilemma. They all make assumptions about the future price volatility that might not hold true.

MARKET DEVELOPMENTS

During the late 1980s the market for currency options was refined further. Some of the product developments catered to clients engaged in competitive bidding situations and provided more applicable option features to these situations. Other product enhancements represented different implicit double option strategies, which through their structure reduced the up-front premium payable on the option hedge. In the competitive market many of the new products had their own peculiarities, whose aim was to differentiate the option product from that offered by competitors. In reality the products are to a large extent based on the same core elements.

Tender to Contract

The *tender to contract,* or the *scout,* solves a problem for the corporation that wants to hedge a potential currency exposure arising in connection with the submission of commercial bids. As already discussed, currency options are ideal in such situations, but the full hedging cost might turn out to be too expensive if the chance of a rejection is high due to the competitive situation.

The tender to contract (TTC) option allows the corporate customer to pay a certain percentage of the option premium, such as 10%, the remaining 90% being payable if the tender bid is accepted. The bank offering the TTC option will then have to sell the same option to other corporations involved in the competitive bidding to cover part of the total option premium. At least the bank should be fairly sure that the option has been sold to the corporation that is eventually awarded the contract, in order to be sure to cover the full premium (otherwise the option represents a potential loss to the writer). Conversely, if the TTC option is sold to the corporation that wins the tender, then the aggregate premiums from the sale of the option to the other bidders represent an additional and excess profit to the seller.

The scout (Shares Currency Option Under Tender) is a variation of the same theme. Here the contract awarder, which could be an overseas government or public entity, buys the option from the bank and reoffers a split option to all the tenderers on the project. Thus the bank is sure that the entity that eventually is awarded the project is among the option buyers, and hence the split premium becomes more competitive for the tenderers. On the contract award date, the successful tenderer is also awarded the option, thereby providing full coverage for the foreign exchange risk. If, for example, the project is being awarded by five firms, then each firm will pay 20% of the normal currency option premium.

The option-on-an-option, often termed a *compound option,* can serve the same purpose. If the underlying currency option is in-the-money, the bank writing the compound option must expect that the holder may want to buy the currency option and exercise it at a profit. Hence, the potential cost of a compound option is lower than or equal to the premium on the underlying currency option. Since there is a chance that the holder might not need or want the currency hedge represented by the currency option, in case the contract is not awarded, the premium is lower than the premium on the underlying option.

Double Option Products

In a *cylinder option,* a receiver of a foreign currency (long position) buys put options on the foreign currency to hedge against a drop in the foreign exchange rate. At the same time the hedger writes call options on the foreign currency at a higher strike price. He pays no premiums on the cylinder because the strike prices on the two underlying option contracts are determined so that the premium paid for the purchase of the put equals the premium received from the sale of the call.

In the cylinder, a short currency position is covered by buying call options on the foreign currency and writing put options at a lower strike price.

Example: A French company wants to hedge U.S. dollar receivables due in six months (a long position). A cylinder option offers rate protection through a U.S. dollar put at 5.5500 Fr. frc./US$. However, if the U.S. dollar foreign exchange rate increases above 5.7200 Fr. frc./US$, the hedger must cover a call option. The hedger pays no premium on the cylinder.

If at the expiry date in 6 months' time the U.S. dollar is

Below 5.5500, the U.S. dollar receivables are converted at 5.5500 Fr. frc./US$.

Between 5.5500 and 5.7200, the U.S. dollar receivables are converted at the prevailing Fr. frc./US$ spot rate.

Above 5.7200, the U.S. dollar receivables are converted at 5.7200 Fr. frc./US$.

The profit and loss profile of the covered position is illustrated in Figure 11.4.

FIGURE 11.4
Profit and Loss Profile of Cylinder Option.

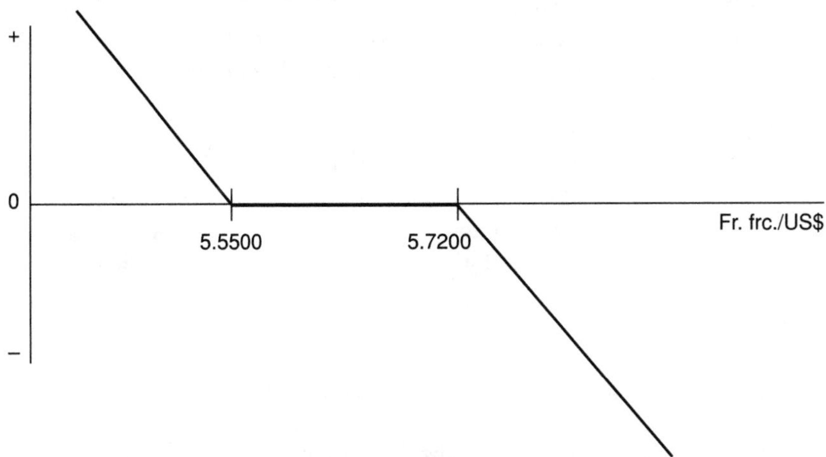

The cylinder option attracts hedgers who cannot be convinced to pay an up-front premium for a single option hedge. Hence, they obtain a downside hedge for free by giving up the upside potential in the underlying currency position over a certain exchange rate.

The so-called *range forward contract* is a variation of exactly the same option product. The contract specifies two foreign exchange rates determining the top and bottom of a range within which the hedger can take advantage of a positive market movement. That is, the currency amount is exchanged at the current spot foreign exchange rate, while maintaining a minimum (the bottom) and a maximum (the top) foreign exchange rate at which the currency exchange can take place.

In practice the hedger will choose either the top or the bottom of the range, while the bank for a given contract maturity will specify the range that applies to a no-cost range forward contract.

Example: A U.S. company has to purchase German marks in two months' time. The current spot rate is 1.6800 DM/US$ (0.5952 US$/DM) and the 2-month forward rate is 1.6949 DM/US$ (0.5900 US$/DM), that is, more favorable than the spot rate. Still, the company is uncertain about the trend, and therefore wants a flexible downside cover. The company wants protection at a bottom foreign exchange rate of 1.6700 DM/US$ (0.5988 US$/DM). The bank defines the zero-cost price range to be between 1.6700 DM/US$ and 1.7150 DM/US$ (0.5831 US$/DM). In other words, 1.6700 DM/US$ is the maximum price the hedger will pay for the German marks. If the spot rate is above 1.6700 DM/US$, then the hedger will exchange currency at the spot rate, but never at a rate exceeding 1.7150 DM/US$. Therefore, if the foreign exchange rate is above the forward foreign exchange rate of 1.6949 DM/US$ at expiry, the hedger will incur a gain as compared to the situation where a full cover at the outright forward rate had been obtained (see Figure 11.5).

Like the range forward, the *participating forward contract* or *forward plus contract* requires no up-front premium payment. The contract constitutes a forward exchange of currencies at an agreed maximum rate. The buyer of the contract pays for the rate protection by reserving less than 100% of the upside rate potential in the option contract. The level of the guaranteed rate depends on the percentage of participation in the upside rate potential.

Example: A Swedish corporation has to buy U.S. dollars in three months' time. The bank offers the following three-month maximum forward rates with a corresponding share of the upside rate potential on the currency option.

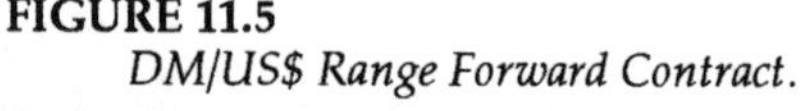

FIGURE 11.5
DM/US$ Range Forward Contract.

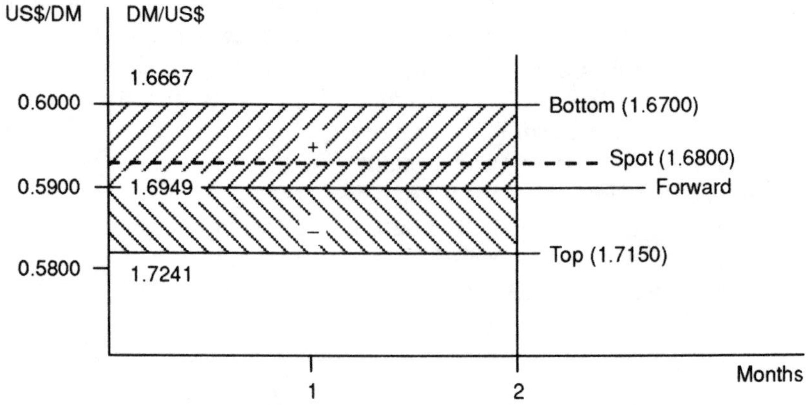

Forward Rate	*Percentage Share*
7.2000	31%
7.8000	53%
7.9000	75%

The corporation chooses the forward rate of 7.8000 SEK/US$ and obtains a hedge position as illustrated in Figure 11.6.

Another variation is the *break forward contract*, or *fox*, which is a forward foreign exchange agreement that can be unwound at the buyer's choice at a predetermined rate. The buyer of a break forward pays a spread on the outright forward rate, against which the bank determines a break rate. The break rate defines the foreign exchange rate at which the buyer can unwind the forward agreement.

Example: A U.K.-based company is to purchase U.S. dollars in three months' time. The company buys a break forward contract at 1.4250 US$/£ stg. [0.7017 £ stg./US$] from a bank at a break rate of 1.4600 US$/£ stg. [0.6849 £ stg./US$]. The forward foreign exchange rate in the market is 1.4450 US$/£ stg. [0.6920 £ stg./US$], so in this case the break forward rate is 200 pips below the quoted outright rate.

If the foreign exchange spot rate at expiry is below the break rate, the U.S. dollars are bought at the fixed rate of 1.4250 US$/£ stg.

If the foreign exchange spot rate at expiry is above the break rate of 1.4600 US$/£ stg., the company will buy dollars spot and sell them to the

FIGURE 11.6

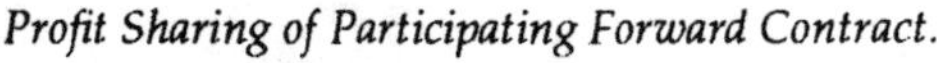

Profit Sharing of Participating Forward Contract.

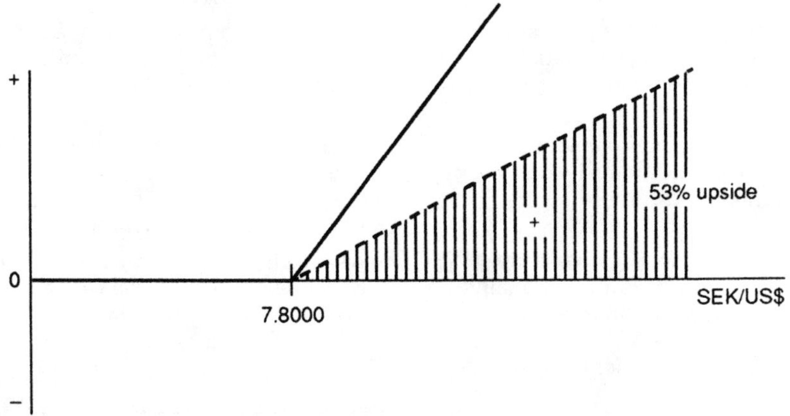

TABLE 11.4
Enhanced Currency Option Agreements.

Tender to Contract or Scout

Option premium is split between tenderers.

Contract award leads to full currency exposure coverage.

Cylinder Option

There is no option premium.

Hedger buys a put and writes a call at a higher strike price (long position).

Hedger buys a call option and writes a put at a lower strike price (short position).

Range Forward

There is no option premium.

Hedger chooses either the bottom or the top foreign exchange rate.

Bank determines the range, specifying the minimum and maximum rates.

Participation Forward or Forward Plus

There is no option premium.

Hedger can obtain maximum or minimum forward rate.

Hedger obtains only part of the upside foreign exchange rate potential.

TABLE 11.5
Comparing Exchange-Traded Options with OTC Option Agreements.

Exchange Options	*OTC Options*
Trading is done on the exchange trading floor and prices are determined by "open outcry."	Banks quote the option premium for the specific option agreement over the phone.
Market participants are unknown to each other, and settlement is done through the exchange clearing entity.	Participants are known to each other and a transaction implies an acceptance of counterparty risk.
Buyers of options pay a premium up front. Option writers pay initial margin and are marked-to-market on a current basis.	Option buyers can pay premium up front or in arrears. So far only limited possibility for writing options.
Option contracts have standard amounts and fixed maturity dates of up to nine months' duration.	Contract size is flexible over a minimum requirement of US$ 1,000,000. Maturity dates are flexible and exceed that of exchange-traded options.
All currency options contracts are quoted against U.S. dollars and only for major currencies. Interest rate options only exist on U.S. Treasuries and 3-month Eurodollar deposits (European type).	Quotes are given on all international currencies against U.S. dollars and on cross rates. Interest rate options are quoted in U.S. dollars.

bank at the break rate, thereby scoring a net gain on the foreign exchange rate differential.

Table 11.4 provides an overview of some of the enhanced option agreements made available in the OTC market.

The emergence of differently packaged hedging instruments has provided the hedger with a large arsenal of OTC hedging products. On the other hand, the hedging possibilities available are more complex than ever, even to an extent that it can be difficult to make suitable comparisons between the market terms of different hedging instruments. Many of the instruments offered can be decomposed into simpler futures and option positions, which can make it possible to make comparisons to the going market rates.

Table 11.5 compares the features of exchange traded contracts and options traded on the OTC-market.

CONCLUSION

OTC options in many ways provide the option buyer with a flexibility that cannot be met by engaging in exchange-traded options, notably with regard to maturities and quotes on cross currencies. On the other hand, OTC contracts are not as easily bought and sold as the highly liquid option exchange options. Although a number of financial institutions offer clients the opportunity to write options over-the-counter, the market is a developing one. So far, the market serves to provide the holder of exchange-traded options with the extra flexibility to close option positions and thereby take advantage of favorable market developments. In the end, the question of which market to approach depends on two things: (1) the organizational resources available to the hedger to monitor current developments on the option exchanges, and (2) how well each market can accommodate true hedges to close specific financial exposure gaps.

12

Interest Rate Agreements

With the appearance of actively traded financial futures markets in, for example, U.S. Treasuries, Eurodollar deposits, and pound sterling gilts, the financial intermediaries have been able to develop different types of hedging services to guarantee the future interest rate level to the buyer. The financial institutions will hedge their exposure by taking up corresponding positions in financial futures or option contracts being offered.

Thus the financial intermediary assumes the basis risk associated with the financial futures and/or options hedge. As experienced exchange dealers, they in effect carry out the handling of the financial futures and/or options hedge, which to most institutions constitutes a resource-intensive function. The client is therefore offered a risk-free interest rate hedging product.

The interest rate hedging services offered by the financial institutions guarantee a maximum future interest rate for borrowers or a minimum future interest rate for investors. As opposed to the hedges that can be arranged by accessing the option exchanges, the OTC services extend the interest rate guarantee for periods exceeding the normal maturities available on the exchanges.

The compensation for a longer-term interest rate guarantee is settled periodically (often quarterly corresponding to the exchange maturities) on a cash basis until the maturity of the agreement. Compensation therefore corresponds to the cash settlement principle prevalent on the financial futures and options exchanges.

The client who has been guaranteed a maximum interest rate level will obtain cash settlement compensation whenever the interest rate exceeds the guaranteed rate. Conversely, the client who has been guaranteed a minimum interest rate level will obtain cash settlement compensation whenever the interest rate falls below the guaranteed rate (see Figure 12.1).

FIGURE 12.1
Graph of Compensation on Guaranteed Rates.

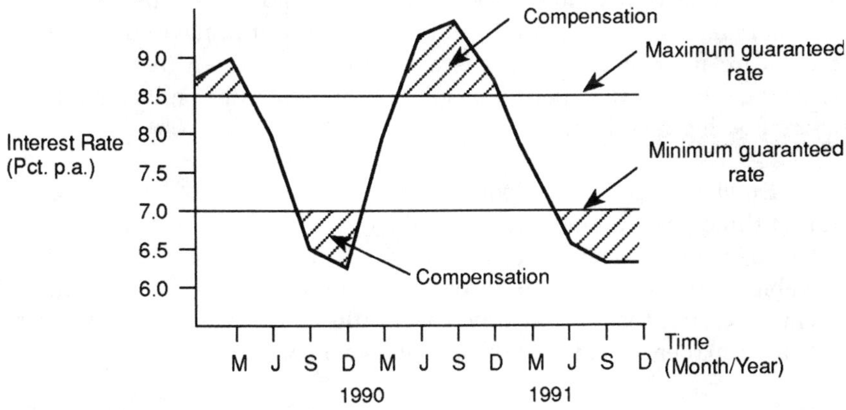

The OTC market also offers services corresponding to the vertical bull and bear spreads, which can be established by trading options contracts on the exchanges (see Chapter 9).

CEILING RATE AGREEMENTS (CAPs)

This type of interest rate agreement provides the holder with a hedge against an increase in the interest rate level without actual delivery of funds taking place. This type of agreement will guarantee a maximum borrowing rate for a period of up to ten years. For this type of hedge the institutional client will pay an up-front fee (sometimes payable quarterly in arrears), quoted as a percentage p.a. on the contract amount. The agreement is often settled quarterly; that is, if at the end of each quarter the actual borrowing rate has exceeded the agreed rate, the bank will pay the client the difference in the interest amount. If the actual borrowing rate is below the agreed rate, nothing will happen (see Figure 12.2).

Settlement:

$$S = (MR - CR) \times A \times T/36{,}000 \qquad MR > CR$$
$$S = 0 \qquad MR < CR$$

where

S^1 = Interest settlement amount.
MR = Market interest rate (reference rate).
CR = Ceiling rate (cap).
A = Contract amount.
T = Number of days in the settlement period.

This type of hedging service is interesting not only to the institution that is planning to raise funds and looking to put a maximum limit on the future interest expense. It is also interesting to an institution that fears the effect of an expected increase in interest rates on its already existing floating rate debt.

Example: A public company has floating rate debt of US$ 10,000,000 raised three years ago with a final bullet repayment maturing five years after drawdown. The loan was obtained at a rate of LIBOR + 1¼%, payable quarterly in arrears throughout the loan period. Now management is fearing that a recent increase in the interest rate level will turn into a permanent trend over the last two years of the loan.

FIGURE 12.2
Hedging with a Ceiling Rate Agreement (*Cap*).

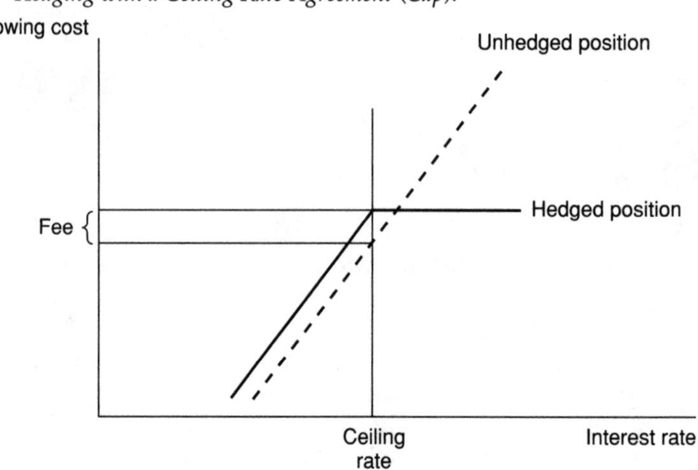

So the company buys a US$ 10,000,000 ceiling rate agreement that guarantees that LIBOR will not exceed a certain level over the next eight quarters. In this case, the LIBOR serves as a rate basis (reference rate) for the quarterly settlement (see Figure 12.3). Assume that rates have been quoted and that the actual interest rate develops as follows:

Period	*Maximum Rate*	*Fee*	*Fee Payable*	*Actual LIBOR*	*Bank Compensation*
3 months in 3 months	9.00% p.a.	½% p.a.	$ 12,500	8.75% p.a.	—
3 months in 6 months	9.10% p.a.	½% p.a.	$ 12,500	9.00% p.a.	—
3 months in 9 months	9.20% p.a.	⅝% p.a.	$ 15,625	9.50% p.a.	$ 7,500
3 months in 12 months	9.30% p.a.	⅝% p.a.	$ 15,625	10.05% p.a.	$ 18,750
3 months in 15 months	9.40% p.a.	¾% p.a.	$ 18,750	10.65% p.a.	$ 32,250
3 months in 18 months	9.50% p.a.	¾% p.a.	$ 18,750	11.25% p.a.	$ 43,750
3 months in 21 months	9.60% p.a.	1% p.a.	$ 25,000	11.85% p.a.	$ 56,250
3 months in 24 months	9.70% p.a.	1% p.a.	$ 25,000	11.50% p.a.	$ 45,000
Total fees			$143,750		
Total bank compensation					$203,500

In the first six months, the actual LIBOR was lower than the maximum rate and hence nothing happened. In the third quarter the actual LIBOR exceeded the maximum rate by 30 basis points and hence the

FIGURE 12.3
Guaranteed Borrowing Rate.

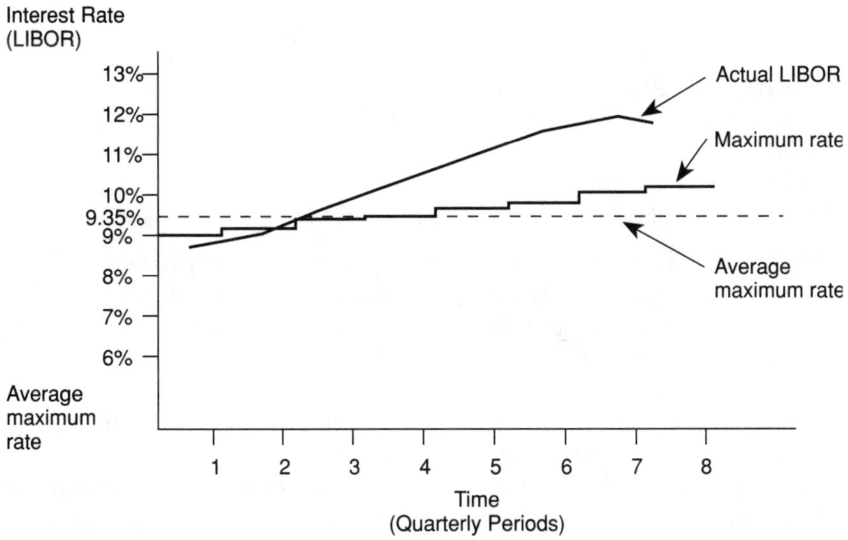

bank paid the company the difference in the interest amount, namely \$7,500 (\$10,000,000 × 0.30/400), and so forth.

The corporation has thus guaranteed a maximum LIBOR on average over the last two years of the loan of 9.35% p.a., that is, a total guaranteed loan rate of 10.60% (9.35 + 1.25). However, the corporation still takes full advantage of the interest rate being lower than the maximum rate. This saved the company \$6,250 in the first quarter and \$2,500 in the second quarter.

FLOOR RATE AGREEMENT

This interest rate agreement provides the holder with a hedge against a decrease in the investment rate. That is, the holder can be guaranteed a minimum return on a certain investment portfolio in a period of up to ten years. The agreement is settled quarterly. If at the end of the quarter the actual investment rate is below the agreed rate, the bank will pay the difference in interest amount. If the actual investment rate is above the agreed rate, nothing happens (see Figure 12.4). For this type of interest rate hedge, the holder will pay up-front fee potentially arranged for payment quarterly in arrears. The fee is usually quoted as a percentage p.a. calculated on the contract amount.

Settlement:

$$S^1 = (FR - MR) \times A \times T/36{,}000 \qquad MR < FR$$
$$S = 0 \qquad MR > FR$$

where

S = Interest settlement amount.
MR = Market interest rate (reference rate).
FR = Floor rate.
A = Contract amount.
T = Number of days in the settlement period.

The agreement is of interest to any institution that has to periodically place excess liquidity or that maintains a fixed maturity floating rate investment and would like to secure a minimum return on the investment in a falling interest rate environment.

Example: A commercial bank is about to extend a two-year floating rate loan of US\$ 15,000,000 at LIBOR + 1½% with interest payable quarterly in arrears, and the management board takes the view that the dollar interest rate will continue its recent declining trend. The bank then buys

FIGURE 12.4
Hedging with Floor Rate Agreement.

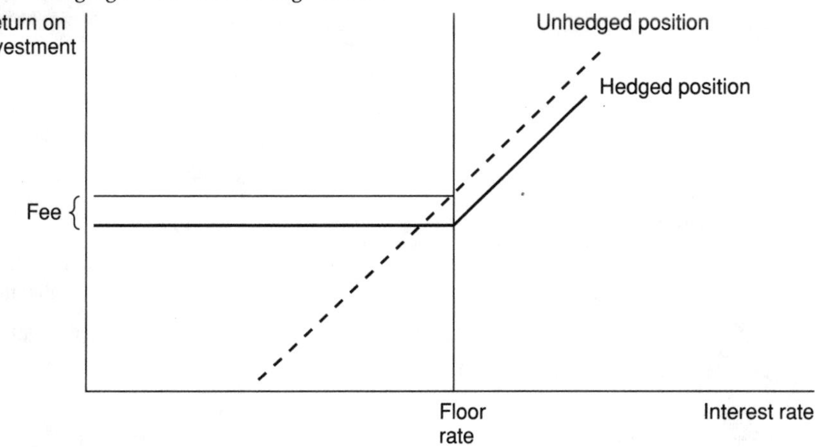

a floor rate agreement of US$ 15,000,000, which guarantees the institution a minimum interest rate on the future loan. Assume that the rates have been quoted and that the actual interest rate developed as follows:

Period	*Minimum Rate*	*Fee*	*Fee Payable*	*Actual LIBOR*	*Bank Compensation*
3 months in 3 months	8.90% p.a.	½% p.a.	$ 18,750	8.55% p.a.	$ 13,125
3 months in 6 months	9.05% p.a.	½% p.a.	$ 18,750	8.45% p.a.	$ 22,500
3 months in 9 months	9.20% p.a.	½% p.a.	$ 18,750	9.10% p.a.	$ 3,750
3 months in 12 months	9.35% p.a.	½% p.a.	$ 18,750	9.50% p.a.	—
3 months in 15 months	9.50% p.a.	⅝% p.a.	$ 23,437	9.00% p.a.	$ 18,175
3 months in 18 months	9.60% p.a.	⅝% p.a.	$ 23,437	8.75% p.a.	$ 31,875
3 months in 21 months	9.65% p.a.	⅞% p.a.	$ 32,812	8.50% p.a.	$ 43,125
3 months in 24 months	9.70% p.a.	1% p.a.	$ 37,500	8.00% p.a.	$ 63,750
Total fee			$192,186		
Total bank compensation					$196,300

In this case the bank has a guaranteed LIBOR in average over the two-year period of 9.37% p.a., which guarantees a return on the loan of minimum 10.87% p.a. [9.37% + 1.50] (see Figure 12.5). However, in case the interest rate exceeds the minimum rate, the holder of the agreement takes full advantage of the excess interest over the guaranteed rate.

As a rule the front-end fee represents the threshold value with which to compare the expected volatility of the interest rate level. If a company buys a two-year ceiling rate agreement at an average fee of

FIGURE 12.5
Guaranteed Investment Rate.

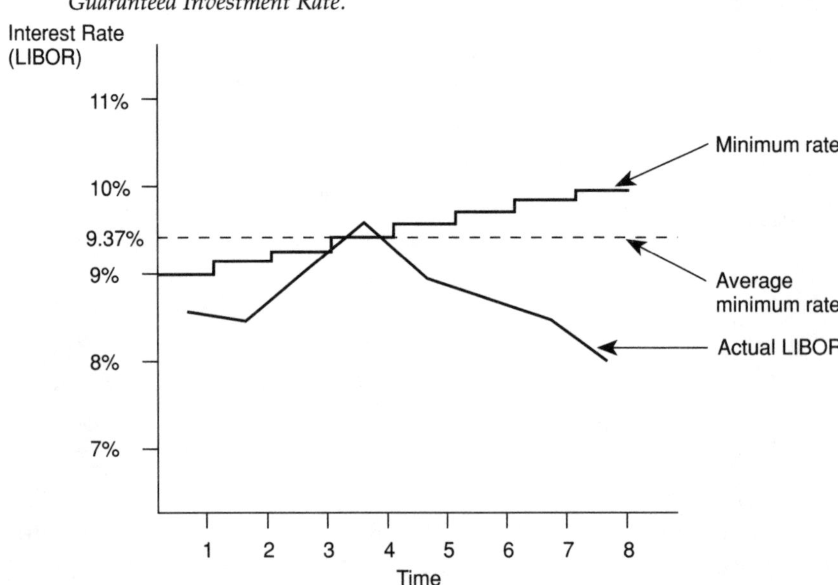

0.72% p.a., then it has taken the view that on average the interest rate will increase by more than 0.72% over the two-year period. Conversely, if a bank buys a floor rate agreement at an average fee of 0.64% p.a., then it fears that on average the interest rate might drop by more than 0.64% over the next two years.

The interest rate agreements can be arranged in different ways by incorporating other interest rate bases for the quarterly settlement or by applying a fixed interest rate for the whole contract period.

The preceding examples illustrate situations in which the advantage to the buyer of the interest rate agreements is significant as calculated on an ex post basis. Obviously such is not always the case. On average the system must be in balance so that gains and losses even out over the long run and at the same time leave a reasonable net gain to cover the transaction and development costs of the market intermediaries. The hedger, however, is willing to pay such a premium to avoid the administrative burden of doing the hedge directly on an exchange and to effectively eliminate the uncertainty of the future interest rate. Whether to engage in an interest rate agreement is an ex ante decision to be analyzed by the financial management given the uncertainty of the future; it involves an evaluation of the potential risks of maintaining an interest rate gapping position. Hence the premium paid for an interest rate agreement will also contain a compensation element for the privilege of obtaining full knowledge or a guarantee on the future interest rate development.

The interbank markets for ceiling (caps) and floor rate agreements have grown over recent years in parallel with the emergence of more efficient FRA markets. Hence, ceiling and floor rates are often quoted in the interbank market with two-way bid and offer prices:

	CAPs						*Floors*			
Reference Rates (6-Month Rates)	*8.00*		*8.25*		*8.50*		*7.50*		*7.75*	
	Bid	*Offer*	*Bid*	*Offer*	*Bid*	*Offer*	*Bid*	*Offer*	*Bid*	*Offer*
2 years	74 –	88	56 –	70	40 –	55	18 –	30	27 –	40
3 years	104 –	137	79 –	106	59 –	85	51 –	74	69 –	95
4 years	123 –	162	93 –	132	68 –	106	93 –	130	122 –	161
5 years	140 –	193	107 –	158	79 –	129	152 –	203	192 –	244

When the contracts are traded on to corporate hedgers, the banks will normally charge a spread around the going interbank rate to cover handling cost and management of counterparty risk (as already discussed).

SCALE-DOWN FLOOR

The *scale-down floor agreement* is made up by a combination of floor rate agreements (put options) with different strike prices and contract amounts, thus effectively establishing a ratio put spread. The position will be most relevant when the market expects a drop in the interest rate level, but gradually, not suddenly. The scale-down floor can be constructed in such a way that the premium paid on the bought floor corresponds to the premium received on the sold floor at a higher contract amount, thus effectively making it a zero cost position. The profit and loss structure of the position is shown in Figure 12.6.

Example: A scale-down floor agreement offers the following terms:

Period of agreement: 2 years
Interest rate basis: 3-month LIBOR
Premium: zero cost

FIGURE 12.6
Profit and Loss Profile of Scale-Down Floor Agreement.

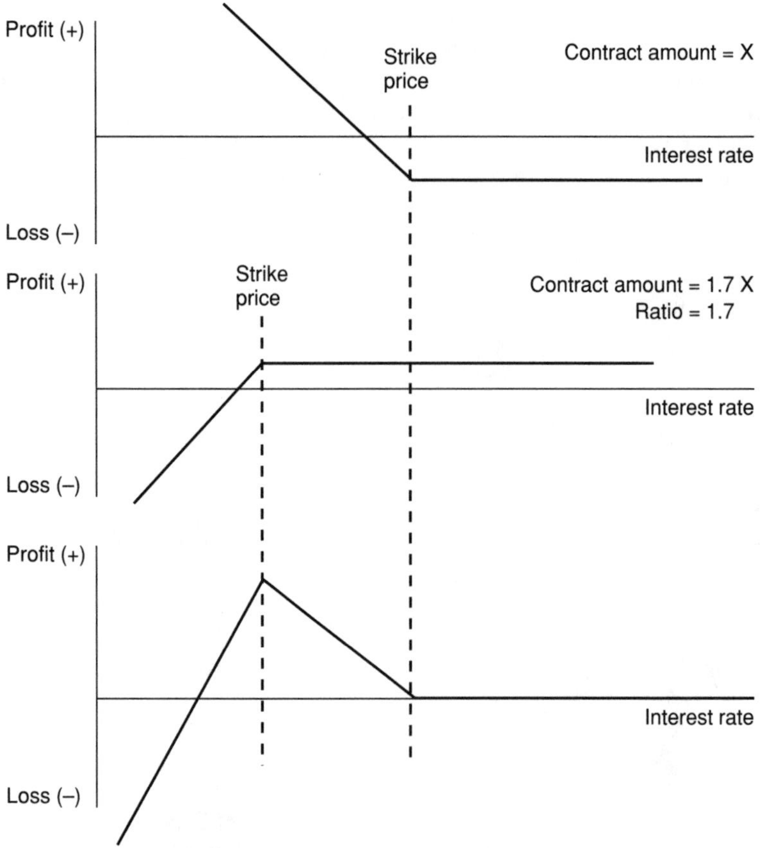

Payments under agreement:

Receive 0.50%, when LIBOR > 8.0%
Receive 0.50% + (8.0 – LIBOR) × 1.5, when 7.5% < LIBOR < 8.0%
Receive LIBOR—6.3%, when 6.3% < LIBOR < 7.5%
Pay 6.3%—LIBOR, when LIBOR < 6.3%

The profit and loss profile of the position is shown in Figure 12.7.

COMBINED CEILING RATE AND FLOOR RATE AGREEMENTS

A *ceiling rate agreement*, or a *cap,* guarantees a maximum borrowing rate and gives the holder the full benefit of a drop in the interest rate below

FIGURE 12.7
Scale-Down Floor Agreement—Profit and Loss Profile (Example).

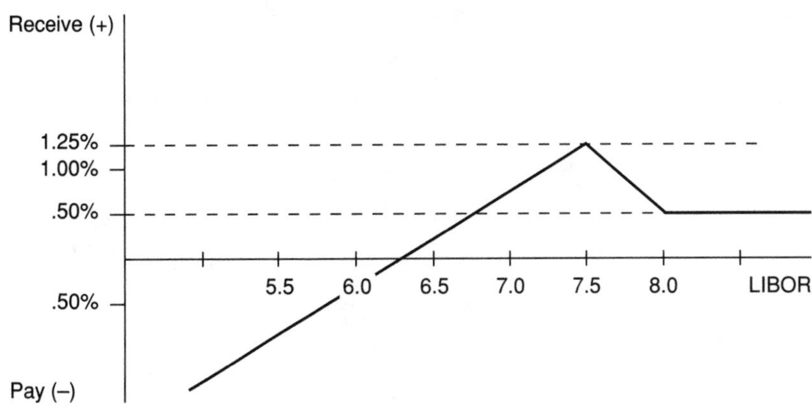

the maximum rate. However, the borrower might take the view that the likelihood of a drop in the interest rate is negligible. So he might want to buy a combined ceiling rate and floor rate agreement. That is, if the rate exceeds the maximum guaranteed level, such as 10% p.a. for a five-year period, the bank will compensate the holder quarterly for the difference in the interest amount. However, if the interest rate drops below, say, 8% p.a. over the same five-year period, the company will compensate the bank quarterly by the difference in the interest amount. Hence the buyer is guaranteed a maximum borrowing rate of 10%. If the interest rate is between 8 and 10% p.a., the buyer will take full advantage of the lower interest rate, but if it drops below 8% p.a., he will incur a loss (see Figure 12.8). (Compare this type of hedge to the vertical bull spread, described in Chapter 9 and to the cylinder option described in Chapter 11.)

Settlement: [at the end of the settlement period]

$$S^1 = (MR - CR) \times A \times T/36{,}000 \qquad MR > CR$$
$$S = 0 \qquad FR < MR < CR$$
$$S = (FR - MR) \times A \times T/36{,}000 \qquad MR < FR$$

where

S = Settlement amount.
MR = Market interest rate (reference rate).
CR = Maximum rate (ceiling).
FR = Minimum rate (floor).
A = Contract amount.
T = Number of days in the settlement period.

FIGURE 12.8
Hedging with a Collar Rate Agreement (Borrower).

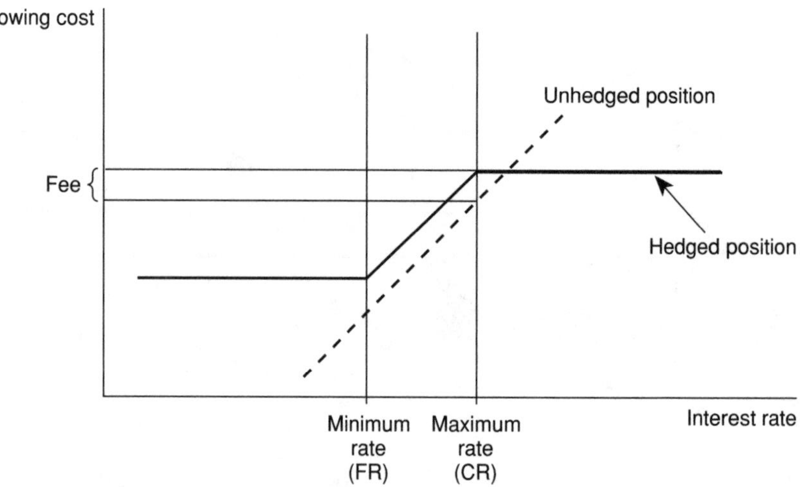

Conversely, a *floor rate agreement* guarantees a minimum investment rate, giving the holder the full benefit of an increase in the interest rate above the minimum rate. Again, if the investor takes the view that an increase in the interest rate is very unlikely, he may want to buy a combination of a floor rate agreement and a ceiling rate agreement. That is, if the interest rate is below the minimum rate of, say, 9% p.a. then the bank will compensate the holder quarterly by paying the difference in the interest amount. If the interest rate is between 9 and 11% p.a., the holder will take full advantage of the higher interest rate. If the interest rate exceeds 11% p.a., the holder will compensate the bank quarterly for the difference in the interest amount (see Figure 12.9). (Compare this type of hedge to the vertical bear spread described in Chapter 9.)

Settlement:

$$S = (FR - MR) \times A \times T/36{,}000 \qquad MR < FR$$
$$S = 0 \qquad FR < MR < CR$$
$$S = (MR - CR) \times A \times T/36{,}000 \qquad MR > CR$$

where

S = Settlement amount.
MR = Market interest rate (reference rate).
CR = Maximum rate (ceiling).

FIGURE 12.9
Hedging with a Collar Rate Agreement (Investor).

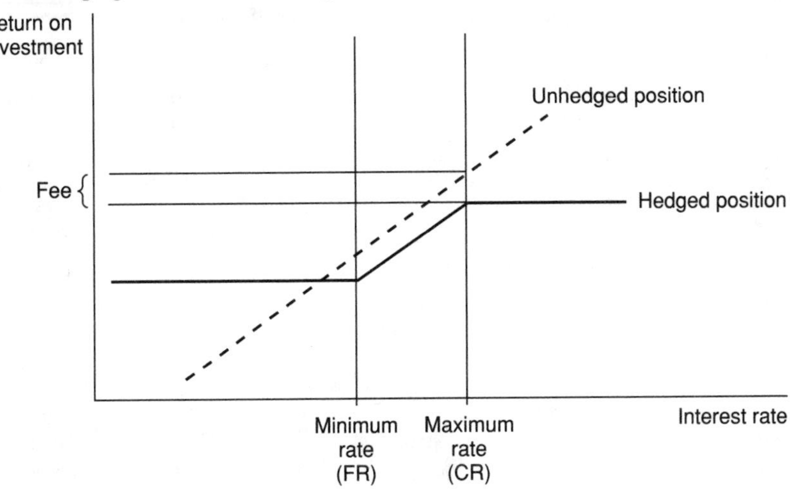

FR = Minimum rate (floor).
A = Contract amount.
T = Number of days in the settlement period.

The combined ceiling rate and floor rate agreement is often termed a *collar rate agreement*. Its advantage is that the front-end fee is lower than the fees on the corresponding ceiling rate agreement or floor rate agreement. Keep in mind, however, that the collar rate agreement does *not* provide a full hedge to the holder.

Case: Interest Rate Agreement: Ceiling Rate (Mortgage Association, Maturity Mismatch Interest Rate Gapping)

In November 1985 the Lauderdale Building Society held a US$ 14,000,000 portfolio of 15-year mortgage loans on its books. The mortgage loans were signed to cover commercial building contracts completed at year-end 1984, and so the final maturity of the loans was determined to be December 1, 1999. Repayment of principal and interest on this specific mortgage portfolio was arranged as 30 equal semiannual annuities with a locked-in rate of 11.50% p.a. Repayment dates were set at June 1 and December 1 each year until maturity (see Table 12.1).

In compliance with normal business practice, Lauderdale Building Society funded most of its long-term commitments through issuance of medium-term savings bonds. However, due to the incremental nature of

TABLE 12.1

Repayment Schedule of US$ 14,000,000, 15-year Mortgage Portfolio.

Date	*Outstanding*	*Annuity*	*Principal*	*Interest*
Dec. 84	14,000,000.00	—	—	—
June 85	13,814,972.66	990,027.34	185,027.34	805,000.00
Dec. 85	13,619,306.25	990,027.34	195,666.41	794,360.93
June 86	13,412,389.02	990,027.34	206,917.23	783,110.11
Dec. 86	13,193,574.05	990,027.34	218,814.97	771,212.37
June 87	12,962,177.22	990,027.34	231,396.83	758,630.51
Dec. 87	12,717,475.07	990,027.34	244,702.15	745,325.19
June 88	12,458,702.55	990,027.34	258,772.52	731,254.82
Dec. 88	12,185,050.61	990,027.34	273,651.94	716,375.40
June 89	11,895,663.68	990,027.34	289,386.93	700,640.41
Dec. 89	11,589,637.00	990,027.34	306,026.68	684,000.66
June 90	11,266,013.79	990,027.34	323,623.21	666,404.13
Dec. 90	10,923,782.24	990,027.34	342,231.55	647,795.79
June 91	10,561,872.38	990,027.34	361,909.86	628,117.48
Dec. 91	10,179,152.70	990,027.34	382,719.68	607,307.66
June 92	9,774,426.64	990,027.34	404,726.06	585,301.28
Dec. 92	9,346,428.83	990,027.34	427,997.81	562,029.53
June 93	8,893,821.15	990,027.34	452,697.68	537,419.66
Dec. 93	8,415,188.53	990,027.34	478,632.62	511,394.72
June 94	7,909,034.53	990,027.34	506,154.00	483,873.34
Dec. 94	7,373,776.68	990,027.34	535,257.85	454,769.49
June 95	6,807,741.50	990,027.34	566,035.18	423,992.16
Dec. 95	6,209,159.30	990,027.34	598,582.20	391,445.14
June 96	5,576,158.62	990,027.34	633,000.68	357,026.66
Dec. 96	4,906,760.40	990,027.34	669,398.22	320,629.12
June 97	4,198,871.78	990,027.34	707,888.62	282,138.72
Dec. 97	3,450,279.57	990,027.34	748,592.21	241,435.13
June 98	2,658,643.31	990,027.34	791,636.26	198,391.08
Dec. 98	1,821,487.96	990,027.34	837,155.35	152,871.99
June 99	936,196.18	990,027.34	936,196.18	53,831.28
Total		29,700,820.20	14,000,000.00	

this commercial transaction and a continued fall in interest rates, the US$ 14,000,000 mortgage loan was being funded through short-term interbank loans at an interest rate determined at the going money market rate plus ¼–½% spread.

The Treasurer of the Lauderdale Building Society, Mr. Fitzgerald, was well aware of the ups and downs in the interbank money market rates, which from year to year—and even from month to month by historical experience—could fluctuate widely. Fitzgerald analyzed the short term interest rate structure and usually based his intermediate funding strategy on a short-term view of the interest rate movement. Given presently declining interest rates, he had funded the portfolio by rolling over 3-month money market loans in the view that the interest rate level at least in the short to medium term would continue to drop (see Table 12.2 and Figure 12.10).

The money market funding strategy would obviously provide flexibility to "play" the market by switching short-term funding maturities according to changes in the interest rate structure. It had led to an overall lower-than-average funding cost over the past year in the falling interest rate environment. However, Mr. Fitzgerald was also aware that a 15-year fixed rate commitment represents considerable interest rate risk in case

TABLE 12.2
Last 20 Months' Midmonth Closing Rates (3-Month Money Market Rate + 1/4% Spread).

Mar. 15, 84	10 13/16%
Apr. 16, 84	10 1/4%
May 15, 84	9 11/16%
June 15, 84	9 3/8%
July 16, 84	8 15/15%
Aug. 15, 84	8 3/4%
Sept. 14, 84	8 5/8%
Oct. 15, 84	8 1/2%
Nov. 15, 84	8 11/16%
Dec. 14, 84	9 1/8%
Jan. 15, 85	9 1/4%
Feb. 15, 85	9 3/8%
Mar. 15, 85	9 1/4%
Apr. 15, 85	9 7/16%
May 15, 85	9 1/2%
June 14, 85	9 1/8%
July 15, 85	8 3/4%
Aug. 15, 85	8 11/16%
Sept. 16, 85	8 7/8%
Oct. 15, 85	8 1/2%

FIGURE 12.10
Interest Rate Structure, Money Market Rates.

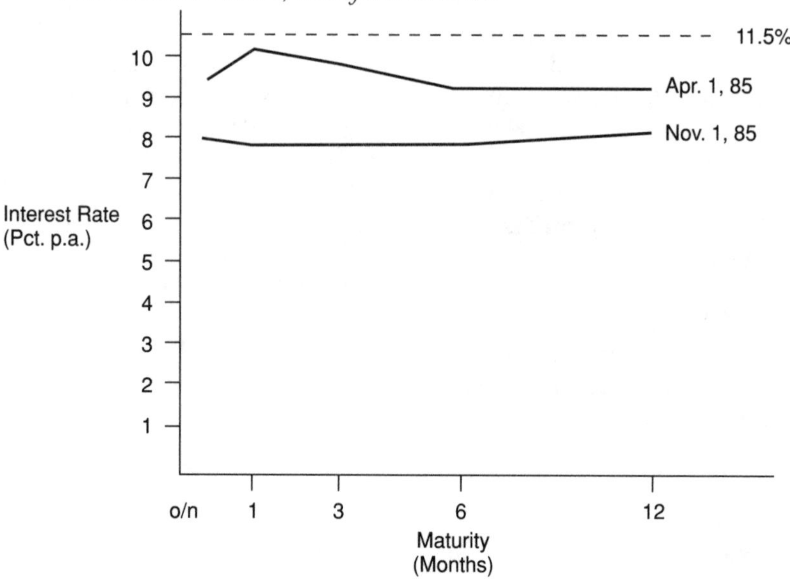

the short-term interbank money market rate increased above the fixed return of 11.50% p.a. on the mortgage portfolio.

As Mr. Fitzgerald expressed it:

> The interest rate gapping concerned us and senior management, and the whole issue had been discussed at several board meetings since the fall of 1984.

In early November 1985 the all-in six-month funding rate was around 8½% p.a., thus securing a reasonable interest rate differential to the Lauderdale Building Society in the short to medium term. The prevailing interest rate outlook favored a continued drop in the interest rate level, but with some uncertainties (see Table 12.3).

Hence the board, meeting on Mr. Fitzgerald's recommendation, decided to fund short term for an interim period of two years and to lock in the interest rate differential for the remaining 12½ years to maturity from June 1987 onward.

To guarantee a maximum funding rate, Mr. Fitzgerald contacted a few money center banks to obtain quotes on ceiling rate agreements which would approximately match the funding need of the building contract until maturity. Take into consideration the periodic annuity pay-

TABLE 12.3

Money Markets (Financial Times).

"Volcker Causes Some Confusion"

In New York the Federal funds rate was high, at around 8 percent, as payment was made for bills and bonds bought at Treasury auctions, withdrawing money from the banking system. This caused a distortion to the general interest rate picture, leaving no clues about monetary policy following the Federal Open Market Committee meeting at the beginning of the week.

An unexpected fall of $2.2 bn in the U.S. M1 money supply measure has been running well above target, but Mr. Paul Volcker, chairman of the Federal Reserve Board, indicated the target will be ignored, and the Fed will not move to aggressively tighten monetary policy.

This caused some confusion in financial markets, because in the light of the policy aimed at weakening the dollar it was not expected that rates would be increased. Signs of a sluggish economy has led to speculation the Fed may well cut its discount rate before year end but Mr. Volcker's comments were interpreted as suggesting a slight tightening by the FOMC.

Mr. Karl Otto Poehl, president of the German Bundesbank, said during the week there was no intention of following Japan in raising interest rates. The central bank drained a little liquidity in Frankfurt, by not fully replacing a maturing securities repurchase agreement, keeping interest rates around 4.5 percent. But as expected the Bundesbank council left monetary policy unchanged.

ments coming in and the interest payments on the short-term funding going out (see Table 12.4).

By assuming an average funding rate of 8½% p.a., Mr. Fitzgerald obtained an approximate estimate of the current funding need of the building contracts. Liquidity flows would balance around year 10 and so he obtained ceiling rate quotes up to June 1995 (see Table 12.5).

The Lauderdale Building Society signed the ceiling rate agreements and was henceforth guaranteed a maximum future funding cost at the quoted rates. Assuming a short-term funding rate in the money market until December 1987 of 8½% p.a., the ceiling rate agreements secured Lauderdale Building Society an average maximum funding rate of around 8.65% p.a. In addition, the Lauderdale Building Society paid a

TABLE 12.4
Cash Flow Analysis.

Date	Short-Term Funding Need	Annuity Payment	Interest on Funding*
Dec. 84	14,000,000	990,027	595,000
June 85	13,604,973	990,027	578,210
Dec. 85	13,193,156	990,027	560,709
June 86	12,763,838	990,027	542,463
Dec. 86	12,316,274	990,027	523,442
June 87	11,849,689	990,027	503,612
Dec. 87	11,632,274	990,027	482,939
June 88	11,125,186	990,027	472,820
Dec. 88	10,607,979	990,027	450,839
June 89	10,068,791	990,027	427,924
Dec. 89	9,506,688	990,027	404,034
June 90	8,920,695	990,027	379,130
Dec. 90	8,309,798	990,027	353,166
June 91	7,672,937	990,027	326,100
Dec. 91	7,009,000	990,027	297,881
June 92	6,316,855	990,027	268,466
Dec. 92	5,595,294	990,027	237,800
June 93	4,843,067	990,027	205,830
Dec. 93	4,058,870	990,027	172,502
June 94	3,241,345	990,027	137,757
Dec. 94	2,389,075	990,027	101,535
June 95	1,500,584	990,027	63,775
Dec. 95	574,332	990,027	24,409
June 96	– 391,286	990,027	– 16,630
Dec. 96	– 1,364,683	990,027	– 57,999
June 97	– 2,412,709	990,027	–102,540
Dec. 97	– 3,505,276	990,027	–148,974
June 98	– 4,644,277	990,027	–197,382
Dec. 98	– 5,831,686	990,027	–247,847
June 99	– 7,069,560	990,027	–300,456
Dec. 99	– 8,360,043	990,027	–355,302

* Assuming an 8.5% short-term funding rate until Dec. 1987.

TABLE 12.5
Ceiling Rate Quotes.

Date	Contract Size ($1,000,000)	Contract Periods (Months in Years)	Guaranteed Rate	Fee
Dec. 87	11.1	6 months in 2.5 years	8.90%	0.60%
June 88	10.6	6 months in 3.0 years	8.90%	0.60%
Dec. 88	10.0	6 months in 3.5 years	8.90%	0.60%
June 89	9.5	6 months in 4.0 years	9.10%	0.75%
Dec. 89	8.9	6 months in 4.5 years	9.10%	0.75%
June 90	8.3	6 months in 5.0 years	9.25%	1.20%
Dec. 90	7.6	6 months in 5.5 years	9.25%	12.2%
June 91	7.0	6 months in 6.0 years	9.25%	1.20%
Dec. 91	6.3	6 months in 6.5 years	9.50%	1.50%
June 92	5.6	6 months in 7.0 years	9.50%	1.50%
Dec. 92	4.8	6 months in 7.5 years	9.75%	1.80%
June 93	4.0	6 months in 8.0 years	9.75%	1.95%
Dec. 93	3.2	6 months in 8.5 years	10.00%	2.25%
June 94	2.4	6 months in 9.0 years	10.20%	2.55%
Dec. 94	1.5	6 months in 9.5 years	10.25%	2.70%
June 95	0.6	6 months in 10.0 years	10.50%	2.85%

contract fee that was calculated on the total funding need over the life of the building contracts; this amounted on average to around 0.90% p.a. Hence the Lauderdale Building Society effectively guaranteed a maximum funding rate of less than 10% p.a. on the 15-year building contracts, given that the short-term interest rate gapping would hold. The guaranteed future funding rate based on funding over the interbank market appeared to be relatively favorable as compared to other alternative sources of funding.

The break-even rate on the money market funding over the coming two-year period until December 1987 was around 14.5% p.a. which under the general interest rate outlook at the time comforted management of the Lauderdale Building Society. Due to the interest rate uncertainties over the longer term until the maturity of the mortgage loans in December 1999, however, the management of the Lauderdale Building Society preferred to lock in or guarantee a maximum future long-term funding rate.

MARKET DEVELOPMENTS

As in the foreign exchange market, there has been a further development of the standard hedging instruments in the debt market.

Captions

Captions are the debt market's parallel to the currency market's option-on-an-option concept. A caption is an option giving the holder the right to acquire or sell a ceiling rate (cap) or a floor rate agreement with a predetermined strike, maturity, interest period, and contract amount.

A *call caption on a ceiling* (*cap*) gives the holder the right to buy a ceiling rate agreement.

A *put caption on a ceiling* (*cap*) gives the holder the right to sell a ceiling rate agreement.

A *call caption on a floor rate* gives the holder the right to buy a floor rate agreement.

A *put caption on a floor rate* gives the holder the right to sell a floor rate agreement.

Normally captions are European-type options. The contracts are primarily used in connection with public bidding situations, where a tenderer wants to secure project funding at a guaranteed maximum interest expense in case the project is awarded to them. Consequently, almost all captions are call captions on a ceiling rate.

Barrier Options

A *barrier option* is an ordinary option agreement with the added feature that a second predetermined rate determines whether the option can be exercised by the holder at the strike price. There are two types of barrier options: *drop-in options* and *drop-out options*.

A *drop-in call* option *can* be exercised if once before the maturity date the market rate drops below the second rate. The second rate is lower than the strike price.

A *drop-in put* option *can* be exercised if once before the maturity date the market rate goes above the second rate. The second rate is above the strike price.

A *drop-out call* option *cannot* be exercised if once before the maturity date the market rate is below the second rate.

A *drop-out put* option *cannot* be exercised if once before the maturity date the market rate exceeds the second rate.

Look-Back Options

A *look-back option* is an option agreement that at the maturity date will be settled at the market rate during the life of the option which is most favorable to the option holder (normal options settle at the prevailing market price at maturity).

Average Rate Options

An *average rate option* agreement (*arrow*) is settled at maturity at the average market rate during the life of the option agreement. The average can be based on daily, weekly, or monthly rates. This type of option can be useful in hedging an institution's exposure that arises on a current basis, such as overdraft facilities and the like.

Example: A company has bought a traditional call option with a strike at price of 58. At maturity the holder will incur a gain of 3.75 (= 61.75 – 58), because the market price has moved to 61.75 (see Figure 12.11).

A drop-in call with a second price of 56 would not be exercised, because the market price has not been below this price during the period. A drop-out call with a switch price of 56, on the other hand, would be exercised. A look-back call option would be exercised with a gain of 6.65 (= 64.65 – 58), because 64.65 was the highest market price during the period.

An arrow would be exercised at a gain of 2.80 (= 60.80 – 58), since the average price over the period amounts to 60.80.

FIGURE 12.11

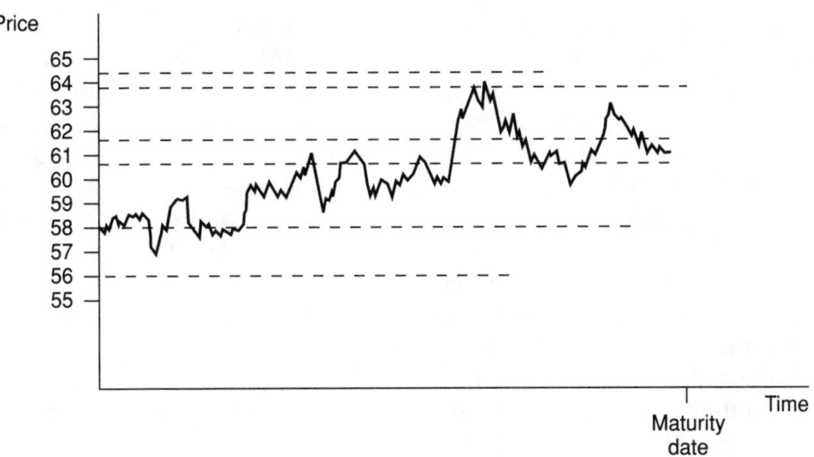

13

Interest Rate and Currency Swaps

In the early 1980s investment bankers and brokerage houses developed techniques that enabled institutions to switch assets and liabilities from one type of interest rate basis into another and/or from one currency denomination to another. At first, the market developed as pure counterparty transactions where two, three, or more institutions with different asset and liability profiles were matched to provide each institution with a more suitable exposure.[1] This type of arrangement could involve, for example, a Japanese airline, an American shipping company, and an Asian sovereign borrower—to mention just one possible constellation. In general the greater the contact with a diversified world-wide customer base, the higher the potential was for a successful match of interests in the initial stages of the swap market's development. This obviously favored the large international financial institutions in the early development of the swaps market. However as transaction volume has increased and the concept has become more familiar to potential benefactors, an active interbank market has developed for the most common types of swap transactions.

INTEREST RATE SWAP AGREEMENTS

By entering into an interest rate swap agreement, an institution can switch an asset or liability from a fixed rate basis to a floating rate basis in the same currency or vice versa. By finding two institutions with opposite interests, an intermediary can arrange a swap transaction.

Example: A construction company has raised US$ 40,000,000 five-year floating rate debt to fund a future project and would like to lock in the future interest expense related to the project. Conversely, a commercial bank has launched a five-year fixed coupon Eurodollar issue of US$ 40,000,000 to fund its portfolio of floating rate loans. These two counterparties can enter an interest rate swap through an intermediary and obtain the type of liability that each is looking for.

This is done simply by having each of the two institutions service the other's interest payments throughout the life of the loans. Since the two liabilities are in the same currency, there is no exchange of principal in the swap. The construction company pays fixed rate interest to the intermediary, and the intermediary pays the floating rate interest to the company to service its floating rate liability. The commercial bank pays floating rate interest to the intermediary, and the intermediary pays fixed interest to the commercial bank to service its fixed rate liability. The outcome is that the construction company has obtained a fixed rate liability, and the commercial bank has obtained a floating rate liability resulting in a better match of the interest rate basis of their assets and liabilities.

The two counterparties, who usually are unknown to each other, deal solely with the intermediary, and their contractual obligations with regard to the swap transaction are solely made against the intermediary. Conversely, the intermediary assumes the counterparty risk of the two counterparties. The intermediary will sometimes charge a front-end fee, fixed as a percentage of the transaction amount, for performing the brokerage function and for managing the counterparty risk in the transaction (see Figure 13.1).

Very often two exactly matching counterparties cannot be found, and several institutions have to be matched together to cover the transaction. As the transaction volume has increased, however, it has become common practice for the intermediaries to run short-term open positions, which to some extent can be hedged in the financial futures or the FRA market. Today two-sided bid and offer quotes are given by the major swap intermediaries in all the major international currencies. The basis for the quotes is usually a common fixed rate indicator of the currency in question. An interest rate swap in U.S. dollars is typically quoted around

FIGURE 13.1
Interest Rate Swaps.

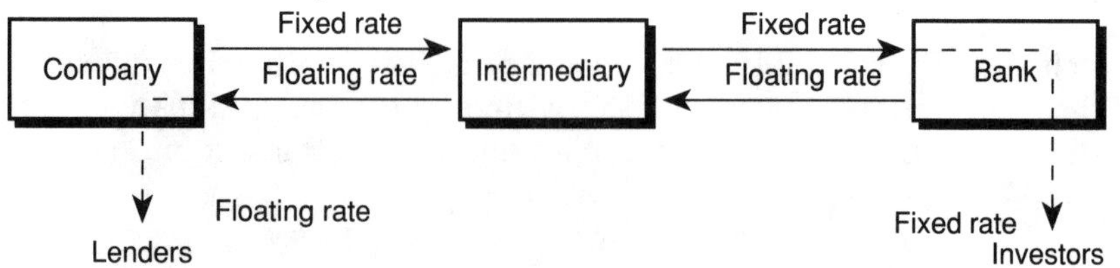

the going U.S. Treasury bill rate, whereas pound sterling quotes relate to the gilt rate, German mark quotes to the Schuldschein rate, and so on (see Table 13.1).

The *bid* rate marks the basis point spread over the U.S. Treasury bill rate of the corresponding maturity, and indicates the fixed rate payment the quoting bank will *pay* for 6-month LIBOR payments. Similarly, the *offer* rate indicates the fixed rate spread over treasuries that the quoting bank will *receive* from the counterparty for the delivery of LIBOR payments. Hence, the U.S. dollar swap yield curve will follow the yield curve of the U.S. Treasury bills, including the swap spread (see Figure 13.2).

A 3-year U.S. dollar interest rate swap quoting 50–70 indicates:

1. The intermediary bids for a dollar floating rate interest at LIBOR by providing fixed rate interest at the going U.S. Treasury bill rate plus 50 basis points.
2. It offers a dollar floating rate interest at LIBOR against receipt of fixed rate interest at the U.S. Treasury bill rate plus 70 basis points.

Example: An institutional investor holds a 3-year floating rate dollar portfolio at LIBOR + 1/4% and would like to fix the return on the investment over the three-year period. The investor has received the preceding quote for a fixed-floating U.S. dollar interest rate swap. The investor would then provide the intermediary with interest at LIBOR. In return he would receive a fixed interest payment equal to the going U.S. Trea-

TABLE 13.1
U.S. Dollar Interest Rate Swaps

	Bid	*Offer*
1 year	52	72
2 years	53	73
3 years	50	70
5 years	55	75
7 years	58	78
10 years	60	80

FIGURE 13.2
Treasury Yield Versus Swap Yield—February 19, 1993. (Source: Chemical Bank Global Derivatives Group; reprinted by permission of IFR, International Financing Review)

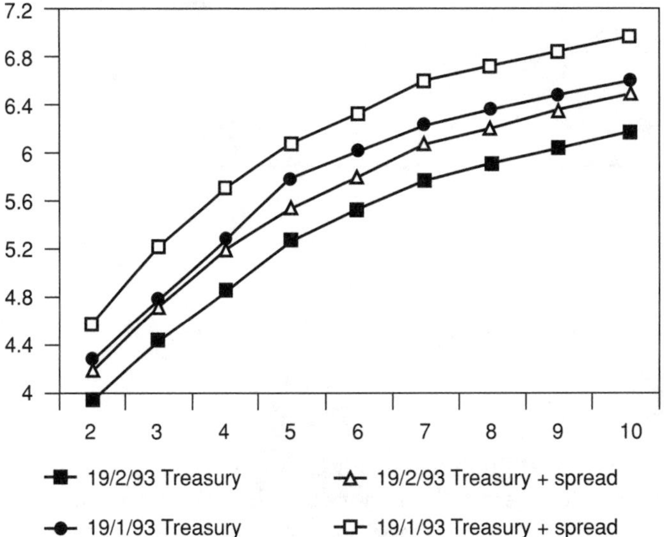

sury bill rate at the time of signing the swap agreement plus 50 basis points. To reach the total fixed rate expense, the investor should add the 25 basis points spread over LIBOR. If the 3 year U.S. Treasury bill rate at the time of signing is 5.25%, the return on the investment has been effectively locked in at a rate of 6% p.a. (5.25 + 0.50 + 0.25) over the three-year period.

Typically the bank providing the swap quote will charge a front-end fee, or subtract a spread from the fixed rate payment. The hedging position is illustrated in Figure 13.3.

Example: A corporation has engaged in a 5-year LIBOR-based U.S. dollar loan. Interest is paid at the 6-month LIBOR plus a spread of ⅜% p.a. The corporation fears that the interest rate level is increasing, and therefore wants to engage in a fixed-floating interest rate swap to convert the floating rate payments to fixed rate payments. The 5-year swap quote is 55–75; that is, the bank will make LIBOR payments against receipt of the U.S. Treasury rate plus 75 basis points. Hence with a 5-year treasury bill rate of 6.25%, the borrower's total fixed rate cost amounts to 7.375% [= 6.25 + 0.75 + 0.375].

The bank charges a front-end fee or adds a spread to the fixed rate quote. The hedging position is illustrated in Figure 13.4.

FIGURE 13.3
Interest Rate Swap Hedge (Investor).

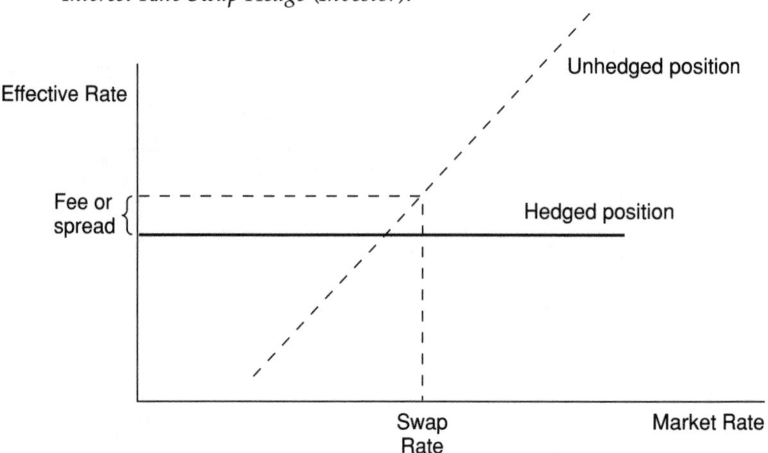

The Treasury yield rate indication (for example, the resulting fixed rate of 7% in the preceding example) is normally indicated on a semiannual interest rate basis. To convert this to an annual interest rate basis, the following calculation must be performed: $\{[1 + 7.375/200)]^2 - 1\} \times 100 = 7.51\%$ p.a. This rate is indicated on an annual bond basis, that is, 360/360 days. Therefore, if the rate is to be brought on to a comparable money market rate, the calculation of which is based on actual days in a

FIGURE 13.4
Interest Rate Swap Hedge (Borrower).

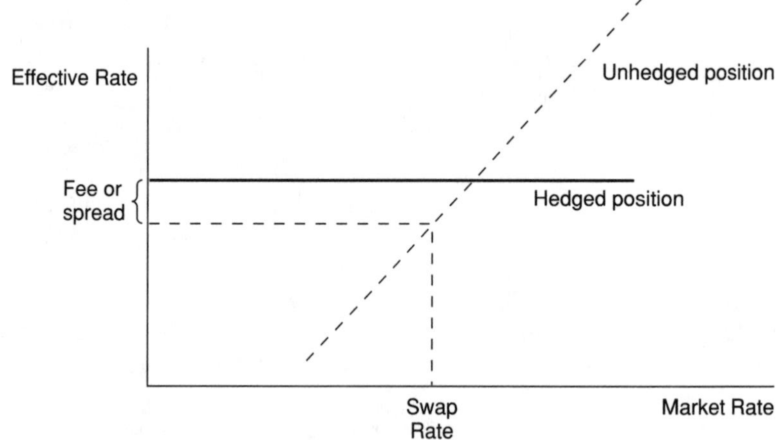

year of 360 days, the following adjustment must be made: [7.51 × 360/365] = 7.41% p.a.

The conversion between semiannual and annual compound interest can be formalized in the following way:

$$i_s = [(i_a/100 + 1)^{1/2} - 1] \times 200$$

$$i_a = [(i_s/200 + 1)^2 - 1] \times 100$$

where

i_s = Semiannual interest rate.
i_a = Annual compound interest rate.

The fixed bond base rate for most currencies (U.S. dollars, Swiss francs, German marks, French francs, Dutch guilders, and so on) is calculated on the basis of a year with 12 months of 30 days each, that is, 360/360 days per year, whereas rates in the money market are based on actual number of days in a 360 day year, that is, 365/360 days per year. Hence, the conversion between annual bond basis (BB) and money market (MM) basis can be formalized as follows:

$$MM = BB \times 365/360$$

$$BB = MM \times 365/360$$

Interest Rate Basis Swaps

Institutions that engage in transactions with different interest rate basis on assets and liabilities incur an interest rate basis gap. This could, for example, be a commercial bank making prime-based corporate loans while funding them on a floating rate LIBOR basis. Usually changes in the prime rate lag behind changes in the interest rates of the interbank market, and the changes will be less frequent than those of the day-to-day money market changes. Hence, a bank lending on these terms can get into a rate squeeze in a scenario of increasing interest rates. The bank can eliminate this exposure by engaging in a prime-LIBOR interest rate swap.

The intermediating bank providing the interest rate basis swap might be in a position in which the swap transaction with the corporation can be covered through reverse interest rate flows with two other counterparts (see Figure 13.5).

CURRENCY SWAP AGREEMENTS

By entering into a currency swap agreement an institution can switch an asset or a liability from one currency to another. The swap transaction

FIGURE 13.5
Interest Rate Basis Swap (Example).

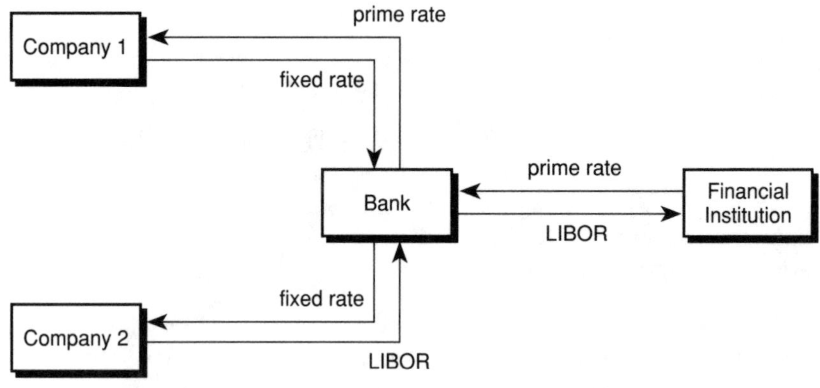

can be done in the same interest rate basis (that is, fixed into fixed rate or floating into floating rate), or the swap can switch from a fixed interest basis to a floating rate basis in the other currency, or from a floating rate basis into a fixed rate basis in the other currency (see Table 13.2).

The currencies are swapped initially through a normal spot foreign exchange transaction so that each of the counterparties have full availability of the currencies they are seeking. Throughout the life of the two obligations, each of the counterparties pay the other's interest obligations in accordance with the swap agreement. At maturity the currencies are swapped back to the original currencies through a forward foreign exchange transaction, usually effectuated at the initial spot exchange rate.

Example: A public entity has acquired a 7-year fixed coupon US$ 35,000,000 loan. It would like to switch it into floating rate Swiss francs to diversify the loan portfolio among different currencies and to take advantage of an expected decrease in the interest rate level. Concurrently a corporate entity has just issued a 7-year Sw. frc. 100,000,000 floating rate note. It seeks to switch it into a fixed rate U.S. dollar liability to lock in the funding cost and to match the company's dollar receivables.

In this situation the currencies will be swapped initially at the current spot exchange rate of 2.8571 Sw. frc./US$ (0.3500 US$/Sw. frc.). The public entity will pay US$ 35,000,000 to the intermediary against receipt of Sw. frc. 100,000,000. Conversely, the corporation will pay Sw. frc. 100,000,000 to the intermediary against receipt of US$ 35,000,000. At this point the two counterparties have the currencies they want. See Figure 13.6(1).

TABLE 13.2
Summary of Interest Rate and Currency Swaps.

Interest Rate Swaps

Fixed interest payments into floating interest payments in the same currency.

Or

Floating interest payments into fixed interest payments in the same currency.

Or

Interest payments on an interest rate basis into another interest rate basis in the same currency.

Currency Swaps

One currency into another currency,

And

Fixed interest payments into fixed interest payments in the other currency.

Or

Fixed interest payments into floating interest payments in the other currency.

Or

Fixed interest payments into floating interest payments in the other currency.

Or

Floating interest payments into fixed interest payments in the other currency.

Or

Interest payments on one interest rate basis into another interest rate basis in the other currency.

Throughout the seven years of the two loans, the public entity will pay floating rate Swiss franc interest to the intermediary against receipt of fixed rate U.S. dollar interest from the intermediary to service the fixed rate dollar loan. The corporation will pay fixed rate dollar interest to the intermediary against receipt of floating rate Swiss franc interest payments from the intermediary to service the floating rate franc loan. See Figure 13.6(2).

At maturity of both loans, the two principal currency amounts are again swapped back at the initial spot exchange rate of 0.3500 US$/Sw. frc. The public entity pays Sw. frc. 100,000,000 to the intermediary against receipt of US$ 35,000,000 for repayment of the dollar loan. The corporation pays US$ 35,000,000 to the intermediary against receipt of Sw. frc. 100,000,000 for repayment of the franc note. See Figure 13.6(3).

Through this swap, the public entity has performed a debt service as if it had on its books a floating rate Swiss franc liability, and the corporation has acted as if it had a fixed rate dollar liability. However, the pub-

FIGURE 13.6
Interest Rate and Currency Swap.

1. Receiving proceeds from initial loan:

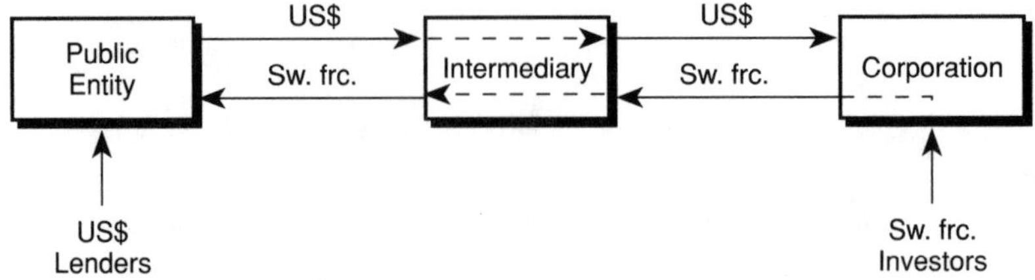

2. Paying interest throughout the life of the loan:

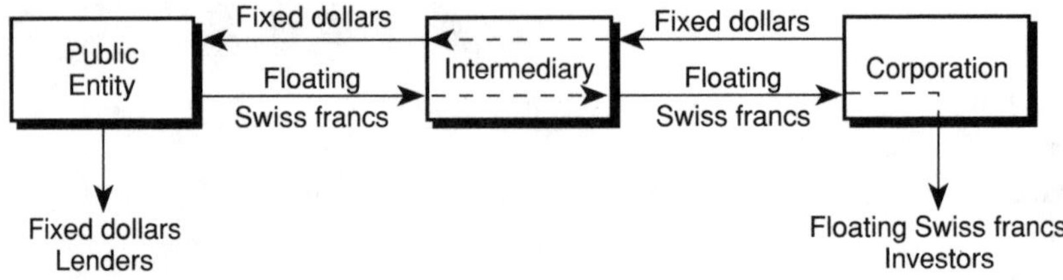

3. Paying back principal at maturity:

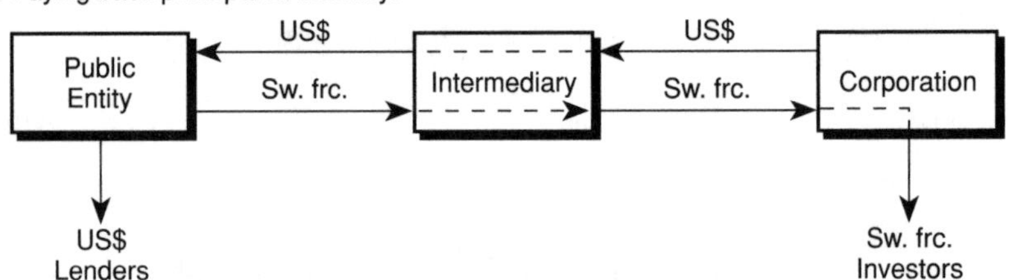

lic entity—and only the public entity—is fully liable for the dollar loan against the lenders, and only the corporation is liable for the Swiss franc note against the investors. Because each of the two counterparties in all likelihood is unknown to the other, the intermediary assumes the counterparty risk. The swap arrangement is solely negotiated with the intermediary and each of the counterparts have no obligations to each other. The intermediary will charge an up-front fee for performing the broker role and for assuming the counterparty risk of the transaction.

The currency swap is an especially flexible hedging arrangement when an asset or a liability represents a combined interest rate and currency exposure. The cash flow statement providing the institution's liquidity forecast would reveal such exposures. For example, a German institution has a net outflow in U.S. dollars emanating from a floating rate loan agreement. If it is in the interest of the German institution to lock in the future cash outflow in German marks, then it could engage in a currency swap agreement bringing the floating rate U.S. dollar commitment into a fixed rate mark commitment. As is obvious by now, currency swap agreements have their particular strength when hedging international financial commitments. Although they can be useful for other hedging purposes, the vast majority of swap agreements are closed to hedge existing financial commitments or to optimize new financial arrangements for borrowers and investors.

The swap markets have other advantages and uses. Swap arrangements can furnish cheaper financing to an institution raising new funds because it can approach the cheapest financial market to raise its debt and then swap it into the type of liability wanted initially. The swap technique can also be used to take advantage of expected changes in foreign exchange rates and the interest rates. If the institution's expectation favors an increase in the interest rate level, investors could swap fixed rate assets into floating rate assets and borrowers could swap floating rate liabilities into fixed rate liabilities in order to take advantage of expected future interest rate movements. Conversely, if the interest rate level is expected to drop, the investors could swap floating rate assets into fixed rate assets, and borrowers could switch fixed rate liabilities into floating rate liabilities. Also, if the market believes that the interest rate will go up, it might indicate a favorable time for a floating rate investor to lock in the higher future rate. Conversely, if the general market outlook favors an interest rate drop, it could signal an opportune moment for the floating rate borrower to lock in a lower future rate. Hence the swap technique can be used to take advantage of expected rate movements or to lock in future rates when the market appears to be favorable. It goes without saying that the currency swaps can be similarly applied to take advantage of favorable foreign exchange rate expectations.

For the major international currencies, the currency swaps are quoted with two-way bid and offer rates in the interbank market (see Table 13.3). The bank providing swap quotes to client counterparts will usually charge an up-front fee or include a swap spread to cover transaction cost and management of counterparty risk. The currency swap quotes are based on fixed annual rate payments in the currency against 6-month U.S. dollar LIBOR payments.

The swap market has often been utilized by borrowers issuing securities in the Euromarket. If the Eurobonds provide favorable funding to the borrower, the loan can be converted into a currency that is more suitable to the borrower's currency exposure on similarly favorable terms in that currency. In the Euromarket, bonds denominated in high coupon currencies have had particular interest among investors, thereby providing good funding opportunities for high-quality borrowers.

TABLE 13.3
Interbank Currency Swaps.

German Marks	*Bid*	*Offer*
3 years	5.86	5.95
5 years	6.29	6.42
7 years	6.75	6.93
Swiss Franc		
3 years	5.22	5.37
5 years	5.47	5.65
7 years	5.62	5.85
Australian Dollar		
3 years	13.84	14.12
5 years	13.64	13.92

Example: A corporation obtains a 5-year fixed coupon Eurobond loan in Australian dollars at an effective cost of 13.40% p.a. A bank quotes 5-year A$/US$ currency swaps at 13.54–14.02, that is, the corporation receives fixed rate A$ at 13.54% p.a. against payment of US$ LIBOR. The corporation earns approximately 14 basis points on the A$ payments [= 13.54 – 13.40], providing the borrower with an effective floating rate cost of LIBOR – 0.14% (see Figure 13.7).

The market opportunities in the currency swap market arise from a variety of reasons.

- *Market inefficiencies:* Different capital markets often have different appetites for different types of borrowers. One type of institutional borrowers may have tapped one capital market extensively, leading to weakening demand for such financing among the investors providing the funds. In this case another type of borrower might get better borrowing terms in that market. Hence it might be an advantage for the initial borrower to approach another capital market and swap the proceeds with the new borrower in the initial market.
- *Availability of a certain type of financing:* In situations where market access is restricted by queuing arrangements, a potential borrower,

FIGURE 13.7
A$/US$ Currency Swap.

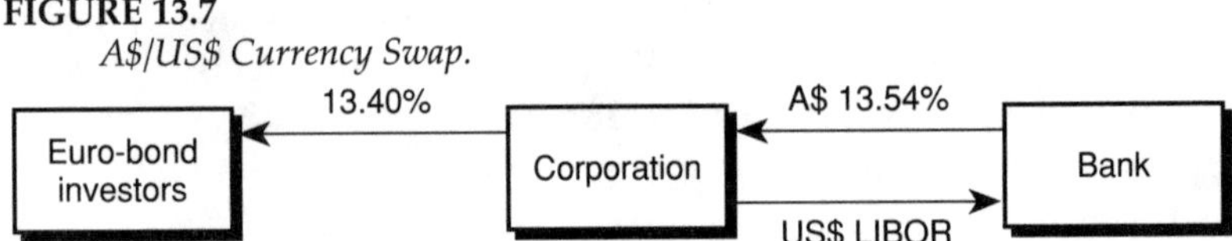

which ranks high on the queuing list, might swap loan proceeds with a newcomer to the market, which otherwise might have to wait very long to get the wanted financing.

- *Subsidized lending:* Many national export credit institutions lend the domestic currency at favorable rates. The beneficiary might not need this currency, but would rather obtain a liability in another currency.
- *Interest rate discrepancies:* Differences between the domestic interest rate level and the rates on the Euromarkets.

These are just some of the possible causes leading to the development of a currency swap market.

Case: Currency-Interest Rate Swap: Manufacturing Company, Currency-Interest Rate Gapping

The Atlanta-based moulding company, A&T Manufacturing, Inc., had just signed a contract with a major German supplier in August 1985 for the delivery of tools and equipment at a total value of DM 13,900,000—close to US$ 5,000,000 at the going exchange rate. The German exporter had guaranteed a favorable 3-year mark loan on the total amount of the purchase price to commence upon delivery. However, if A&T Manufacturing accepted this financing option, the loan would have to be repaid in DM and hence the loan repayment would represent a currency exposure on the part of the borrower (see Table 13.4). In August 1985 the foreign exchange rate was around 2.7800 DM/US$, but there was considerable uncertainty as to the future movement of the U.S. dollar exchange rate. As the Chief Financial Officer of A&T Manufacturing, Sam Bariolli, expressed it:

> We received a very attractive medium-term loan offer from our German supplier. The loan was to be repaid semiannually at an interest rate equivalent to the DM interbank offered rate, which at that time was around 5% p.a. and hence considerably lower than the equivalent U.S. interest rate. However, the DM loan at the same time presented us with a dilemma because the foreign exchange exposure from this loan was extremely difficult to evaluate. The dollar continued to be relatively strong despite recent drops, but there seemed to be increasing political pressure to deflate the strength of the dollar exchange rate further. We feared that the dollar might weaken considerably over the coming years which would make a DM loan unattractive to us despite the favorable interest terms.

TABLE 13.4
Loan Structure—DM Loan (2.78 DM/US$ Constant Exchange Rate).

Date	*Outstanding (DM)*	*Assumed Repayment (DM)*	*Interest 6-month DM Rate*	*Payments (DM)*	*Total DM Payment*
Jan. 86	13,900,000	—	5.00%	—	—
Jul. 86	11,583,334	2,316,666	4.90%	347,500	2,664,166
Jan. 87	9,266,667	2,316,667	4.80%	283,792	2,600,459
Jul. 87	6,950,000	2,316,667	4.80%	222,400	2,539,067
Jan. 88	4,633,334	2,316,666	4.75%	166,800	2,483,466
Jul. 88	2,316,667	2,316,667	4.75%	110,042	2,426,709
Jan. 89	0	2,316,667		55,021	2,371,688
		DM 13,900,000		DM 1,185,555	DM 15,085,555
	(In US$ Equivalent)				
Jan. 86	5,000,000	—		—	—
Jul. 86	4,166,667	833,333		125,000	958,333
Jan. 87	3,333,334	833,333		102,084	935,417
Jul. 87	2,500,000	833,334		79,999	913,333
Jan. 88	1,666,667	833,333		60,000	893,333
Jul. 88	883,334	883,333		39,584	872,917
Jan. 89	0	883,334		19,791	853,125
		$5,000,000		$426,458	$5,426,458

> We really wanted to know the exact cost of the equipment in order to refine our cost-benefit evaluation of the plant and to create certainty at least as far as our financial charges were concerned.

In this situation A&T Manufacturing contacted their major bank to get a comparative offer for a three-year fixed rate loan in U.S. dollars to fund the import purchase. It turned out that a fixed rate dollar offer would cost around 9.75% p.a. based on the same repayment structure as proposed by the German exporter. At the same time an equivalent dollar variable rate offer could be done at a rate of around 8.50% p.a. for the first six-month period, considerably higher than the DM alternative.

As Sam Bariolli engaged in further discussions with the bank on the matter, it appeared to the bank representative that they could take advantage of the favorable DM offer from the German exporter by swapping the variable payments in DM into a more favorable fixed rate payment structure in U.S. dollars. By engaging in a US$/DM fixed/floating rate swap, it turned out that A&T Manufacturing could get away with paying a fixed dollar rate of 8.25% p.a.—considerably lower than the alternative fixed rate proposal and even lower than the variable rate offer

FIGURE 13.8

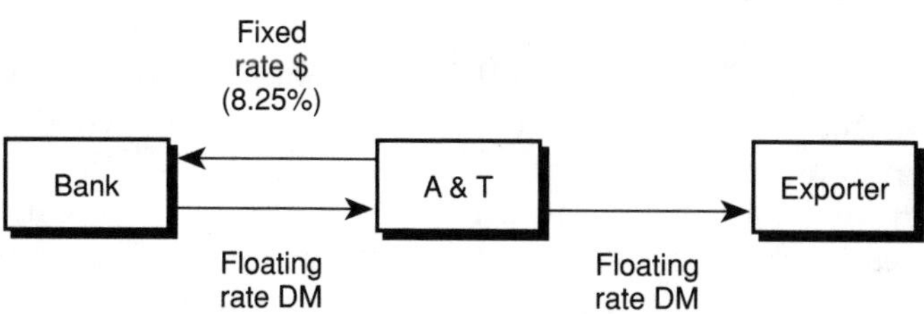

at 8.50% p.a. Under this scheme A&T Manufacturing Inc. exchanged the DM principal into dollars at the current exchange rate. Throughout the life of the loan, the company paid fixed rate dollar interest to the bank which in turn passed variable rate DM payments to A&T Manufacturing, which was used for loan repayments to the German exporter. Principal amounts would be exchanged at the initial foreign exchange rate at which the loan amount was exchanged on due dates (see Figure 13.8).

By engaging in a fixed rate dollar/floating rate German mark swap, A&T Manufacturing obtained the best of two worlds. It eliminated the uncertainty of the DM/US$ exchange rate, and it managed to lock in and convert the favorable DM interest rate into an equivalently favorable U.S. dollar fixed interest rate (see Table 13.5).

Case: Currency-Interest Rate Swap: Financial Institution, Pass-Through Structure, Currency-Interest Rate Gapping

Algemene Bank Institut, an expanding European financial intermediary, for the first time could establish an international bond issue for a

TABLE 13.5
Comparative Analysis (Loan Repayment).

	Unchanged $ Rate (2.78)	*5% drop in $ Rate (2.64)*	*10% drop in $ Rate (2.50)*	*Direct Fixed (9.75%)*	*Swap Payment (8.25%)*
Jan. 86	—	—	—	—	—
Jul. 86	958,333	1,009,154	1,065,666	1,077,083	1,039,583
Jan. 87	935,417	985,022	1,040,184	1,031,266	1,005,208
Jul. 87	913,333	961,768	1,015,627	991,698	970,834
Jan. 88	893,333	940,707	993,386	952,130	936,458
Jul. 88	872,917	919,208	970,684	912,563	902,083
Jan. 89	853,125	898,367	948,675	872,995	867,709
	5,426,458	5,714,226	6,034,222	5,837,735	5,721,875

major international borrower. The bank offered a unique 10-year fixed rate issue totalling DM 300,000,000 at an all-in rate of 6.70% p.a. Since this was the first time this major and well reputed borrower was introduced in the bond market, the funding rate obtained was very favorable compared to the going market rate at the time of issue. Also, the Algemene Bank Institut was able to attract new investors to this issue through its domestic bank associates, and it could therefore offer even better terms than normally was the case for this type of issue.

However, the borrower maintained the major part of its cash flows in U.S. dollars and hence would prefer to obtain the funding in U.S. dollars to eliminate the currency exposure at loan repayment. The view of the borrower at that time was that the U.S. interest rate would decline further over the coming 12–24 months and would therefore favor a floating rate funding proposal (see Figure 13.9).

As the head of the International Bond Department expressed it:

> We were in a situation where we could arrange fixed rate long-term funding in DM to a major international borrower on very favorable terms with the fixed funding rate being something like ⅛–¼ percentage points below the current market rate for a similar issue. As the borrower was likely to give preference to a floating rate dollar proposal, we proceeded to arrange a currency/interest rate swap con-

FIGURE 13.9
Interest Rate Development over Past 12 Months. (End of Month, 3 months US$ LIBID).

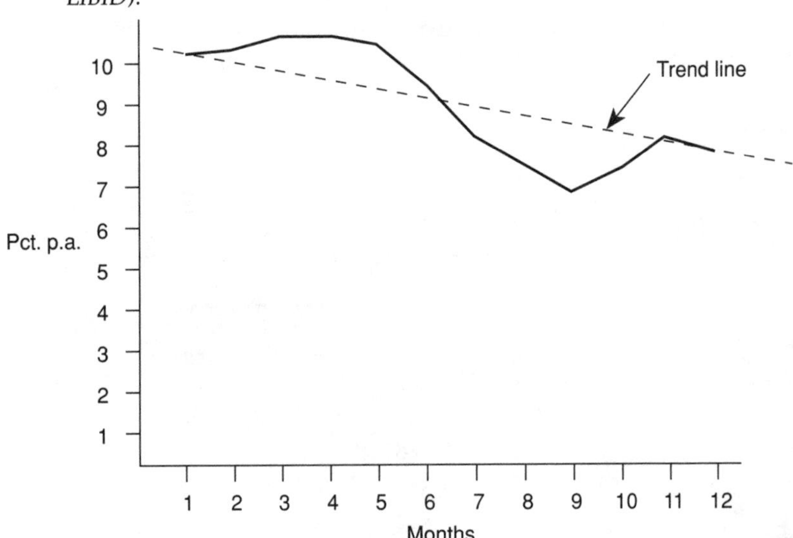

TABLE 13.6
Interest Rate Structure.

Bundesbank Bond Yield:		*6.2% p.a.*
Eurodollar Interbank BID Rate:	1 month	8.05% p.a.
	3 months	7.96% p.a.
	6 months	7.92% p.a.
	1 year	7.98% p.a.
	2 years	8.50% p.a.
	5 years	8.85% p.a.

verting the fixed rate DM funding into a floating rate dollar proposal.

Algemene Bank Institut approached several major international financial institutions to obtain quotes for a DM/US$ fixed/floating rate swap. The most competitive offer was obtained from a well-known London-based merchant banking group proposing to provide DM payments at the Bundesbank bond yield plus 0.60% corresponding to 6.80% (see Table 13.6) against receipt of U.S. dollar payments at three months LIBOR. This meant that the 6.70% fixed rate DM payments could be converted into LIBOR – 0.10% = LIBID, which represented a very favorable variable funding rate in dollars (see Figure 13.10).

Thus Algemene Bank Institut was able to offer a 10-year US$ 100,000,000 (approximate dollar value at current DM/US$ foreign exchange rate) funding proposal at a rate of three-month LIBID. The borrower considered this a very interesting proposal and accepted the offer.

FIGURE 13.10
Interest Rate Structure.

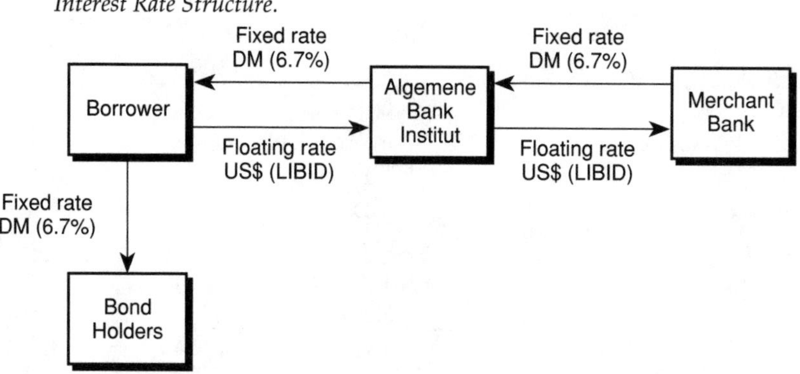

Case: Interest Rate Swap: Financial Institution, Asset and Liability Mismatch, Interest Basis Gapping

Since Mid State Bank Corp. acquired a 25% stake in a bank conglomerate in the London market in 1981, the bank increasingly looked to the Eurocurrency market as a potential source of funding—although being a conservative bank, it had not engaged heavily in this type of cross currency funding. The majority of the short-term loans booked carried a variable interest rate which would vary in accordance with movements in the domestic short-term interest rates. For longer-term commitments, the bank usually based the interest rate on the bank's prime rate. The prime rate was a variable rate but not as volatile as the short-term money market rates which could periodically move whimsically.

This was the problem. The management of Mid State Bank was aware that the prime rate—which, to a large extent, is determined by domestic competitive forces—is by nature very difficult to adapt to immediate changes in the short-term market rates. To the extent that the bank funded longer-term loans by obtaining short-term money market placements, the interest rate margin could get squeezed in periods when the interbank market was experiencing an upward move in interest rates. This factor would only be reflected in the prime rate after a considerable time lag and then only if the upward move in interest rates was longer-term and persistent in character.

In November of 1985 the Mid State Bank Corp. had booked a four-year committed loan structure to a major corporate client totalling US$ 25,000,000 with annual repayments of principal and interest on November 10. The interest calculation on the loan was based on the going Mid State Bank prime rate plus ⅞%. The incremental funding for this loan was

TABLE 13.7

Mid State Bank Corp. Balance Sheet (US$ 1,000,000)

Assets		*Liabilities*	
Cash	214.5	Deposits	3,349.6
Interbank Placements	259.7	Interbank placements	
		—Foreign banks	442.5
Securities	466.0	—Domestic banks	189.9
Loans & advances	3,529.8	Other liabilities	219.9
Other assets	150.3	Total liabilities	4,001.9
		Net Worth	418.4
Total assets	4,620.3	Total liabilities & NW	4,420.3

obtained from the London affiliate at LIBOR. Since the loan was booked, the London interbank rate had seen both upward and downward moves and in March 1986 the market carried a bullish sentiment with continued expectations of an interest rate drop. With the prime rate largely fixed with a view to domestic competition, management had envisaged the risk of a squeeze on the interest rate margin as LIBOR increased from 8 to 9% from November 1985 to January 1986. They also thought that the percent drop in the interest rate in March 1986 to 7⅝% could represent a good time to close the interest rate gap (see Table 13.8).

TABLE 13.8
Interest Rate Development.

	Nov. 1985	*Jan. 1986*	*Mar. 1986*
The U.S. prime rate	9½	9½	9½
3-months Eurodollar Offered Rate	8 1/16	8 15/16	7⅝

Charles Hoover, CEO of the Mid State Bank Corp., voiced his concern for a potentially unfavorable interest rate development:

> Even if there is a natural interlinkage between the domestic interest rate level and the rate prevalent in the Eurocurrency markets, our prime rate is influenced by other factors than simply the movement in the short-term interbank rate on the international money markets. Therefore, as we increasingly obtain funding on LIBOR basis to expand our portfolio of domestic loans based on the prime rate, the interest differential will be vulnerable to different movements in the two interest rates.

The Mid State Bank Corp. found that the solution to the basis risk issue was to engage in an interest rate basis swap with one of the major money center banks. Mid State Bank obtained quotes from several money center banks on interest rate swaps converting the prime rate into a LIBOR-based rate. In this specific case Mid State Bank Corp. accepted to exchange LIBOR for prime—1.25%. The swap arrangement was adapted specifically to the repayment structure of the four-year $25,000,000 loan. Under the swap arrangement Mid State Bank Corp. at each maturity date would pay the interest amount on the principal outstanding, based on prime—1.25%. In turn it would receive from the money center bank the equivalent interest amount based on LIBOR (see Figure 13.11).

By engaging in this interest basis swap, Mid State Bank Corp. effec-

FIGURE 13.11

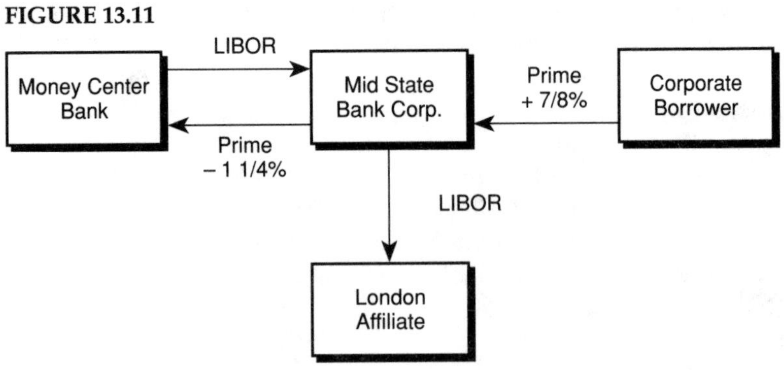

tively locked in an interest rate spread of 2⅛% on the $25 million loan, thus securing lifetime earnings on the loan during the four years to maturity in November 1989 of $1.3 million (see Table 13.9).

TABLE 13.9
US$ 25,000,000 Loan Repayment Schedule.

Date	*Outstanding*	*Net Interest Revenue (Spread 2⅛%)*
Nov. 10, 1985	$25,000,000	—
Nov. 10, 1986	$18,750,000	$ 531,250.00
Nov. 10, 1987	$12,500,000	$ 398,437.50
Nov. 10, 1988	$ 6,250,000	$ 265,625.00
Nov. 10, 1989	0	$ 132,812.50
Locked-in net interest revenue		$1,328,125.00

LONG DATED FORWARD AGREEMENTS

In principle long-dated forward agreements function in the same way as standard forward agreements. The difference, as the name indicates, is that long-dated forwards exceed the normal length of interbank forward agreements with contracts in special cases maturing up to 20 years hence. The main transaction volume, however, is concentrated in maturities from three to seven years. The financial service is used by international institutions to hedge long-term assets and liabilities in foreign currencies and thus represents a close substitute to currency swap agreements.

The problem for the financial institutions offering long-dated forwards is that interbank money markets with maturities over three years are practically nonexistent. Consequently the transaction cannot be hedged in the traditional way by accessing the two currencies' money markets, as with currency forwards. So the long-dated forward market, like the currency swap market, has developed as counterparty transactions where the financial institution offering long-dated forward agreements tries to match the transactions among a group of counterparties. However, financial institutions increasingly take open positions in long-dated forwards in the expectation of future transaction volume which will eventually close the gaps. The periodic open positions can be partly hedged in the financial futures market. For the same reason there is no developed interbank market for long-dated forward agreements.

A long dated forward is quoted as a premium or discount on the going spot foreign exchange rate (see Chapter 10).

Example: A non-American international trading company is expecting periodic cash inflows of US$ 10,000,000 every year over the next seven years. The company will get a long-dated forward quote for each of the seven years, which effectively lock in the future cash inflow in the domestic currency.

Conversely, a non-Swiss sovereign borrower has obtained a 15-year 9% fixed coupon bullet loan of Sw. frc. 100,000,000 with annual interest payments. The sovereign entity can obtain 15 long-dated forward quotes for the Sw. frc. 9,000,000 coupon payments and one quote for the principal repayment of the Sw. frc. 100,000,000 due in 15 years and engage into long-dated forward contracts. Hereby the sovereign entity effectively has tied the future cash outflow into the domestic currency.

Compared to the currency swap market, the long-dated forward agreements are less flexible, since swap transactions can change the interest rate basis and at the same time be applied to almost any cash flow pattern. However, the long-dated forward agreement can provide an efficient mechanism to lock in long-term future cash flows in many international cross currencies.

SWAPTIONS

A *swaption* is an option on a swap. The holder of a swaption has the right to engage in a future defined swap transaction within a fixed time period.

A *call swaption* gives the holder the right to buy a swap, that is, the right to buy LIBOR payments. This is sometimes termed a *payers,* since it gives the right to pay fixed interest against receipt of floating rate.

A *put swaption* gives the holder the right to sell a swap, that is, the right to sell LIBOR payments. This is sometimes termed a *receivers,* since it gives right to receive fixed interest against payment of floating rate.

Example: A borrower has issued a floating rate liability to take advantage of an expected drop in interest rates. As the interest rate outlook is somewhat uncertain, the borrower would like the opportunity to swap into a fixed interest rate basis after 12 months. This is done by buying a 12-month call swaption.

DIFFERENTIAL SWAPS

A *differential swap,* also termed a *diff swap* or a *quanto swap,* is an interest rate and currency swap transaction by which one of the interest rate payments can be made in a currency that is different from the currency of the interest rate basis.

Example: An institution has a 5-year loan denominated in German marks paying interest on a 6-month LIBOR basis. The borrower would like to take advantage of the lower U.S. dollar interest rate without changing the present currency exposure. This is done by engaging in a quanto swap with a bank. In the quanto swap, the bank pays 6-month DM LIBOR to the borrower. The borrower in return pays 6-month US$ LIBOR plus a spread to the bank, where the interest payments are made in German marks (see Figure 13.12).

To hedgers the differential swap can be attractive, because it enables them to take advantage of differences in the interest rate level of different currencies without imposing any new currency risk on the hedger.

FIGURE 13.12
US$-DM Differential or Quanto Swap.

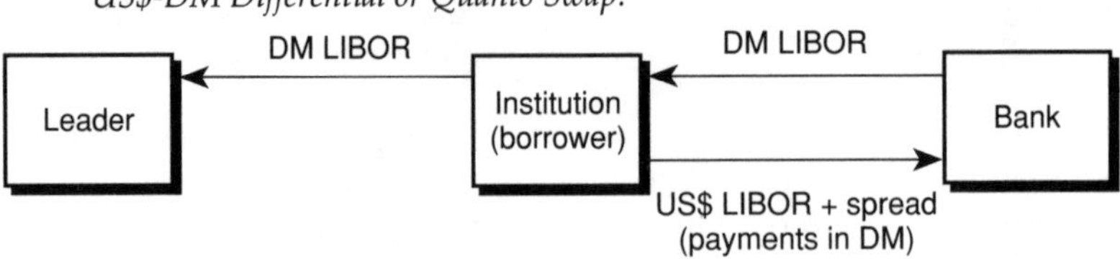

FIGURE 13.13
DM and US$ Yield Curves (Example).

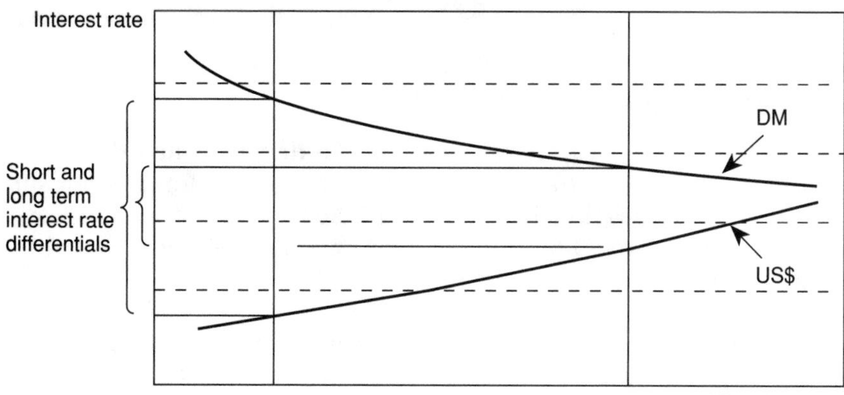

The differential swap takes advantage of the different yield curve shapes of, for example, the U.S. dollar and £ sterling with upward sloping yield curves, and other currencies, such as German marks, French francs, and European Currency Units with upward sloping yield curves.

Due to conversely sloping yield curves, the 6-month rate spread is much higher than, for example, the 5-year spread or the difference between the 5-year fixed interest rate swap quotes in the two currencies (see Figure 13.13).

The challenge to the banks offering differential swaps is to hedge the foreign exchange risk arising from the interest payments received in another currency (see Figure 13.14). Since there is no natural hedge to

FIGURE 13.14
U.S. Dollar-German Mark Differential Swap.

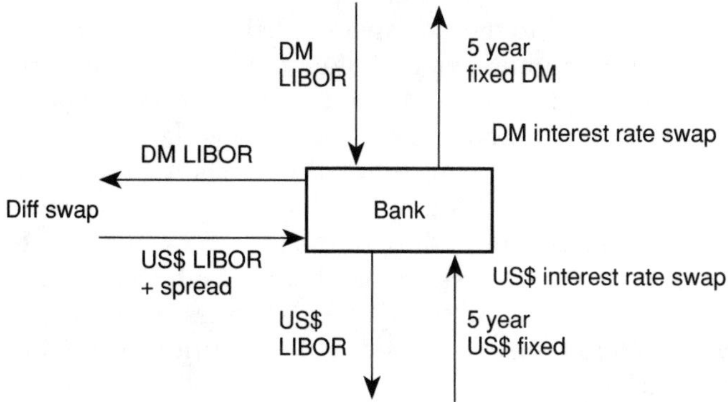

this exposure, only a few banks offer the differential swaps, and consequently there is limited liquidity in the instrument.

HEDGING PORTFOLIOS WITH SWAPS

The duration of a swap is calculated as the time-weighted discounted cashflows of the swap transaction (see Chapter 2). The duration measure is additional; that is, the duration of a portfolio with a swap attached is calculated as the weighted sum of the duration of the portfolio and the duration of the swap.

A *fixed to floating rate* swap will *reduce* the duration of the modified portfolio, and hence the relationship between the durations is:

Duration (modified portfolio) = Duration (portfolio) – duration (swap)

A *floating to fixed rate* swap will *increase* the duration of the modified portfolio. The relationship between the duration is:

Duration (modified portfolio) = duration (portfolio) + duration (swap)

The longer the maturity of the swap, the higher will be the duration of the swap. Hence the nominal swap amount required to adjust the duration of a portfolio is smaller for longer times to swap maturity, and larger for shorter times to the swap maturity. Interest rate swaps can be used as a tool in managing the duration of both investment and loan portfolios without changing the underlying portfolios.

CONCLUSION

The OTC market offers institutional clients a wide variety of interest rate and currency hedging services which provide these institutions with complete hedges. As opposed to the exchange-traded hedging contracts, there is no basis risk and no unknown cash flow implications. Also, the complexity of exchange trading rules are avoided, since dealings are done on a bilateral basis with a known financial intermediary. The OTC market is less flexible than the exchange-traded contracts with regard to selling off an established hedging position which is rarely possible in the OTC market. However, the lack of trading flexibility can be outweighed by the wide range of financial services offered, many of which are tailor-made and cannot be obtained by accessing the exchanges. A major part of the OTC services offered are long-dated, with maturities exceeding those of the futures exchanges.

14

Comparative Analysis

When facing the challenge of hedging interest rate and currency exposures, management must analyze the impact of different hedging instruments and alternative hedging solutions on an ex ante basis. As always, it is hard to know what the future market scenarios will bring, but an analysis that takes into consideration the impact of different hedging possibilities will contribute to the shaping of a final decision. However, in every hedging situation the decision must take a market view into consideration. On the basis of a market outlook, management must act in accordance with the risk parameters established in the corporation. We will try to describe some of these initial evaluations by means of a few examples.

CURRENCY RISK

Example: A French corporation importing goods to be used in the current production is to pay U.S. dollars 10,000,000 in three months' time. The prevailing spot rate is 5.5525 Fr. frc./US$. The importer has three basic alternatives in this situation:

1. Maintain an open position (short U.S. dollars).
2. Engage in a forward foreign exchange agreement.
3. Buy a currency option agreement.

Maintaining an open position means that the importer will benefit if the U.S. dollar weakens against the French franc over the three-month period. Conversely, he will lose if the U.S. dollar strengthens. Therefore, an open position should be maintained only if the importer is fairly sure that the U.S. dollar foreign exchange rate in general will weaken.

The importer can hedge the open currency position by engaging in a *forward foreign exchange rate agreement* at the going 3-month outright rate of 5.5750 Fr. frc./US$. This effectively determines the foreign exchange rate in three months' time. If the spot rate exceeds the outright rate of 5.5750 Fr. frc./US$ after three months, then the hedge paid off. If, on the other hand, the spot rate is below the forward rate, then it would have been cheaper not to engage in the forward agreement. Hence, the importer should engage in a forward foreign exchange agreement only with a strong expectation that the U.S. dollar will strengthen.

The importer could also buy a *currency call option* at a strike price of 5.5800 Fr. frc./US$ (slightly out of the money) at a premium of 0.1200 Fr. frc. per US$. Hence, the importer would be better off by this hedge, if the foreign exchange rate exceeds 5.7000 Fr. frc./US$ (= 5.5800 + 0.1200). If the spot rate falls below the outright rate of 5.5750 Fr. frc./US$—say, down to 5.5000 Fr. Frc./US$—in three months' time, then he does not have to exercise the currency option and can therefore take full advantage of the improved market conditions. The currency option provides the importer with a reasonable cover against a strengthening of the U.S. dollar against the French franc, while at the same time restoring the full upside potential from a favorable development in the Fr. frc./US$ exchange rate. Hence hedgers should choose an option solution if they are somewhat uncertain about the future foreign exchange rate development, but want to establish a reasonable cover against an unfavorable market development, while maintaining the upside potential from a favorable rate development.

The three alternative positions are illustrated in Figure 14.1.

The comparative analysis could be further refined by including a variety of other more developed hedging instruments, but the basic principle in evaluating the choice of hedging solution remains the same. The correspondence between the choice of hedging solution (resulting currency exposure) and market views is combined in Table 14.1. This table shows how it becomes very difficult to make a choice about hedging instruments without establishing a view on the market. If a company, due to established policy rules, automatically and always hedges by engaging in forward foreign exchange agreements without taking the market view into consideration, then it might incur very high opportunity cost if

FIGURE 14.1
Hedging Alternatives (Short US$ Position).

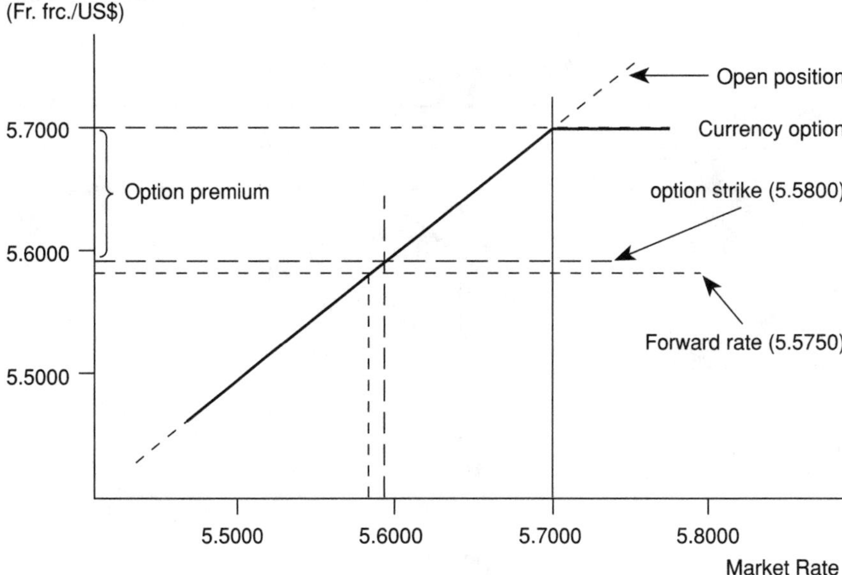

the foreign exchange rate moves in a favorable direction. This can be managed on an ex ante basis by analyzing the markets to establish a view or by seeking professional advice on market trends. If the market outlook appears too uncertain, various currency option products can add further flexibility to the hedging position.

A cylinder option with a ceiling foreign exchange rate of 5.6750 Fr. frc./US$, and a floor rate of 5.5250 Fr. frc./US$ can be acquired by the importer with no up-front payment of premium. In this case the full upside potential from a favorable foreign exchange rate development is limited to the rate of 5.5250 Fr. frc./US$ (see Figure 14.2). Hence, a cylinder could be utilized when the hedger is relatively uncertain about the upside potential of the underlying cash position.

TABLE 14.1
Hedging Position and Market View (Example).

Hedging choice:	*Open Position*	*Forward Agreement*	*Currency Option*
Market view:	Strong expectation of a weakening U.S. dollar	Expectation of a strengthening U.S. dollar	Uncertainty about currency movements

FIGURE 14.2
Hedging with Cylinder and Forward Plus.

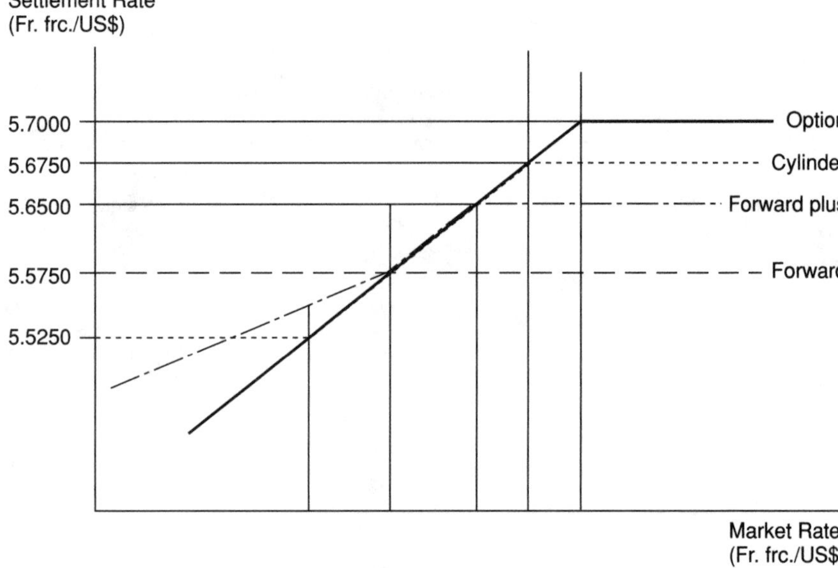

The bank also offers a forward plus rate of 5.6500 Fr. frc./US$ with a share rate of 48% on the upside potential from a favorable development in the foreign exchange rate (see Figure 14.2). The forward plus gives the hedger a better protection against an unfavorable foreign exchange rate development compared to the cylinder, but it provides less immediate gain from a favorable rate movement. Hence, the forward plus could be used when the importer is slightly more worried about the currency risk.

Similar analyses and market considerations should be performed in evaluating any other hedging situation.

INTEREST RATE RISK

When assessing the inherent interest rate risk of a given institution's assets and liabilities, management again must have an awareness of the trends in the financial markets to assess the applicable hedging positions. However, a few general observations can be made on asset and liability hedging. The individual institutions, regardless of their status as net lenders or net borrowers, will (if they behave rationally) try to maximize the return on the assets and to minimize the financing cost of the liabilities. Hence, a set of market behaviors can be scheduled as a function of the prevailing market view (see Table 14.2).

TABLE 14.2

Market View	*Rate Basis*	*Maturity (duration)*	*Lock-in or Cap Rate*
Falling interest rates	*Assets:* Fixed rate	*Assets:* Long	*Assets:* Lock-in rate
	Liablts: Floating rate	*Liablts:* Short	—
Uncertain	*Assets:* Floating rate	*Assets:* Short	*Assets:* Floor rate
	Liablts: Floating rate	*Liablts:* Short	*Liablts:* Ceiling rate
Increasing interest rates	*Assets:* Floating rate	*Assets:* Short	—
	Liablts: Fixed rate	*Liablts:* Long	*Liablts:* Lock-in rate

When the interest rates are expected to fall, the hedger will have a preference for long-term fixed rate investments and for floating rate funding instruments. By engaging in different hedging instruments, the hedger will try to adapt the existing assets and liabilities so that they take on the optimal interest rate and maturity characteristics.

When interest rates are expected to increase, the hedger will prefer short-term floating rate investments, and long-term fixed rate funding instruments. Again the hedger will apply a variety of hedging instruments to change the characteristics of the assets and liabilities favorably.

Example: A borrower has a 5-year floating rate debt portfolio and considers various possible hedging opportunities. The borrower is considering the following alternatives:

1. Maintain position.
2. Engage in interest rate swap and fix the rate.
3. Buy a ceiling rate agreement.
4. Buy a collar rate agreement.

If the position is maintained, the funding cost will drop when the interest rate level decreases, but will go up if the interest rate rises. Hence, an open position should be maintained only if the borrower has a strong view that the interest rates are going to fall.

The borrower can obtain a fixed-floating rate swap from a bank, which will effectively lock in the LIBOR-based funding cost at a 5-year fixed rate of 9.52% p.a. By fixing the interest rate for the five-year period, the borrower will not take advantage of a potential drop in the interest rate level. Hence, the rate should be locked in if the borrower expects interest rate to rise in the future.

The bank also offers an interest rate cap providing a ceiling rate of 9.15% against the payment of an up front premium of 4.40%, corresponding to an annual interest payment of approximately 1.25% over the 5 year period. Therefore, if the short-term interest rate exceeds 10.40%

(= 9.15 + 1.25), the borrower will have a net benefit from the cap while at the same time maintaining the full benefit from a potential drop in the interest rate. Hence, the cap is relevant if the borrower is somewhat uncertain about the future interest rate development, but would like to have some coverage against unfavorable interest rate movements.

The borrower has also received an offer for a collar rate agreement providing a ceiling rate of 9.15% and a floor rate of 6.65% against the payment of an up front premium of 2.70%, corresponding to an annual interest rate of approximately 0.75%. Therefore, the collar is advantageous to the borrower if the interest rate exceeds 9.90% (= 9.15 + 0.75). On the other hand, if the rate falls below 6.65%, the borrower will not get any part of the upside potential below this interest rate. Hence, the collar reflects a slightly more negative view in the interest rate development, since it gives better protection against rising rates, but gives away some of the upside potential from a falling interest rate.

The different hedging positions are illustrated in Figure 14.3.

The final decision as to which of the hedging alternatives to choose must be determined on the basis of the borrower's interest rate outlook and risk policies. Given a high expectation of rising interest rates, then the interest rate swap appears to be a viable solution. If the market outlook is more uncertain, then the cap or collar agreement might be better suited to the situation.

FIGURE 14.3

Interest Rate Hedging Alternatives (*Borrower*).

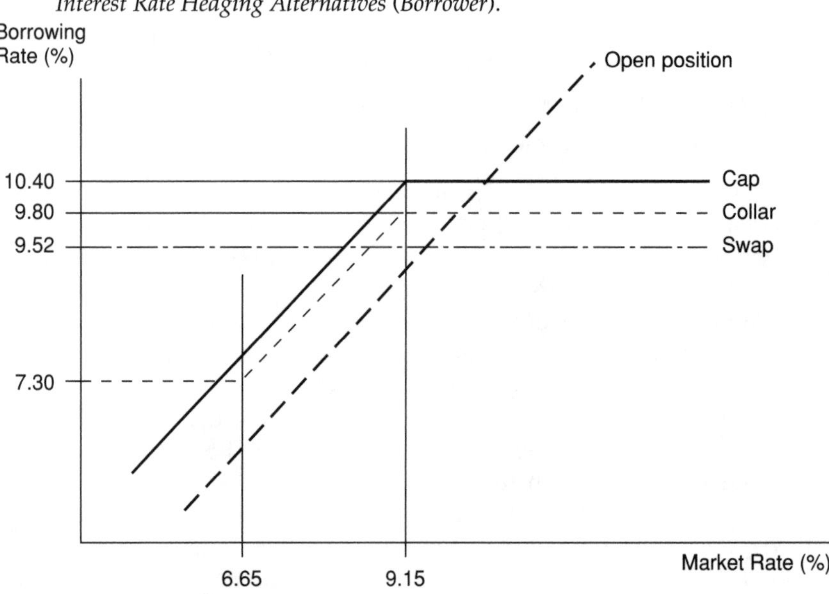

15

Concluding Remarks

The development of the international financial markets over the past decades has been characterized by volatile interest and foreign exchange rates, which impose a significant financial exposure on institutions holding international commitments.

In response, the first financial futures contracts were introduced in the United States in the mid-1970s to provide a hedging mechanism to the financially exposed institutions. The financial futures markets have gone through a geographical expansion both through the establishment of independent futures exchanges in other currency jurisdictions and through cooperation with existing futures exchanges.

During the early 1990s, the futures market has seen the establishment and rapid expansion of various European futures and option exchanges trading in local currency debt instruments. This has contributed to a reduction of the American exchanges' dominance. Consequently their global market share fell from around 80% in the late 1980s to around 50% in the early 1990s. The overseas market expansion does not necessarily represent a threat to the American exchanges, but is rather a reflection that the futures market initially started in the United States, and that the need for local futures products has been largely satisfied through the creation of new exchanges outside the States.

Financial futures contracts provide an efficient means of locking in the future interest or foreign exchange rate. However, hedging over the financial futures market exposes the hedger to a basis risk because the price of the futures contract is not necessarily fully correlated with the price movement of the financial commitment being hedged. Financial futures contracts carry a standard denomination and fixed maturities, and consequently they can be difficult to adapt fully to the specific asset and liability characteristics to be hedged. Hedging in the financial futures market locks in the future rate and hence covers downside risks, but at the same time it limits any upside potential for gains.

The markets for exchange-traded option contracts were established in the early 1980s. The special feature of the option is that it covers the downside risk of an unfavorable price movement, and at the same time leaving open the upside potential for a gain from a favorable price development. As in the financial futures markets, the option contracts have a standard denomination and fixed contract maturities. Exchange-traded option contracts can be written and bought, providing participants with added flexibility to arrange suitable hedging positions. The maximum term of the exchange-traded futures and option contract is typically 9 to 12 months. The limited life places some restrictions on the hedging opportunities.

Despite certain attempts to ease the interaction between the different futures and option exchanges, there is no overall consensus on denomination and market practice. The denomination of futures and option contracts were initially introduced on the exchanges in similar or comparable denominations representing multiples of each other. For example, the currency option contracts of the Philadelphia Stock Exchange make up one-half the size of the corresponding CME futures contracts.

Some exchanges are already directly interlinked. For example, the Singapore International Monetary Exchange (SIMEX) is linked to the International Monetary Market in Chicago. A direct linkage through the same clearing entity and the compatibility of contract characteristics enable exchanges to provide close to 24 hours of trading in the major contracts offered. A refinement of electronic linkages between exchanges, would also allow for the possibility of placing stop orders on option deals that can be transferred automatically from exchange to exchange as opening hours change during the day.

The possibility of establishing interlinkages between U.S.-based, European, and Far Eastern exchanges continues to be investigated. Such development, however, has been delayed by the fact that the various exchanges use different trading practices, contract standards, are backed by different clearing organizations with different contract delivery systems and cost structures, and are under the supervision of different national regulatory bodies.

The increased activity on the financial futures and option exchanges inspired international banks to offer new financial hedging services, whose maturities often exceed those of the exchange-traded contracts, directly to the client over-the-counter. The size, term, and exercise price of these financial agreements can be tailor-made to meet the specific financial needs of the customer. Such financial agreements provide the buyers with hedges, with no basis risk for the holders of the agreements.

The continued growth of OTC derivatives and swaps has been considered a major threat to the exchange-traded contracts. The OTC products have to a large extent provided customer-adapted solutions that could otherwise not be made available in the futures market.

In response to this trend, certain product developments have taken place to increase the reach and flexibility of financial futures and option contracts. Many exchanges have introduced contracts on underlying medium-term interest rate instruments to fill the gap between contracts on short-term money market instruments and longer-term government bonds. A number of exchanges are seeking to expand the maturity date of the futures and option contracts to extend the use of the contracts for hedging purposes. This includes the LEAPS traded on the Chicago Board Options Exchange and selected currency options on the Philadelphia Stock Exchange. Other attempts have been made to increase the flexibility of the traded option contracts through the introduction of *BOUNDS* and *CAPS* (instruments on packaged buy-write strategies) and *FLEX* options (which will allow customers to individually specify the expiry date and strike price). The latter instrument increases the customization of the traded option contract. However, the increased flexibility could be obtained at the expense reduced liquidity in the instruments. In response to the expanding OTC swap market, the Chicago Board of Trade introduced standardized interest rate swap futures contracts, which, due to the nature of the product, will not engage the futures trader in any counterparty exposures, and hence in this regard has a competitive edge on the OTC swap agreements.

The OTC swap market has grown at a phenomenal pace from an estimated total value of outstanding swap agreements in notional amounts of around US$ 1 trillion in 1987 to an estimated contract volume in 1992 of around US$ 5 trillion. The significant counterparty exposures in the swap market have in recent years had the attention of the regulatory authorities, and in the professional market considerable effort has been devoted to managing and reducing the counterparty risks. There are different views on the continued potential for expansion in the swap market. Some argue that the original arbitrage opportunities, which laid the groundwork for the market, disappeared with the development of an efficient swap interbank market, and that consequently the rapid growth of the swap market has come to a halt. Others argue that the swap instruments have become an integral part of the foreign exchange and money markets and hence will serve to fulfill a growing need to manage interest rate and currency risks.

There has been no market consensus regarding the type of trading being practiced on the different exchanges and consequently no general consensus regarding contract compatibility. The Chicago Board of Trade and LIFFE are leaning to open outcry trading, whereas, for example, the Deutsche Terminsbörse is a wholly electronic market place. The Chicago Mercantile Exchange's introduction of the electronic Reuter-supported trading system Globex and the link-up of MATIF provide some perspective for a globalization of some of the futures and option exchanges.

The rapid expansion and development of derivative interest rate and currency instruments have paved the way for new opportunities in financial risk management.

The apparent competition between the standardized exchange-traded futures and option contracts and the more flexible interest rate and currency agreements sold over the counter should not be exaggerated. The different markets for hedging instruments should be judged on their own merits. There is a significant interrelationship between the exchange-traded contracts and the OTC instruments. A large portion of the exposures incurred by the financial institutions offering OTC hedging services are based on counter hedges on the financial futures and option exchanges. Consequently it is difficult to imagine the development of the OTC market without the initial and parallel development of the markets for financial futures and option contracts.

The reason for the rapid expansion of the OTC products is to be found in the flexibility of the instruments that can be tailor-made to individual users in terms of amount, maturity, and price, and which typically are being sold on a client relationship basis. The financial futures and option contracts to a large extent cater to professional market participants who have the necessary market insights to perform efficiently on the exchanges.

The range of hedging instruments made available today provides for efficient ways to manage any corporation's inherent interest rate and currency exposures. A prerequisite for any hedging exercise is that the financial exposures are effectively and accurately registered. The application of different hedging instruments requires an evaluation of prevailing market trends, which should be set against the institution's accepted risk parameters. Hedging does not necessarily imply that all exposures should be closed, but rather that currency and interest rate exposures should be monitored and managed prudently on a current basis.

The wide scope of hedging instruments will no doubt expand further over the coming years, thereby providing increased potential for the astute hedger.

I

Forecasting Techniques

1. ECONOMETRIC MODELS

The econometric models have been developed during the 1960s and 1970s as extensions of the Keynesian economic model relationships. The econometric models are based on linear economic relationships which in their simplest form can be presented in the following way.

$$C_t = a_0 + a_1(Y_t - T_t)$$
$$I_t = b_0 + b_1 Y_{t-1}$$
$$Y_t = C_t + I_t + G_t$$

where

C_t = Total consumption in period t.
I_t = Total investments in period t.
Y_t = National income in period t.
T_t = Taxes on income in period t.
G_t = Government expenditure in period t.
a_0, a_1, b_0, b_1 = Coefficients.

The set of three relationships consists of two economic relationship equations and one definition. The variables T and G are termed *exogenous* variables, reflecting the fact that these are determined by the policy makers. *C, I,* and *Y* are termed *endogenous* variables since they are determined by solving the economic relationship equations for a given set of exogenous variables. Hence, the econometric model can stipulate the consequences of certain policy measures (the exogenous variables) on real economic factors (the endogenous variables). The preceding equation system, in its simple form, represents three equations with three unknown variables (the endogenous variables), which can be solved by applying ordinary algebra. However, the equation systems can be extended to involve a very large number of endogenous variables to reflect more complicated economic relationships. These equation systems in principle can be solved by applying matrix algebra as long as the number of endogenous variables corresponds to the number of relationships or equations in the model. The model with *n* equations can then be presented in the matrix form as follows:

$$y = Xb + r$$

or

$$\begin{bmatrix} y_1 \\ y_2 \\ \vdots \\ y_i \\ \vdots \\ y_n \end{bmatrix} = \begin{bmatrix} 1x_{21} \ldots x_{m1} \\ 1x_{22} \ldots x_{m2} \\ \vdots\vdots \\ 1x_{2i} \ldots x_{mi} \\ \vdots\vdots \\ 1x_{2n} \ldots x_{mn} \end{bmatrix} \begin{bmatrix} b_1 \\ b_2 \\ \vdots \\ b_i \\ \vdots \\ b_n \end{bmatrix} + \begin{bmatrix} r_1 \\ r_2 \\ \vdots \\ r_i \\ \vdots \\ r_n \end{bmatrix}$$

where

$y = n$ endogenous variables.
$X = m \times n$ exogenous variables (some of which in the equation system can correspond to endogenous variables).
$b = n$ residuals (actual observations of y minus the estimated values of y).

In practice, the model is solved by applying the least square estimate, the technique known from linear regression analysis. The coefficients are then determined at the values that, based on the statistical material, provides the smallest value of r^2:

$$r^2 = \sum_{i=1}^{n} r^2{}_i$$

where

$r_i = y_i - (b_1 + b_2X_{2i} + \ldots + b_iX_{mi})$.
$i = 1,2, \ldots , n.$

To provide a better fit to the linear equation system, it is often an advantage to manipulate the statistical data to fit better into the least square requirement. This can be done, for example, by basing the model calculations on the logarithmic values of the underlying statistical material, their reciprocal values, and other factors.

The further extensions of the econometric methods quickly become very technical and, to pursue this further, guidance should be sought in specialized literature on the subject.[1]

2. *AUTOREGRESSIVE INTEGRATED MOVING AVERAGE (ARIMA) MODELS*

To this category of time series forecasting techniques belongs the *auto regressive integrated moving average* processes, the so-called ARIMA models, developed among others by Box and Jenkins during the early 1970s. A *moving average* (*MA*) *model* is a weighted average of a series of historical observations, which in its simplest form is described as follows:

$$X_t = Z_t + bZ_{t-1}$$

where

X_t = Moving average at time t.
Z_t = Observation at time t.
b = Coefficient (weight).

An *autoregressive* (*AR*) *model* is basically a regression equation where the explanatory variables are the historical observations themselves. In its simplest form, this model is expressed as follows:

$$X_t = aX_{t-1} + Z_t$$

where

X_t = Observed value at time t.
X_{t-1} = Observed value at time $t-1$.
a = Coefficient.
Z_t = The discrepancy between the forecasted value at time t and the actual value at time t.

These two models can now be combined to make an auto regressive moving average (ARMA) model, expressed simply as follows:

$$X_t = aX_{t-1} + Z_t + bZ_{t-1}$$

Often a nonstationary (that is, it follows a trend of some sort) time series can be made stationary by taking the difference between all observations and applying the time series analysis to the differentiated values. This means that one has to integrate or sum up the differentiated model to get back to the nonstationary model. A simple differentiation of observations is as follows:

$$Y_t = (X_t - X_{t-1})$$

Hence the autoregressive integrated moving average (ARIMA) model, in its simple form, can be expressed as:

$$Y_t = aY_{t-1} + Z_t + bZ_{t-1}$$
$$(X_t - X_{t-1}) = a(X_{t-1} - X_{t-2}) + Z_t + bZ_{t-1}$$
$$X_t = (1 + a)X_{t-1} - aX_{t-2} + Z_t + bZ_{t+1}$$

This equation represents the simplest form of an ARIMA model containing an autoregressive process with one time lag, as well as a moving average process with one time lag and with the analysis based on the once differentiated observations.

These equations can be extended to include as many time lags as is found necessary to make a good model. The general model can therefore be represented as follows:

$$Y_t = a_1Y_{t-1} + a_2Y_{t-2} + \dots a_nY_{t-n} + Z_t + b_1Z_{t-1} + b_2Z_{t-2} + \dots + b_nZ_{t-n}$$

where

$Y_t = (X_t - X_{t-1})$.
n = Number of time lags.

A substantial amount of literature describes and discusses the analysis of time series in order to establish the optimal models, a task that soon becomes fairly technical.[2]

3. *MODELS BASED ON CHAOS THEORY*

The chaos theory in its simple form tries to establish a nonlinear relationship in a given time series through a repetitive iterative process. The following formula provides a general presentation of such a process:

$$P_t = f(P_{t-1})$$

where

P_t = Price in period t.
f = Functional relationship describing the current period's price in terms of previous period's price.

The following formula represents a relatively simple nonlinear relationship of the type just described:

$$y = bx^2 - a$$

where

y = Variable to be forecasted.
b = Constant number.
x = Number between 0 and 1 (an initial value).
a = Constant number.

For example, the equation could take the form of:

$$dP_t = 1.75 \times dP^2_{t-1} - 1 \quad \text{for } t > 1$$

where

$P_t = P_{t-1} + dP_t$

hence

$$dP_1 = 1.75 \times 0.55^2 - 1$$
$$= -0.47$$

Calculating the iterations in accordance with the formula gives the following values for P_t:

t	dP_t	P_t
0	—	83.16
1	–0.47	82.69
2	–0.61	82.08
3	–0.34	81.74
4	–0.79	80.92
5	0.10	81.05
6	–0.98	80.07
7	0.68	80.75
8	–0.19	80.56
9	–0.93	79.63
10	0.54	80.17
11	–0.49	79.68
12	–0.57	79.11
13	–0.43	78.68
14	–0.68	78.00
15	–0.18	77.82

t	dP_t	P_t
16	–0.94	76.58
17	0.55	77.43
18	–0.47	76.96
19	–0.62	76.34
20	–0.33	76.01
21	–0.81	75.20
22	0.14	75.34
23	–0.96	74.38
24	0.63	75.01
25	–0.31	74.70
26	–0.83	73.87
27	0.21	74.08
28	–0.93	73.15
29	0.50	73.65
30	–0.57	73.08
31	–0.44	72.64
32	–0.66	71.98
33	–0.24	71.74
34	–0.90	70.84
35	0.42	71.26
36	–0.69	70.57
37	–0.16	70.41
38	–0.95	69.46
39	0.59	70.05
40	–0.38	69.67
41	–0.74	68.93
42	–0.03	68.90
43	–0.99	67.91
44	0.74	68.65
45	–0.03	68.62
46	–0.99	67.63
47	0.74	68.37
48	–0.03	68.34
49	–0.99	67.35
50	0.74	68.09

As it appears, this simple model loses its descriptive power after the 40th iteration, after which point it shows a fixed downward moving price pattern. Hence, the models do not have a strong long-term predictive value. By changing the variables (in the simple model a, b, and x), the model will get quite different characteristics. Even small changes in the variables can have a significant impact on the predicted values. The interesting thing is that the time interval between each observation/forecast period (t) can be reduced to very small time fractions, such as 1-minute each or longer intervals, say, 1-day. In other words, the model works the same way in a small perspective as it does in a larger perspective. The same phenomena can be observed in natural science, such as in the build-up of a snow flake or the branching of a large tree, where a lot of repetitive processes of the same simple pattern can create very complex structures. For a further description of potential financial applications, refer to specialized readings on the topic.[3]

II

Establishing Different Option Strategies on Cash Market Positions

Various option strategies can be established by applying existing long or short positions in the cash market or equivalent long or short futures positions. The following presents some of these option positions and indicates how they are established around a cash market (futures) position through the purchase or sale of different option contracts.

S = strike price

1. *Bought call* (C) = Long future (F) + Buy put (P)

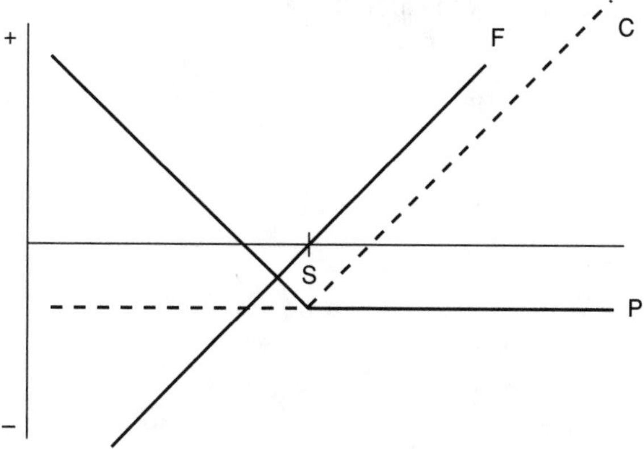

2. *Sold call* (*C*) = Short future (*F*) + Sold put (*P*)

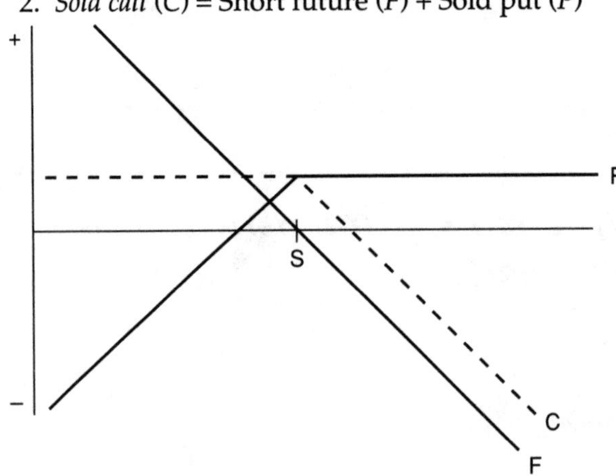

3. *Bought put* (*P*) = Short future (*F*) + Bought call (*C*)

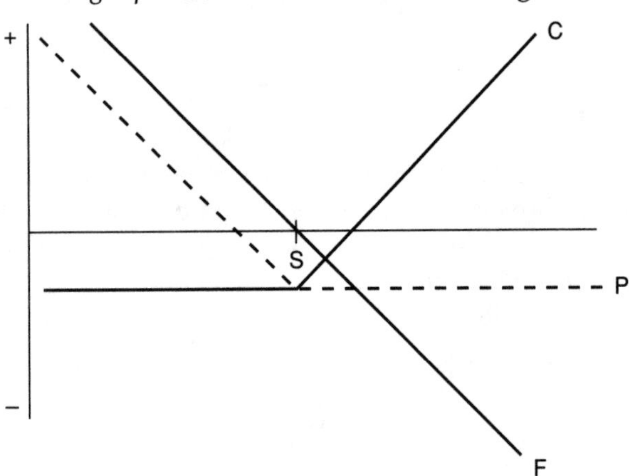

4. *Sold put* (*P*) = Long future (*F*) + Sold call (*C*)

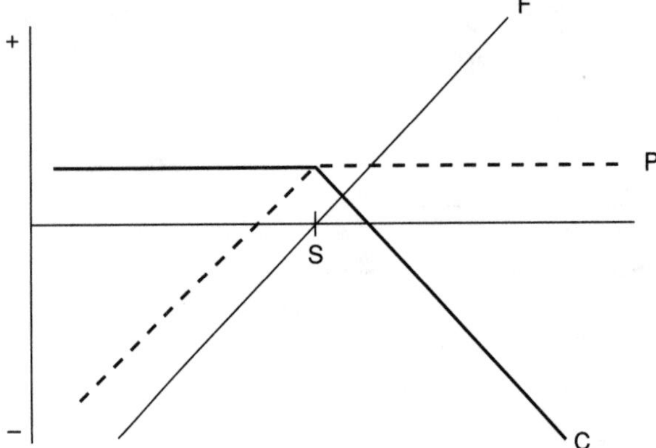

5. *Bull spread* = Long future (S_2) + Sold put (S_1) + Bought put (S_2)
   or = Long future (S_1) + Sold call (S_1) + Bought call (S_2)
   or = Long 2 futures ($S_1 + S_2$) + Sold call (S_1) + Bought put (S_2)

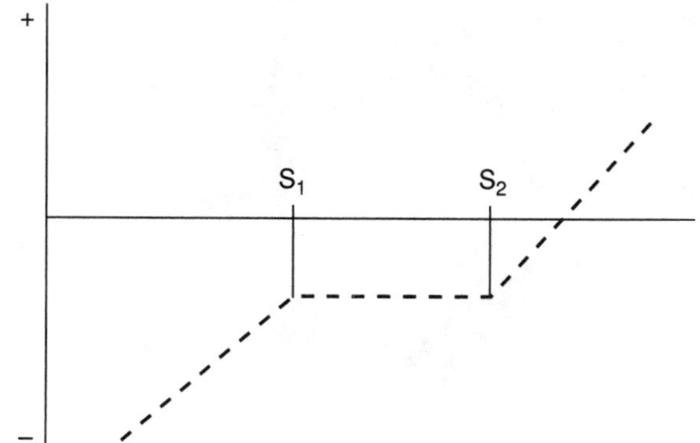

6. *Limited bull spread* = Long future (S_1) + Bought put (S_1) + Sold call (S_2)
   or = Short future (S_2) + Bought call (S_1) + Sold put (S_2)

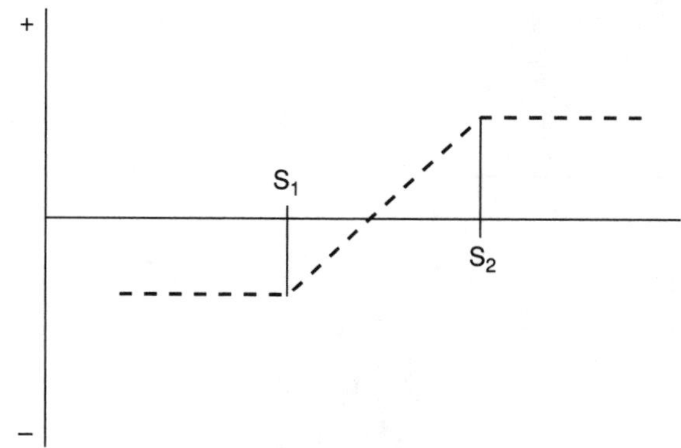

7. *Bear spread* = Short future (S_1) + Bought call (S_1) + Sold call (S_2)
   or = Short future (S_2) + Bought put (S_1) + Sold put (S_2)
   or = Short 2 futures ($S_1 + S_2$) + Bought call (S_1) + Sold put (S_2)

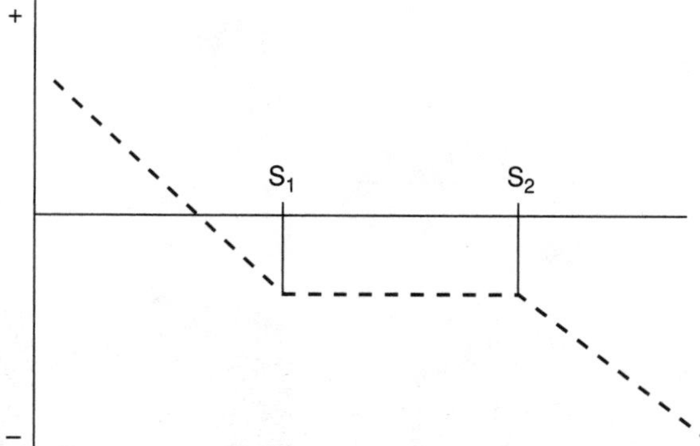

8. *Limited Bear spread* = Short future (S_1) + Sold put (S_1) + Bought call (S_2)
   or = Long future (S_2) + Sold call (S_1) + Bought put (S_2)

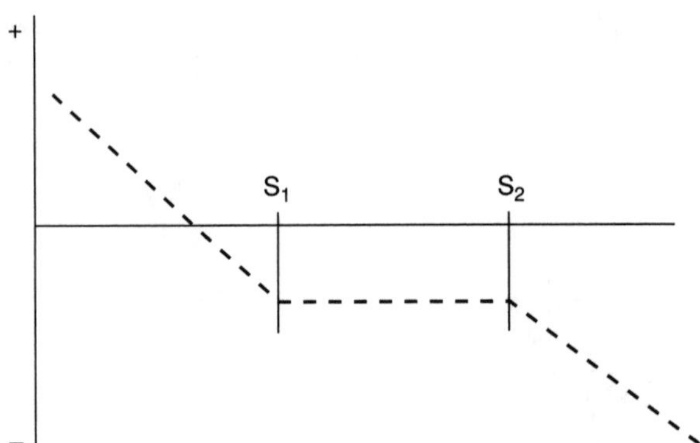

9. *Long Straddle* = Long future + Long 2 puts
   or = Short future +Long 2 calls

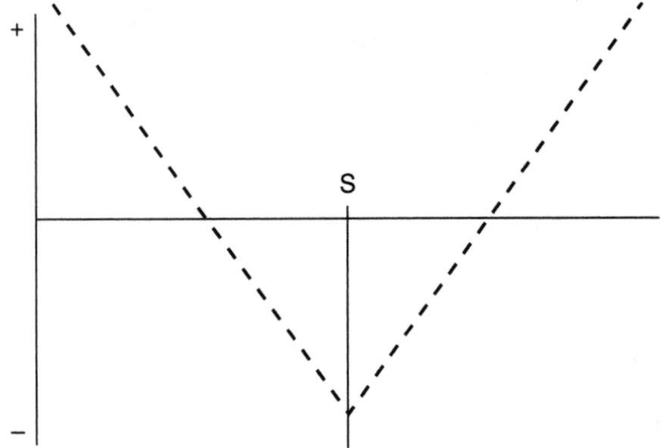

10. *Long Strangle* = Long future (S_2) + Bought put (S_1) + Bought put (S_2)
    or = Short future (S_1) + Bought call (S_1) + Bought call (S_2)

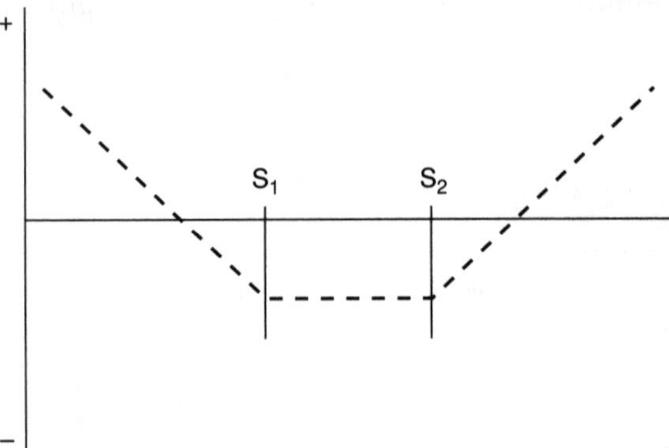

11. *Long butterfly spread* = Long future (S_1) + Sold call (S_1) + Bought put (S_2) + Bought call (S_2) + Sold call (S_3)
    or = Short future (S_2) + Sold call (S_3) + Bought 2 calls (S_2) + Sold put (S_1)
    or = Short future (S_2) + Sold put (S_1) + Bought 2 calls (S_2) + Sold call (S_3)
    or = Long future (S_2) + Sold call (S_1) + Bought 2 puts (S_2) + Sold put (S_3)
    or = Long future (S_2) + Sold put (S_1) + Bought 2 puts (S_2) + Sold call (S_3)
    or = Short future (S_3) + Sold put (S_1) + Bought put (S_2) + Bought call (S_2) + Sold put (S_3)

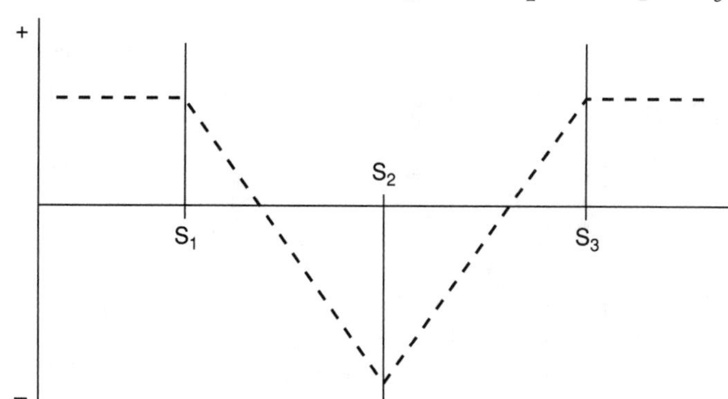

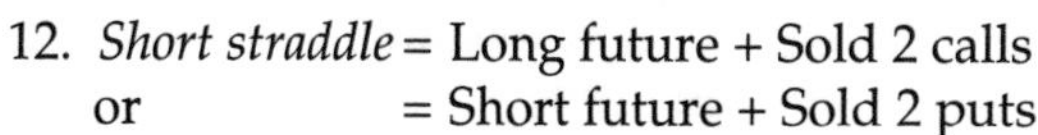

12. *Short straddle* = Long future + Sold 2 calls
    or = Short future + Sold 2 puts

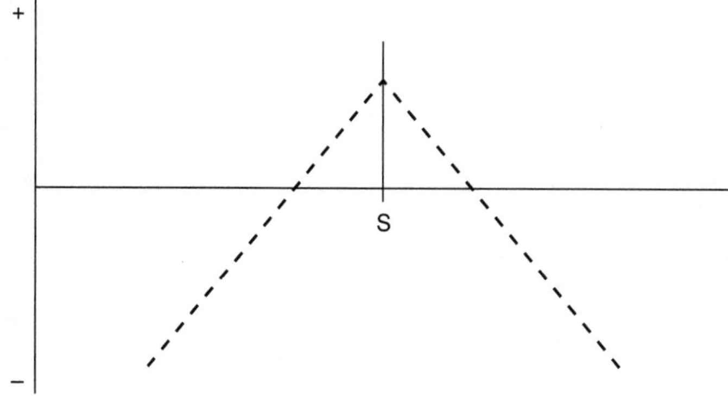

13. *Short strangle* = Long future (S_1) + Sold call (S_1) + Sold call (S_2)
    or = Short future (S_2) + Sold put (S_1) + Sold put (S_2)

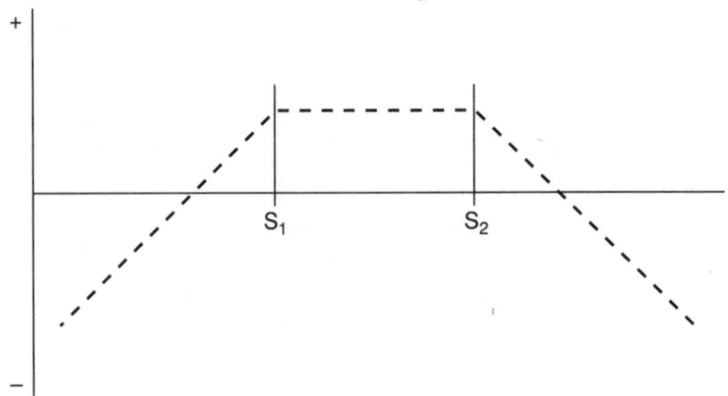

14. *Short butterfly spread* = Short future (S_1) + Bought call (S_1) + Sold put (S_2) + Sold call (S_2) + Bought call (S_3)
    or = Long future (S_3) + Bought put (S_1) + Sold put (S_2) + Sold call (S_2) + Bought put (S_3)
    or = Long future (S_2) + Bought put (S_1) + Sold 2 calls (S_2) + Bought call (S_3)
    or = Short future (S_2) + Bought put (S_1) + Sold 2 puts (S_2) + Bought call (S_3)
    or = Long future (S_2) + Bought call (S_1) + Sold 2 calls (S_2) + Bought put (S_3)
    or = Short future (S_2) + Bought call (S_1) + Sold 2 puts (S_2) + Bought put (S_3)

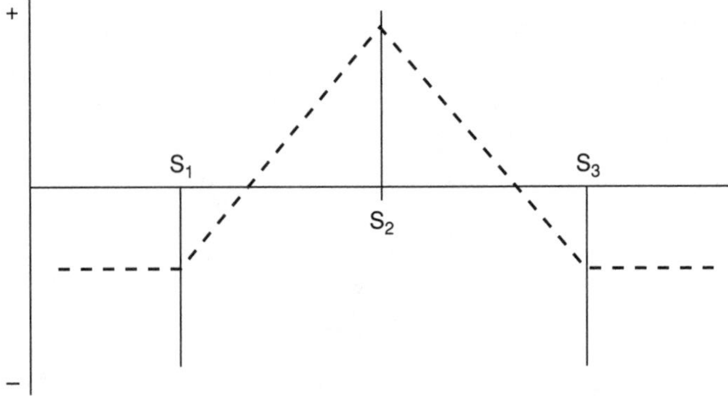

III

Standard Documentation

In 1985 the British Bankers' Association (BBA) took the initiative to establish standardized documentation on forward rate agreements, and in 1992 BBA introduced new standard documentation on international currency options being traded in the important London Interbank Market. This documentation is generally accepted as market standard and is widely used.

In 1985 the International Swap Dealers Association (ISDA) introduced a standardized Interest Rate and Currency Exchange Agreement, which since has established itself as the prevailing swap documentation among international swap counter parties. This documentation has been revised in the 1992 ISDA Master Agreement.

The permission to incorporate in this book the text of the *Forward Rate Agreements ("FRABBA" terms)* and the *International Currency Option Market (ICOM) Master Agreement* has kindly been granted by the **British Bankers' Association.** The permission to reproduce the *ISDA Master Agreement* has kindly been granted by the **International Swap Dealers Association, Inc.**

FORWARD RATE AGREEMENTS ("FRABBA" terms)

BRITISH BANKERS' ASSOCIATION (in association with the Foreign Exchange and Currency Deposit Brokers' Association) August, 1985

LONDON INTERBANK FORWARD RATE AGREEMENTS RECOMMENDED TERMS AND CONDITIONS "FRABBA TERMS"

As recommended by the Forward Rate Agreements Working Party of the British Bankers' Association, endorsed by the Foreign Exchange Committee, and approved by the Executive Committee of that Association in August, 1985

Whilst every care has been taken in the preparation of this booklet, the British Bankers' Association gives no representation or warranty as to the suitability of the recommended FRABBA terms herein for any particular transaction or that FRABBA terms will cover every or any eventuality. The B.B.A. cannot be liable for any losses suffered by contracting on FRABBA terms or arising from the presence of any errors or omissions in this booklet or the non-availability of, or any error or omission in, or miscalculation of, the B.B.A. Interest Settlement Rate.

Contents

A. Introduction

1. *Terms of Reference.*

During 1984 it became apparent that an increasing number of banks were trading actively in a variety of relatively new market instruments, notably Forward Rate Agreements, Interest Rate Swaps and Foreign Currency Options. The F.R.A. market had been in existence since 1983 and was developing rapidly. In London it was very largely in the hands of the banks operating in the interbank eurocurrency and money markets, though deposit brokers had increasingly acted to bring counterparties together. Whilst recognising that such instruments brought more business and greater depth to the London interbank market, it was felt that further growth could be inhibited unless a measure of uniformity was introduced to the documentation which most banks had developed individually. The market might otherwise have become inhibited by the practice whereby transactions are documented in detail after telex confirmation of particulars agreed in principle over the telephone, either directly or through a broker. A number of banks had already begun trading solely on the basis of telex confirmations.

Accordingly, in October 1984, the B.B.A. established, through their Foreign Exchange Committee, three Working Parties to liaise with market interests, including the Foreign Exchange and Currency Deposit Brokers Association, with a view to drawing up recommended Terms and Conditions for such contracts and to provide guidance on market practice. The Bank of England was represented as an observer on each Working Party.

2. *Recommendations.*

The Working Party which has been considering Forward Rate Agreements concluded that it would be realistic to attempt to devise a set of recommendations covering most of the aspects of F.R.A.s which had become sufficiently common in the London interbank market to benefit from the adoption of standardised Terms and Conditions. This Booklet therefore embodies the recommendations of the Working Party relating to interbank Forward Rate Agreements.

The resultant B.B.A. standard for Forward Rate Agreements set out in the following pages, to be known as "FRABBA terms", should in future be treated as normal market practice for interbank transactions falling within the categories covered. Banks are, of course, free to deal on other terms if they wish, but should consider themselves under an obligation to make clear to any would-be counterparty in what way their terms for such transactions differ from FRABBA terms. In the absence of such clarification banks and brokers in the London interbank market are expected to follow what in future will be the normal custom of the market by quoting on the basis of FRABBA terms.

The Working Party has mainly confined itself to the London interbank market, and has not been directly concerned with the terms and conditions which individual banks may elect to quote to their customers or to banks abroad, although FRABBA terms could be utilised in such circumstances.

3. *Interest Settlement Rates.*

In addition, the Forward Rate Agreements and Interest Rate Swaps Working Parties have together recommended definitions and procedures for establishing daily interest settlement rates to be fixed by reference to market rates for deposits in the London interbank market. These fixings will be made at 11.00 a.m. each day on the basis of quotations provided by eight out of a panel of twelve banks designated by the B.B.A. as reference banks. An information vendor nominated by the B.B.A. will calculate and broadcast the fixings through its screen service. Initially, daily fixings will be made available for each monthly deposit maturity between one and twelve months in the FRABBA currencies listed in the Appendix.

In the event that the rates are unobtainable through this medium, they will be available from a member of the Foreign Exchange and Currency Deposit Brokers' Association (in liaison with members of the Sterling Brokers Association) nominated from time to time by their Hon. Secretary.

The method of calculating the interest settlement rate will be as follows:—

the middle four of the quotations from the reference banks will be averaged and the result rounded up, if necessary, to the fifth decimal place. In order to avoid any confusion with the practice of establishing LIBOR on a fractions basis, the rates fixed for F.R.A.s and Interest Rate Swaps (see separate booklet) will be known as "BBA Interest Settlement Rates".

In the unlikely event of an error in a BBA Interest Settlement Rate, the nominated information vendor will have a period of one hour, following the screened publication time, in which to screen an amendment, after which time all rates will be regarded as fixed firm.

4. *Impact of FRABBA Terms.*

Under FRABBA terms a legally binding contract is established at the point when the parties agree terms. This will most often be by telephone but may also be by telex or other means. FRABBA terms provide for an exchange of confirmations and it is important to appreciate their function. Without diminishing the importance of these confirmations, participants should be aware that, under FRABBA terms, confirmations only evidence the particulars of an already established contract and do not constitute the contract itself.

With effect from 2nd September, 1985 banks and brokers should consider FRABBA terms as constituting normal market practice. Thereafter, in the absence of clarification to the contrary, banks and brokers in the London interbank market will be assumed to be operating on FRABBA terms for F.R.A.s.

A broker or other intermediary, acting for any non-London counterparty, should establish from the outset whether FRABBA terms are to apply and should indicate to any prospective London counterparty, at the start of negotiations, if this is not to be the case.

5. *Future Developments.*

The Working Party will continue to survey developments in the F.R.A.s market and will make further recommendations as it considers appropriate.

B. Definitions (as denoted by initial capital letters in all texts in this booklet)

"BBA Designated Banks"	means the panel of not less than twelve banks as designated from time to time by the British Bankers' Association for the purpose of establishing the BBA Interest Settlement Rate.
"BBA Interest	means, in respect of the Contract Period, the rate cal-

Settlement Rate" culated, and published, by the information vendor for the time being designated by the British Bankers' Association to make such calculation. The information vendor shall calculate such rate by taking the rates quoted to it by eight BBA Designated Banks as being in their view the offered rate at which deposits in the Contract Currency for such Contract Period are being quoted to prime banks in the London interbank market at 11.00 a.m. on the relevant Fixing Date for Settlement Date value and eliminating the two highest (or, in the event of equality, two of the highest) and the two lowest (or, in the event of equality, two of the lowest), taking the average of the remaining four rates and then (if necessary) rounding the resultant figure upwards to five decimal places.

"Broken Date" means a Contract Period of a different duration from that used in the fixing of the BBA Interest Settlement Rate, and any Contract Period exceeding 1 year.

"Business Day" means any day (other than a Saturday or a Sunday) on which banks are open for business in London.

"Buyer" means the bank seeking to protect itself against a future rise in interest rates.

"Contract Amount" means the notional sum on which the F.R.A. is based.

"Contract Currency" means the currency in which the F.R.A. is based (see Appendix).

"Contract Period" means the period from the Settlement Date to the Maturity Date.

"Contract Rate" means the forward rate of interest for the Contract Period as agreed between the parties.

"Fixing Date" means the day which is two Business Days prior to the Settlement Date except for Pounds Sterling for which the Fixing Date and the Settlement Date are the same.

"F.R.A." means Forward Rate Agreement (sometimes referred to as Future Rate Agreement) as defined in Section D. 1.2 below.

"FRABBA" means F.R.A.s written on B.B.A. terms as laid down in Section D of this booklet.

"Maturity Date" means the date on which the Contract Period ends.

If the Maturity Date originally agreed upon shall prove not to be both a Business Day and a day on which banks are open for business in the principal financial centre of the country of the Contract Currency, then the Maturity Date shall be the immediately succeeding day which is both a Business Day and a day in which banks are so open, unless, in the case of all currencies except Pounds Sterling, such date falls in the next calendar month in which case the Maturity Date shall be the immediately preceding day which is both a Business Day and a day on which banks are so open.

"Seller" — means the bank seeking to protect itself against a future fall in interest rates.

"Settlement Date" — means the date from which the Contract Period commences, being the date on which the Settlement Sum is paid.

If the Settlement Date originally agreed upon shall prove not to be both a Business Day and a day on which banks are open for business in the principal financial centre of the country of the Contract Currency, then the Settlement Date shall be the immediately succeeding day which is both a Business Day and a day in which banks are so open, unless, in the case of all currencies except Pounds Sterling, such date falls in the next calendar month in which case the Settlement Date shall be the immediately preceding day which is both a Business Day and a day on which banks are so open.

"Settlement Sum" — means an amount equal to the difference between:

(a) an amount representing interest calculated at the Contract Rate in respect of the Contract Amount for the Contract Period and on the basis of the actual number of days in the Contract Period and a year of 360 days (or 365 days where the Contract Currency is Pounds Sterling, or any other currency where the period is so calculated in accordance with London market custom); and

(b) an amount representing interest calculated at the BBA Interest Settlement Rate in respect of the Contract Amount for the Contract Period on such basis,

which amount shall be discounted in accordance with the formula shown in Section D. 4.

C. Conventional Style of Price Quotation

The normal Contract Periods for F.R.A. quotations, unless otherwise specified, will be based on the conventional value dates applicable to each subsequent month for the currency concerned in the London interbank deposit market on the day of negotiation.

Any F.R.A. having a Contract Period with a duration different from the normal Contract Period, as described above, will be construed as a Broken Date F.R.A., which requires that the procedures followed shall be in compliance with Section D. 4.2.

D. Recommended Terms and Conditions

1. *Scope.*

1.1 These recommended Terms and Conditions shall apply to all Forward Rate Agreements (F.R.A.s) between participants operating in the U.K. interbank market and shall be deemed to be incorporated in any contract, whether oral or written, entered into relating to a F.R.A. Unless otherwise stated all F.R.A. deals will be regarded as having been written on "FRABBA terms". ANY VARIATION FROM THESE RECOMMENDED TERMS AND CONDITIONS MUST BE CLEARLY AGREED AT THE TIME OF THE DEAL AND SPECIFIED IN THE DOCUMENTATION.

1.2 A F.R.A. is an agreement between any two banks seeking to protect themselves against a future interest rate movement in the currencies listed in the Appendix, for an agreed Contract Amount, for a specified Contract Period at an agreed Contract Rate; and requires that settlement is effected between the parties in accordance with Section D. 4. For the purpose of the F.R.A. there is no commitment made by either party to lend or borrow the Contract Amount.

1.3 It is understood that both parties have entered into this F.R.A. in accordance with normal banking practice.

2. *Representations and Warranties.* Each party represents and warrants to the other that:—

i) it has full power and authority (corporate and otherwise) to enter into this F.R.A. and to exercise its rights and perform its obligations hereunder and has obtained all authorisations and consents necessary for it so to enter, exercise rights and perform obligations and such authorisations and consents are in full force and effect;

ii) the obligations expressed to be assumed by it under this F.R.A. are legal and valid obligations binding on it in accordance with their terms; and

iii) as of the date of this F.R.A. all payments to be made by it hereunder may be made free and clear of, and without deduction for or on account of, any taxes whatsoever.

3. *Confirmation/Notification.* F.R.A.s may be entered into either orally or in writing and any demand may be made orally or in writing. Each of the parties shall be bound (but without prejudice to the binding nature thereof) to give confirmation in writing of any F.R.A. or demand concluded or made orally. Where such confirmation or demand is made or confirmed by letter it shall be deemed to have been properly made or confirmed to the counterparty, if posted, addressed to the counterparty's registered office or such other address as may be notified and shall be deemed to have been given or made at the time at which it would, in the ordinary course of post, have been delivered. Where such a confirmation or demand is made by telex (or other agreed telegraphic means) it shall be deemed properly made at the time of transmission provided the telex (or other transmission) was sent to the last published number of the recipient and, in the case of telex, the last published answer back of the recipient appears thereon. (For examples see Section F.)

4. *Settlement* (for contract periods in excess of one year see Section E).

4.1 Wherever two parties enter into a F.R.A. the Buyer will agree to pay to the Seller on the Settlement Date (if the Contract Rate exceeds the BBA Interest Settlement Rate), and the Seller will agree to pay to the Buyer on the Settlement Date (if the BBA Interest Settlement Rate exceeds the Contract Rate) an amount calculated in accordance with the following formula:

(a) when L is higher than R

$$\frac{(L-R)\times D\times A}{(B\times 100)+(L\times D)}$$

or

(b) when R is higher than L

$$\frac{(R-L)\times D\times A}{(B\times 100)+(L\times D)}$$

where

L = BBA Interest Settlement Rate (expressed as a number and not a percentage, e.g. 10.11625 and not 10.11625%
R =Contract Rate (expressed as a number and not a percentage)
D = Days in Contract Period
A = Contract Amount
B = 360 except where the Contract Currency is Pounds Sterling (or any other currency where the contract rate is calculated on 365 days according to market custom) when 'B' = 365.

4.2 *Broken Dates.* In the event that no BBA Interest Settlement Rate is available for the Contract Period, then it will be the responsibility of both parties to agree both the basis for establishing an alternative rate and the reference banks to be used for this purpose; and to specify the Settlement Date and the Maturity Date at the time of dealing.

4.3 *Subsequent Declaration of Non-Business Day.* If a Contract Period ceases to be eligible for settlement under recommended FRABBA terms owing to circumstances where the original Settlement Date ceases to be a normal business day (e.g. the announcement, subsequent to the contract date, of a public holiday and/or a market closure in London or in the other relevant financial centre) the settlement rate will be obtainable for the revised Fixing Date from a member of FECDBA (in liaison with members of the Sterling Brokers Association) as specified from time to time by their Hon. Secretary.

5. *Payment.*

Any payments shall be made for value on the Settlement Date when due in the Contract Currency and be immediately available, freely transferable and freely convertible by credit to the counterparty's specified account.

6. *Cancellation/Compensation.*

Subject to mutual agreement between both parties, an existing F.R.A. can be cancelled, at which time the method of calculating the Settlement Sum must be agreed by both parties. In the event that agreement cannot be reached there will be no cancellation.

7. *Events of Default.*

7.1 The occurrence of any one or more of the following circumstances in respect of either party (the "Defaulting Party") shall be an Event of Default:

i) an order of a competent court is made or an effective resolution is passed for the winding up or dissolution of the Defaulting Party other than for the purpose of a reconstruction or amalgamation previously approved in writing by the other party, such approval not to be unreasonably withheld; or

ii) the initiation of proceedings under any applicable bankruptcy, reorganisation, composition or insolvency law by (in respect of itself) or against the Defaulting Party, provided that such proceedings have not been discharged or stayed within 30 days, or the appointment of a receiver over all or any part of the undertaking or any property, assets or revenues of the Defaulting Party; or

iii) any representation made or warranty given by the Defaulting Party pursuant to Clause 2 is or proves to have been materially incorrect or misleading when made.

7.2 *Notice of Event of Default.* Each of the parties undertakes with the other that it will promptly notify the other of any occurrence which constitutes an Event of Default by it. Upon an Event of Default occurring in respect of either party, the other (the "non-Defaulting Party") may, by notice to the Defaulting Party, elect to terminate this F.R.A. immediately whereupon each party shall be released and discharged from its obligations hereunder, providing always that the foregoing shall be without prejudice to any rights, obligations or liabilities under this F.R.A. of the parties hereto which may have accrued up to and including the date of such notice.

8. *Indemnity.*

The Defaulting Party shall fully indemnify (and keep indemnified) the non-Defaulting Party from and against any and all expense, cost, loss, damage or liability incurred by the non-Defaulting Party arising out of the termination of a F.R.A. pursuant to Clause 7 by the non-Defaulting Party which the non-Defaulting Party incurs as a consequence (directly or indirectly) of the occurrence of any Event of Default in respect of the Defaulting Party and/or such termination including, but without limitation, any legal or out-of-pocket expenses, and any amount required to compensate the non-Defaulting Party for any losses sustained and/or costs incurred by the non-Defaulting Party in making alternative arrangements to secure the financial equivalent of the payments and receipts contemplated by Clause 4. In each case, the certificate of the non-Defaulting Party as to the amount of any such costs and/or losses shall be conclusive in the absence of manifest error. Each party expressly recognises that the other is or may become party to one or more transactions which are the reverse of the transactions contemplated in this F.R.A. to which that party may refer for the purpose of computing its expenses, costs, losses, damage or liability.

9. *Rights and Remedies.*

9.1 These Terms and Conditions shall be binding upon and enure to the benefit of both parties and their respective successors and assigns. The rights and obligations of each party may not be assigned (whether by way of charge or otherwise) or transferred without the prior written consent of the other party.

9.2 No delay or omission by either party in exercising any right, power or privilege conferred upon it by this F.R.A. shall impair the same nor shall any single or partial exercise thereof preclude any further exercise thereof or the exercise of any other right power or privilege. The rights and the remedies herein provided are cumulative and not exclusive of any rights or remedies provided by law.

10. *Governing Law.* F.R.A.s entered into under these Terms and Conditions shall be governed by and construed in accordance with the laws of England.

E. Forward Rate Agreements with a Contract Period in Excess of 1 Year: Recommended Calculation Procedure

Example: 2½ year F.R.A.

L = Settlement rate (expressed as a number and not a percentage)
R = Contract Rate (expressed as a number and not a percentage)
A = Contract Amount
B = 36000 (or if Pounds Sterling 36500)
$D1$ = Number of days in year 1
$D2$ = Number of days in year 2
$D3$ = Number of days in year 3
$SS1$ = Discounted Interest Differential due for year 1
$SS2$ = Discounted Interest Differential due for year 2
$SS3$ = Discounted Interest Differential due for year 3

Formulae

$$\frac{(L-R)\times D1\times A}{B+(L\times D1)} = SS1$$

$$\frac{(L-R)\times D2\times A}{B+(L\times D2)} = SS2$$

$$\frac{(L-R)\times D3\times A}{B+(L\times D3)} = SS3$$

$$\text{Settlement} = \frac{SS3}{\left(1+\left(\frac{D2\times L}{B}\right)\right)\left(1+\frac{D1\times L}{B}\right)} + \frac{SS2}{1+\left(\frac{D1\times L}{B}\right)} + SS1$$

N.B.

The above formula calculates the discounted interest differential for each period (SS1, SS2 and SS3) and then discounts each discounted sum back to start date.

F. 1. Examples of Confirmations

PART I

To Be Used on the Agreement Date

F.R.A. CONTRACT *AGREEMENT DATE*
CONFIRMATION NOTICE
TO:—
FROM:—

We are pleased to confirm the following Forward Rate Agreement ('F.R.A.') made between ourselves as per FRABBA Recommended Terms and Conditions dated 1985. (Direct/Broker..)

CONTRACT CURRENCY & AMOUNT ....
FIXING DATE ....
SETTLEMENT DATE............................ MATURITY DATE.....................................
CONTRACT PERIOD (DAYS) ....
CONTRACT RATE............................... % per annum on an actual over 360/365 days basis (as applicable)
SELLER'S NAME ....
BUYER'S NAME ....
NON-STANDARD TERMS & CONDITIONS (IF ANY) ....

Any payment to be made to us under the F.R.A. hereby confirmed should be credited to our Account Number ....
at ....

PLEASE ADVISE BY TELEX, OR CABLE US IMMEDIATELY, SHOULD THE PARTICULARS OF THIS CONFIRMATION NOT BE IN ACCORDANCE WITH YOUR UNDERSTANDING.

Either:— Or:—

SIGNED:... TESTED TELEX CONFO
FOR AND ON BEHALF OF
....

2. *Examples of Confirmations*

PART II

To Be Used on the Settlement Date

F.R.A. CONTRACT AGREEMENT DATE

CONFIRMATION NOTICE—SETTLEMENT

TO:—

FROM:—

We refer to the following Forward Rate Agreement ('F.R.A.') made between ourselves as per FRABBA Recommended Terms and Conditions dated 1985. (Direct/Broker ....)

CONTRACT CURRENCY & AMOUNT ....

FIXING DATE ....

SETTLEMENT DATE............................ MATURITY DATE....................................

CONTRACT PERIOD (DAYS)

CONTRACT RATE............................... % per annum on an actual over 360/365 days basis (as applicable)

SELLER'S NAME ....

BUYER'S NAME ....

NON-STANDARD TERMS & CONDITIONS (IF ANY) ....

SETTLEMENT RATE .... % per annum

SETTLEMENT SUM............................. ($/£ etc.)

SETTLEMENT INSTRUCTIONS:–

☐ WE PAY THE SETTLEMENT SUM ON THE SETTLEMENT DATE TO YOUR ACCOUNT NO. .... AT ....

☐ WE RECEIVE THE SETTLEMENT SUM ON THE SETTLEMENT DATE AT OUR ACCOUNT NO. .... AT ....

Please tick as applicable

Either:– Or:–

SIGNED:.. TESTED TELEX CONFO

FOR AND ON BEHALF OF

....

APPENDIX: FRABBA Currencies

U.S. Dollars
Pounds Sterling
Deutschemarks
Swiss Francs
Japanese Yen

Additions or amendments to the list of FRABBA currencies may be announced by the B.B.A. from time to time.

THE BRITISH BANKERS' ASSOCIATION
AND
THE FOREIGN EXCHANGE COMMITTEE

INTERNATIONAL CURRENCY OPTIONS MARKET (ICOM) MASTER AGREEMENT AND GUIDE
April 1992

Table of Contents

Preface

The International Currency Options Market (ICOM) Master Agreement is intended to serve as a model foreign exchange options contract in the United States and the United Kingdom. The agreement defines key terms and addresses formation, exercise, and settlement procedures for foreign exchange options as well as procedures for the event of default. This model agreement will provide a basis upon which dealers operating in the United States and the United Kingdom can trade foreign currency options with a wide range of dealing counterparties on both sides of the Atlantic without the need to negotiate costly bilateral agreements. Where necessary the agreement can also be modified to allow the terms to be extended to dealers' customers.

The agreement and the accompanying guide were prepared by a group of attorneys working under the auspices of the Foreign Exchange Committee in New York in conjunction with the British Bankers' Association and represents an important first step in cooperation between financial centers. Work in the United Kingdom was carried out by a working party of the British Bankers' Association. The Foreign Exchange Committee in New York sponsored the work of a group of attorneys in the United States, which included the following members:

Ruth Ainslie (Bankers Trust)

Michael Bannon (Chase Manhattan Bank)

Marc Baum (Merrill Lynch)

Rakesh Bhala (Federal Reserve Bank of New York)

Joshua A. Cohn, Esq. (Dai-ichi Kangyo Bank)

John Emert (Citibank)

Laurie Ferber (Goldman, Sachs)

Margaret Grieve (Chase Manhattan Bank)
Marjorie Gross (Chemical Bank)
Douglas Harris (Morgan Guaranty Trust)
Jess Hungate (The Royal Bank of Canada)
Philip Levy (Manufacturers Hanover Trust)
Jeffrey Lillien (First National Bank of Chicago)
Ernest T. Patrikis (Federal Reserve Bank of New York)
Jim Roselle (First National Bank of Chicago)
Garland D. Sims (Chase Manhattan Bank)

INTERNATIONAL CURRENCY OPTIONS MARKET MASTER AGREEMENT

MASTER AGREEMENT dated as of ________________, 19__, by and between ____, a ______________________________, and ___________________________, a ______________________________.

1. *Definitions*

In this Agreement, unless otherwise required by the context, the following terms shall have the following meanings:

"American Style Option"	An Option which may be exercised on any Business Day up to and including the Expiration Time;
"Base Currency"	The currency specified as such by a Party in Part IV of the Schedule hereto;
"Base Currency Rate"	For any day, the average rate at which overnight deposits in the Base Currency are offered by major banks in the London interbank market as of 11:00 a.m. (London time) on such day or such other rate as shall be agreed by the Parties, in either case as determined in good faith by the Non-Defaulting Party;
"Business Day"	For purposes of: (i) Section 4.2 hereof, a day which is a Local Banking Day for the applicable Designated Office of the Buyer; (ii) Section 5.1 hereof and the definition of American Style Option and Exercise Date, a day which is a Local Banking Day for the applicable Designated Office of the Seller; (iii) the definition of Event of Default, a day which is a Local Banking Day for the Non-Defaulting Party; and (iv) any other provision hereof, a day which is a Local Banking Day for the applicable Designated Office of both

	Parties; *provided, however,* that neither Saturday nor Sunday shall be considered a Business Day hereunder for any purpose;
"Buyer"	The owner of an Option;
"Call"	An option entitling, but not obligating, the Buyer to purchase from the Seller at the Strike Price a specified quantity of the Call Currency;
"Call Currency"	The currency agreed as such at the time an Option is entered into;
"Confirmation"	A confirmation of an Option substantially in the form of *Exhibit I* hereto, which confirmation shall be in writing (which shall include telex or other electronic means from which it is possible to produce a hard copy);
"Currency Pair"	The two currencies which may be potentially exchanged upon the exercise of an Option, one of which shall be the Put Currency and the other the Call Currency;
"Designated Office"	As to either Party, the office or offices specified on Part I of the Schedule hereto and any other office specified from time to time by one Party and agreed to by the other as an amendment hereto as a Designated Office on Part I of the Schedule hereto;
"European Style Option"	An Option for which Notice of Exercise may be given only on the Option's Expiration Date up to and including the Expiration Time, unless otherwise agreed;
"Event of Default"	The occurrence of any of the following with respect to a Party (the "Defaulting Party"): (i) the Defaulting Party shall default in any payment hereunder (including, but not limited to, a Premium payment) to the other Party (the "Non-Defaulting Party") with respect to any Option and such failure shall continue for two (2) Business Days after written notice of non-payment by the Non-Defaulting Party; (ii) the Defaulting Party shall commence a voluntary case or other proceeding seeking liquidation, reorganization or other relief with respect to itself or to its debts under any bankruptcy, insolvency or similar law, or seeking the appointment of a trustee, receiver, liquidator, conservator, administrator, custodian or other similar official (each, a "Custodian") of it or any substantial part of its assets; or shall take any corporate action to authorize any of the foregoing; (iii) an involuntary case or other proceeding shall be commenced against the Defaulting Party seeking liquidation, reorganization or other relief with respect to it or its debts under any bankruptcy, insolvency or other similar law or seeking the ap-

pointment of a Custodian of it or any substantial part of its assets; (iv) the Defaulting Party is bankrupt or insolvent; (v) the Defaulting Party shall otherwise be unable to pay its debts as they become due; (vi) the failure by the Defaulting Party to give adequate assurances of its ability to perform its obligations with respect to an Option within two (2) Business Days of a written request to do so when the Non-Defaulting Party has reasonable grounds for insecurity; (vii) the Defaulting Party or any Custodian acting on behalf of the Defaulting Party shall disaffirm or repudiate any Option; or (viii) any representation or warranty made or deemed made pursuant to Section 3 of this Agreement by the Defaulting Party shall prove to have been false or misleading in any material respect as at the time it was made or given or deemed made or given and the Non-Defaulting Party shall have given the Defaulting Party one (1) Business Day's prior written notice thereof;

"Exercise Date" The Business Day on which a Notice of Exercise received by the applicable Designated Office of the Seller becomes effective pursuant to Section 5.1;

"Expiration Date" The date specified as such in a Confirmation;

"Expiration Time" The latest time on the Expiration Date on which the Seller must accept a Notice of Exercise as specified in a Confirmation;

"In-the-money Amount" (i) In the case of a Call, the excess of the Spot Price over the Strike Price, multiplied by the aggregate amount of the Call Currency to be purchased under the Call, where both prices are quoted in terms of the amount of the Put Currency to be paid for one unit of the Call Currency; and (ii) in the case of a Put, the excess of the Strike Price over the Spot Price, multiplied by the aggregate amount of the Put Currency to be sold under the Put, where both prices are quoted in terms of the amount of the Call Currency to be paid for one unit of the Put Currency;

"Local Banking Day" For any currency or Party, a day on which commercial banks in the principal banking center of the country of issuance of such currency or in the location of the applicable Designated Office of such Party, respectively, are not authorized or required by law to close;

"Notice of Exercise" Telex, telephonic or other electronic notification (excluding facsimile transmission), providing assurance of receipt, given by the Buyer prior to or at the Expiration Time, of the exercise of an Option, which notification shall be irrevocable;

"Option"	A Put or a Call, as the case may be, including any unexpired Put or Call previously entered into by the Parties, which shall be or become subject to this Agreement unless otherwise agreed;
"Parties"	The parties to this Agreement; and the term "Party" shall mean whichever of the Parties is appropriate in the context in which such expression may be used;
"Premium"	The purchase price of the Option as agreed upon by the Parties, and payable by the Buyer to the Seller thereof;
"Premium Payment Date"	The date specified as such in the Confirmation;
"Put"	An option entitling, but not obligating, the Buyer to sell to the Seller at the Strike Price a specified quantity of the Put Currency;
"Put Currency"	The currency agreed as such at the time an Option is entered into;
"Seller"	The Party granting an Option;
"Settlement Date"	In respect of: (i) an American Style Option, the Spot Date of the Currency Pair on the Exercise Date of such Option; and (ii) a European Style Option, the Spot Date of the Currency Pair on the Expiration Date of such Option;
"Spot Date"	The spot delivery day for the relevant Currency Pair as generally used by the foreign exchange market;
"Spot Price"	The price at the time at which such price is to be determined for foreign exchange transactions in the relevant Currency Pair for value on the Spot Date, as determined in good faith: (i) by the Seller, for purposes of Section 5 hereof; and (ii) by the Non-Defaulting Party, for purposes of Section 8 hereof;
"Strike Price"	The price specified in a Confirmation at which the Currency Pair may be exchanged.

2. *General*

2.1 The Parties (through their respective Designated Offices) may enter into Options (neither being obliged to do so) for such Premiums, with such Expiration Dates, at such Strike Prices and for the purchase or sale of such quantities of such currencies, as may be agreed subject to the terms hereof.

2.2 Each Option shall be governed by the terms and conditions set forth in this Master Agreement and in the Confirmation relating to such Option. Each Confirmation shall supplement and form a part of this Master Agreement and shall be read and construed as one with this Master Agreement and with each other Confirmation, so that this Master Agreement and all Confirmations, Schedules and amendments hereto constitute a single agreement between the Parties (collectively referred to as this "Agreement"). The Parties acknowledge that all Options are entered into in reliance upon such fact, it being understood that the Parties would not otherwise enter into any Option.

2.3 Options shall be promptly confirmed by the Parties by Confirmations exchanged by mail, telex, facsimile or other electronic means. Unless either Party objects to the terms contained in any Confirmation within the earlier of (i) the time period recognized by local market practice or (ii) three (3) Business Days of receipt thereof, the terms of such Confirmation shall be deemed correct absent manifest error, unless a corrected Confirmation is sent by a Party within such three day period, in which case the Party receiving such corrected Confirmation shall have three (3) Business Days after receipt thereof to object to the terms contained in such corrected Confirmation. Failure by either Party to issue a Confirmation shall not alter the rights and obligations of either Party under an Option to which the Parties have agreed. In the event of any conflict between the terms of a Confirmation and this Agreement, such Confirmation shall prevail, except for purposes of this Section 2.3 and Section 6 hereof.

2.4 Neither Party may assign its rights nor delegate its obligations under any Option to a third party without the prior written consent of the other Party.

3. Representations and Warranties; Contractual Status

Each Party represents and warrants to the other Party as of the date hereof and as of the date of each Option that: (i) it has authority to enter into this Master Agreement and such Option; (ii) the persons executing this Master Agreement and entering into such Option on its behalf have been duly authorized to do so; (iii) this Master Agreement and such Option are binding upon it and enforceable against it in accordance with their respective terms and do not and will not violate the terms of any agreements to which such Party is bound; (iv) no Event of Default, or event which, with notice or lapse of time or both, would constitute an Event of Default has occurred and is continuing with respect to it; and (v) it acts as principal in entering into and exercising each and every Option.

4. The Premium

4.1 Unless otherwise agreed in writing by the Parties, the Premium related to an Option shall be paid on its Premium Payment Date.

4.2 If any Premium is not received on the Premium Payment Date, the Seller may elect either: (i) to accept a late payment of such Premium; (ii) to give written notice of such non-payment and, if such payment shall not be received within two (2) Business Days of such notice, treat the related Option as void; or (iii) to give written notice of such non-payment and, if such payment shall not be received within two (2) Business Days of such notice, treat such non-payment as an Event of Default under clause (i) of the definition of Event of Default. If the Seller elects to act under either clause (i) or (ii) of the preceding sentence, the Buyer shall pay all out-of-pocket costs and actual damages incurred in connection with such unpaid or late Premium or void Option, including, without limitation, interest on such Premium in the same currency as such Premium at the then prevailing market rate and any other costs or expenses incurred by the Seller in covering its obligations (including, without limitation, a delta hedge) with respect to such Option.

5. Exercise and Settlement of Options

5.1 The Buyer may exercise an Option by delivery to the Seller of a Notice of Exercise. Subject to Section 5.4 hereof, if an Option has not been exercised prior to or at the Expiration Time, it shall expire and become void and of no effect. Any Notice of Exercise shall (unless otherwise agreed): (i) if received prior to 3:00 p.m. on a Business Day, be effective upon receipt thereof by the Seller; and (ii) if received after 3:00 p.m. on a Business Day, be effective only as of the opening of business of the Seller on the first Business Day subsequent to its receipt.

5.2 An exercised Option shall settle on its Settlement Date. Subject to Section 5.3 and 5.4 hereof, on the Settlement Date, the Buyer shall pay the Put Currency to the Seller for value on the Settlement Date and the Seller shall pay the Call Currency to the Buyer for value on the Settlement Date.

5.3 An Option shall be settled at its In-the-money Amount if so agreed by the Parties at the time such Option is entered into. In such case, the In-the-money Amount shall be determined based upon the Spot Price at the time of exercise or as soon thereafter as possible. The sole obligations of the Parties with respect to such Option shall be to deliver or receive the In-the-money Amount of such Option on the Settlement Date.

5.4 Unless the Seller is otherwise instructed by the Buyer, if an Option has an In-the-money Amount at its Expiration Time that equals or exceeds the product of (x) 1% of the Strike Price and (y) the amount of the Call or Put Currency, as appropriate, then the Option shall be deemed automatically exercised. In such case, the Seller may elect to settle such Option either in accordance with Section 5.2 of this Agreement or by payment to the Buyer on the Settlement Date for such Option of the In-the-money Amount, as determined at the Expiration Time or as soon thereafter as possible. In the latter case, the sole obligations of the Parties with respect to such Option shall be to deliver or receive the In-the-money Amount of such Option on the Settlement Date. The Seller shall notify the Buyer of its election of the method of settlement of an automatically exercised Option as soon as practicable after the Expiration Time.

5.5 Unless otherwise agreed by the Parties, an Option may be exercised only in whole.

6. Discharge and Termination of Options

Unless otherwise agreed, any Call Option or any Put Option written by a Party will automatically be terminated and discharged, in whole or in part, as applicable, against a Call Option or a Put Option, respectively, written by the other Party, such termination and discharge to occur automatically upon the payment in full of the last Premium payable in respect of such Options; *provided that* such termination and discharge may only occur in respect of Options:

(a) each being with respect to the same Put Currency and the same Call Currency;

(b) each having the same Expiration Date and Expiration Time;

(c) each being of the same style, i.e. either both being American Style Options or both being European Style Options;

(d) each having the same Strike Price; and

(e) neither of which shall have been exercised by delivery of a Notice of Exercise;

and, upon the occurrence of such termination and discharge, neither Party shall have any further obligation to the other Party in respect of the relevant Options or, as the case may be, parts thereof so terminated and discharged. In the case of a partial termination and discharge (i.e., where the relevant Options are for different amounts of the Currency Pair), the remaining portion of the Option which is partially discharged and terminated shall continue to be an Option for all purposes of this Agreement, including this Section 6.

7. Payment Netting

7.1 If, on any date, and unless otherwise mutually agreed by the Parties, Premiums would otherwise be payable hereunder in the same currency between respective Designated Offices of the Parties, then, on such date, each Party's obligation to make payment of any such Premium will be automatically satisfied and discharged and, if the aggregate Premium(s) that would otherwise have been payable by such Designated Office of one Party exceeds the aggregate Premium(s) that would otherwise have been payable by such Designated Office of the other Party, replaced by an obligation upon the Party by whom the larger aggregate Premium(s) would have been payable to pay the other Party the excess of the larger aggregate Premium(s) over the smaller aggregate Premium(s).

7.2 If, on any date, and unless otherwise mutually agreed by the Parties, amounts other than Premium payments would otherwise be payable hereunder in the same currency between respective Designated Offices of the Parties, then, on such date, each Party's obligation to make payment of any such amount will be automatically satisfied and discharged and, if the aggregate amount that would otherwise have been payable by such Designated Office of one Party exceeds the aggregate amount that would otherwise have been payable by such Designated Office of the other Party, replaced by an obligation upon the Party by whom the larger aggregate amount would have been payable to pay the other Party the excess of the larger aggregate amount over the smaller aggregate amount.

8. Default

8.1 If an Event of Default has occurred and is continuing, then the Non-Defaulting Party shall have the right to liquidate and/or to deem to liquidate all, but not less than all (except to the extent that in the good faith opinion of the Non-Defaulting Party certain of such Options may not be liquidated under applicable law), outstanding Options by notice to the Defaulting Party. The previous sentence notwithstanding, in the case of an Event of Default specified in clauses (ii), (iii) or (iv) of the definition thereof, such liquidation and/or deemed liquidation shall be automatic as to all outstanding Options, except where the relevant voluntary or involuntary case or other proceeding or bankruptcy or insolvency giving rise to such Event of Default is governed by a system of law which contains express provisions enabling close-out in the manner respect of the Defaulting Party's obligations hereunder against the net payment calculated in accordance with clause (iii) above which the Defaulting Party owes to the Non-Defaulting Party, if any, and, at the option of the Non-Defaulting Party, any Margin held by the Defaulting Party (including the liquidated value of any non-cash Margin) in respect of the Non-Defaulting Party's obligations hereunder; *provided,* that, for purposes of such set-off, any Margin denominated in a currency other the Non-Defaulting Party's Base Currency shall be converted into such currency at the rate specified in clause (ii) above.

8.2 The net amount payable by one Party to the other Party pursuant to the provisions of Section 8.1 above shall be paid by the close of business on the Business Day following such liquidation and/or deemed liquidation of all such Options (converted as required by applicable law into any other currency, any such costs of conversion to be borne by, and deducted from any payment to, the Defaulting Party). To the extent permitted by applicable law, any amounts owed but not paid when due under this Section 8 shall bear interest at the Base Currency Rate plus 1% per annum (or, if conversion is required by applicable law into some other currency, either (x) the average rate at which overnight deposits in such other currency are offered by major banks in the London interbank market as of 11:00 a.m. (London time) plus 1% per annum or (y) such other rate as may be prescribed by such applicable law) for each day for which such amount remains unpaid.

8.3 Without prejudice to the foregoing, so long as a Party shall be in default in payment or performance to the other Party hereunder or under any Option and the Non-Defaulting Party has not exercised its rights under this Section 8, or during the pendency of a reasonable request to a Party for adequate assurances of its ability to perform its obligations hereunder or under any Option, the other Party may, at its election and without penalty, suspend its obligation to perform hereunder or under any Option.

8.4 The Party required to make a payment to the other Party pursuant to Sections 8.1 and 8.2 above shall pay to the other Party all out-of-pocket expenses incurred by such other Party (including fees and disbursements of counsel and time charges of attorneys who may be employees of such other Party) in connection with any reasonable collection or other enforcement proceedings related to such required payment.

8.5 The Parties agree that the amounts recoverable under this Section 8 are a reasonable pre-estimate of loss and not a penalty. Such amounts are payable for the loss of bargain and the loss of protection against future risks and, except as otherwise provided in this Agreement, neither Party will be entitled to recover any additional damages as a consequence of such losses.

8.6 The Non-Defaulting Party's rights under this Section 8 shall be in addition to, and not in limitation or exclusion of, any other rights which the Non-Defaulting Party may have (whether by agreement, operation of law or otherwise), and the Non-Defaulting Party shall have a general right of set-off with respect to all amounts owed by each Party to the other Party, whether due or not due (provided that any amount not due at the time of such set-off shall be discounted to present value in a commercially reasonable manner by the Non-Defaulting Party).

9. Parties to Rely on Their Own Expertise

Each Option shall be deemed to have been entered into by each Party in reliance only upon its judgment. Neither Party holds out itself as advising, or any of its employees or agents as having its authority to advise, the other Party as to whether or not it should enter into any such Option (whether as Seller or Buyer) or as to any subsequent actions relating thereto or on any other commercial matters concerned with any currency options or transactions, and neither Party shall have any responsibility or liability whatsoever in respect of any advice of this nature given, or views expressed, by it or any of such persons to the other Party, whether or not such advice is given or such views are expressed at the request of the other Party.

10. Illegality, Impossibility and Force Majeure

If either Party is prevented from or hindered or delayed by reason of force majeure or act of State in the delivery or payment of any currency in respect of an Option or if it becomes unlawful or impossible for either Party to make or receive any payment in respect of an Option, then the Party for whom such performance has been prevented, hindered or delayed or has become illegal or impossible shall promptly give notice thereof to the other Party and either Party may, by notice to the other Party, require the liquidation and close-out of each affected Option in accordance with the provisions of Section 8 hereof and, for such purposes, the Party unaffected by such force majeure, act of State, illegality or impossibility shall be considered the Non-Defaulting Party and, for purposes of this Section 10, such Non-Defaulting Party shall perform the calculation required under Section 8.

11. Miscellaneous

11.1 Unless otherwise specified, the times referred to herein shall in each case refer to the local time of the relevant Designated Office of the Seller of the relevant Option.

11.2 Unless otherwise specified, all notices, instructions and other communications to be given to a Party hereunder shall be given to the address, telex (if confirmed by the appropriate answerback), facsimile (confirmed if requested) or telephone number and to the individual or Department specified by such Party in Part II of the Schedule attached hereto. Unless otherwise specified, any notice, instruction or other communication, shall be effective upon receipt if given in accordance with this Section 11.2.

11.3 All payments to be made hereunder shall be made in same day (or immediately available) and freely transferable funds and, unless otherwise specified, shall be delivered to such office of such bank and in favor of such account as shall be specified by the Party entitled to receive such payment in Part III of the Schedule attached hereto or as specified by such Party by notice given in accordance with Section 11.2. Time shall be of the essence in this Agreement.

11.4 The receipt or recovery by either Party of any amount in respect of an obligation of the other Party in a currency other than the Base Currency (other than receipt by the Defaulting Party pursuant to Sections 8.1 and 8.2 of a payment in the Non-Defaulting Party's Base Currency), whether pursuant to a judgment of any court or pursuant to Section 8 hereof, shall discharge such obligation only to the extent that, on the first day on which such party is open for business immediately following such receipt, the recipient shall be able, in accordance with normal banking procedures, to purchase the Base Currency with the currency received. If the amount of the Base Currency so purchasable shall be less than the original Base Currency amount calculated pursuant to Section 8 hereof, the obligor shall, as a separate obligation and notwithstanding any judgment of any court, indemnify the recipient against any loss sustained by it. The obligor shall in any event indemnify the recipient against any costs incurred by it in making any such purchase of the Base Currency.

11.5 The Parties agree that each may electronically record all telephonic conversations between them and that any such recordings may be submitted in evidence to any court or in any proceeding for the purpose of establishing any matters pertinent to any Option.

11.6 This Agreement shall supersede any other agreement between the Parties with respect to the subject matter hereof and all outstanding

Options between the Parties on the date hereof shall be subject hereto, unless otherwise expressly agreed by the Parties.

11.7 A margin agreement between the Parties may apply to obligations governed by this Agreement. If the Parties have executed a margin agreement, such margin agreement shall be subject to the terms hereof and is hereby incorporated by reference herein. In the event of any conflict between a margin agreement and this Agreement, this Agreement shall prevail, except for any provision in such margin agreement in respect of governing law.

11.8 In the event any one or more of the provisions contained in this Agreement should be held invalid, illegal or unenforceable in any respect, the validity, legality and enforceability of the remaining provisions contained herein shall not in any way be affected or impaired thereby. The Parties shall endeavor in good faith negotiations to replace the invalid, illegal or unenforceable provisions with valid provisions the economic effect of which comes as close as possible to that of the invalid, illegal or unenforceable provisions.

12. Law and Jurisdiction

12.1 This Agreement shall be governed by, and construed in accordance with, the laws of [the State of New York] [England and Wales] without giving effect to conflicts of law principles.

12.2 With respect to any suit, action or proceedings ("Proceedings") relating to any Option or this Agreement, each Party irrevocably (i) [submits to the non-exclusive jurisdiction of the courts of the State of New York and the United States District Court located in the Borough of Manhattan in New York City,] [agrees for the benefit of the other Party that the courts of England shall have jurisdiction to determine any Proceeding and irrevocably submits to the jurisdiction of the English courts] and (ii) waives any objection which it may have at any time to the laying of venue of any Proceedings brought in any such court, waives any claim that such Proceedings have been brought in an inconvenient forum and further waives the right to object, with respect to such Proceedings, that such court does not have jurisdiction over such Party. Nothing in this Agreement precludes either Party from bringing Proceedings in any other jurisdiction nor will the bringing of Proceedings in any one or more jurisdictions preclude the bringing of Proceedings in any other jurisdiction.

12.3 Each Party hereby irrevocably waives any and all right to trial by jury in any legal proceeding arising out of or relating to this Agreement or any Option.

12.4 Each Party hereby irrevocably waives, to the fullest extent permitted by applicable law, with respect to itself and its revenues and assets (irrespective of their use or intended use), all immunity on the grounds of sovereignty or other similar grounds from (i) suit, (ii) jurisdiction of any court, (iii) relief by way of injunction, order for specific performance or for recovery of property, (iv) attachment of its assets (whether before or after judgment) and (v) execution or enforcement of any judgment to which it or its revenues or assets might otherwise be entitled in any Proceedings (as defined in Section 12.2 hereof) in the courts of any jurisdiction and irrevocably agrees, to the extent permitted by applicable law, that it will not claim any such immunity in any Proceedings.

IN WITNESS WHEREOF, the Parties have caused this Agreement to be duly executed by their respective authorized officers as of the date first written above.

____

By: ___________________________
Title:

____

By: ___________________________
Title:

EXHIBIT I

Currency Option Confirmation

To: ____________________

______________________________ hereby confirms the following terms of a currency option:

Reference:

Trade Date (DD/MMM/YY):

Buyer:

Seller:

Option Style (European or American):

Option Type (Put or Call):

Put Currency and Amount:

Call Currency and Amount:

Strike Price:

Expiration Date (DD/MMM/YY):

Expiration Time:

Expiration Settlement Date (DD/MMM/YY):

Premium:

Price:

Premium Payment Date (DD/MMM/YY):

Premium Payment Instructions:

Other terms and conditions:

This Option is subject to the International Currency Options Market Master Agreement between [us] [__________________ and __________________, dated as of ______________, 19__].

Please confirm to us by return telex, mail, facsimile or other electronic transmission that the above details are correct.

SCHEDULE

Part I: Designated Offices

Each of the following shall be a Designated Office:

Part II: Notices

Address

Telephone Number

Telex Number

Facsimile Number

Name of Individual or Department to whom Notices are to be sent

Part III: Payment Instructions

Name of Bank and Office, Account Number and Reference with respect to relevant Currencies

Part IV: Base Currency

ISDA®
International Swap Dealers Association, Inc.
MASTER AGREEMENT

dated as of ____________________

____________________ and ____________________

have entered and/or anticipate entering into one or more transactions (each a "Transaction") that are or will be governed by this Master Agreement, which includes the schedule (the "Schedule"), and the documents and other confirming evidence (each a "Confirmation") exchanged between the parties confirming those Transactions.

Accordingly, the parties agree as follows:—

1. *Interpretation*

(a) *Definitions.* The terms defined in Section 14 and in the Schedule will have the meanings therein specified for the purpose of this Master Agreement.

(b) *Inconsistency.* In the event of any inconsistency between the provisions of the Schedule and the other provisions of this Master Agreement, the Schedule will prevail. In the event of any inconsistency between the provisions of any Confirmation and this Master Agreement (including the Schedule), such Confirmation will prevail for the purpose of the relevant Transaction.

(c) *Single Agreement.* All Transactions are entered into in reliance on the fact that this Master Agreement and all Confirmations form a single agreement between the parties (collectively referred to as this "Agreement"), and the parties would not otherwise enter into any Transactions.

2. *Obligations*

(a) *General Conditions.*

(i) Each party will make each payment or delivery specified in each Confirmation to be made by it, subject to the other provisions of this Agreement.

(ii) Payments under this Agreement will be made on the due date for value on that date in the place of the account specified in the relevant Confirmation or otherwise pursuant to this Agreement, in freely transferable funds and in the manner customary for payments in the required currency. Where settlement is by delivery (that is, other than by payment), such delivery will be made for receipt on the due date in the manner customary for the relevant obligation unless otherwise specified in the relevant Confirmation or elsewhere in this Agreement.

(iii) Each obligation of each party under Section 2(a)(i) is subject to (1) the condition precedent that no Event of Default or Potential Event of Default with respect to the other party has occurred and is continuing, (2) the condition precedent that no Early Termination Date in respect of the relevant Transaction has occurred or been effectively designated and (3) each other applicable condition precedent specified in this Agreement.

(b) *Change of Account.* Either party may change its account for receiving a payment or delivery by giving notice to the other party at least five Local Business Days prior to the scheduled date for the payment or delivery to which such change applies unless such other party gives timely notice of a reasonable objection to such change.

(c) *Netting.* If on any date amounts would otherwise be payable:—

(i) in the same currency; and

(ii) in respect of the same Transaction,

by each party to the other, then, on such date, each party's obligation to make payment of any such amount will be automatically satisfied and discharged and, if the aggregate amount that would otherwise have been payable by one party exceeds the aggregate amount that would otherwise have been payable by the other party, replaced by an obligation upon the party by whom the larger aggregate amount would have been payable to pay to the other party the excess of the larger aggregate amount over the smaller aggregate amount.

The parties may elect in respect of two or more Transactions that a net amount will be determined in respect of all amounts payable on the same date in the same currency in respect of such Transactions, regardless of whether such amounts are payable in respect of the same Transaction. The election may be made in the Schedule or a Confirmation by specifying that subparagraph (ii) above will not apply to the Transactions identified as being subject to the election, together with the starting date (in which case subparagraph (ii) above will not, or will cease to, apply to such Transactions from such date). This election may be made separately for different groups of Transactions and will apply separately to each pairing of Offices through which the parties make and receive payments or deliveries.

(d) *Deduction or Withholding for Tax.*

(i) ***Gross-Up.*** All payments under this Agreement will be made without any deduction or withholding for or on account of any Tax unless such deduction or withholding is required by any applicable law, as modified by the practice of any relevant governmental revenue authority, then in effect. If a party is so required to deduct or withhold, then that party ("X") will:—

(1) promptly notify the other party ("Y") of such requirement;

(2) pay to the relevant authorities the full amount required to be deducted or withheld (including the full amount required to be deducted or withheld from any additional amount paid by X to Y under this Section 2(d)) promptly upon the earlier of determining that such deduction or withholding is required or receiving notice that such amount has been assessed against Y;

(3) promptly forward to Y an official receipt (or a certified copy), or other documentation reasonably acceptable to Y, evidencing such payment to such authorities; and

(4) if such Tax is an Indemnifiable Tax, pay to Y, in addition to the payment to which Y is otherwise entitled under this Agreement, such additional amount as is necessary to ensure that the net amount actually received by Y (free and clear of Indemnifiable Taxes, whether assessed against X or Y) will equal the full amount Y would have received had no such deduction or withholding been required. However, X will not be required to pay any additional amount to Y to the extent that it would not be required to be paid but for:—

(A) the failure by Y to comply with or perform any agreement contained in Section 4(a)(i), 4(a)(iii) or 4(d); or

(B) the failure of a representation made by Y pursuant to Section 3(f) to be accurate and true unless such failure would not have occurred but for (I) any action taken by a taxing authority, or brought in a court of competent jurisdiction, on or after the date on which a Transaction is entered into (regardless of whether such action is taken or brought with respect to a party to this Agreement) or (II) a Change in Tax Law.

(ii) ***Liability.*** If:—

(1) X is required by any applicable law, as modified by the practice of any relevant governmental revenue authority, to make any deduction or withholding in respect of which X would not be required to pay an additional amount to Y under Section 2(d)(i)(4);

(2) X does not so deduct or withhold; and

(3) a liability resulting from such Tax is assessed directly against X,

then, except to the extent Y has satisfied or then satisfies the liability resulting from such Tax, Y will promptly pay to X the amount of such liability (including any related liability for interest, but including any related liability for penalties only if Y has failed to comply with or perform any agreement contained in Section 4(a)(i), 4(a)(iii) or 4(d)).

(e) *Default Interest; Other Amounts.* Prior to the occurrence or effective designation of an Early Termination Date in respect of the relevant Transaction, a party that defaults in the performance of any payment obligation will, to the extent permitted by law and subject to Section 6(c), be required to pay interest (before as well as after judgment) on the overdue amount to the other party on demand in the same currency as such overdue amount, for the period from (and including) the original due date for payment to (but excluding) the date of actual payment, at the Default Rate. Such interest will be calculated on the basis of daily compounding and the actual number of days elapsed. If, prior to the occurrence or effective designation of an Early Termination Date in respect of the relevant Transaction, a party defaults in the performance of any obligation required to be settled by delivery, it will compensate the other party on demand if and to the extent provided for in the relevant Confirmation or elsewhere in this Agreement.

3. *Representations*

Each party represents to the other party (which representations will be deemed to be repeated by each party on each date on which a Transaction is entered into and, in the case of the representations in Section 3(f), at all times until the termination of this Agreement) that:—

(a) *Basic Representations.*

(i) ***Status.*** It is duly organised and validly existing under the laws of the jurisdiction of its organisation or incorporation and, if relevant under such laws, in good standing;

(ii) ***Powers.*** It has the power to execute this Agreement and any other documentation relating to this Agreement to which it is a party, to deliver this Agreement and any other documentation relating to this Agreement that it is required by this Agreement to deliver and to perform its obligations under this Agreement and any obligations it has under any Credit Support Document to which it is a party and has taken all necessary action to authorise such execution, delivery and performance;

(iii) ***No Violation or Conflict.*** Such execution, delivery and performance do not violate or conflict with any law applicable to it, any provision of its constitutional documents, any order or judgment of any court or other agency of government applicable to it or any of its assets or any contractual restriction binding on or affecting it or any of its assets;

(iv) ***Consents.*** All governmental and other consents that are required to have been obtained by it with respect to this Agreement or any Credit Support Document to which it is a party have been obtained and are in full force and effect and all conditions of any such consents have been complied with; and

(v) ***Obligations Binding.*** Its obligations under this Agreement and any Credit Support Document to which it is a party constitute its legal, valid and binding obligations, enforceable in accordance with their respective terms (subject to applicable bankruptcy, reorganisation, insolvency, moratorium or similar laws affecting creditors' rights generally and subject, as to enforceability, to equitable principles of general application (regardless of whether enforcement is sought in a proceeding in equity or at law)).

(b) *Absence of Certain Events.* No Event of Default or Potential Event of Default or, to its knowledge, Termination Event with respect to it has occurred and is continuing and no such event or circumstance would occur as a result of its entering into or performing its obligations under this Agreement or any Credit Support Document to which it is a party.

(c) *Absence of Litigation.* There is not pending or, to its knowledge, threatened against it or any of its Affiliates any action, suit or proceeding at law or in equity or before any court, tribunal, governmental body, agency or official or any arbitrator that is likely to affect the legality, validity or enforceability against it of this Agreement or any Credit Support Document to which it is a party or its ability to perform its obligations under this Agreement or such Credit Support Document.

(d) *Accuracy of Specified Information.* All applicable information that is furnished in writing by or on behalf of it to the other party and is identified for the purpose of this Section 3(d) in the Schedule is, as of the date of the information, true, accurate and complete in every material respect.

(e) *Payer Tax Representation.* Each representation specified in the Schedule as being made by it for the purpose of this Section 3(e) is accurate and true.

(f) *Payee Tax Representations.* Each representation specified in the Schedule as being made by it for the purpose of this Section 3(f) is accurate and true.

4. *Agreements*

Each party agrees with the other that, so long as either party has or may have any obligation under this Agreement or under any Credit Support Document to which it is a party:—

(a) *Furnish Specified Information.* It will deliver to the other party or, in certain cases under subparagraph (iii) below, to such government or taxing authority as the other party reasonably directs:—

(i) any forms, documents or certificates relating to taxation specified in the Schedule or any Confirmation;

(ii) any other documents specified in the Schedule or any Confirmation; and

(iii) upon reasonable demand by such other party, any form or document that may be required or reasonably requested in writing in order to allow such other party or its Credit Support Provider to make a payment under this Agreement or any applicable Credit Support Document without any deduction or withholding for or on account of any Tax or with such deduction or withholding at a reduced rate (so long as the completion, execution or submission of such form or document would not materially prejudice the legal or commercial position of the party in receipt of such demand), with any such form or document to be accurate and completed in a manner reasonably satisfactory to such other party and to be executed and to be delivered with any reasonably required certification,

in each case by the date specified in the Schedule or such Confirmation or, if none is specified, as soon as reasonably practicable.

(b) *Maintain Authorisations.* It will use all reasonable efforts to maintain in full force and effect all consents of any governmental or other authority that are required to be obtained by it with respect to this Agreement or any Credit Support Document to which it is a party and will use all reasonable efforts to obtain any that may become necessary in the future.

(c) *Comply with Laws.* It will comply in all material respects with all applicable laws and orders to which it may be subject if failure so to comply would materially impair its ability to perform its obligations under this Agreement or any Credit Support Document to which it is a party.

(d) *Tax Agreement.* It will give notice of any failure of a representation made by it under Section 3(f) to be accurate and true promptly upon learning of such failure.

(e) *Payment of Stamp Tax.* Subject to Section 11, it will pay any Stamp Tax levied or imposed upon it or in respect of its execution or performance of this Agreement by a jurisdiction in which it is incorporated, organised, managed and controlled, or considered to have its seat, or in which a branch or office through which it is acting for the purpose of this Agreement is located ("Stamp Tax Jurisdiction") and will indemnify the other party against any Stamp Tax levied or imposed upon the other party or in respect of the other party's execution or performance of this Agreement by any such Stamp Tax Jurisdiction which is not also a Stamp Tax Jurisdiction with respect to the other party.

5. *Events of Default and Termination Events*

(a) *Events of Default.* The occurrence at any time with respect to a party or, if applicable, any Credit Support Provider of such party or any Specified Entity of such party of any of the following events constitutes an event of default (an "Event of Default") with respect to such party:—

(i) ***Failure to Pay or Deliver.*** Failure by the party to make, when due, any payment under this Agreement or delivery under Section 2(a)(i) or 2(e) required to be made by it if such failure is not remedied on or before the third Local Business Day after notice of such failure is given to the party;

(ii) ***Breach of Agreement.*** Failure by the party to comply with or perform any agreement or obligation (other than an obligation to make any payment under this Agreement or delivery under Section 2(a)(i) or 2(e) or to give notice of a Termination Event or any agreement or obligation under Section 4(a)(i), 4(a)(iii) or 4(d)) to be complied with or performed by the party in accordance with this Agreement if such failure is not remedied on or before the thirtieth day after notice of such failure is given to the party;

(iii) ***Credit Support Default.***

(1) Failure by the party or any Credit Support Provider of such party to comply with or perform any agreement or obligation to be complied with or performed by it in accordance with any Credit Support Document if such failure is continuing after any applicable grace period has elapsed;

(2) the expiration or termination of such Credit Support Document or the failing or ceasing of such Credit Support Document to be in full force and effect for the purpose of this Agreement (in either case other than in accordance with its terms) prior to the satisfaction of all obligations of such party under each Transaction to which such Credit Support Document relates without the written consent of the other party; or

(3) the party or such Credit Support Provider disaffirms, disclaims, repudiates or rejects, in whole or in part, or challenges the validity of, such Credit Support Document;

(iv) ***Misrepresentation.*** A representation (other than a representation under Section 3(e) or (f)) made or repeated or deemed to have been made or repeated by the party or any Credit Support Provider of such party in this Agreement or any Credit Support Document proves to have been incorrect or misleading in any material respect when made or repeated or deemed to have been made or repeated;

(v) ***Default under Specified Transaction.*** The party, any Credit Support Provider of such party or any applicable Specified Entity of such party (1) defaults under a Specified Transaction and, after giving effect to any applicable notice requirement or grace period, there occurs a liquidation of, an acceleration of obligations under, or an early termination of, that Specified Transaction, (2) defaults, after giving effect to any applicable notice requirement or grace period, in making any payment or delivery due on the last payment, delivery or exchange date of, or any payment on early termination of, a Specified Transaction (or such default continues for at least three Local Business Days if there is no applicable notice requirement or grace period) or (3) disaffirms, disclaims, repudiates or rejects, in whole or in part, a Specified Transaction (or such action is taken by any person or entity appointed or empowered to operate it or act on its behalf);

(vi) ***Cross Default.*** If "Cross Default" is specified in the Schedule as applying to the party, the occurrence or existence of (1) a default, event of default or other similar condition or event (however described) in respect of such party, any Credit Support Provider of such party or any applicable Specified Entity of such party under one or more agreements or instruments relating to Specified Indebtedness of any of them (individually or collectively) in an aggregate amount of not less than the applicable Threshold Amount (as specified in the Schedule) which has resulted in such Specified Indebtedness becoming, or becoming capable at such time of being declared, due and payable under such agreements or instruments, before it would otherwise have been due and payable or (2) a default by such party, such Credit Support Provider or such Specified Entity (individually or collectively) in making one or more payments on the due date thereof in an aggregate amount of not less than the applicable Threshold Amount under such agreements or instruments (after giving effect to any applicable notice requirement or grace period);

(vii) ***Bankruptcy.*** The party, any Credit Support Provider of such party or any applicable Specified Entity of such party:—

(1) is dissolved (other than pursuant to a consolidation, amalgamation or merger); (2) becomes insolvent or is unable to pay its debts or fails or admits in writing its inability generally to pay its debts as they become due; (3) makes a general assignment, arrangement or composition with or for the benefit of its creditors; (4) institutes or has instituted against it a proceeding seeking a judgment of insolvency or bankruptcy or any other relief under any bankruptcy or insolvency law or other similar law affecting creditors' rights, or a petition is presented for its winding-up or liquidation, and, in the case of any such proceeding or petition instituted or presented against it, such proceeding or petition (A) results in a judgment of insolvency or bankruptcy or the entry of an order for relief or the making of an order for its winding-up or liquidation or (B) is not dismissed, discharged, stayed or restrained in each case within 30 days of the institution or presentation thereof; (5) has a resolution passed for its winding-up, official management or liquidation (other than pursuant to a consolidation, amalgamation or merger); (6) seeks or becomes subject to the appointment of an administrator, provisional liquidator, conservator, receiver, trustee, custodian or other similar official for it or for all or substantially all its assets; (7) has a secured party take possession of all or substantially all its assets or has a distress, execution, attachment, sequestration or other legal process levied, enforced or sued on or against all or substantially all its assets and such secured party maintains possession, or any such process is not dismissed, discharged, stayed or restrained, in each case within 30 days thereafter; (8) causes or is subject to any event with respect to it which, under the applicable laws of any jurisdiction, has an analogous effect to any of the events specified in clauses (1) to (7) (inclusive); or (9) takes any action in furtherance of, or indicating its consent to, approval of, or acquiescence in, any of the foregoing acts; or

(viii) ***Merger Without Assumption.*** The party or any Credit Support Provider of such party consolidates or amalgamates with, or merges with or into, or transfers all or substantially all its assets to, another entity and, at the time of such consolidation, amalgamation, merger or transfer:—

(1) the resulting, surviving or transferee entity fails to assume all the obligations of such party or such Credit Support Provider under this Agreement or any Credit Support Document to which it or its predecessor was a party by operation of law or pursuant to an agreement reasonably satisfactory to the other party to this Agreement; or

(2) the benefits of any Credit Support Document fail to extend (without the consent of the other party) to the performance by such resulting, surviving or transferee entity of its obligations under this Agreement.

(b) *Termination Events.* The occurrence at any time with respect to a party or, if applicable, any Credit Support Provider of such party or any Specified Entity of such party of any event specified below constitutes an Illegality if the event is specified in (i) below, a Tax Event if the event is specified in (ii) below or a Tax Event Upon Merger if the event is specified in (iii) below, and, if specified to be applicable, a Credit Event Upon Merger if the event is specified pursuant to (iv) below or an Additional Termination Event if the event is specified pursuant to (v) below:—

(i) ***Illegality.*** Due to the adoption of, or any change in, any applicable law after the date on which a Transaction is entered into, or due to the promulgation of, or any change in, the interpretation by any court, tribunal or regulatory authority with competent jurisdiction of any applicable law after such date, it becomes unlawful (other than as a result of a breach by the party of Section 4(b)) for such party (which will be the Affected Party):—

(1) to perform any absolute or contingent obligation to make a payment or delivery or to receive a payment or delivery in respect of such Transaction or to comply with any other material provision of this Agreement relating to such Transaction; or

(2) to perform, or for any Credit Support Provider of such party to perform, any contingent or other obligation which the party (or such Credit Support Provider) has

under any Credit Support Document relating to such Transaction;

(ii) ***Tax Event.*** Due to (x) any action taken by a taxing authority, or brought in a court of competent jurisdiction, on or after the date on which a Transaction is entered into (regardless of whether such action is taken or brought with respect to a party to this Agreement) or (y) a Change in Tax Law, the party (which will be the Affected Party) will, or there is a substantial likelihood that it will, on the next succeeding Scheduled Payment Date (1) be required to pay to the other party an additional amount in respect of an Indemnifiable Tax under Section 2(d)(i)(4) (except in respect of interest under Section 2(e), 6(d)(ii) or 6(e)) or (2) receive a payment from which an amount is required to be deducted or withheld for or on account of a Tax (except in respect of interest under Section 2(e), 6(d)(ii) or 6(e)) and no additional amount is required to be paid in respect of such Tax under Section 2(d)(i)(4) (other than by reason of Section 2(d)(i)(4)(A) or (B));

(iii) ***Tax Event Upon Merger.*** The party (the "Burdened Party") on the next succeeding Scheduled Payment Date will either (1) be required to pay an additional amount in respect of an Indemnifiable Tax under Section 2(d)(i)(4) (except in respect of interest under Section 2(e), 6(d)(ii) or 6(e)) or (2) receive a payment from which an amount has been deducted or withheld for or on account of any Indemnifiable Tax in respect of which the other party is not required to pay an additional amount (other than by reason of Section 2(d)(i)(4)(A) or (B)), in either case as a result of a party consolidating or amalgamating with, or merging with or into, or transferring all or substantially all its assets to, another entity (which will be the Affected Party) where such action does not constitute an event described in Section 5(a)(viii);

(iv) ***Credit Event Upon Merger.*** If "Credit Event Upon Merger" is specified in the Schedule as applying to the party, such party ("X"), any Credit Support Provider of X or any applicable Specified Entity of X consolidates or amalgamates with, or merges with or into, or transfers all or substantially all its assets to, another entity and such action does not constitute an event described in Section 5(a)(viii) but the creditworthiness of the resulting, surviving or transferee entity is materially weaker than that of X, such Credit Support Provider or such Specified Entity, as the case may be, immediately prior to such action (and, in such event, X or its successor or transferee, as appropriate, will be the Affected Party); or

(v) ***Additional Termination Event.*** If any "Additional Termination Event" is specified in the Schedule or any Confirmation as applying, the occurrence of such event (and, in such event, the Affected Party or Affected Parties shall be as specified for such Additional Termination Event in the Schedule or such Confirmation).

(c) *Event of Default and Illegality.* If an event or circumstance which would otherwise constitute or give rise to an Event of Default also constitutes an Illegality, it will be treated as an Illegality and will not constitute an Event of Default.

6. *Early Termination*

(a) *Right to Terminate Following Event of Default.* If at any time an Event of Default with respect to a party (the "Defaulting Party") has occurred and is then continuing, the other party (the "Non-defaulting Party") may, by not more than 20 days notice to the Defaulting Party specifying the relevant Event of Default, designate a day not earlier than the day such notice is effective as an Early Termination Date in respect of all outstanding Transactions. If, however, "Automatic Early Termination" is specified in the Schedule as applying to a party, then an Early Termination Date in respect of all outstanding Transactions will occur immediately upon the occurrence with respect to such party of an Event of Default specified in Section 5(a)(vii)(1), (3), (5), (6) or, to the extent analogous thereto, (8), and as of the time immediately preceding the institution of the relevant proceeding or the presentation of the relevant petition upon the occurrence with respect to such party of an Event of Default specified in Section 5(a)(vii)(4) or, to the extent analogous thereto, (8).

(b) *Right to Terminate Following Termination Event.*

(i) ***Notice.*** If a Termination Event occurs, an Affected Party will, promptly upon becoming aware of it, notify the other party, specifying the nature of that Termination Event and each Affected Transaction and will also give such other information about that Termination Event as the other party may reasonably require.

(ii) ***Transfer to Avoid Termination Event.*** If either an Illegality under Section 5(b)(i)(1) or a Tax Event occurs and there is only one Affected Party, or if a Tax Event Upon Merger occurs and the Burdened Party is the Affected Party, the Affected Party will, as a condition to its right to designate an Early Termination Date under Section 6(b)(iv), use all reasonable efforts (which will not require such party to incur a loss, excluding immaterial, incidental expenses) to transfer within 20 days after it gives notice under Section 6(b)(i) all its rights and obligations under this Agreement in respect of the Affected Transactions to another of its Offices or Affiliates so that such Termination Event ceases to exist.

If the Affected Party is not able to make such a transfer it will give notice to the other party to that effect within such 20 day period, whereupon the other party may effect such a transfer within 30 days after the notice is given under Section 6(b)(i).

Any such transfer by a party under this Section 6(b)(ii) will be subject to and conditional upon the prior written consent of the other party, which consent will not be withheld if such other party's policies in effect at such time would permit it to enter into transactions with the transferee on the terms proposed.

(iii) ***Two Affected Parties.*** If an Illegality under Section 5(b)(i)(1) or a Tax Event occurs and there are two Affected Parties, each party will use all reasonable efforts to reach agreement within 30 days after notice thereof is given under Section 6(b)(i) on action to avoid that Termination Event.

(iv) ***Right to Terminate.*** If:—

(1) a transfer under Section 6(b)(ii) or an agreement under Section 6(b)(iii), as the case may be, has not been effected with respect to all Affected Transactions within 30 days after an Affected Party gives notice under Section 6(b)(i); or

(2) an Illegality under Section 5(b)(i)(2), a Credit Event Upon Merger or an Additional Termination Event occurs, or a Tax Event Upon Merger occurs and the Burdened Party is not the Affected Party,

either party in the case of an Illegality, the Burdened Party in the case of a Tax Event Upon Merger, any Affected Party in the case of a Tax Event or an Additional Termination Event if there is more than one Affected Party, or the party which is not the Affected Party in the case of a Credit Event Upon Merger or an Additional Termination Event if there is only one Affected Party may, by not more than 20 days notice to the other party and provided that the relevant Termination Event is then continuing, designate a day not earlier than the day such notice is effective as an Early Termination Date in respect of all Affected Transactions.

(c) *Effect of Designation.*

(i) If notice designating an Early Termination Date is given under Section 6(a) or (b), the Early Termination Date will occur on the date so designated, whether or not the relevant Event of Default or Termination Event is then continuing.

(ii) Upon the occurrence or effective designation of an Early Termination Date, no further payments or deliveries under Section 2(a)(i) or 2(e) in respect of the Terminated Transactions will be required to be made, but without prejudice to the other provisions of this Agreement. The amount, if any, payable in respect of an Early Termination Date shall be determined pursuant to Section 6(e).

(d) *Calculations.*

(i) ***Statement.*** On or as soon as reasonably practicable following the occurrence of an Early Termination Date, each party will make the calculations on its part, if any, contemplated by Section 6(e) and will provide to the other party a statement (1) showing, in reasonable detail, such calculations (including all relevant quotations and specifying any amount payable under Section 6(e)) and (2) giving details of the relevant account to which any amount payable to it is to be paid. In the absence of written confirmation from the source of a quotation obtained in determining a Market Quotation, the records of the party obtaining such quotation will be conclusive evidence of the existence and accuracy of such quotation.

(ii) ***Payment Date.*** An amount calculated as being due in respect of any Early Termination Date under Section 6(e) will be payable on the day that notice of the amount payable is effective (in the case of an Early Termination Date which is designated or occurs as a result of an Event of Default) and on the day which is two Local Business Days after the day on which notice of the amount payable is effective (in the case of an Early Termination Date which is designated as a result of a Termination Event). Such amount will be paid together with (to the extent permitted under applicable law) interest thereon (before as well as after judgment) in the Termination Currency, from (and including) the relevant Early Termination Date to (but excluding) the date such amount is paid, at the Applicable Rate. Such interest will be calculated on the basis of daily compounding and the actual number of days elapsed.

(e) *Payments on Early Termination.* If an Early Termination Date occurs, the following provisions shall apply based on the parties' election in the Schedule of a payment measure, either "Market Quotation" or "Loss", and a payment method, either the "First Method" or the "Second Method". If the parties fail to designate a payment measure or payment method in the Schedule, it will be deemed that "Market Quotation" or the "Second Method", as the case may be, shall apply. The amount, if any, payable in respect of an Early Termination Date and determined pursuant to this Section will be subject to any Set-off.

(i) ***Events of Default.*** If the Early Termination Date results from an Event of Default:—

(1) *First Method and Market Quotation.* If the First Method and Market Quotation apply, the Defaulting Party will pay to the Non-defaulting Party the excess, if a positive number, of (A) the sum of the Settlement Amount (determined by the Non-defaulting Party) in respect of the Terminated Transactions and the Termination Currency Equivalent of the Unpaid Amounts owing to the Non-defaulting Party over (B) the Termination Currency Equivalent of the Unpaid Amounts owing to the Defaulting Party.

(2) *First Method and Loss.* If the First Method and Loss apply, the Defaulting Party will pay to the Non-defaulting Party, if a positive number, the Non-defaulting Party's Loss in respect of this Agreement.

(3) *Second Method and Market Quotation.* If the Second Method and Market Quotation apply, an amount will be payable equal to (A) the sum of the Settlement Amount (determined by the Non-defaulting Party) in respect of the Terminated Transactions and the Termination Currency Equivalent of the Unpaid Amounts owing to the Non-defaulting Party less (B) the Termination Currency Equivalent of the Unpaid Amounts owing to the Defaulting Party. If that amount is a positive

number, the Defaulting Party will pay it to the Non-defaulting Party; if it is a negative number, the Non-defaulting Party will pay the absolute value of that amount to the Defaulting Party.

(4) *Second Method and Loss.* If the Second Method and Loss apply, an amount will be payable equal to the Non-defaulting Party's Loss in respect of this Agreement. If that amount is a positive number, the Defaulting Party will pay it to the Non-defaulting Party; if it is a negative number, the Non-defaulting Party will pay the absolute value of that amount to the Defaulting Party.

(ii) ***Termination Events.*** If the Early Termination Date results from a Termination Event:—

(1) *One Affected Party.* If there is one Affected Party, the amount payable will be determined in accordance with Section 6(e)(i)(3), if Market Quotation applies, or Section 6(e)(i)(4), if Loss applies, except that, in either case, references to the Defaulting Party and to the Non-defaulting Party will be deemed to be references to the Affected Party and the party which is not the Affected Party, respectively, and, if Loss applies and fewer than all the Transactions are being terminated, Loss shall be calculated in respect of all Terminated Transactions.

(2) *Two Affected Parties.* If there are two Affected Parties:—

(A) if Market Quotation applies, each party will determine a Settlement Amount in respect of the Terminated Transactions, and an amount will be payable equal to (I) the sum of (a) one-half of the difference between the Settlement Amount of the party with the higher Settlement Amount ("X") and the Settlement Amount of the party with the lower Settlement Amount ("Y") and (b) the Termination Currency Equivalent of the Unpaid Amounts owing to X less (II) the Termination Currency Equivalent of the Unpaid Amounts owing to Y; and

(B) if Loss applies, each party will determine its Loss in respect of this Agreement (or, if fewer than all the Transactions are being terminated, in respect of all Terminated Transactions) and an amount will be payable equal to one-half of the difference between the Loss of the party with the higher Loss

("X") and the Loss of the party with the lower Loss ("Y").

If the amount payable is a positive number, Y will pay it to X; if it is a negative number, X will pay the absolute value of that amount to Y.

(iii) ***Adjustment for Bankruptcy.*** In circumstances where an Early Termination Date occurs because "Automatic Early Termination" applies in respect of a party, the amount determined under this Section 6(e) will be subject to such adjustments as are appropriate and permitted by law to reflect any payments or deliveries made by one party to the other under this Agreement (and retained by such other party) during the period from the relevant Early Termination Date to the date for payment determined under Section 6(d)(ii).

(iv) ***Pre-Estimate.*** The parties agree that if Market Quotation applies an amount recoverable under this Section 6(e) is a reasonable pre-estimate of loss and not a penalty. Such amount is payable for the loss of bargain and the loss of protection against future risks and except as otherwise provided in this Agreement neither party will be entitled to recover any additional damages as a consequence of such losses.

7. *Transfer*

Subject to Section 6(b)(ii), neither this Agreement nor any interest or obligation in or under this Agreement may be transferred (whether by way of security or otherwise) by either party without the prior written consent of the other party, except that:—

(a) a party may make such a transfer of this Agreement pursuant to a consolidation or amalgamation with, or merger with or into, or transfer of all or substantially all its assets to, another entity (but without prejudice to any other right or remedy under this Agreement); and

(b) a party may make such a transfer of all or any part of its interest in any amount payable to it from a Defaulting Party under Section 6(e).

Any purported transfer that is not in compliance with this Section will be void.

8. Contractual Currency

(a) *Payment in the Contractual Currency.* Each payment under this Agreement will be made in the relevant currency specified in this Agreement for that payment (the "Contractual Currency"). To the extent permitted by applicable law, any obligation to make payments under this Agreement in the Contractual Currency will not be discharged or satisfied by any tender in any currency other than the Contractual Currency, except to the extent such tender results in the actual receipt by the party to which payment is owed, acting in a reasonable manner and in good faith in converting the currency so tendered into the Contractual Currency, of the full amount in the Contractual Currency of all amounts payable in respect of this Agreement. If for any reason the amount in the Contractual Currency so received falls short of the amount in the Contractual Currency payable in respect of this Agreement, the party required to make the payment will, to the extent permitted by applicable law, immediately pay such additional amount in the Contractual Currency as may be necessary to compensate for the shortfall. If for any reason the amount in the Contractual Currency so received exceeds the amount in the Contractual Currency payable in respect of this Agreement, the party receiving the payment will refund promptly the amount of such excess.

(b) *Judgments.* To the extent permitted by applicable law, if any judgment or order expressed in a currency other than the Contractual Currency is rendered (i) for the payment of any amount owing in respect of this Agreement, (ii) for the payment of any amount relating to any early termination in respect of this Agreement or (iii) in respect of a judgment or order of another court for the payment of any amount described in (i) or (ii) above, the party seeking recovery, after recovery in full of the aggregate amount to which such party is entitled pursuant to the judgment or order, will be entitled to receive immediately from the other party the amount of any shortfall of the Contractual Currency received by such party as a consequence of sums paid in such other currency and will refund promptly to the other party any excess of the Contractual Currency received by such party as a consequence of sums paid in such other currency if such shortfall or such excess arises or results from any variation between the rate of exchange at which the Contractual Currency is converted into the currency of the judgment or order for the purposes of such judgment or order and the rate of exchange at which such party is able, acting in a reasonable manner and in good faith in converting the currency received into the Contractual Currency, to purchase the Contractual Currency with the amount of the currency of the judgment or order actually received by such party. The term "rate of exchange" includes, without limitation, any premiums and costs of exchange payable in connection with the purchase of or conversion into the Contractual Currency.

(c) *Separate Indemnities.* To the extent permitted by applicable law, these indemnities constitute separate and independent obligations from the other obligations in this Agreement, will be enforceable as separate and independent causes of action, will apply notwithstanding any indulgence granted by the party to which any payment is owed and will not be affected by judgment being obtained or claim or proof being made for any other sums payable in respect of this Agreement.

(d) *Evidence of Loss.* For the purpose of this Section 8, it will be sufficient for a party to demonstrate that it would have suffered a loss had an actual exchange or purchase been made.

9. *Miscellaneous*

(a) *Entire Agreement.* This Agreement constitutes the entire agreement and understanding of the parties with respect to its subject matter and supersedes all oral communication and prior writings with respect thereto.

(b) *Amendments.* No amendment, modification or waiver in respect of this Agreement will be effective unless in writing (including a writing evidenced by a facsimile transmission) and executed by each of the parties or confirmed by an exchange of telexes or electronic messages on an electronic messaging system.

(c) *Survival of Obligations.* Without prejudice to Sections 2(a)(iii) and 6(c)(ii), the obligations of the parties under this Agreement will survive the termination of any Transaction.

(d) *Remedies Cumulative.* Except as provided in this Agreement, the rights, powers, remedies and privileges provided in this Agreement are cumulative and not exclusive of any rights, powers, remedies and privileges provided by law.

(e) *Counterparts and Confirmations.*

(i) This Agreement (and each amendment, modification and waiver in respect of it) may be executed and delivered in counterparts (including by facsimile transmission), each of which will be deemed an original.

(ii) The parties intend that they are legally bound by the terms of each Transaction from the moment they agree to those terms (whether orally or otherwise). A Confirmation shall be entered into as soon as practicable and may be executed and delivered in counterparts (including by facsimile transmission) or be created by an exchange of telexes or by an exchange of electronic messages on an electronic messaging system, which in each case will be sufficient for all purposes to evidence a binding supplement to this Agreement. The parties will specify therein or through another effective means that any such counterpart, telex or electronic message constitutes a Confirmation.

(f) *No Waiver of Rights.* A failure or delay in exercising any right, power or privilege in respect of this Agreement will not be presumed to operate as a waiver, and a single or partial exercise of any right, power or privilege will not be presumed to preclude any subsequent or further exercise, of that right, power or privilege or the exercise of any other right, power or privilege.

(g) *Headings.* The headings used in this Agreement are for convenience of reference only and are not to affect the construction of or to be taken into consideration in interpreting this Agreement.

10. Offices; Multibranch Parties

(a) If Section 10(a) is specified in the Schedule as applying, each party that enters into a Transaction through an Office other than its head or home office represents to the other party that, notwithstanding the place of booking office or jurisdiction of incorporation or organisation of such party, the obligations of such party are the same as if it had entered into the Transaction through its head or home office. This representation will be deemed to be repeated by such party on each date on which a Transaction is entered into.

(b) Neither party may change the Office through which it makes and receives payments or deliveries for the purpose of a Transaction without the prior written consent of the other party.

(c) If a party is specified as a Multibranch Party in the Schedule, such Multibranch Party may make and receive payments or deliveries under any Transaction through any Office listed in the Schedule, and the Office through which it makes and receives payments or deliveries with respect to a Transaction will be specified in the relevant Confirmation.

11. *Expenses*

A Defaulting Party will, on demand, indemnify and hold harmless the other party for and against all reasonable out-of-pocket expenses, including legal fees and Stamp Tax, incurred by such other party by reason of the enforcement and protection of its rights under this Agreement or any Credit Support Document to which the Defaulting Party is a party or by reason of the early termination of any Transaction, including, but not limited to, costs of collection.

12. *Notices*

(a) *Effectiveness.* Any notice or other communication in respect of this Agreement may be given in any manner set forth below (except that a notice or other communication under Section 5 or 6 may not be given by facsimile transmission or electronic messaging system) to the address or number or in accordance with the electronic messaging system details provided (see the Schedule) and will be deemed effective as indicated:—

(i) if in writing and delivered in person or by courier, on the date it is delivered;

(ii) if sent by telex, on the date the recipient's answerback is received;

(iii) if sent by facsimile transmission, on the date that transmission is received by a responsible employee of the recipient in legible form (it being agreed that the burden of proving receipt will be on the sender and will not be met by a transmission report generated by the sender's facsimile machine);

(iv) if sent by certified or registered mail (airmail, if overseas) or the equivalent (return receipt requested), on the date that mail is delivered or its delivery is attempted; or

(v) if sent by electronic messaging system, on the date that electronic message is received,

unless the date of that delivery (or attempted delivery) or that receipt, as applicable, is not a Local Business Day or that communication is delivered (or attempted) or received, as applicable, after the close of business on a Local Business Day, in which case that communication shall be deemed given and effective on the first following day that is a Local Business Day.

(b) *Change of Addresses.* Either party may by notice to the other change the address, telex or facsimile number or electronic messaging system details at which notices or other communications are to be given to it.

13. Governing Law and Jurisdiction

(a) *Governing Law.* This Agreement will be governed by and construed in accordance with the law specified in the Schedule.

(b) *Jurisdiction.* With respect to any suit, action or proceedings relating to this Agreement ("Proceedings"), each party irrevocably:—

(i) submits to the jurisdiction of the English courts, if this Agreement is expressed to be governed by English law, or to the non-exclusive jurisdiction of the courts of the State of New York and the United States District Court located in the Borough of Manhattan in New York City, if this Agreement is expressed to be governed by the laws of the State of New York; and

(ii) waives any objection which it may have at any time to the laying of venue of any Proceedings brought in any such court, waives any claim that such Proceedings have been brought in an inconvenient forum and further waives the right to object, with respect to such Proceedings, that such court does not have any jurisdiction over such party.

Nothing in this Agreement precludes either party from bringing Proceedings in any other jurisdiction (outside, if this Agreement is expressed to be governed by English law, the Contracting States, as defined in Section 1(3) of the Civil Jurisdiction and Judgments Act 1982 or any modification, extension or re-enactment thereof for the time being in force) nor will the bringing of Proceedings in any one or more jurisdictions preclude the bringing of Proceedings in any other jurisdiction.

(c) *Service of Process.* Each party irrevocably appoints the Process Agent (if any) specified opposite its name in the Schedule to receive, for it and on its behalf, service of process in any Proceedings. If for any reason any party's Process Agent is unable to act as such, such party will promptly notify the other party and within 30 days appoint a substitute process agent acceptable to the other party. The parties irrevocably consent to service of process given in the manner provided for notices in Section 12. Nothing in this Agreement will affect the right of either party to serve process in any other manner permitted by law.

(d) *Waiver of Immunities.* Each party irrevocably waives, to the fullest extent permitted by applicable law, with respect to itself and its revenues and assets (irrespective of their use or intended use), all immunity on the grounds of sovereignty or other similar grounds from (i) suit, (ii) jurisdiction of any court, (iii) relief by way of injunction, order for specific performance or for recovery of property, (iv) attachment of its assets (whether before or after judgment) and (v) execution or enforcement of any judgment to which it or its revenues or assets might otherwise be entitled in any Proceedings in the courts of any jurisdiction and irrevocably agrees, to the extent permitted by applicable law, that it will not claim any such immunity in any Proceedings.

14. Definitions

As used in this Agreement:—

"Additional Termination Event" has the meaning specified in Section 5(b).

"Affected Party" has the meaning specified in Section 5(b).

"Affected Transactions" means (a) with respect to any Termination Event consisting of an Illegality, Tax Event or Tax Event Upon Merger, all Transactions affected by the occurrence of such Termination Event and (b) with respect to any other Termination Event, all Transactions.

"Affiliate" means, subject to the Schedule, in relation to any person, any entity controlled, directly or indirectly, by the person, any entity that controls, directly or indirectly, the person or any entity directly or indirectly under common control with the person. For this purpose, "control" of any entity or person means ownership of a majority of the voting power of the entity or person.

"Applicable Rate" means:—

(a) in respect of obligations payable or deliverable (or which would have been but for Section 2(a)(iii)) by a Defaulting Party, the Default Rate;

(b) in respect of an obligation to pay an amount under Section 6(e) of either party from and after the date (determined in accordance with Section 6(d)(ii)) on which that amount is payable, the Default Rate;

(c) in respect of all other obligations payable or deliverable (or which would have been but for Section 2(a)(iii)) by a Non-defaulting Party, the Non-default Rate; and

(d) in all other cases, the Termination Rate.

"Burdened Party" has the meaning specified in Section 5(b).

"Change in Tax Law" means the enactment, promulgation, execution or ratification of, or any change in or amendment to, any law (or in the application or official interpretation of any law) that occurs on or after the date on which the relevant Transaction is entered into.

"consent" includes a consent, approval, action, authorisation, exemption, notice, filing, registration or exchange control consent.

"Credit Event Upon Merger" has the meaning specified in Section 5(b).

"Credit Support Document" means any agreement or instrument that is specified as such in this Agreement.

"Credit Support Provider" has the meaning specified in the Schedule.

"Default Rate" means a rate per annum equal to the cost (without proof or evidence of any actual cost) to the relevant payee (as certified by it) if it were to fund or of funding the relevant amount plus 1% per annum.

"Defaulting Party" has the meaning specified in Section 6(a).

"Early Termination Date" means the date determined in accordance with Section 6(a) or 6(b)(iv).

"Event of Default" has the meaning specified in Section 5(a) and, if applicable, in the Schedule.

"Illegality" has the meaning specified in Section 5(b).

"Indemnifiable Tax" means any Tax other than a Tax that would not be imposed in respect of a payment under this Agreement but for a present or former connection between the jurisdiction of the government or taxation authority imposing such Tax and the recipient of such payment or a person related to such recipient (including, without limitation, a connection arising from such recipient or related person being or having been a citizen or resident of such jurisdiction, or being or having been organised, present or engaged in a trade or business in such jurisdiction, or having or having had a permanent establishment or fixed place of business in such jurisdiction, but excluding a connection arising solely from such recipient or related person having executed, delivered, performed its obligations or received a payment under, or enforced, this Agreement or a Credit Support Document).

"law" includes any treaty, law, rule or regulation (as modified, in the case of tax matters, by the practice of any relevant governmental revenue authority) and ***"lawful"*** and ***"unlawful"*** will be construed accordingly.

"Local Business Day" means, subject to the Schedule, a day on which commercial banks are open for business (including dealings in foreign exchange and foreign currency deposits) (a) in relation to any obligation under Section 2(a)(i), in the place(s) specified in the relevant Confirmation or, if not so specified, as otherwise agreed by the parties in writing or determined pursuant to provisions contained, or incorporated by reference, in this Agreement, (b) in relation to any other payment, in the place where the relevant account is located and, if different, in the principal financial centre, if any, of the currency of such payment, (c) in relation to any notice or other communication, including notice contemplated under Section 5(a)(i), in the city specified in the address for notice provided by the recipient and, in the case of a notice contemplated by Section 2(b), in the place where the relevant new account is to be located and (d) in relation to Section 5(a)(v)(2), in the relevant locations for performance with respect to such Specified Transaction.

"Loss" means, with respect to this Agreement or one or more Terminated Transactions, as the case may be, and a party, the Termination Currency Equivalent of an amount that party reasonably determines in good faith to be its total losses and costs (or gain, in which case expressed as a negative number) in connection with this Agreement or that Terminated Transaction or group of Terminated Transactions, as the case may be, including any loss of bargain, cost of funding or, at the election of such party but without duplication, loss or cost incurred as a result of its terminating, liquidating, obtaining or reestablishing any hedge or related trading position (or any gain resulting from any of them). Loss includes losses and costs (or gains) in respect of any payment or delivery required to have been made (assuming satisfaction of each applicable condition precedent) on or before the relevant Early Termination Date and not made, except, so as to avoid duplication, if Section 6(e)(i)(1) or (3) or 6(e)(ii)(2)(A) applies. Loss does not include a party's legal fees and out-of-pocket expenses referred to under Section 11. A party will determine its Loss as of the relevant Early Termination Date, or, if that is not reasonably practicable, as of the earliest date thereafter as is reasonably practicable. A party may (but need not) determine its Loss by reference to quotations of relevant rates or prices from one or more leading dealers in the relevant markets.

"Market Quotation" means, with respect to one or more Terminated Transactions and a party making the determination, an amount determined on the basis of quotations from Reference Market-makers. Each quotation will be for an amount, if any, that would be paid to such party (expressed as a negative number) or by such party (expressed as a positive number) in consideration of an agreement between such party (taking into account any existing Credit Support Document with respect to the obligations of such party) and the quoting Reference Market-maker to enter into a transaction (the "Replacement Transaction") that would have the effect of preserving for such party the economic equivalent of any payment or delivery (whether the underlying obligation was absolute or contingent and assuming the satisfaction of each applicable condition precedent) by the parties under Section 2(a)(i) in respect of such Terminated Transaction or group of Terminated Transactions that would, but for the occurrence of the relevant Early Termination Date, have been required after that date. For this purpose, Unpaid Amounts in respect of the Terminated Transaction or group of Terminated Transactions are to be excluded but, without limitation, any payment or delivery that would, but for the relevant Early Termination Date, have been required (assuming satisfaction of each applicable condition precedent) after that Early Termination Date is to be included. The Replacement Transaction would be subject to such documentation as such party and the Reference Market-maker may, in good faith, agree. The party making the determination (or its agent) will request each Reference Market-maker to provide its quotation to the extent reasonably practicable as of the same day and time (without regard to different time zones) on or as soon as reasonably practicable after the relevant Early Termination Date. The day and time as of which those quotations are to be obtained will be selected in good faith by the party obliged to make a determination under Section 6(e), and, if each party is so obliged, after consultation with the other. If more than three quotations are provided, the Market Quotation will be the arithmetic means of the quotations, without regard to the quotations having the highest and lowest values. If exactly three such quotations are provided, the Market Quotation will be the quotation remaining after disregarding the highest and lowest quotations. For this purpose, if more than one quotation has the same highest value or lowest value, then one of such quotations shall be disregarded. If fewer than three quotations are provided, it will be deemed that the Market Quotation in respect of such Terminated Transaction or group of Terminated Transactions cannot be determined.

"Non-default Rate" means a rate per annum equal to the cost (without proof or evidence of any actual cost) to the Non-defaulting Party (as certified by it) if it were to fund the relevant amount.

"Non-defaulting Party" has the meaning specified in Section 6(a).

"Office" means a branch or office of a party, which may be such party's head or home office.

"Potential Event of Default" means any event which, with the giving of notice or the lapse of time or both, would constitute an Event of Default.

"Reference Market-makers" means four leading dealers in the relevant market selected by the party determining a Market Quotation in good faith (a) from among dealers of the highest credit standing which satisfy all the criteria that such party applies generally at the time in deciding whether to offer or to make an extension of credit and (b) to the extent practicable, from among such dealers having an office in the same city.

"Relevant Jurisdiction" means, with respect to a party, the jurisdictions (a) in which the party is incorporated, organised, managed and controlled or considered to have its seat, (b) where an Office through which the party is acting for purposes of this Agreement is located, (c) in which the party executes this Agreement and (d) in relation to any payment, from or through which such payment is made.

"Scheduled Payment Date" means a date on which a payment or delivery is to be made under Section 2(a)(i) with respect to a Transaction.

"Set-off" means set-off, offset, combination of accounts, right of retention or withholding or similar right or requirement to which the payer of an amount under Section 6 is entitled or subject (whether arising under this Agreement, another contract, applicable law or otherwise) that is exercised by, or imposed on, such payer.

"Settlement Amount" means, with respect to a party and any Early Termination Date, the sum of:—

(a) the Termination Currency Equivalent of the Market Quotations (whether positive or negative) for each Terminated Transaction or group of Terminated Transactions for which a Market Quotation is determined; and

(b) such party's Loss (whether positive or negative and without reference to any Unpaid Amounts) for each Terminated Transaction or group of Terminated Transactions for which a Market Quotation cannot be determined or would not (in the reasonable belief of the party making the determination) produce a commercially reasonable result.

"Specified Entity" has the meaning specified in the Schedule.

"Specified Indebtedness" means, subject to the Schedule, any obligation (whether present or future, contingent or otherwise, as principal or surety or otherwise) in respect of borrowed money.

"Specified Transaction" means, subject to the Schedule, (a) any transaction (including an agreement with respect thereto) now existing or hereafter entered into between one party to this Agreement (or any Credit Support Provider of such party or any applicable Specified Entity of such party) and the other party to this Agreement (or any Credit Support Provider of such other party or any applicable Specified Entity of such other party) which is a rate swap transaction, basis swap, forward rate transaction, commodity swap, commodity option, equity or equity index swap, equity or equity index option, bond option, interest rate option, foreign exchange transaction, cap transaction, floor transaction, collar transaction, currency swap transaction, cross-currency rate swap transaction, currency option or any other similar transaction (including any option with respect to any of these transactions), (b) any combination of these transactions and (c) any other transaction identified as a Specified Transaction in this Agreement or the relevant confirmation.

"Stamp Tax" means any stamp, registration, documentation or similar tax.

"Tax" means any present or future tax, levy, impost, duty, charge, assessment or fee of any nature (including interest, penalties and additions thereto) that is imposed by any government or other taxing authority in respect of any payment under this Agreement other than a stamp, registration, documentation or similar tax.

"Tax Event" has the meaning specified in Section 5(b).

"Tax Event Upon Merger" has the meaning specified in Section 5(b).

"Terminated Transactions" means with respect to any Early Termination Date (a) if resulting from a Termination Event, all Affected Transactions and (b) if resulting from an Event of Default, all Transactions (in either case) in effect immediately before the effectiveness of the notice designating that Early Termination Date (or, if "Automatic Early Termination" applies, immediately before that Early Termination Date).

"Termination Currency" has the meaning specified in the Schedule.

"Termination Currency Equivalent" means, in respect of any amount denominated in the Termination Currency, such Termination Currency amount and, in respect of any amount denominated in a currency other than the Termination Currency (the "Other Currency"), the amount in the Termination Currency determined by the party making the relevant determination as being required to purchase such amount of such Other Currency as at the relevant Early Termination Date, or, if the relevant Market Quotation or Loss (as the case may be), is determined as of a later date, that later date, with the Termination Currency at the rate equal to the spot exchange rate of the foreign exchange agent (selected as provided below) for the purchase of such Other Currency with the Termination Currency at or about 11:00 a.m. (in the city in which such foreign exchange agent is located) on such date as would be customary for the determination of such a rate for the purchase of such Other Currency for value on the relevant Early Termination Date or that later date. The foreign exchange agent will, if only one party is obliged to make a determination under Section 6(e), be selected in good faith by that party and otherwise will be agreed by the parties.

"Termination Event" means an Illegality, a Tax Event or a Tax Event Upon Merger or, if specified to be applicable, a Credit Event Upon Merger or an Additional Termination Event.

"Termination Rate" means a rate per annum equal to the arithmetic mean of the cost (without proof or evidence of any actual cost) to each party (as certified by such party) if it were to fund or of funding such amounts.

"Unpaid Amounts" owing to any party means, with respect to an

Early Termination Date, the aggregate of (a) in respect of all Terminated Transactions, the amounts that became payable (or that would have become payable but for Section 2(a)(iii)) to such party under Section 2(a)(i) on or prior to such Early Termination Date and which remain unpaid as at such Early Termination Date and (b) in respect of each Terminated Transaction, for each obligation under Section 2(a)(i) which was (or would have been but for Section 2(a)(iii)) required to be settled by delivery to such party on or prior to such Early Termination Date and which has not been so settled as at Early Termination Date, an amount equal to the fair market value of that which was (or would have been) required to be delivered as of the originally scheduled date for delivery, in each case together with (to the extent permitted under applicable law) interest, in the currency of such amounts, from (and including) the date such amounts or obligations were or would have been required to have been paid or performed to (but excluding) such Early Termination Date, at the Applicable Rate. Such amounts of interest will be calculated on the basis of daily compounding and the actual number of days elapsed. The fair market value of any obligation referred to in clause (b) above shall be reasonably determined by the party obliged to make the determination under Section 6(e) or, if each party is so obliged, it shall be the average of the Termination Currency Equivalents of the fair market values reasonably determined by both parties.

IN WITNESS WHEREOF the parties have executed this document on the respective dates specified below with effect from the date specified on the first page of this document.

______________________________	______________________________
(Name of Party)	(Name of Party)
By: ______________________________	By: ______________________________
Name:	Name:
Title:	Title:
Date:	Date:

Endnotes

Chapter 2

[1] See, for example, David K. Eiteman and Arthur I. Stonehill, *Multinational Business Finance* (Addison-Wesley Publishing Co, 1979), Chapter 3.

[2] The cash flows denominated in foreign currencies could, for example, represent export receivables where amounts and due dates are predetermined, or it could represent principal and interest payments on financial commitments. In case a financial commitment is established on a floating rate basis, the future cash flow in the currency of accounting is uncertain not only because the foreign exchange rate is volatile, but also because the interest rate applied is likely to fluctuate.

In circumstances where the foreign currency cash flows represent predetermined receivables or payables the sole consideration would be the foreign exchange exposure. In the case of a foreign-currency-denominated financial commitment, one would have to consider both the currency and interest rate gapping aspects. The interest rate gapping in foreign currencies is an especially important consideration to many financial institutions.

[3] Torben Juul Andersen and Rikky Hasan, *Interest Rate Risk Management* (IFR Publishing Ltd., London, 1989).

[4] See, for example, "Risk Management in Financial Services", *OECD,* Paris, 1992.

Chapter 4

[1] The delivery date of the futures contracts differs from exchange to exchange and also varies for different types of contracts as shown by the following examples:

Type of Futures Contract (Exchange)	*Delivery Date*
3-month Eurodollar time deposit (IMM)	2nd London business day before the 3rd Wednesday of the delivery month.
3-month Eurodollar time deposit (LIFFE)	2nd Wednesday of delivery month.
3-month certificate of deposit (IMM)	15th through last business day of delivery month.
3-month U.S. Treasury bill (IMM)	1st day when 13-week T bills are issued in the delivery month (or one-year T bills have 13 weeks to maturity).
U.S. Treasury bonds (CBOT/LIFFE)	Any business day in the delivery month.

[2] Calculation of par value multipliers:

A. 8% coupon/15 years to maturity

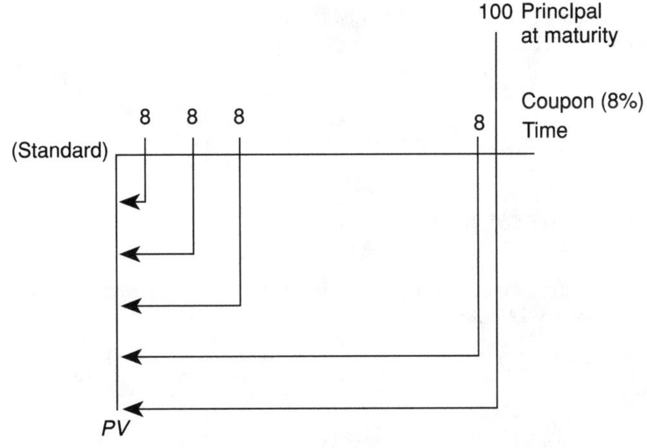

$$PV = \frac{8}{1.08} + \frac{8}{1.08^2} + \ldots \frac{8}{1.08^{15}} + \frac{100}{1.08^{15}}$$

$$= 8 \times \frac{\overline{(1-1.08)^{15}}}{0.08} + \frac{100}{1.08^{15}} = 8 \times 8.5595 + \frac{100}{3.1722}$$

$$= 68.48 + 31.52 = 100 = \text{Principal}$$

B. 7% coupon / 15 years to maturity:

$$PV = 7 \times 8.5595 + \frac{100}{3.1722} = 59.92 + 31.52 = 91.44$$

The par value multiplier is .9144.

C. 7% coupon / 20 years to maturity:

$$PV = 7 \times 9.8181 + \frac{100}{1.08^{20}} = 68.7267 + 21.4548 = 90.18$$

The par value multiplier is .9018.

D. 9% coupon / 15 years to maturity:

$$PV = 9 \times 8.5595 + \frac{100}{3.1722} = 77.04 + 31.52 = 108.56$$

The par value multiplier is 1.0856.

[3] For an excellent discussion of the interest rate parity theory, for example, refer to Jan H. Giddy, "An Integrated Theory of Exchange Rate Equilibrium," in *International Financial Management, Theory and Application,* ed. by Donald R. Lessard (Warren, Gorham & Lamont, 1980).

[4] For example, the Standard & Poors (S&P) 500 index is made up of 500 stocks representing industry, public utilities, transportation, and financial companies in relation to their proportions in the stock market. The shares represent around 80% of the value traded on the New York Stock Exchange.

The index is calculated by multiplying the number of stocks outstanding for each of the 500 institutions multiplied by their market prices. The total market value of these shares is then compared to the market value of the stocks outstanding in 1941–43. The index value for the base period is set at 10. Hence the S&P 500 index (x) is calculated as follows:

$$x = \frac{MV_p}{MV_{41-43} \times 10}$$

where

MV_p = Total market value of the 500 stocks at present.
MV_{41-43} = Total market value of the 500 stocks during the base period 1941–43.

[5] To illustrate the diversity of stock indexes, see the following listing from *The Wall Street Journal* (Europe) of February 12, 1985.

	1985		*Change*	*1984*
N.Y.S.E. Composite	104.50	–0.89	–0.84%	89.28
Industrial	120.40	–1.06	–0.87%	103.70
Utility	53.28	–0.25	–0.47%	45.20
Transp.	100.66	–1.64	–1.60%	85.09
Financial	109.45	–1.16	–1.05%	89.50
Am. Ex. Mkt Val Index	229.53	–1.52	–0.66%	205.02
Nasdaq OTC Composite	287.43	–0.92	–0.32%	250.57
Industrial	311.39	–1.04	–0.33%	282.94
Insurance	319.66	–1.08	–0.34%	244.71
Banks	251.26	–0.88	–0.35%	205.23
Nasdaq Natl Mkt Comp	122.64	–0.52	–0.41%	...
Industrial	117.71	–0.52	–0.44%	...
Standard & Poor's 500	180.51	–1.68	–0.92%	154.95
400 Industrial	201.85	–1.95	–0.96%	174.18
Value Line Index	198.97	–1.00	–0.50%	178.77
Wilshire 5000 Equity	1,865.081	–14.442	–0.77%	1,611.709

Note the difference in the index value, which is influenced by the choice of base period, the index value of the base period, and the development in share prices of the underlying stock portfolio. The change figures refer to the absolute changes (– or +) in the index value and the corresponding percentage change from the previous trading day.

[6] For a general description of the commodity futures markets, see, for example, William F. Sharpe, *Investments*, 2nd ed. (Prentice-Hall, 1981).

[7] The following ten exchanges are among those with the highest turnover of commodity futures contracts in the 1980s:

The Chicago Mercantile Exchange (CME)
The Chicago Board of Trade (CBOT)
The Commodity Exchange Inc. (COMEX)
The Coffee, Sugar & Cocoa Exchange (CS&C)
The New York Mercantile Exchange (NYMEX)
The Mid America Commodity Exchange (MIDAM)
The New York Cotton Exchange (NYCE)
The Kansas City Board of Trade (KCBOT)
The Minneapolis Grain Exchange (MGE)
The New Orleans Commodity Exchange (NOCE)

Chapter 5

[1] For a discussion of this, see, for example, Mark J. Powers, *Inside the Financial Futures Markets*, 2nd ed. (John Wiley & Sons, Inc., 1984).

[2] For a 15-year 8% coupon with \$100 nominal value, to yield 11.00% p.a., it should be sold at a discount price of \$78.43 ($^{14}/_{32}$). (The calculations here assume that coupon is paid annually.)

$$8\frac{1-\frac{1}{1.11^{15}}}{0.11}+\frac{100}{1.11^{15}}=57.527+20.900=78.43$$

When investing US\$ 10,000,000, one achieves a nominal value of 100/78.427 × 10,000,000 equals \$12,750,710.85, or rather by investing \$9,960,230 one achieves a nominal value of \$12,700,000. Applying the present value formula, the following present value calculations are worked out.

$$PV=\text{Coupon}\frac{\left[1-\frac{1}{(1+i)^{n}}\right]}{i}+\frac{\text{Principal}}{(1+i)^{n}} \quad \text{Coupon}=8\%\text{ p.a., Principal}=100$$

	n=15	n=14	(Change)
i = 12.0%	54.487 + 18.270 = 72.76	53.025 + 20.462 = 73.49	(2.71)
i = 11.5%	55.974 + 19.538 = 75.51		
i = 11.0%	—	55.855 + 23.199 = 79.05	(2.85)
i = 10.5%	59.151 + 22.365 = 81.52	57.361 + 24.713 = 82.07	(3.02)

Example 1: Actual return is calculated as follows:

Amount invested ($10,000,000)	$9,960,230
Current market price at year-end (12,700,000 × 0.7349)	$9,333,230
Loss from reduction in market price	$ (627,000)
Interest payment	$ 800,000
	$ 173,000

[3] *Example 2:* Actual return is calculated as follows:

Current market price at year-end (12,700,000 × 0.8207)	$10,422,890
Amount invested ($10,000,000)	$ 9,960,230
Capital gain from increase in market	$ 462,660
Interest payment	$ 800,000
	$ 1,262,660

[4] Principal = $20,000,000

Semiannual coupon = $800,000 (8% p.a.)

Maturity = 15 years

$$PV = 800,000 \times \frac{1-\frac{1}{1.05375^{30}}}{0.05375} + \frac{20,000,000}{1.05375^{30}} \quad i = 10.75\% \text{ p.a.}$$

$$= 11,789,267.94 + 4,158,171.21 = \$15,947,439.15$$

This implies sale at a discount price of

$$15,947,439.15/20,000,000 \times 100 = 79.74\%.$$

[5] $$PV = 800,000 \times \frac{1-\frac{1}{1.055^{30}}}{0.055} + \frac{20,000,000}{1.055^{30}} \quad i = 11.00\% \text{ p.a.}$$

$$= 11,626,996.13 + 4,012,880.31 = \$15,639,876.44$$

This implies sale at a discount price of

$$15,639,876.44/20,000,000 \times 100 = 78.2\%.$$

and a loss on the issue of

($15,947,439.15 – $15,639,876.44) = $307,562.71

[6] Of all the eligible bonds to be delivered under the U.S. Treasury bond contract, it is generally true to assume that sellers will deliver the bond cheapest for them. In general it is the security with the lowest value, calculated by taking the current cash market price and dividing it by the appropriate conversion factor.

[7] For more information on regression analysis, see, for example, Ronald J. Wannacott and Thomas H. Wannacott, *Econometrics* (John Wiley & Sons, Inc., 1970).

[8] Applying the present value formula

$$PV = \text{Coupon} \times \frac{1-\frac{1}{(1+i)^n}}{i} + \frac{\text{Principal}}{(1+i)^n}$$

the following calculations are performed assuming that the present interest rate for both the Eurobonds and the Treasury bonds is 12% p.a.

Eurobond:

Nominal amount = 20,000,000
Coupon = 7% (annual payment)
Maturity= 20 years

i = 12% PV = 12,530,556.38

i = 12.01% PV = 12,520,306.28, change = – 10,250.10

i = 11.99% PV = 12,540,820.30, change = + 10,263.92

Treasury bond:

Nominal amount = 20,000,000
Coupon = 8% (annual payment)
Maturity= 20 years

i = 12% PV = 14,024,445.10

i = 12.01% PV = 14,013.12, change = – 11,185.98

i = 11.99% PV = 14,035,645.89, change = + 11,200.79

[9] See London International Financial Futures Exchange, "US Treasury Bond Futures," LIFFE Ltd., 1984.

[10] In fact, the axiom only holds when the duration is calculated on the basis of the zero-coupon interest rate as opposed to the effective yield. However, the discrepancies will usually be relatively small.

[11] Remember here that the spot exchange rate quotation for all currencies is indicated as number of currency units per U.S. dollars with the exception of commonwealth currencies like the pound sterling, which is quoted as US$/£ stg.

The futures contract prices, however, are always quoted in U.S. dollars. That is, a cash futures price of $0.0952 for a French franc contract implies a spot exchange rate of 10.5042 Fr. frc./US$, and the cross rate is calculated as 1.0750 × 10.5042 (Fr. frc./US$ × $/£ stg.) = 11.2920 Fr. frc./£ stg.

[12] The price variance of a stock portfolio is mathematically presented as follows:

$$\text{Var}(P) = \frac{1}{N^2}\sum_{i=1}^{N}\sum_{j=1}^{N}\text{Cov}(P_i, P_j)$$

where

Var (P) = Price variation of stock portfolio P.
Cov (P_i, P_j) = Price covariance of stock category i and j.

$$= \frac{1}{n-1}\sum_{k=1}^{n}(P_{i,k} - \overline{P}_{i,k})(P_{j,k} - \overline{P}_{j,k})$$

where

$i = 1,2,\ldots, N$.
$j = 1,2,\ldots, N$.
i, j = Denotes specific categories of stock.
N = Total number of stock categories.

$k = 1,2,\ldots, n$.
n = Total number of events in the statistical sample.
P_i = Average stock price of category i.
P_j = Average stock price of category j.

Then

Lim Var $(P) = 0$ given a finite price fluctuation level for N approaching infinity.

When the number of stock categories in the portfolio increases, the price variation of the portfolio goes toward zero.

Chapter 6

[1] See, for example, a standard finance textbook like J. Fred Weston, Eugene F. Brigham, Poul Halpern, *Essentials of Canadian Managerial Finance* (Holt, Rinehart & Winston of Canada, Ltd., 1979).

[2] For a further discussion on the valuation of call options on stocks, refer to William F. Sharpe, *Investments*, 2nd ed. (Prentice-Hall, 1981).

[3] For a discussion of the Black-Scholes option evaluation equation, refer, for example, to Thomas E. Copeland and J. Fred Weston, *Financial Theory and Corporate Policy* (Addison-Wesley Publishing Co., 1979); or to the original source, F. Black and M. Scholes, "The Pricing of Options and Corporate Liabilities," *Journal of Political Economy* (May/June 1973), pp. 637–659.

Example: Say the following data reflects the present market environment:

P = US$ 120.
E = US$ 120.5.
$T = 0.50$ (six months being half a year).
$rt = 10\%$ (reflecting the going interest rate on U.S. Treasury bills).
$s^2 = 33.5$.

The price variance is calculated on the basis of the past year's end-of-month quotes on the stock price.

Month (*t*)	*Market Price* (*P*)	$(Pt/Pt-1)$
1	119.75	—
2	119.95	0.00167
3	121.00	0.00872
4	120.85	–0.00124
5	119.65	–0.00979
6	118.95	–0.00587
7	118.00	–0.00802
8	117.45	0.00467
9	118.05	0.05096
10	118.35	0.00254
11	119.15	0.00674
12	119.50	0.00293
13	120.00	0.00418
	Mean =	0.00401
	Variances =	0.00232
	Standard deviation (*s*) =	0.01589
	Annual standard deviation =	$0.01589 \times \sqrt{12} = 0.05504$

$$
\begin{aligned}
x_1 &= [\ln 120/120.5) + (0.05504\,^2/2).50)]/(0.05504\sqrt{.50} \\
&= (0.00416 + 0.10076)/0.03892 \\
&= 2.48 \\
x_2 &= (\ln(120/120.5) + [0.10 - (0.05504\,^2/2)0.50]/(0.05504\sqrt{0.50})(-0.00416 + 0.09924)/0.03892 \\
&= 2.44 \\
w &= 120 \times N(2.48) - e^{-0.10\times 0.5} \times 120.5 \times N(2.44) \\
&= 120 \times 0.9934 - 0.9512 \times 120.5 \times 0.9927 \\
&= 19.21 - 113.78 = \underline{\$5.43}
\end{aligned}
$$

[4] Refer, for example, to Lawrence G. McMillan, *Options as a Strategic Investment*, 3rd ed. (New York Institute of Finance, 1992).

Chapter 8

[1] See, for example, Jack D. Schwager, A Complete Guide to the Futures Markets (John Wiley & Sons, Inc., 1984).

[2] Refer to Lawrence G. McMillan, *Options as a Strategic Investment*, 3rd ed. (New York Institute of Finance, 1992).

Chapter 9

[1] We have ignored the funding cost of the up-front premium from May to September. Assuming a per-annum rate of 10%, the four months' interest cost amounts to $500, which is relatively small compared to the premium itself.

[2] In this discussion the initial margin payment required to write an option has not been included in the profit and loss analysis. However, it is very important for option writers to fully understand the margin requirements of the exchange before engaging in any trading activities.

[3] It should be noted that the additionality of the duration strictly speaking only holds if the duration calculations are based on a zero-coupon bond structure. However, the use of effective interest rates will normally not lead to excessive discrepancies.

Chapter 10

[1] In this calculation, however, we make an assumption that the dollar deposit interest amount in six months' time can be converted into Swiss francs at the spot foreign exchange rate prevalent at the date of the transaction initiation. To be precise, what should be done is to buy spot an amount of dollars that, including the six-month deposit-interest amount, is equal to the required $1,000,000. Applying this principle the transaction looks as follows:

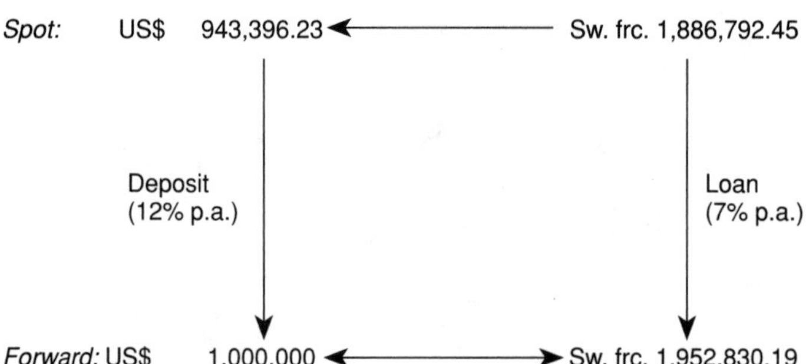

Hence the true outright rate is Sw. frc./US$ 1.9528 and the swap is 0.0472 as opposed to 0.0500. However, the difference is considered too small to be material for general purposes.

[2] It is important to use the correct foreign exchange rate denomination when applying the general rules. In this example we trade U.S. dollars, so that the "price" (foreign exchange rate) of the "goods" (US$) are denominated as Sw. frc./US$.

Chapter 11

[1] These and other relationships are discussed further in an excellent unpublished paper by Jan H. Giddy, "Foreign Exchange Options," Columbia University and Claremont Economics Institute (September 1982).

Chapter 12

[1] If the settlement is made in the beginning of the settlement period then the interest settlement amount is calculated in the following way, which is similar to the FRA settlement calculation (see Chapter 10):

$$S = (MR - CR) \times A \times T/(36{,}000 + MR \times T) \text{ when } MR > CR$$

or

$$S = (FR - MR) \times A \times T/(36{,}000 + MR \times T) \text{ when } MR < FR$$

Chapter 13

[1] For a very good overview of the counterparty technique behind swap transactions, for example, David Pritchard, "Swap Financing Techniques," *Euromoney* (May 1984).

Appendix I

[1] See, for example, J. Johnston, *Econometric Methods,* 2nd ed. (McGraw-Hill, 1972) or Henri Theil, *Principles of Econometrics* (North-Holland Publishing Company, 1979).

[2] Charles R. Nelson, *Applied Time Series Analysis for Managerial Forecasting* (Holden-Day, 1973).

C. Chatfield, *The Analysis of Time Series, Theory and Practice* (Chapman and Hall, 1975).

C.W.J. Granger and Paul Newbold, *Forecasting Economic Time Series* (Academic Press, 1977).

George E.P. Box and Gwillyn M. Jenkins, *Time Series Analysis, Forecasting and Control,* Revised Edition (Holden-Day, 1976).

[3] See, for example, Edgar Peters, *Chaos and the Capital Markets* (John Wiley and Sons, Inc., 1991).

Index